D0551175

WOLSEY

WOLSEY

THE LIFE OF KING HENRY VIII'S CARDINAL

JOHN MATUSIAK

All that hate me whisper together against me:
against me do they devise my hurt.

Psalm xli. 7

In memory of Margaret Czarnecki

10.7.1923 - 11.6.2014

Cover illustrations: *Front:* Thomas Wolsey (Alamy); *Back:* Embarkation of
King Henry VIII at Dover.

First published 2014

The History Press
The Mill, Brimscombe Port
Stroud, Gloucestershire, GL5 2QG
www.thehistorypress.co.uk

© John Matusiak, 2014

The right of John Matusiak to be identified as the Author
of this work has been asserted in accordance with the
Copyright, Designs and Patents Act 1988.

British Library Cataloguing in Publication Data.
A catalogue record for this book is available from the British Library.

ISBN 978 0 7524 9884 3

Typesetting and origination by The History Press
Printed in Great Britain

Contents

1

'This Ipswich Fellow'

In a report of 1519 which echoed the universal prejudice of the day, the Venetian ambassador Sebastiano Giustiniani noted tersely that Thomas Wolsey was of 'low origin'. Yet in terms of the rarefied courtly world that he frequented, the Italian's remark could hardly have been more apt, for the cardinal who by then had come to vie with princes is said to have grown up above a butcher's shop in the provincial port and market town of Ipswich, 'at the left corner of a little avenue leading down to the churchyard' of St Nicholas. According to the Court Rolls relating to the borough, the premises had cost a total of £8 6s 8d to purchase, which, by the humble standards of the day, was no mean sum for any moderately successful tradesman to acquire. But if it smacked of thrift and earnest endeavour, the amount involved was hardly suggestive of grace or privilege. And the common well that the property shared with the neighbouring family of a certain Edward Winter provides ample proof of its limitations.

By contrast, the date of Wolsey's birth is altogether more uncertain. In the same report, Giustiniani observed that the cardinal was 'about' 46 years of age, placing his birth towards the end of 1472 or in the early part of 1473. But the Abbot of Winchcombe's claim in August 1514 that Wolsey was then under 40 indicates a slightly later alternative. And calculations based upon the date of his ordination in March 1498 offer little further assistance, for if the minimum age of admission into the priesthood was 24, the only certainty is that Wolsey cannot have been born later than 1474.

Nevertheless, some inspired guesses have stood the test of time and two in particular are worthy of special consideration. Writing in 1724, it was

Sir Richard Fiddes who first suggested that Wolsey's Christian name might well be linked to the feast of St Thomas Aquinas on 7 March and this particular notion has always had its fair share of advocates. The year, on the other hand, has often been reckoned at 1471 from the evidence of George Cavendish, a trusted member of the cardinal's household who would later become his most notable biographer. Neither proposal, therefore, is without a respectable pedigree. But it is not until the two dates are used in combination that their full interest emerges, for if England's most remarkable statesman really did make his entrance in March 1471 or thereabouts, he could hardly have done so in more inauspicious circumstances.

Only two months earlier a marvellous blazing star, marked by 'a white flame of fire fervently burning', was said to have lit up the sky for twelve nights on end, while throughout March itself 'great storms and tempests from the sea' raged continually. For some while, too, an outbreak of bubonic plague had been delivering what Sir John Paston considered 'the most universal death' he had ever witnessed in England. Most ominously of all, however, this was a time when the peace of the realm was hanging by the slenderest of threads. Little more than a year before, the Earl of Warwick, the 'Kingmaker', had changed sides to depose his sovereign, and though Edward IV soon returned in triumph it would require two grim battles, at Barnet and Tewkesbury, not to mention the violent death of Henry VI in the Tower, to restore temporary peace.

Yet, for all its tribulations, this was also a time of rich opportunity for any thrusting individual suitably endowed with an eagle eye for advancement. And Robert Wolsey – who, like his son, would always spell his name 'Wulcy' – was, it seems, just such a person. Throughout the fifteenth century, in fact, successive generations of Suffolk Wolseys had fashioned modest livings as butchers, while at Dunwich, Yoxford and Blythburgh the more enterprising of them had also made their way as innkeepers. But despite his sturdily plebeian roots, Thomas Wolsey's father was not, it seems, inclined to mediocrity and for this reason he moved as a young man to Ipswich from his native village of Combs, near Stowmarket, bent on making good. Furthermore, by the time that Thomas – the first of his four children – was born, he was already combining the roles of butcher, innkeeper and grazier, and, in the process, confidently outstripping his forebears.

Crucially, he had achieved a lucrative marriage to a member of a well-connected East Anglian family that had come over the years to dominate several local villages, and though Joan Daundy was not quite of gentle stock, her dowry was nevertheless a more than handy acquisition. Indeed, a potent combination of her father's means and her husband's methods would soon be yielding such solid dividends that by 1475 the Wolseys had moved from the parish of St Mary Elms, where their famous son was born, to the more central location where he was to spend his childhood. By around 1480, moreover, an Ipswich monk named Fetherstone was referring to a local squire called 'Wolci' who, besides fattening cattle on his meadow near the town, was also selling wool to the English market in Calais. Indeed, well before his death in the autumn of 1496, 'Squire' Wolsey had, it seems, actually acquired sufficient means to retire in comparative comfort.

The rest from his life's labours was surely welcome, too, for the head of the Wolsey household had striven long and hard to better himself, and suffered his fair share of indignities along the way. As a newcomer to Ipswich, possibly unfamiliar with the tangle of civic ordinances impeding his enterprise and doubtless keen to make his mark in any event, it had not been long before he was making regular appearances before the local magistracy. Arraigned at first for keeping a *'hospicium'* or inn, where he is said to have sold victuals for excessive gain, he also found himself in court shortly afterwards when he and a Stowmarket butcher by the name of John Wood were accused of selling bad pies.

Although the fines involved were comparatively light, by the time that Thomas was 9 his father was said to be 'the greatest offender before the leet'. Not only had he gone on to brew ale and sell it in illegal measures, he had also supplied horse feed for excessive profit, permitted his pigs to wander at large within the borough precincts and failed to maintain the guttering in front of his house. Later, he would be indicted yet again: first, for defiling the highway with filth from his stables instead of placing it within the public pits provided for the purpose, and then, as a final flourish, for 'fostering harlots and adulterers within his house against the king's peace'.

Despite these scrapes and setbacks, however, Robert Wolsey continued to grow in wealth and came ultimately to be something of a fixture in the community. No doubt, too, the son beheld in his father's progress signs of what was required by the times, for a bold head and stout heart could, it seems, open many a door. Though he would never manage to become a free burgess of the borough of Ipswich and thereby gain the right to vote, Wolsey senior still served his turn for three years as churchwarden of St Nicholas and acquired further property at St Mary Stoke, along with farmland at Sternfield-by-Farnham, a village some 24 miles away.

Likewise, at his death he was not only able to bequeath funds for a painting of an archangel above the altar of his parish church but also to leave other money to guarantee that masses should be sung for both him and his friends over the space of one whole year. And if his house just down from the Cornhill, past

Rosemary Lane and Dog's Head Street, provided a somewhat modest address for any aspiring bourgeois, at least it stood at the heart of things. Nearby rose the massive church of St Peter and behind that the humbler but still august edifice of Ipswich Grammar School, founded in 1476 by a local mercantile elite which was thriving at that time as never before.

Certainly, the town of Thomas Wolsey's birth was one where any industrious individual had scope to prosper. Situated 70 miles north-east of London and benefiting from good access to the sea along the Gipping and Orwell rivers, it was a sheltered port, through which thousands of tightly stuffed woolsacks passed continually to the great duchy of Burgundy and the English-held port of Calais. For all of two centuries, in fact, Ipswich merchants had been taking wool, hides, corn and cheese either to Brittany in return for salt, or to the Low Countries from which they returned with finished cloth.

Just as Ipswich had long served as a window on the Continent, so it had also become over many years a magnet for foreign traders and craftsmen – a goodly number of whom would surely have lodged at Robert Wolsey's premises. In this truly cosmopolitan community, wine merchants from Bordeaux rubbed shoulders with arms traders from Hamburg and dealers in horses' hides from Cologne. Spanish vessels, too, were regular visitors and the town also boasted its own thriving community of Flemings who had drifted there throughout the fifteenth century, marrying local brides and occupying themselves with industries such as brewing, carving and hat-making.

Predictably, the material benefits accruing from such a bustle of commercial activity had been considerable, particularly since 1404, when Ipswich became one of the few towns in the kingdom permitted to export wool to the Continent. Thereafter, Ipswich merchants had also begun to send their ships on the lucrative 'long Iceland' voyage, selling their cargoes of stockfish to London merchants at St Gregory's Fair in Sudbury, or to the Suffolk gentry. Others made good profits from the canvas trade, and such were the resulting surplus funds available to the host of newly rich burgesses that every one of Ipswich's churches would be rebuilt during these plentiful years. Indeed, the Perpendicular churches and half-timbered town houses with their ornately carved corner posts, which form such a prominent part of Suffolk's architectural heritage, still bear ample testimony to a sustained commercial boom that would cause average incomes in the area to rise fourfold during the century.

Meanwhile, as Ipswich continued to hum with commercial activity the town charter, granted by King John on 25 May 1200, further reinforced its robustly independent outlook. Protected from the interference of powerful magnate families, such as the Mowbrays, de la Poles, de Veres and Howards,

Ipswich's 5,000 inhabitants were almost always smugly dismissive of the high politics associated with the Wars of the Roses. Tending mainly to support the Yorkist cause – albeit in a lukewarm manner – through the influence of Sir John Howard, or 'Jockey of Norfolk' as he was known, the town gained from Edward IV and Richard III the privileges it prized and quietly ignored the greater tides of national affairs.

Thus, when Edward IV returned from his foreign exile the annals of the town recorded only that a certain Ingell Bolton was fined 'for nuisance done to the highway at Cole Dunghill, by laying muck therein'. On other occasions, too, while the country at large was being rocked by faction and assassination, we hear in Ipswich mainly of stiff fines for the likes of John Maughteld, a local shoemaker, found guilty of eavesdropping under the paneless windows of the overhanging upper stories of a wealthy merchant's house. And when news came finally that the murdered corpse of Henry VI had been brought to St Paul's and 'bled on the pavement there', the same report was swift to return to more pressing local concerns, warning earnestly that 'the town millers are, at their peril, to take no excessive toll'.

It was here, then, in the midst of the pealing bells of Ipswich's fifteen churches and a whole wide world away from Westminster and its distracted turnings that Thomas Wolsey was reared. Here, as an eldest son, he was schooled, no doubt, in all the finer points of his father's trades, learning to barter shrewdly at local market stalls, tending to the foreign merchants at the family inn and rinsing the bloodied floor of the shop in St Nicholas Street when required. Here, too, as he grew through boyhood, he will doubtless have learned of human nature at his father's side and been shaped and moulded in other ways by the rhythms and spectacles of the everyday world around him.

Bordered by the old Buttermarket and the shambles, the hub of town life for the common people of Ipswich and for young Wolsey, too, was the Cornhill. It was the site of regular wheat and cattle markets and the favourite resort of public preachers and travelling showmen. It was also the place where fairs occurred in summer and the hustings were held from time to time. Less happily, it was home to the stocks, the pillory and the bull ring, and occasionally it heaved with crowds who came to witness a bear-baiting or public execution. By and large, offenders were dispatched unceremoniously enough by the hangman's noose in Ipswich, but for those criminals who refused to plead, there was also the prospect of death by crushing under heavy stones – the so-called punishment of '*delapidaretur*' or '*peine forte et dure*'.

No local butcher's son could have failed to know the sights and sounds of the Cornhill anything other than intimately and, like any young boy, Wolsey is certain to have drunk deeply of what he saw and heard there. No less surely, he must also have gained first-hand experience of some of the town's other idiosyncracies. According to one local ordinance, for instance, it was deemed an offence to sell the flesh of any bull that had not been baited by dogs for at least an hour prior to slaughter. This savage and noisy practice was said to add flavour to the meat, and it provided its share of daily spectacle as well, for if the tormented animal were not dead within the allocated time, it would be finished off in full public view by a butcher.

But if the world of Wolsey's boyhood was filled with more than its fair share of cruelty, there were also pockets of prayer and contemplation all around him, which were clearly not without their influence either. The Carmelites or 'White Friars' lived out their lives of learning and austerity not far from his house, in a priory whose precincts stretched from St Stephen's Lane and the Buttermarket towards the town jail. Closer still to Wolsey's home were the mendicant Franciscans, who resided near the western wall of the town, immediately west of the parish church of St Nicholas. Then there were the 'Black' or Dominican Friars, who were established in the town by Henry III back in the thirteenth century, as well as the Austin canons whose priors seem to have led the way in organising the town's many open-air processions.

Ipswich also boasted its very own religious shrine, located in Lady Lane, only a stone's throw away from where Wolsey lived. Early historical records abound, in fact, with references to the 'miraculous powers' and 'many marvels' associated with the Shrine of Our Lady of Grace at Ipswich, and make it clear that the Lady Lane chapel was 'much resorted to by pilgrims' and 'second only to Walsingham' in popularity. Long after Wolsey had left his home town, Sir Thomas More would visit Ipswich and sing the shrine's praises, observing how he had seen the daughter of Sir Roger Wentworth, a local landowner, freed from demonic possession: 'her mouth drawn aside, and her eyes laid out upon her cheeks [...] a terrible sight to behold'.

This is not to say that Wolsey's Ipswich was without its lighter side. Indeed, there was an abundance of festivities and local customs to lighten the everyday struggle for survival. On so-called 'Hockmondays', for instance, the women of St Nicholas ward would stretch a chain across a chosen street and hold all passing men to ransom. The guild feasts for which Ipswich was well known are certain to have been another highlight of Thomas Wolsey's childhood. They were a time for remembrance of dead brethren and an occasion, too, for contrition and reflection. But above all, they were a time for public display and junketing on the grandest scale.

On the day of Corpus Christi 1479, for instance, it is hard to believe that Wolsey's father was not among those walking slowly behind their guild symbols through the town's crowded streets: the mariners, merchants and brewers following the sign of the ship; the cloth makers, dyers, drapers, mercers and other men of similar trades making their way behind the effigy of the Virgin Mary; and the butchers and tallow chandlers being led, appropriately enough, by a bull. In the feasting that followed, moreover, young Thomas would almost certainly have enjoyed his share of the lamb, veal, goose, pork, chicken, bread, spices and honey supplied, so we are told, to the families of all guild members on that day.

Most spectacular of all, however, were those rarer occasions when a mighty lord would come to visit Ipswich amid brilliant colours, beating drums and blaring fanfares. By and large, the local landed elite kept their distance from the town, preferring to maintain an Olympian detachment on their extensive estates. Nevertheless, occasional displays of might and splendour remained a crucial element of their mystique and on days such as these the butcher's son may well have caught a fleeting glimpse of the youthful Thomas Howard, his future nemesis. The two were, after all, almost exact contemporaries and Ipswich itself was surrounded by Howard properties, the most notable of which at this time was the manor of Stoke-by-Nayland a dozen miles to the south-west.

But it was Wolsey's potential as a budding scholar that would eventually lead him, around the age of 11, to abandon the sights and novelties of his Ipswich home once and for all. Precisely when he embarked upon his education and who was responsible for his earliest tuition are both uncertain, although a number of guild chaplains are known to have doubled as grammar masters, and there were certainly independent schoolmasters within the borough to teach the 'petties' or little ones the alphabet. In any event, it was at the town's grammar school that he received his first formal instruction for a fee of eightpence a quarter under the supervision of a headmaster who had, it seems, only been appointed on condition that he arrange the construction of latrines for his pupils' use. In a house standing beside the gate of the Friars Preachers, then, Wolsey learnt his Latin primers, memorised his psalter and possibly developed his first love of music as a chorister, since the will of the school's main benefactor, Richard Felaw, had stipulated that the pupils should sing a Mass of Our Lady at six o'clock each morning in the neighbouring Dominican church.

Wolsey's stay, however, would not be a long one, and though the precise circumstances of his removal are unclear, it seems that he must have shone sufficiently at his studies to come to the attention of James Goldwell, who had been Bishop of Norwich since 1472. Goldwell, a former principal secretary to Edward IV, is known to have taken a keen interest in the grammar school at Ipswich and he is known, too, to have held in his gift four places at Magdalen College School each year. In all likelihood, young Wolsey's name would have been put forward by John Squyer, Master of the grammar school, and the funds of the Daundy family may also have been enlisted to help with the costs involved. Ever keen to identify and reward scholars of potential, Goldwell was thus persuaded to select the butcher's son as a likely candidate for study at Oxford.

There can be little doubt either that Wolsey's father would have fully appreciated the considerable possibilities that admission to the university and eventual entry into the priesthood might open up for his firstborn. The Church, after all, offered a career not only to lowly parsons and curates in every one of England's parishes, but also to canons in cathedral chapters, to chantry priests singing lucrative private masses for the souls of dead benefactors, and even to the chaplains of the nobility. That a clerical career might eventually make his son one of the most influential figures in Christendom would, however, surely have exceeded even Robert Wolsey's wildest expectations.

The College of St Mary Magdalen, which had been established twenty-six years earlier, was still being built when its fresh-faced resident from Ipswich arrived there to spend the next eighteen years or so. A small turreted fragment of the college's school, which was founded in 1479, remains to this day, but apart from a single large room the original building consisted of little more than the chambers of the headmaster and usher, along with a kitchen. It was in this Grammar Hall that Wolsey, along with a handful of timid boys, would have received his first instruction. And though the frequent references in the college accounts to the repair of broken windows suggest that the boys remained a spirited bunch, they were subjected to a rigorous academic diet, which was imposing enough to intimidate even the most avid of young scholars.

The standard curriculum seems to have emphasised the acquisition of a thorough grounding in Latin by means of a steadily ascending progress through Terence, Virgil, Cicero's letters and the histories of either Sallust or Caesar, up to and including Horace's epistles and Ovid's *Metamorphoses* or *Fasti*. Ultimately, pupils were then expected to study the science of grammar proper in Donatus or Valla. Yet just how far Thomas Wolsey progressed along this set path is unknown, for shortly after his arrival, presumably as a result of his unusual progress, he was transferred to the college itself, where he began his studies to qualify as a Bachelor of Arts.

The regime awaiting him will have been a particularly austere one. As Bishop of Winchester and Lord Chancellor of England, William Waynflete, the college's founder, had been a tireless patron of learning who was determined to purge his beloved university of disorderly elements by imposing the rigour and discipline of enclosed community life upon its members. Before the establishment of colleges, the students of Oxford had not been compelled to live in any one place and, in consequence, their dissolute behaviour had become a considerable cause of scandal. Now, however, entry to the university became in effect a species of custodial sentence.

Statutes enacted around the time that Wolsey entered Oxford forbade swearing, games of chance, 'unhonest garrulities', being out after eight o'clock in the winter and nine o'clock in the summer and speaking English except on feast days. Likewise, all were required to hear Mass daily and to attend sermons, while clothes were regulated and long hair strictly condemned. Card playing, too, was prohibited and failure to prepare for lessons, as well as playing, laughing or talking in lectures, not to mention lateness or non-attendance at chapel, could lead to corporal punishment at the discretion of the college authorities. Books, meanwhile, were still so valuable that punishments were imposed for leaving them open.

Around a thousand young scholars in all attended the colleges, halls and associated semi-monastic institutions which constituted the university, while at Magdalen itself the student community consisted of some forty postgraduates, thirty undergraduates and another twenty *commensales* – the sons of noble and powerful friends of the college – who received private tuition. Not surprisingly, living conditions for all but the wealthy handful were rudimentary. Undergraduates were housed two or three to a chamber, with cubicles or 'studies' partitioned off for reading, and those, like Wolsey, who were under the age of fifteen were expected to share a bed.

But at least basic board and lodging was cheap. An individual's room rent, for instance, ran to no more than sixpence a year, and his share of 'commons' – the basic food and drink bought each week for members of the hall or college – amounted to less than a penny a day. Moreover, the food on offer was, it seems, wholesome enough. A contemporary described a typical Oxford dinner as a 'penye pece of byefe amongst iiii, hauying a few porage made of the broth of the same byefe with salte and otemell'. As for other basics, each student provided his own bedding, knives, spoons and candlesticks, along with a lantern, a pair of bellows and a coffer for his books.

Certainly, the teaching Wolsey received will have done much to mould his later reputation for both endurance and intellectual rigour. Consisting of lectures and disputations, the main aim was to encourage an appreciation of semantics, alongside a training in logical analysis and argument. And in the process, no quarter was afforded to clumsy thinking of any kind, while the highest premium was set upon control of detail.

At lectures, masters focused their delivery upon interpretations and glosses on a set text, which were followed by *quaestiones*, or investigations, into its aspects. Disputations and exercises in oratory, on the other hand, were held on so-called *dies disputabilis*. A disputation on theology, for instance, was held weekly in the chapel, along with two further debates on logic or moral philosophy in the college's central hall. On such occasions, before a hushed audience of young scholars, masters and bachelors argued on either side of an interpretation or proposition – usually one proponent and two opponents – until the presiding master gave his determination or final judgement.

Moreover, in the unlikely event that the student from Ipswich did not already appreciate the full meaning of hard work and long hours before his arrival at the college, his Oxford education will soon have rid him of any illusions on that score. The first lecture, which was often conducted 'in the dark without artificial light', began at six o'clock in the morning and only the handful of more fortunate students will have faced its three hours' duration with the benefit of a breakfast beforehand. Then, following dinner at ten o'clock, two further lectures usually occurred from noon onwards, lasting until five o'clock, when supper was served.

Thereafter, Wolsey and his fellows were free to take their pleasure until eight or nine o'clock. Chess and other homemade amusements, such as storytelling and carol singing, were considered suitable, as was the reading of 'poems, chronicles of the realm, or wonders of the world'; morality plays and pageants, along with comedies by Plautus and Aristophanes were especially encouraged. But the day itself would necessarily have ended with prayers. Before retiring to bed, therefore, all students chanted the *Salve Regina* or some similar antiphon to the Virgin Mary.

Predictably, such a sternly structured environment sometimes proved intolerable, and punishments, as well as expulsions and banishments, were not infrequent. Indeed, though there is no record of any misdemeanour on Wolsey's part, it was said that on the roads round about Oxford, gangs of expelled scholars roamed abroad fecklessly, while others, it seems, had even chosen to swap their studies for more lucrative careers as highwaymen. Certainly, it was not unknown for less colourful students to poach in the royal forests at Shotover and Woodstock, and the fact that colleges imposed fines for bringing unsheathed knives to table and doubled them if blood was shed in a brawl says something about the simmering undercurrents that must have existed.

Yet Magdalen was far from being merely the academic gulag it might at first appear. In fact, it had been expressly established for the study of philosophy and divinity, in the hope that it would serve the Church as a bastion against heresy, and in this respect its impact had been impressive. Oxford was, after all, still shadowed by the catastrophic impact of heresy originating with John Wycliffe's challenge to Roman doctrines half a century earlier. And if its founder had, indeed, intended Magdalen to be frozen in permanent intellectual stasis, he was to be roundly disappointed, for while Wolsey was living and growing there, the college was being thoroughly renewed and energised under the influence of some of the leading exponents of the so-called 'New Learning'.

Not content with intellectual subservience to tradition and the arid logic-chopping of their medieval predecessors, humanist scholars at Wolsey's Oxford were busily condemning corruption and obscurantism in the Church. In place of error and superstition, they advocated a thorough purification of doctrine, which could only be achieved, they argued, by studying biblical sources and philosophical texts in their original Greek form. Furthermore, the scale of the subsequent transformation at the university was quite apparent to the celebrated scholar Erasmus when he made his first visit there in either 1497 or 1498. The scholarship on offer was no longer, it seems, 'of the outworn, commonplace sort', but of the 'profound, accurate kind', and the Dutchman went on to express his genuine amazement at 'how thickly this standing grain of ancient letters now ripens to harvest'.

Thomas Wolsey's intellect would therefore be shaped in the midst of a powerful array of cutting-edge thinkers. William Grocyn, for instance – the most venerated of Magdalen's illuminati – was a reader in divinity there from 1481 to 1488. For two years he had studied at Florence under Demetrius Chalcondylas and Politian, and on his return to Oxford he gave what is likely to have been the first ever set of lectures on the Greek language delivered there. Laconic in his speech and a man of the strictest ascetic habits, his fame rested purely on his lectures, for he never published any of his works. Thomas Linacre, that other great champion of English humanism, was also at Oxford between 1480 and 1485. Having graduated in medicine from the University of Padua, he had spent some further time in Italy as a member of Lorenzo the Magnificent's 'academy' before returning to his homeland, where he eventually taught Thomas More and gave Erasmus his knowledge of Greek.

But these were only two of the outstanding scholars who helped frame Wolsey's intellectual horizons during his stay at Oxford. John Colet, for instance, probably studied and taught at Magdalen between 1483 and 1493 before making the Italian tour, which had become virtually obligatory for all aspiring scholars. The first Englishman to historicise the gospels, his public lectures on St Paul's Epistle to the Romans in 1497 represented a seminal contribution to the development of English religious life. Then there was William Lily, a godson of Grocyn, who studied at Magdalen from 1486 to 1490 before being selected by Colet as high master of St Paul's School after his tour of Jerusalem and the classical shrines of the Latin world. And William Latimer, friend and travelling companion of both Linacre and Grocyn, was yet another contemporary Oxford man rightfully numbered among the leading lights of learning in his time.

Wolsey's intellect therefore had every opportunity to grow and ripen in a near-perfect climate as he received at first hand the fresh wisdom that was blowing through every portico of his current home. No doubt, too, he will have absorbed in full the urbanity as well as the affectation that came with academic status. And this was by no means all that the boy from Ipswich was likely to have absorbed during these years, for he also began, on occasion, to witness at close quarters a new world of power and display that would ultimately prove utterly intoxicating to him. In July 1483, for instance, no less a figure than the newly crowned Richard III visited Oxford on a royal progress and, in accordance with its statutes, Magdalen College duly entertained him and became his temporary residence. Halls were cleared and extra food laid in, and the most prestigious scholars were duly paraded to engage in solemn disputations on moral philosophy and divinity.

Such was Thomas Wolsey's very first introduction to a stirring mixture of worlds. On the one hand there was the weighty realm of scholarship and philosophy; on the other, the glittering sphere of pomp and politics. To those, like Grocyn, who made their mark by the glibness of their tongues, King Richard bestowed his benevolences liberally. But for Wolsey there would eventually be little doubt where primacy lay in the greater scheme of things. While scholars might hold sway within the narrow confines of Magdalen, there was nevertheless a wider, more enticing world outside, far beyond their grasp and altogether more substantial than their arid quibblings.

Before Thomas Wolsey could come to dominate either, however, he would have to obtain his degree and by the tender age of 15 he appears to have done precisely that. Moreover, if George Cavendish recorded this singular achievement correctly, it was indeed 'a rare thing and seldom seen', for the examination which led to the award of a bachelor's degree was both elaborate and exacting. Under the supervision of a Master of Arts, Wolsey was made to stand before a desk for at least seven days between nine o'clock and twelve in the morning and from one o'clock until five in the afternoon. His task, quite simply, was to defend a formidable range of propositions against all comers, impressing observers and holding firm against each and every challenge.

It was an arrangement that encouraged both ostentation of mind and extreme resourcefulness, and the training it involved will certainly have played a major part in helping to hone Wolsey's so-called 'filed tongue'. Nor should it be forgotten that the whole process was conducted under conditions of extreme pressure, for unless he became a Bachelor of Arts in this way, Wolsey would need an extra year beyond the standard seven to gain a Master of Arts degree. Conversely, if he did well in his examination, he might himself attract students for his future lectures or catch the notice of wealthy patrons.

That a 15-year-old would come through such an exacting challenge says much about his talent and precocity. But it also raises tantalising questions about the possible impact of such newfound celebrity upon his self-image and ambitions. Although Wolsey would always enjoy the company of learned men and in later life became a generous patron of education in his own right, it would be misleading to depict him as a truly outstanding scholar. Nevertheless, he would now be known to all as the 'boy bachelor'. Furthermore, the degree brought to the lad who achieved it a good deal more personal liberty than might have been accorded to his peers, as well as certain privileges.

Henceforth the poorer students, known as 'batudents, who were required to wait on others before sitting down to table themselves, would tend his needs assiduously. He might also don distinctive livery and sport stylish fur-trimmed cloaks in preference to the plain clerical garb of undergraduates. All in all, then, the accolade bestowed on a callow 15-year-old after such an arduous test of wits served to single him out very visibly from his peers and lifted him to special heights within the college community as a whole. Here, it already seemed, was a student who might well come to occupy a lofty place in the counsels of the mighty.

Curiously, however, for the next eleven years or so until the day in 1497 when his name came to adorn the college rolls once more, the record of Thomas Wolsey's activities and achievements is largely a blank sheet. There is no suggestion of his returning to Ipswich even once, nor any record of his continuing study abroad at Paris, Padua, or any other European university for that matter. Nor is there the slightest hint that he gained temporary employment as a member of some great household, lay or ecclesiastical, though this may not have been for want of trying, since useful contacts for a butcher's son from Ipswich were hardly likely to have been easy to come by.

Yet clearly at some point during this period he gained his Master of Arts degree – possibly in as little as two years, according to some authorities. It is also highly likely that he specialised in divinity rather than law, however odd that may seem for someone destined to become Lord Chancellor of England.

Clearly, a grounding in divinity would have fitted him for a career within the highest ranks of the Church and would also help explain his close familiarity with the writings of Thomas Aquinas and the other scholastic philosophers whose books he would later encourage Henry VIII to read. But whatever his chosen specialism, the qualification itself was the key consideration for its owner, since it carried with it the stamp of genuine authority, along with all the accompanying dignities.

It might well seem, then, that while the Battle of Bosworth was being won and thereafter while Henry Tudor was consolidating his grip on the crown, Thomas Wolsey had simply locked himself away at Oxford and set his sights firmly on a life of scholarship and teaching. It was certainly George Cavendish's belief that Wolsey spent these years 'prospering and increasing in learning', and there was also no denying that the degree of Master of Arts at Oxford – with the comprehensive grounding it provided in grammar, rhetoric, logic, arithmetic, music, astronomy and geometry – rendered its holders well suited to all kinds of teaching opportunities. Indeed, it was a university requirement that any scholar of this rank should offer to tutor others.

Yet if some, like Wycliffe, considered Oxford 'the Vineyard of the Lord for its learning and its beauty' – 'a place, gladsome and fertile, suitable for a habitation of the Gods' – it was patently too sterile and hidebound to hold the likes of Thomas Wolsey indefinitely. Academic distinction was one thing, a lifetime of largely anonymous scholarship altogether another, and it was no coincidence that the young man from Ipswich seems to have made no effort to gain a doctorate or even to become a Bachelor of Divinity, both of which would have been crucial qualifications for an academic career.

Nevertheless, any appearance of mere hibernation during this period is deceptive. In a *Liber Nominum*, or dinner-book, of 1497 Wolsey is recorded as a Master of Arts and fourteenth on the list of fellows, and the success which this indicates leaves no doubt that he had been both busy and successful throughout his years of anonymity. He had clearly consolidated his earlier academic reputation and been of exemplary character, too, for the slightest hint of incontinence would almost certainly have barred him from election. And we can also surmise that since there are the names of five other fellows on the list after his, he is likely to have been elected to his new role one or two years previously, making him perhaps no more than 24 at the time of his promotion.

But this was not the only advance that Wolsey made during these years. By the autumn of 1498, for instance, he had also served as master of Magdalen College School, succeeding Andrew Scarbott, strongly suggesting that he had indeed already accumulated some other teaching experience. And though, according to the so-called *'Liber Computi'*, he seems to have held this particular post for only six months, there is nothing whatsover to suggest that his record was anything other than commendable. Indeed, the same register also mentions him holding the position of third bursar around this time – a post which made him one of the treasurers and managers of Magdalen's property and gave him his first significant grounding in administration.

It appears, then, that Wolsey had been steadily distinguishing himself as a talented and earnest member of his college community, and there is every indication that, with continued dedication and laborious clean-living, further gradual advancement would have been his for the taking. Yet the self-made man who had helped him on his way to Oxford did not live to witness his son's most recent progress. Robert Wolsey had made his will on 30 September 1496 and died only a few days later.

Not altogether surprisingly, the death of Wolsey's father seems to have had little obvious impact on his own life. The two men's worlds had, after all, long since parted company and if the usual rules applied, neither is likely to have experienced much ease in the other's presence, if indeed their paths had ever crossed at all in the immediately preceding years. For the older Wolsey, his refined and eloquent son had almost certainly become a figure of increasing incomprehension as the years unfolded. He may also, for that matter, have eventually become a source of some mild vexation, since he had failed to take holy orders at the earliest opportunity and was therefore failing to offer a speedy return on the already considerable investment expended on him. For the son, on the other hand, his father was firmly planted in a way of life and outlook that he himself had long since superseded.

Whether there was any outright resentment is anyone's guess, but the will that Robert Wolsey left might possibly bear such an interpretation. The son was duly appointed an executor, along with a man named Cade, but while there were several bequests to church charities, he himself received no legacy other than his father's freehold land to which he was, in any case, automatically entitled by law. And at a time when any extra financial assistance would almost certainly have been most welcome, the absence of any other bequest to the eldest son is, at least odd. All other property was bequeathed to Thomas's mother Joan, who soon afterwards married a certain William Patient.

Equally curious in its way is the stipulation that if Thomas were to become a priest within a year, he was to receive the sum of ten marks for singing Masses for his dead father's soul over the next twelve months. If, however, the young man had not by then taken holy orders as required, it was also laid down that some other priest should receive the fee. Why such a potentially niggling incentive should have been employed is hard to explain unless Thomas was for some reason dragging his feet in a way that may have exasperated his father. And the fact that he still failed to enter the priesthood within the period specified reinforces this suspicion.

In the event, it was not until 10 March 1498 that Wolsey was finally ordained at the church of St Peter in Marlborough by the Bishop of Sarum's suffragan; the entry on folio 113 of the bishop's register is the earliest precise date for any event in Wolsey's career. But if the man whose name is synonymous with meteoric rises and honours in abundance was expecting early windfalls from his ordination, he was to be at least temporarily frustrated, for one full year after his ordination he was still without a benefice of any kind. Furthermore, when the time eventually came he was appointed only to the very subordinate position of rural dean in the diocese of Norwich.

Even so, it was not long before Wolsey's own university provided him with recognition of a much more substantial kind when he was appointed senior bursar, a post which he would hold from 29 September 1499 to the same date of the following year. He had obviously been a success in his earlier role as third bursar and the administrative skill which would become his trademark was clearly expected to prove invaluable at a time when Magdalen College was involved in extensive building operations. The construction of the college's new tower was by any standards a particularly ambitious project, and though it had been progressing steadily under the direction of the great Oxford mason, William Orchard, Wolsey was now entrusted to expedite matters, which he duly did, albeit in a manner that would lead to his prompt dismissal.

Tradition has it that Wolsey was removed from his new post after exceeding his authority and misallocating funds to speed the tower's construction. In his favour, there is no hint that he had sought any personal gain and he appears, strictly speaking, to have been not so much sacked as reassigned, for at the time of his removal in 1500 he was offered the post of dean of divinity. Yet even if Wolsey's dismissal has sometimes been wrongly exploited by his detractors to confirm his dishonesty, the story itself does have a distinct ring of truth about it, not least of all because extravagant building projects would remain one of his lifelong passions. Much more significantly still, however, the whole unfortunate incident reflects two other enduring tendencies on Wolsey's part: firstly, an ongoing preparedness to take on tasks that intimidated others, and secondly an unerring willingness to take irregular shortcuts to get things done.

Nor should the impact of this first reverse be minimised, since Wolsey was at that crucial stage when defining decisions had to be made about the overall direction of his life. And however venial the offence, a shadow had been cast not only over his methods but, to a lesser degree, his integrity too. Doubtless, his pride will have been wounded – possibly grievously – and for a man like Wolsey that may well have been too much to take, especially if there were other options on offer. Was not the response of the authorities to his 'creativity' therefore final proof that the time had finally come for him to move on to new and better things?

2

The Wide Ocean of Opportunity

In the midwinter of 1499 spring came unexpectedly, it seems, for Thomas Wolsey. Until comparatively recently the privileged sons of England's elite had usually been spared the soggy tedium and vexations of university life; as long as they had mastered the intricacies of courtly manners and were skilled in sport and war, their fathers invariably considered them more than adequately prepared for the narrow world of power and privilege in which they were to move. Indeed, the bristling contempt for study and contemplation so prevalent among many men of high rank was vividly captured by one contemporary scholar who recorded with resignation how he had heard a certain gentleman proudly airing his scorn for the written word. 'By the body of God,' the man is said to have declared, 'I would sooner have my son be hanged than a bookworm. It is a gentleman's calling to be able to blow the horn, to hunt and to hawk. He should leave learning to the clodhoppers.'

Change was in the air, however, and for three of the seven sons of Thomas Grey, first Marquess of Dorset, things would be very different. All had been sent to Oxford to acquire precisely that subtlety of mind which others of their class were still so ready to despise. Nor did their arrival within Magdalen's high stone walls go unnoticed by the masters immured with them: no ambitious teacher, after all, could fail to realise that a marquess stood only below a duke and the king himself in terms of rank. The opportunities for preferment and patronage that might suddenly open up, if the right services were rendered and the proper signals sent, were plain for all to see.

On this occasion, however, the good fortune on offer was to be all Thomas Wolsey's, since the three young Greys had been given over wholly to his personal care and tuition. Faced with what he surely now considered the tepid possibilities of academic life and soon to be embarrassed by his falling short as college bursar, opportunity had therefore knocked loudly for the newly fledged schoolmaster and was not to be lightly ignored.

None could deny that the Marquess of Dorset was a well-known figure at court who boasted considerable influence in the country at large. Not only was he widely regarded as 'a good and prudent man', but as Elizabeth Woodville's son he was also the half-brother of Henry VII's queen, Elizabeth of York. Moreover, as a stepson of Edward IV he had fought alongside the king at Tewkesbury and received his current title four years later.

There had, it is true, once been venomous rumours about his loyalty at the time of Lambert Simnel's treason, but his rehabilitation had since been complete and from that time forth he had received various tokens of royal confidence. He had been present, for instance, at the christening of Prince Arthur, the heir to the throne, and in 1492 he had taken part in a difficult expedition to extricate the Holy Roman Emperor Maximilian from a fruitless campaign against the French. At home, too, he had been busily loyal, serving in the forces assembled by Henry VII in 1497 to quell an ominous rebellion fomented by the men of Cornwall. For some time, then, his reputation had been high and he now enjoyed the firmest confidence the king could repose in him – a royal commission to have troops under his personal command.

But, as the marquess well knew, loyalty and courage were only two of three essential qualities required of a worthy lord. Generosity was also a crucial hallmark of true nobility, and this was the best of news for Thomas Wolsey, for now his efforts on his students' behalf were to be fittingly rewarded. He had, we are told, attended his three noble charges so dutifully and exercised such diligent care in all respects that at the start of the Christmas vacation of 1499 he received an invitation from the marquess to accompany his pupils on their journey back to Bradgate Park, 7 miles to the west of Leicester.

The passage from Oxford to the Grey country seat involved a round trip of more than 100 miles and the presence of the tutor was therefore of considerable reassurance to the father. But if it was a comfort to the marquess, it would prove nothing less than a heavenly deliverance to Wolsey himself, for here, it seemed, was the perfect chance to pose and profit. By now he was a more than becoming young man – hearty, eloquent and personable – for whom the great house at Bradwell Park might well prove the gateway to greater things. And in spite of first appearances to the contrary, the opportunity which was about to come his way would ultimately have undreamt-of consequences.

Some 150 miles away in Somerset lay the parish church of Limington, near Ilchester, the income and profits of which were in the gift of Wolsey's host. To all intents and purposes, such a parish was typical of the kind that slowly consumed the energies of so many packhorse priests throughout England at this time, and until his recent death it had been a certain John Borde who tended the simple needs of his flock there. When not preaching and administering the sacraments, it was Borde who taught local children and adults alike the Lord's Prayer and Hail Mary, as well as the Ten Commandments. It was he, too, who ensured that common folk knew how to cross themselves appropriately and comport themselves with due reverence at Mass. There were baptisms for him to conduct, petty confessions to hear and trifling wills to write, while the government in its turn would have expected him from time to time to read out bulletins from his pulpit. And then, of course, there were the more practical chores of everyday survival for Borde to attend to; chores which involved, among other things, the farming of his so-called 'glebe', as well as the many tasks associated with the everyday upkeep of his humble parson's dwelling.

With all its remoteness and inconveniences, not to mention the wearisome routine of its parish life, the church of St Mary at Limington was therefore hardly the most attractive of destinations, especially for a fellow of Magdalen who was currently serving as college bursar and would soon turn down the opportunity to become dean of divinity there. A thirteenth-century construction of sturdy stone with a nave measuring 87ft by 24ft and a chantry on its north side, St Mary's remains to this day a handsome enough edifice, possessing to the west a perpendicular tower with six bells which continues to impress as a miniature imitation of something vast. But, in spite of the building's brave attempt to proclaim itself, the more humdrum truth could not be altogether obscured.

Even as a first appointment, and taking into account the importance of the benefactor who controlled it, this would remain an unlikely outpost for anyone of real ambition. Yet, however humble the living it might have offered, Limington was a living all the same and one, moreover, which now presented both freedom and opportunity to the newly liberated tutor from Oxford. When, therefore, the Marquess of Dorset offered Wolsey this quiet parish in a remote part of the kingdom – 'in reward for his diligence' – he did not hesitate to accept. And, as always, he would prove more than capable of squeezing advantage from the most unlikely of circumstances.

It was, in any case, a good time to be gone from Magdalen, and not simply because Wolsey's term as senior bursar was about to end unhappily. He had already defended the president of the college, Richard Mayhew, when his leadership was called into question, and he had also taken the president's side against detractors in a dispute between the colleges of Magdalen and Merton over the ownership of a mill. But Mayhew's administration had nevertheless ended in disorder and confusion. There had been other internal controversies involving charges and counter-charges, and it was in the midst of the petty sniping and bickering which now consumed the place that Wolsey was finally accused of improperly diverting funds to the completion of the college's new tower.

Worse still, these troubles marked only the beginning of Magdalen's steady descent into acrimony and disrepute. Indeed, when the college was formally inspected in 1507, a number of its members were rebuked and told to reform, while others suffered penalties for various breaches of statutes, including sleeping in chapel, keeping ferrets and perjury. On the other hand, more serious complaints against members included charges of adultery and receiving stolen goods, and in one case a charge of concealing a thief was also successfully upheld. Another member, meanwhile, was charged with baptising a cat in order to discover by occult means the whereabouts of a treasure. In all likelihood, then, Wolsey had read the writing on the wall long before this and was more than ready for a fleeting sojourn in far-off Somerset before the call to better things arrived.

Besides which, if the new rector of Limington did not care to minister to his bumpkin flock, there would be ample opportunity for him to employ a vicar or curate to perform his duties. Absentee rectors, no less than absentee bishops, were commonplace at this time; indeed, such arrangements had become almost the norm in most outlying parishes of the day. A wretched stand-in could usually be employed for a modest sum of around £5 per year and might even be persuaded to swear that he would not ask for a larger stipend during his tenure. So although the church of St Mary at which Thomas Wolsey was duly instituted on 10 October 1500 still houses a plaque proudly displaying his name as rector there until 1509, it seems that for at least eight of those years he came nowhere near the place. Indeed, in little more than a twelvemonth he had gone, leaving his cipher on the panels of the parish pews and his initials on some parsonage windows, which remained intact until the eighteenth century.

But within that time he had once again pushed his luck, it seems, and according to tradition paid a price far more galling than the one he had already incurred at his old college. Quite apart from the mediocrity of his everyday routine, the parish priest of a backwater parish like Limington also had other more worrying things to press upon his mind, for although the Roman Catholic

Church was still a massive institution claiming universal sway, the reality in such far-flung outposts was altogether different, and vulnerable, exposed priests might not always be treated with anything like due deference. On the contrary, most parishes were corporations in which clergy had to be ever-mindful of secular patrons and local bigwigs of all kinds. In theory at least, no lords of the manor or political personages were intended to hold any power or authority over the serving priest. But in times of change and in specific situations, long-honoured principles were sometimes subject to challenge and though mighty prelates were still, for the time being at least, secure enough in their palaces, assaults like the one now made on Wolsey by Sir Amyas Paulet in 1501 were by no means unheard of.

Paulet was a knight and local worthy who lived 10 miles from Limington at Hinton St George. He had been a Lancastrian in the intermittent Wars of the Roses, and after Buckingham's rebellion at the beginning of the reign of Richard III he had been attainted by his Yorkist foes. After the triumph of Henry Tudor at the Battle of Bosworth, however, he had been duly rewarded for his support by being appointed sheriff of both Dorset and Somerset – an area of personal suzerainty that should have been adequate even for a man of his bristling temperament. But Paulet's star was still rising, it seems, for after the Battle of Stoke Field he had been knighted.

At the same time, the scope of his operations was also beginning to expand as the king, with an ever-peeled eye for easy income, looked for willing henchmen to levy fines upon those who had dared espouse the cause of Perkin Warbeck, pretender to the throne. Revenues gained from Somerset and the four adjoining counties equalled an amount sufficient to run the royal household for well over a year, and those who might yield moneys for their transgressions in the Warbeck affair were therefore ruthlessly hunted down by the king's collectors. Foremost among those prowling the country and ferreting out fines – sometimes by rough means – had been Sir Amyas Paulet.

Not altogether surprisingly, the arrival of pastor Wolsey in a local parish – fresh from Oxford and the protégé of a marquess – will have attracted the attention of this puffed-up, nosy knight soon enough. But what is supposed to have followed in the summer of 1501 was truly extraordinary, since, according to George Cavendish, Paulet 'took an occasion of displeasure' against Wolsey and 'was so bold to set the schoolmaster by the feet during his pleasure'. In other words, the future Lord Chancellor of England apparently suffered the indignity of being confined in the stocks at Paulet's behest.

Naturally enough, in the reign of Elizabeth I, Wolsey's detractors made much of this alleged incident. Sir John Harrington, for instance, would claim that

Wolsey had been involved a drunken fray and paid the price accordingly. Yet from all we know of the man – his intense application, not to mention his desire to stand well with those in positions of power – such a tale does not ring altogether true. Not least, it seems highly unlikely that Wolsey would have compromised himself in this way within only a few months of obtaining the favour of so influential a patron as the Marquess of Dorset. Furthermore, at no time before or after this event was the charge of drunkenness ever brought against him, even by the bitterest contemporary critics.

Nor is another explanation, originating with Sir Roger Wilbrahim, Master of Requests to Queen Elizabeth, much more convincing. Writing some eighty years after the event, Wilbrahim would claim that Wolsey was punished for fornication. But although this particular story is not altogether implausible, a courtier of Anne Boleyn's daughter like Wilbrahim was hardly more likely than Harrington to advance a wholly disinterested explanation. In any event, it would have been most unusual and irregular for a parish rector to be placed in the stocks for this or any other offence – and particularly at the order of some secular authority. The rural dean of Bath and Wells, it should be remembered, had full authority to refer all clerical misdemeanours to the bishop's consistory court. Equally significantly, Wolsey's numerous enemies once again made no attempt to produce the charge against him while he was alive. Later on, indeed, even John Skelton, his most scathing of detractors, made no mention of it whatsoever in any of his foul-mouthed tirades.

There is certainly much about the whole episode that is, at the very least, both mysterious and surprising. The stocks were regularly used as a punishment for members of the lower classes who had committed some comparatively minor misdemeanour not sufficiently serious to warrant a prison sentence. By 1501, however, Wolsey was no longer 'a poor scholar of base condition', but a person of some substance in his own right who enjoyed the patronage of the queen's half-brother, and the marquess himself could hardly have overlooked the matter if Wolsey had actually been punished in the way described. There can be little doubt either that Dorset would surely have heard about the incident from Paulet or from Wolsey himself, if it had indeed occurred, and thereafter he would have had no choice but to take the part of one or other. The result could only have been disgrace for Wolsey, or the kind of almighty clash between powerful personages that was unlikely to have gone entirely unrecorded in the way it did.

So where does the truth lie? It needs to be remembered, above all, that although Cavendish states on several occasions how incidents reported by him were told by Wolsey himself, he makes no such claim on this occasion.

On the contrary, the story may well have been gleaned from idle gossip current in Wolsey's own household, to which Cavendish, as gentleman usher, would doubtless have been privy.

Yet there is still no reason to disbelieve that an incident of some sort may indeed have occurred back in Somerset and that both its causes and consequences are likely to have been of genuine significance. From the scanty evidence available, we can only infer that Wolsey, with characteristic independence and self-assertiveness, had in some way or other raised the hackles of a notoriously touchy and pompous local magnate, resulting possibly in a threat from Paulet to place his enemy in the stocks. Years later, members of Wolsey's household – well acquainted with his haughty manner, his mistress and his bastards – may then have seen fit to embroider the story with a trumped-up tale of their low-born master's final comeuppance.

However, even if Wolsey's discomfiture did not extend as far as outright public ridicule, the clash itself may well have confirmed him once and for all in his lifelong belief that the secular authorities should not be allowed to over-assert themselves in their dealings with the clergy. They must be met head-on and faced down strenuously, if need be. Nor was the victim prepared to turn the other cheek even in the long term, it seems, for years later, with one of those delectable ironies that life sometimes produces, he would gain and take his opportunity to be avenged.

In 1515, while Lord Chancellor, Wolsey is said to have sent for Paulet 'and after many sharp and heinous words enjoined him to attend upon the Council until he were by them dismissed, and not to depart without license upon urgent pain and forfeiture'. In all fairness to Wolsey he was far too prudent to stir up muddy waters, if he had, indeed, been guilty of some shameful misdemeanour or other back in 1501. But by this time Paulet had nevertheless become treasurer of the Middle Temple at the Inns of Court and was thus wholly at the Lord Chancellor's mercy.

According to Cavendish, therefore, Wolsey coolly confined his former adversary to the Inn over some five or more years during which time Paulet was said to have been so chastened that he saw fit to supervise the building of a splendid gatehouse there – duly adorned with Wolsey's arms and cognisances – in hope of forgiveness. 'Now may this be,' wrote Cavendish, 'a good example and precedent to men in authority, who will sometimes work their will without wit, to remember in their authority how authority may decay.' 'Who would have thought,' he added, 'that when Amyas Paulet punished this poor scholar, that ever he should have attained to be Chancellor of England, considering his baseness in every condition?' Who indeed? And who would have thought, too, that Wolsey's memory of old scores might have stretched so far and lead ultimately to such flagrant abuse of his authority?

For the time being, however, if the incident back in Limington had jarred Wolsey, it by no means checked the momentum of his rise. Preparing the way for what would eventually become a flood of extra benefices, he had already applied for the necessary papal dispensation, which was duly granted on 3 November 1500. Moreover, Wolsey had been making a string of additional contacts through the Marquess of Dorset, and when the marquess died in September 1501 what might have been a blow to the priest's hopes proved nothing of the kind, for very soon afterwards he was appointed as one of two chaplains to Henry Deane, the new Archbishop of Canterbury – a post of much influence and a definite stepping-stone for any man of genuine promise. The clear implication is that Limington's new rector was already thinking far beyond his parish's limited horizons from the moment he arrived there.

Archbishop Deane, for his part, enjoyed a solid reputation as a man of clear principles and firm loyalties, although he was without flair and rarely, if ever, asserted himself. Descended apparently from the ancient family of Dene in the Forest of Dean, he had been a reforming prior of the house of Austin canons at Llanthony Abbey near Gloucester until Henry VII had sent him to Ireland as deputy governor, providing him with the modest revenues of the see of Bangor between 1496 and 1500. And here, to his credit, he had embarked on the refurbishment of the cathedral and restitution of a diocese which had lain devastated for the greater part of a century since the rising of Owain Glyn Dŵr.

Thereafter, in the last year of the century, he had been translated to the diocese of Salisbury, only to be appointed Archbishop of Canterbury almost at once as Cardinal Morton's successor. But he was never officially installed, either for lack of funds to meet the huge expense involved or because he wished to save his money for what he took to be his impending demise. He was, after all, around 70 years of age by this time and had grown infirm during his long period of service to the Crown. Indeed, he had already prepared minute directions for his funeral, intending, it seems, that it should be the biggest event of his life.

Yet if Canterbury held little attraction for Deane, it was most definitely a glimpse of the Promised Land for his new chaplain. Administratively, Canterbury held sixteen dioceses under its control, while the junior archiepiscopal province of York contained only three: York, Durham and Carlisle. And, as if this was not enough to confirm the gulf in status between the two archbishoprics, it had long been established by custom that the man appointed primate of all England should also serve *ex officio* as Lord Chancellor and Keeper of the Great Seal, thereby embodying the key offices of both Church and State. Any individual serving on the staff of such a man would therefore have every chance to observe at close hand the methods by which the crucial business of the kingdom was conducted. And if his mind were sufficiently alert and open, he might well become an apprentice to power in his own right.

For the eighteen months of Deane's tenure, then, Thomas Wolsey resided at Lambeth Palace and soaked up the full authority of the great institutions of the day. It was during Wolsey's stay at Lambeth, for instance, that the archbishop entertained Catherine of Aragon on her way to London after her stormy passage from Spain to marry Prince Arthur. And it was Henry Deane, too, who conducted the marriage ceremony of Catherine and Arthur in November 1501. Henceforth, whenever grand ceremonial was called for Wolsey would be in close attendance and he would also have his first taste of weightier political affairs, accompanying the archbishop to Edinburgh, for instance, in order to negotiate the Treaty of Perpetual Peace with Scotland, which resulted in the marriage of Princess Margaret and James IV.

No less importantly, Wolsey could now savour to his heart's content the full pomp and glory that made Canterbury so much more than a mere administrative centre within the English Church. Not least of all, the cathedral boasted one of the great sights and wonders of the Christian world. The tomb of St Thomas Becket, said one Italian visitor, 'notwithstanding its great size, is entirely covered with plates of pure gold', and the same awe-struck witness noted, too, that 'the gold is scarcely visible from the variety of precious stones with which it was studded'. 'These beauties of nature,' he concluded, 'are enhanced by human skill, for the gold is carved and engraved in beautiful designs …'

Nor was such extravagance misplaced, since Becket was England's most revered saint – one in whose life and death the whole drama of Church–State rivalry had been played out in most spectacular fashion. Indeed, it is no exaggeration to say that in the martyrdom and canonisation of Thomas Becket the ultimate pre-eminence of the clergy had never been embodied more emphatically. And when pilgrims made their slow and tortuous journey to Canterbury in their thousands, they were reminded continually of the transcendent authority of any prelate backed by the moral power of the Church. By the same token, no clergyman seeking high state office would ever find a fitter subject for solemn reflection.

But wherever Wolsey was concerned, events always seemed to move too fast for lengthy contemplation of any kind and in February 1503 the old archbishop died, only one week after the king's wife, Elizabeth of York, had also breathed her last. Once again, however, what might have seemed a serious setback would prove to be another rich opportunity for advancement. Indeed, even the funeral itself was turned to good advantage by the man who would so often refashion adverse circumstances to suit his own ends.

Having been appointed one of Deane's executors, Wolsey now served as chief mourner and duly helped to carry out the elaborate instructions for his master's final journey. In fact £500 had been laid aside in anticipation by the deceased archbishop, who had even written a play to commemorate his own passing. With no trouble spared, it was arranged that the body be carried by water from Lambeth to Faversham by thirty sailors, all dressed in black, and then taken on a hearse to Canterbury to be buried with great pomp in the cathedral. Following hard upon the queen's funeral, this particular send-off therefore called for surpassing skill in management and the fact that Wolsey executed all with such solemnity and pomp could not have gone unnoticed in high places.

By the time that Archbishop Deane was snugly interred, therefore, his favourite chaplain had already secured another valuable position. And any claim that Thomas Wolsey's next appointment represented some kind of downgrading in his status could not be more misleading. He had already seen both Church and State in operation at close hand and now it made perfect sense to gain a grasp of business and diplomacy. As such, his appointment to the staff of Sir Richard Nanfan, Deputy Lieutenant of Calais, was merely one more remarkable opportunity. Indeed, it represented nothing less than the finishing touch in his preparation for royal service.

The Deputy of Calais had always served, in effect, as the gatekeeper to the kingdom of England from the time that Edward III had wrested the old town and harbour from the French following the Battle of Crécy in 1346. Having besieged the town for eleven months, the English had swiftly expelled the native French inhabitants, and though by 1503 foreigners – especially Flemish traders – were once again numerous, a high proportion of the town's population of 1,200 was still descended from the first settlers of a century and a half ago. Now, moreover, the English were as determined as ever to hold the place at any cost. 'When shall the Frenchman Calais win?' ran the inscription above one of the town's gates. 'When iron and lead like cork will swim', the same inscription concluded stridently.

Calais was at the hub of English affairs, both commercially and diplomatically, as well as militarily. Known as 'the brightest jewel in the English crown', it was the portal to the Netherlands and the rest of Europe for England's tin, lead, cloth and wool trades, and its customs revenue alone amounted to no less than a third of the English government's income. Not surprisingly, therefore, it was duly represented in Parliament and also formed part of the diocese of Canterbury, a fact which may explain Wolsey's transfer there upon the death of

Archbishop Deane. Furthermore, since 1453 it was the only territory in France which was still in English hands and its continued possession by English kings was a crucial justification for their claim to the title 'King of France'.

Stretching along the coast for about 25 miles and inland for some six, the so-called 'Pale of Calais' encompassed the fortress of Guisnes on the French border, along with a number of scattered villages. To the south and west, meanwhile, it was surrounded by France, and in the east by the Holy Roman Emperor's territories in the Netherlands, which extended as far as the imperial border towns of Gravelines and St Omer. There was also a permanent military garrison, both in the town of Calais itself and in Guisnes, and there was frequently tension with the rival French garrison in Ardres just across the border. Most significantly of all, however, every local government body within the Pale of Calais was subordinated to the King's Deputy – a fact which would now offer limitless opportunities for Wolsey.

No matter was so minor that it could be allowed to escape official attention. But, in the words of Cavendish, Sir Richard Nanfan soon appears, on account of his 'great age', to have 'committed all the charge of his office' to his assistant, while he himself spent more and more time at home on his Worcestershire estates. This meant that in his superior's absence Wolsey would now be called upon to assume every aspect of the deputy's duties, however grave or trivial. On the one hand, he might well find himself arranging for nothing more than the transfer of two prime stags under diplomatic privilege, if the Archduke of Austria had them to spare for one of the King of England's hunting parks. Very frequently, too, there were routine complaints to be heard about tolls levied by imperial officials at Gravelines on all boats passing between Calais and Flanders. But he might also be called upon to assist the transit of English, French, Spanish and imperial ambassadors, or to supervise any one of a host of other crucial activities or events.

Meanwhile, Wolsey was expected to monitor daily reports from the various keepers of lodging houses about the number and type of guests being accommodated, along with the continual flow of information about seditious utterances within the town's confines. Likewise, details about the condition of the nearby French garrisons were continually processed, alongside information from English spies further afield in France or operating in Flanders. Yet his most pressing task was to examine further daily reports on the state of the town's defences. A fort possessing sluice gates to the sea, which allowed for flooding of the surrounding countryside in the event of French attack, commanded the only road by which Calais could be approached from the south and south-west. And not surprisingly, the maintenance of this fort occupied a special place in the deputy's attention, as did control of the keys of Calais' mighty gates. Each night the keys were received by him and handed over to the night porter, who was told the number of gates to be opened in the morning.

All this, however, was still only part of the workload involved. The king's government in London had, for example, to be reminded constantly of the need to make money available in Calais to pay the soldiers' wages. And when the harvests in England were bad, it was up to the deputy lieutenant to ensure that food supplies were sufficient for the town's garrison and civilian population. In the meantime, the merchants who operated the wool trade had to be pressed to pay their customs dues, and twice a year in May and November the Deputy of Calais received the instalments, amounting to some 25,000 francs, on the king's pensions from France.

The four years that Wolsey spent in such a hive of bureaucratic activity between 1503 and 1507 therefore gave him the ideal opportunity to learn about each and every aspect of government administration. But Calais was more than a training ground, since it also gave Wolsey the perfect platform to parade his efficiency. Now, indeed, he found himself in his natural element: recording, intervening, easing, cajoling and making himself invaluable all the while to the ageing Sir Richard Nanfan, who as early as 1505 was making ready to leave his exacting post and return to England, 'intending to live more at quiet'.

Even so, it was not until January 1507 that Nanfan was finally released from his labours – and only then by death. Nor was it any surprise when Wolsey was appointed his executor, or that any small labour involved should prove such a meagre price to pay. For, prior to Nanfan's demise, he had commended his tireless assistant to the special favour of the king himself, and now at last the world was truly Wolsey's oyster.

3

'At Anchor in the Port of Promotion'

When Thomas Wolsey first took up his new post as royal chaplain in 1507, the capital which greeted him must surely have seemed infinitely exciting and exotic, for although it was still an easy walk to the surrounding fields, London was, without doubt, one of the great cities of Europe. With a population of more than 50,000 jammed inside its crumbling walls and spilling out beyond them, it was a malodorous jumble of slums and ruins. But even if Londoners themselves were quite content to rely on scavenging rooks, ravens and jackdaws to keep their closely packed streets clean, visitors never failed to comment on the special charm of the place. Indeed, its teeming bridge, its serried churches, its splendid public buildings and well-built private houses 'of old time built upon arched vaults with gates of stone' were all universally admired. Even its wildlife, for that matter, attracted glowing praise. According to one foreign visitor, it was reckoned 'a truly beautiful thing to behold one or two thousand swans upon the River Thames'.

Yet the newly arrived priest from Ipswich cannot have failed to notice either that London was manifestly a place of boundless opportunity. An observant Venetian diplomat had remarked some ten years earlier that:

> In one single street named the Strand, leading to St. Paul's, there are fifty-two goldsmiths' shops so rich and full of silver vessels, great and small, that in all the

shops of Rome, Venice and Florence together, I do not think there would be found so many of the magnificence that is to be seen in London.

More significantly still, perhaps, the Venetian would also note how 'these great riches are not occasioned by its inhabitants being noblemen or gentlemen; being all on the contrary, persons of low degree, and artificers who have congregated here from all parts of the island, and from Flanders and from every other place'. Riches of all kinds, then, were readily available for anyone with the gift of acquisition and in Thomas Wolsey's case these riches included political power and influence.

The role of royal chaplain was not, in fact, without possibilities all of its own, especially at this time. For by now Henry VII was shadowed increasingly by old age and sickness, and as his infirmity increased, so his resort to the consolations of religion became ever more pronounced. Though always a devoted son of the Church, one of the king's greatest concerns during his last years was the endowment of the chapel in Westminster that still bears his name. Likewise, the king displayed an increasingly 'singular devotion' to the Blessed Virgin, while his growing preoccupation with his own mortality would also lead him ultimately to make detailed provision for the saying of ten thousand Masses endowed in honour of the Trinity, the Five Wounds of Christ, the nine orders of angels and the Five Joys of Our Lady.

Furthermore, King Henry's superstitious belief in relics and miracles was beginning to border on the obsessional. A piece of the Holy Cross, for instance, brought all the way from Greece, now became one of his most treasured possessions, along with a leg of St George, which had supposedly been captured by Louis of France at the siege of Milan. Inevitably, too, the king's attendance at divine service also occurred with greater regularity than ever. And now it was often Thomas Wolsey who celebrated Mass for his sovereign either in the royal chapel, or more intimately still, in the king's own privy chamber, where an altar stood. On such occasions, moreover – at Richmond, Greenwich or Eltham – Prince Henry, the new heir to the throne, would usually have been present to witness the tall, dignified priest at his imposing best.

But Thomas Wolsey's talents would also have supplied the king's needs in much more significant ways. It was customary for the duties of a royal chaplain to extend well beyond the royal chapel itself, since the household of the first Tudor king, like that of his medieval predecessors, was still crucially important to the governance of the realm. Not least, it served as the normal source from which trained officials were recruited for all sorts of administrative tasks, and any chaplain worth his salt would therefore find himself involved in all kinds of extra duties – especially when he was equipped with the kind of university training that Wolsey could boast. Furthermore, Henry VII was a businessman king who believed, above all else, in the tidy management of his kingdom's affairs, and for this reason he would always value raw ability more highly than nobility in his choice of assistants. An unusual king and exceptional commoner had thus met at a point in history which would lead, in the longer term, to the most extraordinary consequences.

Wolsey's first task, however, was to attach himself to men of influence within the king's circle and this was now brought about by a happy conjunction of circumstances. One layman who was quick to recognise the new chaplain's worth was the witty and avuncular Sir Thomas Lovell, who had joined Henry Tudor during his French exile and gone on to fight for him at the battles of Bosworth and Stoke Field. By the time of Wolsey's arrival at court, Sir Thomas was a veteran in the royal service and the bond between the kindly knight and his sovereign was of the strongest sort. In return for his assistance to the Tudor cause he had, for instance, been appointed Chancellor of the Exchequer for life and Master of the King's Wards. Before that, he had served as Speaker of the House of Commons and since 1502 had been President of the Council. This, then, was a man of many parts and much influence around the throne. And like a number of other 'ancient and grave councillors', Lovell, it seems, came to look upon Wolsey – from the wisdom 'packed in his head' – as 'a meet and apt person to be preferred in witty affairs'.

But it was Richard Fox, Bishop of Winchester and Lord Privy Seal, who became Wolsey's most important patron. By 1507, Fox was 59 years old and had remained on the closest terms with the king for nearly thirty years, having faced exile with him in France during the dark days of Richard III. Indeed, such was the link between the two that it was Fox who had been invited in 1491 to baptise the future Henry VIII. Equally importantly from Thomas Wolsey's point of view, Fox represented the clerical interest at court and, along with William Warham, Archbishop of Canterbury, he was wholeheartedly committed to safeguarding its interests. As a result, he stood out boldly against the old nobility and great landowners, and was keen to groom a suitably talented up-and-coming clergyman to continue his mission in the years ahead.

With rumbles of anticlericalism abroad in the land and growing signs of hostility toward the wealth, privileges and influence of the Church, Fox's chief priority was to see that the Church had a champion at court – one young enough, hopefully, to grow into government over time and one, too, whose power would increase within Church and State simultaneously. For this ultimate purpose a priest who came into the service of the king inconspicuously, and grew through royal favour, was ideal, particularly if he had the kind of application and managerial acumen upon which Henry VII placed such emphasis.

However, there were other respects in which Wolsey was ideally placed to capitalise on Fox's goodwill. As an inspector of Magdalen College, Fox will certainly have known a good deal about his new protégé, and the venerable bishop may well have identified him as a man after his own heart. Like him Wolsey had come from a humble background, and the chaplain was also making his way to the centre of national life via Oxford, just as Fox had done. Even more significantly, perhaps, Wolsey had already accumulated some significant experience of foreign affairs, as a result of his service in Calais, and this coincided perfectly with Fox's own special area of expertise. Indeed, the bishop's experience in this field was second to none and it was he who had successfully concluded the protracted marriage negotiations between the king's eldest son and Catherine of Aragon.

Yet there were other men at court whom Wolsey was much more inclined to watch with suspicion from a distance – and rightly so. One such individual was Thomas Howard, Earl of Surrey, who now acted as the figurehead and spokesman of the old nobility. His father, the first Duke of Norfolk, had been killed with Richard III at Bosworth and his title attainted, while the son himself was deprived of his land and confined to the Tower of London. A year later, however, he was pardoned and given an honourable office in the north of England as lieutenant-general. In this capacity, he had put down the Yorkshire rising of 1489, and then in the autumn of 1496 he had also successfully resisted a Scottish invasion. Thereafter, in return for his sterling services he had been brought back to court, restored to the earldom of Surrey and by 1507 was serving as the Lord High Treasurer of England. Clearly, then, the fact that Howard was in such favour sent an unmistakable signal to all who attended the king that the primacy of the clerical interest at court could no longer be taken wholly for granted. It provided a clear signal, too, that Fox must advance his protégé with some urgency, if he was to guarantee the Church's interests as he desired.

For the time being, however, a much more corrosive role was being played by two men of considerably lower social status. These were Sir Richard Empson, Chancellor of the Duchy of Lancaster, and Sir Edmund Dudley, who had previously been Speaker of the House of Commons, but in 1507 held no official position beyond that arising from some minor sinecures. Dudley, a Sussex gentleman by birth, and Empson, a Northamptonshire commoner, had both been called to the Bar and after successful legal careers entered Henry VII's service, where they were employed, alongside Lovell, in the tax-raising activities of the Court of Exchequer. And before long, these two inveterate chisellers would become the most hated men in England as a result of their offensive manners, their ruthlessness in extracting money and their personal corruption. On all counts, therefore, it was crucial for Thomas Wolsey neither to be associated with these men nor to fall foul of their displeasure.

But while Wolsey watched his back, he also continued to make hay. In fact, with his experience of financial administration and foreign relations at Calais, and his friendship with both Lovell and Fox, he could have been employed equally suitably in handling either the financial or diplomatic aspects of government. As luck would have it, though, he was appointed assistant secretary to Fox, and this was of the greatest significance, since the Bishop of Winchester was now virtually in sole charge of England's foreign policy. Whether Wolsey's appointment was, indeed, pure chance or rather the result of skilful manipulation on his part is unknown, but in any event things would now unfold more favourably for him than even he could possibly have anticipated. Not only would he be able, in the longer term, to claim the title of 'arbiter of Europe', but for the time being he would also be able to avoid close association with the hated activities of Empson and Dudley.

Once assigned to Fox it was not long before Wolsey was engaged in the kind of delicate foreign negotiations at which he would always excel. In the spring of 1508, for instance, he was sent on a tricky diplomatic mission to Scotland, whose international status had risen sharply in recent years. Indeed, its king, James IV, had set out to make his kingdom one of Christendom's leading nations and seemed to be succeeding admirably to this end. He had built a navy, opened gunpowder factories in Fife, intervened boldly in European politics and, for good measure, even gone on in 1503 to marry Henry VII's elder daughter, Margaret. His court was predictably splendid, too, and included among other notables the poets William Dunbar and David Lindsay, not to mention a bevy of beautiful ladies, several of whom he seduced. Somewhat paradoxically, perhaps, he was also very religious and, despite the time he expended upon women, hunting and diplomacy, he still managed, we are told, to attend Mass several times a day. But though his realm boasted three universities as compared to England's two and its scholars taught in universities throughout Europe, it remained for the people of other countries, and particularly England, a mythical land inhabited by 'wild Scots' and bounded in the north by a great field of snow and ice.

It was to this strange and exotic land that Thomas Wolsey was now dispatched, for since his marriage to Princess Margaret, James had continued to keep his options open, and did not, as the English had hoped, repudiate Scotland's 'auld alliance' with France, which had already lasted over 300 years. More than this, he had actually sent his cousin, the Earl of Arran, and Arran's brother, Patrick Hamilton, to France to negotiate a renewal of that alliance.

The problem for James, however, was the simple one of communication with the French. If his envoys travelled by sea, they might find themselves forced by rough weather to shelter in an English port. Travelling by land, on the other hand, would involve either permission from the English government or, alternatively, the risk of making the journey without guarantees of safe conduct. In the event, Arran and Hamilton took the last option and paid the price accordingly. Although they reached France uneventfully, they were apprehended at Kent on their return journey and taken to Henry's court to be detained as 'honoured guests'. When, however, James IV complained about the treatment of his two representatives and added a further swipe at the English authorities in Northumberland for their failure to surrender Scottish fugitives, Wolsey was sent to Edinburgh to iron matters out – the clearest possible evidence of his rapidly growing political status.

The journey itself was a forbidding one which took at least a fortnight, even in the most favourable conditions, for on the rough and muddy roads north, 40 miles a day was the furthest distance that any traveller could normally hope to cover. Yet Wolsey did at least enjoy the company of perhaps the only true friend he ever made during his many years at court. Lord Darcy of Templehurst was an older courtier and privy councillor now serving as Warden of the Eastern Marches who had, it seems, first been thrown into the closest kind of acquaintance with Wolsey, as a result of the inadequate sleeping arrangements caused by the itinerancy of the royal court. Apparently, the two men had sometimes been sleeping companions on arduous royal progresses to remote and inhospitable locations, for Darcy would later write to his friend referring to him as his 'bedfellow' and reflecting upon the discomforts they experienced together on their courtly travels. Interestingly, he also recalled the long hours they had spent revealing their minds and ambitions to each other and talking over their frustrations, each promising to help the other as far as he could.

In view of the general difficulty of travel, both men took their time on this particular trip and carried out other duties as they edged northwards. First, after making their way up the Great North Road by Ware, Huntingdon and Grantham, they made arrangements at York with the Abbot of St Mary's, who acted as the government's banker in that region, for the payment of wages and for the supply of provisions to the border garrisons. Then, before moving on to inspect the fortresses at Norham and Berwick, they stopped at Newcastle to discuss with the Earl of Northumberland his somewhat ineffectual attempts to suppress the lawlessness of the Border country. Thereafter, it was a two-day journey via Dunbar and Haddington to Edinburgh along a road which was more commonly travelled by English armies than English diplomats.

After such an arduous journey, it was no doubt galling but quite predictable that Wolsey would be met upon his arrival with a calculated snub. After waiting five days in Berwick for his guarantee of safe-conduct, he reached Edinburgh on 28 March, only to find the king inspecting a gunpowder factory. As a result, it was another five days before an audience was arranged. But if James IV was cool, Wolsey was nothing if not persistent, calling upon the Scottish king daily for the next eight days in an effort to wear him down with unremitting courtesy. The negotiations made no progress, however, and Wolsey reported to Henry VII that James was moody and changeable. Ultimately, it seems, the Scots were not for compromise and it was made clear that there could be no treaty of friendship until Arran and Hamilton were released.

Back in England, meanwhile, Henry VII remained equally stubborn and it was not until his death a year later that the two Scottish captives were eventually set free. Yet the whole episode had provided tantalising glimpses of Wolsey's merits. Not least of all, he had demonstrated that he could make an honest report, even if it was one that his sovereign might not have relished. Though he went to Scotland to protest, he confessed to Henry that according to the information he had gathered 'the offences of Englishmen were to those of Scotsmen as four to one'. Furthermore, by proposing a face-to-face summit between the kings of England and Scotland, he had also demonstrated a preference for compromise and what would be an ongoing belief in the efficacy of personal contact between monarchs as a means of dispelling distrust. However, while the idea of a direct encounter appears to have found favour with James, there was no enthusiasm for it among his council, and the plan subsequently sank without trace.

Certainly, Wolsey's stock did not fall as a result of his long trek north and by July 1508 he was on his travels once more – this time to the court of the Holy Roman Emperor. After the death of his wife, Elizabeth of York, in 1503, the King of England had soon set his dimming eyes upon another marriage. Initially the Queen of Naples had been considered, and a list of twenty-four criteria had even been drawn up to test her suitability. In particular, Henry's ambassadors were required to 'mark her breasts, whether they be big or small' and, more importantly still, to 'make inquisition and ensearch what land or livelihood the said Queen hath or shall have after the decease of her mother'.

But the good lady appears to have failed on all counts, for Henry soon switched his attention, first to Margaret of Angoulême, and then to the pick of the bunch, Margaret of Savoy. Not only was the latter regent of the Netherlands and daughter of Maximilian I, Holy Roman Emperor, she was also the sister of Philip the Handsome, Archduke of Flanders, who in 1506 had been driven by an adverse wind to take shelter in England, whereupon he had promised Henry his sister's hand. Even the marriage portion of 300,000 crowns had been fixed with each crown to be worth four shillings.

Nevertheless, there remained significant problems to overcome, not the least of which was the considerable wilfulness of the Lady Margaret herself. She had, after all, already seen off two husbands and was in no hurry now to take on the ailing King of England. Some pressure would therefore be needed to bring the marriage off, and it was under these circumstances that Richard Fox and Thomas Lovell had first begun in the spring of 1508 to urge that Wolsey be sent upon a direct embassy to the Emperor Maximilian. The result was an expedition that was remarkable both for the speed and efficiency of its execution, as well as its impact upon the royal chaplain's fortunes.

The story of Wolsey's trip to Flanders in the summer of 1508 is related in a particularly purple patch of George Cavendish's *Life and Death of Cardinal Wolsey*, which extends to some 1,200 words – a little less than half the narrative to that point. According to Cavendish's account, Wolsey had his final instructions from the king at four o'clock in the afternoon at Richmond before taking a barge at once to Gravesend, having ensured in advance that the barge was ready for immediate departure. Post horses had also been arranged at Gravesend for the journey to Dover, where he would embark for passage across the Channel.

With more post horses prepared in relay, Wolsey was said to have reached Dover the next morning at the very moment when his boat for the Channel was ready to weigh anchor. By noon, apparently, he was at Calais, and by late afternoon, having ridden long and hard, he was at the residence of the emperor, whereupon he was said to have been granted an immediate audience, since Maximilian's 'affection to the king of England was such that he was glad of any opportunitie to doe him a curtesy'.

Thereafter, Wolsey briefly discussed the details of his mission and respectfully requested the most expeditious response possible from his host, though even this swiftly conducted dialogue left England's envoy in no doubt about the weasel ways of contemporary diplomacy. And he learned the lesson well, if his future behaviour is anything to judge by. 'There is here so much inconstancy, mutability and little regard of promises and causes,' he observed, 'that in their appointments there is little trust or surety; for things surely determined to be done one day are changed and altered the next.'

Yet the outcome of Wolsey's audience with the emperor and his formidable minister, the Bishop of Gurk, could not have been more encouraging, for not only were Maximilian's responses all favourable, they were delivered early next morning. Leaving immediately for Calais, therefore, in the company of a splendid train of nobles provided by his host, he embarked for England after an uneventful night's rest, to be back at Dover by ten the next morning. That night he slept at Richmond, the whole journey having taken – or so Cavendish would claim - no more than seventy hours.

But there was, it seems, a further twist, for Wolsey rose next morning, ahead of Henry, and presented himself at the royal bedchamber as the king left early for Mass. Seeing him there and thinking him remiss in his duties, the king is said to have inquired why he had not yet set out on his mission, to which Wolsey is said to have replied, 'Sire, if it may stand with your Highness's pleasure, I have already been with the Emperor and dispatched your affairs, I trust to your Grace's liking'. When Henry then enquired further about a messenger he had sent after Wolsey with additional instructions, he was met with the following response: 'I encountered him, Sire, and I made bold, your Grace, upon my own discretion, to dispatch the same. And for as much as I have exceeded your Grace's commission, I most humbly crave your gracious remission and pardon.' To this Henry is said to have replied, 'We do not only pardon you thereof, but also give you our princely thanks, and also for your good and speedy exploit'.

Not surprisingly, the truth of the whole story has been doubted by many historians down the years and there are certainly aspects of the narrative which are not borne out by other evidence. If, for instance, the journey did actually occur in the summer of 1508 it could not have involved a face-to-face meeting with the emperor, since he was not in the Netherlands at this time. Nevertheless, the speed of such a journey is not entirely beyond possibility. Although the distance from Gravesend to Dover was some 50 miles, the road along which Wolsey passed was one of the best in England. Furthermore, a supply of post horses was, indeed, always available at Rochester, Sittingbourne, Faversham and Canterbury for travellers on the king's business. And if the meeting occurred at Gravelines or some other place not far from the frontier – rather than at Bruges or Courtrai, which are some 60 miles from Calais – it is just conceivable that Wolsey could have managed it.

Certainly, if anyone could achieve such a feat, Wolsey – with his boundless drive and determination to impress – would be a good candidate. It is worth noting, too, that Cavendish specifically tells his readers that he heard the tale from Wolsey in person after his eventual fall from power. At any rate, it is too good a story to dismiss entirely, and there can be little doubt that the rising star of English diplomacy saw his efforts on this occasion as a real springboard for his career.

Wolsey would, in fact, be packed off to the Netherlands once more in 1508 in another effort to hasten the marriage with Margaret. In the summer, he had obviously conducted his mission skilfully, because the lady herself had executed the marriage treaty and agreed to fines that should be paid were the marriage not to take place. Nevertheless, Margaret was known to be fickle and promises of marriage soon proved to be as easily broken as made. In consequence, Wolsey was again at the imperial court at Malines from the beginning of October and into November, attempting to iron out the details to his master's satisfaction as well as Margaret's, though in spite of his tireless efforts and a grand embassy headed by the Earl of Surrey, Margaret continued to hesitate. And it was while she dallied that the King of England's health finally collapsed.

At 52 years of age Henry VII's glorious victory at Bosworth Field was now long past and there were very few left who remembered the fair-haired young Welshman who had landed at Milford Haven those many years ago to seize the English throne by force of arms. Racked by 'a disease of the joints', he had complained to his mother as early as 1501 of failing eyesight and apologised for the fact that it had taken him all of three days to write her a letter in his own hand. Then, during 1503, following hard upon the death of his eldest son and heir, he had lost his wife, Elizabeth of York, to that most eager of grim reapers, puerperal fever. It came as no real surprise, therefore, that only one year later the ubiquitous courtly whisperers were suggesting that the king's grace was 'but a weak and sickly man, not likely to be long lived'.

Even so, the voluminous correspondence conducted between Henry and Wolsey leaves no doubt about the extent to which the king had come to appreciate his chaplain's abilities. Around this time, the king would refer to him more and more as 'our trusty and well-beloved chaplain', and saw fit to advance his servant's career accordingly. Henry had, in fact, already established a direct Magdalen connection at court by his appointment of the college's president, Richard Mayhew, as royal almoner, and it was, perhaps, only logical now that the current rising light should receive a similar appointment, possibly with Mayhew's sponsorship. Accordingly, on 3 November 1508 Wolsey, too, became almoner to the king. Moreover, the job of administering the king's charitable works could not have been more significant at this time, for as the king's health deteriorated steadily, so his desire to appease his Maker grew greater than ever.

Like all his predecessors, Henry had always seen fit to cater generously for good causes. Thus, he had not only provided daily alms for the poor and needy, but had also ploughed more considerable sums of money into a range of worthy projects. He had, for instance, built houses for various communities of friars at Richmond, Greenwich, Newark, Canterbury and Southampton, while the library of the Observant Franciscans at Greenwich was also lavishly stocked with books given personally by the king.

Now, however, Henry's charitable plans expanded considerably in scale, which would undoubtedly have increased his almoner's sphere of operation. Just as the king had built the Savoy Hospital, near Charing Cross, to shelter 100 poor folk, he planned urgently in the last year of his life to erect a large hospital in Bath. His will also made detailed provision for a surge of other benefactions. There were, for instance, separate bequests to the Carthusians of London and Sheen, and since the friars of Greenwich could acquire nothing as a result of their vows of poverty, the king made arrangements for their orchard wall to be rebuilt of brick. He also set aside £2,000 for relief of the sick and destitute, half of which was to be distributed at his tomb, the rest taken by hand to the bedridden. To King's College, Cambridge, meanwhile, he left £5,000 and funds were also arranged for improving the main roads between Westminster, Richmond and Canterbury, to make them pilgrims' ways. To Wolsey, in particular, the king requested that 8,000 masses be offered at Oxford and Cambridge, watching in person, we are told, as the money was made over to the almoner.

With Lovell's encouragement, the king soon considered it timely to reward his almoner's efforts with a gift of more special significance. Since he still ranked only as a humble priest – one of a stable of royal chaplains – there was, of course, no question of apportioning Wolsey a slice of royal land or doling out to him any carefully husbanded funds from the crown's coffers. However, the royal influence could easily be wielded to secure a rich promotion within the Church, with the additional benefit that England could continue to enjoy the lucky recipient's talents, while Rome paid his wages.

As it transpired, Wolsey had already been exhibiting for some time what might well be described as his own peculiar species of clerical kleptomania. In 1506, for instance, while he was still resident in Calais, the Benedictine Abbot of Bury St Edmonds had appointed him Vicar of Redgrave in Suffolk - no doubt after the usual requests from Sir Richard Nanfan. And then, in July 1508, he had received a dispensation from the pope to hold a maximum of four benefices simultaneously with leave of absence from all of them, whereupon he had become free to accept the vicarage of Lydd in Kent from the Cistercian Abbot of Tintern. Pluralism of this kind was not of course uncommon, though what was notable in Wolsey's case was that even when he achieved the highest summits in the Church, far from divesting himself of his other benefices he clung to them tenaciously while continuing to collect more and more appointments.

But early in 1509, at the king's personal prompting, a perk of an altogether higher order now came his way. It was on 2 February – the last feast of Candlemas that he would witness – that Henry VII saw fit to make Wolsey Dean of the cathedral church of Lincoln, and six days afterwards, the almoner was presented with a prebend in the same cathedral. Eventually installed by proxy on Lady Day, this was the moment for which Wolsey had been hoping ever since Archbishop Dean's death, and it was news which must have cheered his mother in what would prove to be the last few months of her life.

The reward came only just in time, however, for with the approach of spring in 1509, the wiry and chronically bronchitic Henry VII, whose teeth were by now 'few, poor and blackish', began his creaky descent into a 'consuming sickness'. In 1507, Henry's servants had already despaired of his life after he became seriously ill of a 'quinsy'. But this was only one in a long list of episodes marking the king's final physical collapse. According to Polydore Vergil, for instance, he was greatly incapacitated during the spring in three successive years. In February 1508, moreover, he was said to be in the last stage of consumption, only to rally against all odds. By Holy Week of 1509, however, the king was at last 'utterly without hope of recovery'. For the space of twenty-seven hours, we are told, he endured his final agonies before at last succumbing to the inevitable on 21 April. And all the while that the king endured 'the sharp assaults of death', those about the throne and in the nation at large were anxiously awaiting the new and healthier dawn to come.

4

The Threshold of All Things Great

It was not until 10 May 1509 that Henry VII was finally consigned to dwell 'more richly dead than he did alive' in his splendid tomb of black marble at Westminster. And throughout the grief and gravity of his final agonies, as well as the lavish obsequies which accompanied his passing, Thomas Wolsey was never far removed. While the king lay dying at Richmond Palace, for instance, it was his almoner who had assisted prominently at the Easter services, and during the next harrowing weeks, Wolsey would also play his solemn part in both the shriving of his master's soul and anointing of his body.

Nor was he absent from the final ceremony of interment itself. Snugly flanked by bishops, abbots and representatives of the King's Bench, he duly took his place amid the grand cortège which formed on the evening of 8 May to convey the royal corpse on its final journey. Further ahead, behind the royal standard and a wax effigy of the dead king dressed in his most magnificent robes of state, rode an imposing throng of foreign potentates, courtiers and dignitaries of all kinds, while hooded monks, canons of the cathedral chapter and the choir of the King's Chapel intoned their most mournful Latin dirges.

Past the green parks and great houses of the nobility on the south bank of the Thames, along rows of ornate, well-windowed merchant houses, and through the meaner streets of Southwark where pock-marked whores and reeling drunks usually abounded, the solemn procession wound its way by the light of

600 torches. And when, over the next two nights, the former king's body lay in state at St Paul's, illuminated by 'a goodlie curious Light of Nine Branches', Wolsey was nearby at Westminster to offer up his prayers beside the freshly prepared grave.

Yet as the time approached for the king's wasted remains to be placed beside the bones of his wife, the chaplain's feelings were likely to have been mixed. It was true that he had once more lost a patron, but then again his dead master had always been his own man, and his councillors, just as surely, were men of his mind and making. Moreover, those in his trust, like William Warham, Archbishop of Canterbury; Thomas Ruthall, secretary to the king; and, of course, Richard Fox, were all weighty and substantial figures, anchored permanently in their sovereign's estimation and, as such, not to be outstripped or undermined by any rising force while the crown was still his.

There was also the 66-year-old Thomas Howard, first soldier of England and Lord Treasurer to consider, as well as a host of lesser lights who had hemmed Wolsey in and blocked his way. Sir Edward Poynings, controller of the royal household, had forged a worthy reputation as a soldier and administrator, while George Talbot, Earl of Shrewsbury, had fought bravely beside his sovereign at Stoke Field, and carried with him an illustrious family reputation. Likewise, Sir Henry Marney had stood firm against the rebel host at Blackheath in 1497 and fully confirmed his unflinching loyalty in subsequent years. If, therefore, Henry VII required loyal and capable senior servants, they had been his in abundance.

As such, the demise of the old king spelled opportunity rather than crisis for Thomas Wolsey, particularly when the age and nature of the new monarch were considered. Nine weeks and four days short of his eighteenth birthday, Henry VIII was cut in a clean-contrasting mould to his newly deceased father. Glittering, massive, puffed up and impressionable, his excessive heartiness and exhibitionism were merely the tip of a much more ominous emotional iceberg. Having been reared in comparative isolation under the leaden piety of his careworn grandmother, Lady Margaret Beaufort, he still bore the marks, and, to compound matters, he had suffered a series of losses between the ages of 8 and 12 which cut him deeply. On 11 February 1503, for instance, his mother, Elizabeth of York, had swiftly followed her newborn daughter to the grave, and in June of the same year Henry's favourite sister, Margaret, suffered what appeared to be an equally final fate when she was carried off to Edinburgh to wed the gifted, but philandering King James IV of Scotland.

Furthermore, the death of Arthur, his elder brother, in 1502 had already ushered in a time of upheaval and uncertainty for the boy who now became the sole guarantee of the Tudors' grasp upon the crown. Though the emotional bond between the two brothers had been tenuous to say the least, the impact of the younger prince's elevation upon his subsequent development cannot be doubted. Thereafter, he would live at Westminster under the remorseless gaze of his father and suffer the full rigours of a sheltered upbringing which would ill equip him for the practical tasks of leadership ahead. Nor would the early attempts to break him for government succeed in other respects. On the contrary, they would serve only to reinforce the boy's natural wilfulness and impulsiveness, and, in doing so, store up untold problems for the future. Curbed, cowed and cloistered during the crucial years of his adolescence, Henry VIII would be not so much crowned in 1509 as unleashed.

Nevertheless, though politically raw and prone to violent gusts of enthusiasm, he would be hailed by his subjects as the herald of a golden age of glory, light and learning. And if surface appearances were to be trusted, England's high hopes were by no means unfounded, for everything about the new monarch seemed to declare his careless grace and prowess. Indeed, he could play the roles of Christian scholar, courtly lover or dashing soldier-athlete with equal ease. Tireless in the field, invincible with lance, spear, poleaxe or bow, 'angelic' of face, broad-chested, bejewelled and beringed, there seemed no admirable quality or advantage in which he was lacking.

Equally importantly, he had inherited a stable realm, freed from the shadow of rebellion which had stalked his father, and he was also comfortably equipped with a financial legacy amounting, in all probability, to around £300,000 – the equivalent of some two or three years revenue. 'He is very rich,' wrote one of his innumerable enthusiasts, 'and very liberal, so humane and kind that the poorest person can easily approach him and so made for war, that there is no military exercise in which he does not equal, not to say surpass his soldiers.' The papal tax collector and historian Polydore Vergil was yet another who gushed praise for the new king's 'handsome bearing', 'skill at arms' and 'scholarship of no mean order'. There were even references by the Italian to Henry's 'humanity, benevolence and self-control'. The adulation heaped upon the new king from all quarters was, then, utterly unalloyed, though in the process, his pride and sense of power, as well as his contempt for the foreigner, were all magnified accordingly. And if, when the time came, the old heads of the previous reign might choose to deny him his wishes, he could be counted upon to look elsewhere for counsel.

Yet if any of this might be taken to imply, as it often is, that Thomas Wolsey was already safely set upon a well-paved high road to power under a new, more flamboyant and pliable king, events would soon prove otherwise. For though the young monarch was said to have received him with friendly and familiar conversation upon his regal debut at court, the progress of Henry VII's favourite chaplain and almoner seems to have been squarely baulked thereafter by none other than the new king's grandmother.

It was Lady Margaret Beaufort, Countess of Richmond, who had engineered her son's ascent to the crown before the climactic Battle of Bosworth, and in later overseeing the education and upbringing of her grandson she had firmly established her authority over him. Not surprisingly, then, she was eminently well placed to seize the initiative in those first harried days when that same grandson became king himself. Wise, devout, watchful and controlling, the countess's deep-seated suspicion of fast-rising men at court is likely to have been especially pronounced at this time. And though there was by now little of the parvenu about Thomas Wolsey, for he had long ago grown easy among the great and noble, his questionable beginnings were unlikely to have been ignored entirely by the 'venerable Margaret'. Even more importantly, Wolsey's sponsor had been the old Marquess of Dorset, and for one of the countess's calculating cast of mind and Lancastrian blood, the marquess and his protégés were all automatically tarred with the same Yorkist brush.

In consequence, Wolsey was left to wait edgily in the political wings as the old guard, who were all of the Lady Margaret's age and persuasion, continued to dominate the corridors of power. Indeed, Warham, Fox, Ruthall and Thomas Howard picked up the reins of power just where they had laid them upon the old king's death, leaving Wolsey and others close to him stranded in political limbo. While his friend Darcy, for instance, was superseded as vice-chamberlain, Wolsey himself was not only overlooked as royal chaplain, but also barred from re-appointment as almoner. Indeed, the latter post now became the sole responsibility of Dr John Edenham and, to add insult to injury, Wolsey was bypassed once more in July, following Edenham's untimely demise.

Meanwhile, the absence of Wolsey's name from any lists drawn up for the coronation is no less striking, and it was not until November, almost two months after the death of Edenham's successor, Thomas Hobbes, that Wolsey was finally appointed as Henry VIII's royal almoner. To all appearances, then, his career hung precariously in the balance as the new order took shape during the late spring and summer of 1509.

Even during the ten weeks or so of Lady Margaret Beaufort's dominance, however, a subterranean tide had continued to run in Wolsey's favour. The accession of a handsome and dashing young king in place of his cautious and niggardly father would, for instance, put paid to the two most prominent and unpopular ministers of the previous reign. On 25 April, only three days after the death of Henry VII, a proclamation was issued to the effect that anyone who had previously sustained injury or suffered loss of goods at the hands of his royal commissioners should make due supplication to the new king. Thus were the flood gates opened and all too predictably the popular clamour was now directed in full against Richard Empson and Edmund Dudley.

There followed baying petitions, biting ballads and a hearty collective cry for blood, which England's new sovereign was keen to exploit for popularity's sake. Accordingly, the pair were arrested in July and charged with high treason on the wholly spurious grounds that they had plotted to place the new king under restraint in order to prevent their removal from power. 'Whoever yet saw any man condemned for justice?' complained Empson at the time.

Crucially, though, the death of these two newly rich scapegoats had the effect of sparing Wolsey's own patrons. Richard Fox survived his sovereign's whim and continued as Bishop of Winchester and Lord Privy Seal on Henry VIII's council, while another of Wolsey's sponsors, Sir Thomas Lovell, also managed to emerge unscathed after some anxious weeks, regardless of his former close connection with Empson and Dudley at the Exchequer.

Moreover, even though the remaining personnel were unchanged, the evolving balance of power on the new king's council would suit Wolsey's longer-term needs admirably. Though the Great Seal remained with the Archbishop of Canterbury, William Warham seems, in fact, to have taken little or no part in moulding the new king's outlook. Unambitious and almost certainly weary of twenty years of official life, his hang-dog expression in his most famous portrait implies a long lifetime of mild regrets. Ultimately, he was content to devote himself to his clerical duties while dispensing generous patronage to impecunious authors. And in consequence, the chief place in the direction of affairs belonged to Richard Fox.

Named by Henry VII as one of his executors in return for his considerable services, Fox had also, it seems, been specially commended by the former king to his heir. Even so, the new monarch was wary of Fox, confiding to the Spanish ambassador Caroz that though he trusted him, he knew he did so 'at his risk'. 'Here in England,' added Caroz, 'they think he is a fox and such is his name.' Yet wily or not, such was Fox's undeniable talent that by 1510 Badoer, the Venetian ambassador, was referring to him as '*alter rex*'. And this, of course, could not have been better news for Wolsey, since the bishop had, as we have already seen, marked him out as a rising star of the clerical interest at court.

Fox's primacy was no doubt reinforced, too, by his support for the new king's most passionate early cause – his marriage to his brother Arthur's former wife, Catherine of Aragon. Less than a week into his reign, in fact, Henry VIII boldly announced his intention to marry the Spanish princess, who was five years his senior and had lived in harassed isolation since her husband's death. Negotiations had already been in hand to match Henry with Eleanor of Savoy, thereby hitching England to the Habsburgs in a grand dynastic scheme. But the young king was nothing if not headstrong and would not be deterred from putting his own distinctive stamp on his kingdom's foreign policy. Nor, for that matter, would he be swayed by serious divisions on his council concerning the wisdom of the marriage.

William Warham, for instance, had expressed grave doubts about Pope Julius II's bull, which had originally sanctioned the union back in December 1503. Most seriously of all, it had ignored Catherine's claim that her previous marriage had never been consummated. But it had also been conspicuously slow in arriving and, to make matters worse, its validity had eventually been challenged by none other than young Henry himself, on the eve of his fourteenth birthday. It was no secret either that Henry VII, for all his eagerness to secure the Spanish alliance and dowry, could not ultimately bring even his well-worn conscience to sanction the marriage. It did not take an archbishop, after all, to know that in biblical terms any match between a woman and her dead husband's brother was highly questionable, for, according to the Book of Leviticus, it was an 'unclean thing', which would leave the sinning couple childless.

The new king's decision was therefore as risky as it was momentous and it succeeded in no small part because Richard Fox supported it on practical grounds of statecraft. From the bishop's perspective, moreover, the apparent non-consummation of Catherine's previous marriage served as a clear-cut incentive for the new match. Certainly, there was no conclusive evidence that Catherine and the sickly Arthur had ever lived together as man and wife in the fullest sense. And was not the new king, in any case, someone whose own conscience should be respected and trusted? This, after all, was a prince who, in spite of all his interests and distractions, still found time to hear three Masses per day. And had his theological training not made him a dutiful son of the Church, wholly alert to its laws – someone who had fully imbibed the piety of his dead father?

There were other arguments, too, that could now be raised in favour of the marriage. Henry VII in his death agony was said, for instance, to have beseeched his son to marry Catherine. Likewise, Ferdinand of Spain was eagerly offering to pay up his daughter's dowry, while offering at the same time to betroth his grandson, Charles of Ghent, to young Henry's sister, the Lady Mary. Indeed, such was Ferdinand's keenness that 200,000 crowns were dispatched, not by sea – for fear of delay – but through Italian bankers in bonds and bills of exchange. So Fox, and by implication Wolsey, were surely bound to prevail.

Within two months of his father's funeral, therefore, Henry VIII duly married and brushed aside, at a stroke, eight long years of vacillation. He had gone with his bride to the church of the Observant Franciscans at Greenwich on Barnaby Bright Day, 11 June, and pledged his troth in a ceremony that was remarkable only for its privacy. In fact, no official celebrations at all were arranged and even the traditional ceremony of putting the bride and groom to bed seems to have been waived on this occasion, since the king who could do no wrong was still officially in mourning for his father.

Nevertheless, before the day was done the whole teeming populace of London knew of the marriage. They knew, too, that the bride had been clad in white in token of her virginity. And if Londoners were sorry to have been denied a wedding spectacle, the coronation ceremony which followed two weeks later would more than compensate for any temporary disappointment. In fact, it would set the tone resoundingly for the lavish pageantry which came to characterise the entire reign. Henry had, after all, demanded that his wedding be spoken of in superlatives, and, even though time for preparation was short, the robes and trappings for the procession to Westminster were described by one and all as 'more rich' and 'more curious' than had ever been seen.

On the eve of the midsummer ceremony the royal couple rode through a capital festooned with decorations. At that point in the city known as Old Change, which London's goldsmiths had made their own, young maidens clad in white waved branches of white May, while at Cornhill the lavish display of rich tapestries and cloth of gold was nothing short of breathtaking. As free wine flowed from conduits, Henry rode beneath a canopy borne by the barons of the Cinque Ports, with his heralds going before him and the bearers of his hat and cloak just behind, their mounts trapped with silver cloth under a web of green and gold. Then, we are told, came 'nine children of honour' in blue velvet and fleurs-de-lys on horses decked with the emblems of England and France, Gascony and Guienne, Normandy, Anjou, Cornwall, Wales and Ireland – all the king's dominions, actual or claimed.

Like his gentlemen and household officers, the king himself wore scarlet robes, though his were of the richest velvet and furred with ermine. Sewn into his jacket of raised gold were diamonds, emeralds, pearls and other precious stones, while across his chest he wore a baldric of outsize rubies. The queen, in her turn, was drawn by white palfreys in a litter of cloth of gold, clad once more in white satin, her gleaming hair hanging down her back, 'of a very great length, beautiful and goodly to behold'.

Then, on the day of the ancient ceremony itself, Henry and Catherine walked the short distance to Westminster Abbey along a carpet of striped cloth strewn with flowers, which was later ripped to pieces by the common people in quest of souvenirs. Led to his throne by no fewer than thirty-six bishops, the king was anointed with holy oil before being consecrated by Archbishop Warham with the crown of St Edward the Confessor in a ritual which unfolded over many hours. In a much shorter ceremony, meanwhile, the queen was crowned with a heavy gold diadem set with rubies, pearls and sapphires.

Thereafter it was time for a banquet at Westminster Hall, 'greater than any that Caesar had known', followed by jousts and tournaments over many days. Such was the scale of celebration that in the tiltyard of the palace at Westminster a miniature castle had been erected around which mock battles of various descriptions were fought, the most notable of which involved a combat between the 'Knights of Diana', wearing gold helmets with huge feather plumes, and the 'Knights of Pallas'. At its climax fallow dear were released and killed by greyhounds, after which their carcasses were trussed on poles and presented to the ladies.

But though Wolsey appears to have missed out on this and all else associated with the coronation, he need not have felt too deprived, for soon enough, on 30 July, the pious, creaking roadblock who had so far frustrated him finally made way. Ironically, it may well have been the wedding festivities themselves that put paid to the king's grandmother once and for all. Sixty-eight years old, enfeebled by her spiritual exertions and itching, in any case, for eternity, Lady Margaret Beaufort did not linger long after her collapse, though even on her death bed at the abbot's house of Cheyney Gates at Westminster, where she had been lodged for the duration of the nuptials, she continued to load her grandson with advice. He should take as his mentor, she said, her confessor, Bishop John Fisher, 'the most holy and learned prelate in Christendom', for in her opinion, only he could now help to guide the newly fledged monarch through the trying transition to high authority.

Both the implication and irony of the old lady's words are, of course, clear to see with hindsight. But even the force of a personality like Lady Margaret's could not extend beyond the grave, and her passing duly broke Henry VIII's last remaining link to his childhood. The two dominant figures of his past, his father and his grandmother, were thus swept from his life within months of one another and now he was his own master, for even if he faced the disapproval of his councillors, he was still their king. And the king's word was law.

Henceforth, England's new ruler could at last seek to give his court a style that would be the envy of foreign princes. It would be a home to artists from Italy and the Low Countries, to fine home-grown musicians such as Robert Fairfax, and, above all, it would be a haven for the finest scholars in Europe: a place where humanist lights like Erasmus and More, Linacre, Colet, and Mountjoy could shine brightest. But, much more visibly still, Henry's court was to become a refuge from worldly cares and haven for glorious, youthful excess. Unlike the Holy Roman Emperor, for instance, who was said to be 'frugal and an enemy to pomp', England's king would neither skimp nor scrape in cutting a figure amid his European counterparts. And there was more, it seems, to Henry's high living than mere public relations and international prestige.

Brought up in a household that saved candle ends and ate porridge, and freed now from the tyranny of the schoolroom, regular bedtimes and a meagre allowance, England's new ruler was determined to kick over the traces like a schoolboy on holiday. May Day festivities might henceforth last for four whole days, while two days a week, the Spanish ambassador observed, were devoted to single combat on foot in imitation of Lancelot and Amadis, the heroes of romance. Henry hunted and hawked with equal gusto and when, in May and June, such sport was out of season, he merely redoubled his efforts with the lance or sword. Sheathed extravagantly in the latest German or Italian plate armour, fluted and braced and inlaid with gold, Henry would take to the lists, plumes flying, on his magnificent stallion, gifted to him by the Duke of Mantua. Many young men excelled in such sports, it was said, but among them all 'the most assiduous and the most interested was the king'.

In the evenings, meanwhile, there were elaborate 'masks' at which Henry would indulge his other consuming passion – his love of dressing up. Disappearing with some of his boon companions in the middle of an extravagant banquet, the King of England would presently reappear in glittering disguise in the midst of a party of 'Turks' or 'Moors' or 'Germans', intruding upon the company and demanding to dance with the supposedly astonished ladies thereabouts. Once, it seems, when the court was at Greenwich, a party of masked outlaws all in Kendal green made their entrance, followed, however incongruously, by a band of musicians. The queen and her ladies, the chronicler assures us, were surprised and terrified by the invasion, but courteously danced with the outlaws and were duly amazed and delighted when the king and his nobles eventually unmasked. No matter how often such games occurred, Catherine, it seems, never disappointed her boyishly exuberant spouse by identifying the gigantic Muscovite or wild man or Saracen in her midst, or by failing to be suitably nonplussed or delighted as occasion dictated.

The more the king carolled and cavorted, the more he attracted young nobles of similar mind, as eager to indulge him as to match his lust for play. Though older nobles also began to attend court more regularly, it was especially the younger scions of mighty houses who were prominent from this point onwards, along with newer men, too; young squires from newly risen families or those freshly resurrected by a wealthy marriage. Such characters found themselves just as welcome as their social betters, so long as their wits were sharp and their purses full. Courtenays and Staffords, Howards, Percys, Nevilles and Talbots all rubbed shoulders, therefore, with Comptons, Bryans and Boleyns and men of other names hitherto unknown to court chroniclers. And as they gathered, these young bucks were more prepared than ever to encourage and indulge their sovereign's excess.

In fact, there soon grew up around the king an inner circle of drinking, gaming and sporting companions who acted as raucous elder brothers to their sovereign: an elite fellowship of noble funsters to whom he looked for guidance and by whose standards he gauged his own adulthood and virility. This band of high-spirited heroes – or gaggle of irresponsible braggarts, according to perspective – included William Compton, Charles Brandon, Edward and Henry Guildford, Thomas Knyvet and Edward Howard. Ranging in age in 1509 from 21 to 30, they seemed to exercise an unseemly familiarity with the king and were almost daily involved in incidents which always irritated and sometimes shocked and scandalised.

If, moreover, the Welsh chronicler Elis Gruffydd is to be believed, the king's own little games were soon exceeding the bounds of acceptable behaviour. His cutting of a nobleman's purse, for instance, may well have represented excellent sport for his merry cronies, but it would ultimately end unhappily. 'As a result,' says the Welshman, 'the stealing of purses became so common that [...] if anyone had the chance to do it so skilfully that the owner did not notice or catch him in the act he could only treat it as a laughing matter.' In the event, the foolish craze would have to be checked ultimately on pain of death.

Not altogether surprisingly, then, the king's exuberance did not sit so comfortably with the sentiments and priorities of his councillors, who were said to be firmly set in their dusty ways and sober, seemingly, to a fault: as arthritic in outlook as they were of limb. Yet George Cavendish's suggestion that these men set out to bridle the young king and thereby directly drove him under the more indulgent wing of Thomas Wolsey may not be so certain as is often assumed. According to Cavendish, the council had neither wasted time nor spared any frankness in reminding the king of his regal duties, on the grounds that they feared 'lest such abundance of riches [...] the king was now possessed of should move his young years into a riotous forgetting of himself'. So, said Cavendish, 'they gate him to be present with them to acquaint him with the politique government of the realm, with which at first he could not endure to be much troubled'.

On the other hand, Sir William Paulet, who would become one of the century's great political survivors, referred many years later to another formal debate which supposedly took place at court around this time, led by two great officers of the royal household: John de Vere, Earl of Oxford, a veteran general, councillor and long-time friend of the late king, and Edward Stafford, Duke of Buckingham. The subject once again was the handling of the young monarch and whether he should be tutored in the intricacies of policy and administration or encouraged to devote himself to the creation of a magnificent, cultured court and leave the details of government to his council. According to this account, however, the greybeards in the king's service opted for the latter alternative.

Certainly, such a decision would have had much to recommend it. The realm was fortunate, after all, in having as its monarch a glittering figure who loved display and could parade before the whole of Europe the might and splendour of a renascent England. There would be little benefit, therefore, in immuring him within the council chamber or counting house. The dynasty, moreover, required colour and publicity, and, as such, it made sound sense for the king and his household to flaunt their magnificence.

Likewise, even the more conservative councillors will have been keen to avoid the confusion likely to arise from any sudden lurches of policy, particularly in the conduct of foreign affairs caused by the new king's contributions. When Henry did apply himself to affairs of state, he had already displayed a notably headstrong and impulsive streak. His peremptory decision to marry, for instance, had sent an early warning signal, not only of his intention to take charge of his own destiny but also, more worryingly, of his determination to take sides in the European power struggle and to resume the ancient feud with France. Only a few weeks later he had flown into a rage upon learning that the council had written in his name to Louis XII of France assuring him of England's friendship. Clearly, such barely concealed enmity with the French represented a drastic reversal of Henry VII's policy of avoiding dangerous entanglements, and raised at the same time the spectre of the 'auld alliance' between France and Scotland.

For at least some members of the council, then, the problem was not so much Henry's absence from the council chamber as the fact that his ill-considered interventions in affairs were inclined all too often to act to the detriment of measured and sensible policy-making. As such, Cavendish's suggestion that Wolsey wooed Henry by liberating him from his responsibilities is likely to be at least partially wide of the mark.

Nevertheless, the almoner was still surprisingly well placed for a blind side assault on power, for there was now, undoubtedly, a vacuum at the heart of government into which a man like him could well have been sucked, albeit as much by chance as by design. Technically, the almoner's role was a comparatively inconspicuous one, entailing the distribution of largesse on the king's behalf and dealing with the multitude of supplicants who sought it. In effect, though, royal almoners were factotums, used by monarchs in any way they saw fit, acting alternately as messengers, diplomats and intermediaries. Besides which, this particular almoner was now at liberty to operate on an altogether more imaginative and lavish scale than his predecessors, for there was a dazzling splash of colour about the new regime that was lacking in the old.

The monarchy had, as it were, come out of hiding, affording the king's almoner a new visibility of his own in the new, more generous setting then prevailing. And there were underlings aplenty to handle the more mundane aspects of the almoner's main business. What mattered most about this comparatively humble household post, in fact, was that it secured daily access to the king. From there on it was up to the office holder to use it how he might in his ascent of the gilded staircase to power. In this respect, he might also use his role to enrich himself with benefices and sinecures, for the almonership had already proven a reliable stepping stone to greater things, as it would throughout the sixteenth century.

Thanks to the present king's character this flexible position afforded ampler opportunities than ever before. Though Henry firmly believed that he was naturally endowed with all the gifts required for all the more serious aspects of government, there was a surfeit of niggling chores by which he was unwilling to be distracted, and now the ever-willing Wolsey was always close by to lend a helping and guiding hand. Indeed, since the young man who had come to occupy England's throne was unversed in the day-to-day business of the court, Wolsey could actually assume the role of mentor. Knowing the lie of the royal household already and bolstered by appointments within the Church that gave him a status of sorts, his increasing command of government procedures and protocol enabled him to shepherd the king through the tasks for which he was largely unprepared. Apart from wearisome talks with the dreary grey men who populated his father's parsimonious court, young Henry had, after all, gained little contact with the game of politics. Nor, as we have seen, was this a situation he was overly anxious to remedy.

Government business was, in fact, usually handled by a group of between eight to a dozen councillors, meeting mainly in the Star Chamber at Westminster. Not only was the king rarely present, he was frequently miles away on progress or residing at Greenwich or Richmond. Thus there existed an executive of which Henry VIII was the head *de jure* but seldom *de facto*, and this, in turn, meant that someone was needed to mediate between king and council, gauging the king's inclinations, reporting the outcomes of debates and securing the seal of the royal signet on state documents.

Individuals, such as the Earl of Surrey or Archbishop of Canterbury, could not, of course, be expected to scurry about the countryside on routine matters of this kind, though the potential power which might be wielded by such a 'messenger' was certain to be considerable. More significantly still, a headless executive could not be counted upon to frame policy effectively, and debates in such circumstances might well degenerate into fruitless stalemates between factions and individuals. Though Warham doubtless chaired meetings effectively, the council could not make policy confidently, even with a broad consensus, when it might later be altered by the king. The only answer, therefore, was for a suitable intermediary to become, in effect, the royal mouthpiece. And that, indeed, is precisely what happened.

5

Service and High Favour

When, with the fall of autumn's last leaves in 1509, Thomas Wolsey finally secured his place at Henry VIII's court, there was still, as yet, nothing about him to suggest the overweight and overweening knave of later legend. Most curiously, perhaps, for an age in which looks were beginning to count for more and more, no detailed written description of him was ever produced by contemporaries. Even the colour of his hair remains a mystery. But though he does seem to have developed, at some stage, 'a flap before his eye', which the poet Skelton unkindly attributed to the pox, there is no compelling reason whatsoever to believe that he was either obese or, for that matter, possessed of 'a coarse red face'.

The most famous image of Wolsey to have survived, which was painted by an unknown artist and now hangs in the National Portrait Gallery, certainly suggests a man of bulk. But it shows its subject in later life and was not, in any case, intended to be a lifelike depiction. Besides which, the only other near-contemporary portrait – a French painting of 1567 – indicates a substantially thinner man, while a largely reliable observer, such as Sebastiano Giustiniani, the Venetian ambassador, freely described Wolsey as 'very handsome'.

Likewise, any claims that he was a 'vulgarian' with a 'common accent' seem less than convincing when his educational background and achievements are taken into account. On the contrary, even Wolsey's enemies such as Polydore Vergil granted him distinction, while another Italian had no hesitation in describing him as 'hale and of good presence'. Big, then, and becoming, Wolsey seems, in fact, to have had all the aplomb and polish of the born courtier, so that when the new Marquess of Dorset added his voice in support of the man who had tutored him at Magdalen, the king hesitated no further.

Once committed Henry did not look back, for his new almoner was at once prepared both to echo and to serve him at every turn, boosting his ego, salving his conscience and undermining opposition with well-turned observations at critical moments. Equally, he was an amusing companion who was wholly at ease with the rumbustious crew of courtiers who shaped Henry's mental world at this time. Unlike so many other clerics, he could smile at high jinks and hear a ribald tale without offence. He also conversed charmingly, played the lute and was known, on occasion, to dance. As a former schoolmaster he knew the young. But more than this, as a man who had already seen something of the world, he knew its all too human ways.

Wolsey also had the intellectual credentials which Henry VIII so admired. Indeed, in this respect, he possessed the one thing that most of the king's everyday playfellows sorely lacked: a sophisticated education. Speaking the language of the 'new learning', he displayed a rare appreciation of painting, music, poetry and architecture, and would, in due course, become a prodigious patron of the arts. In fact, it is no exaggeration to say that he was already well on the way to personifying the much-vaunted 'universal' Renaissance man. Certainly, few could deny his winning qualities and none could deny his growing knowledge of European politics.

All in all, then, Wolsey seemed to the young monarch to be exactly the sort of man needed to construct the resplendent image of Tudor kingship that he sought so keenly to project. And just as the king had no doubt that he himself fully grasped the intricacies of foreign policy, theology and canon law, he was equally sure that he had mastered the art of delegation, too. Buoyed up, therefore, by raw talent, loyalty and unstinting effort, the royal chaplain would now be swept to undreamt-of heights on a wave of royal favour. And with rank, of course, came material rewards.

In October 1509, even before his formal appointment as almoner, the king promised Wolsey one of Richard Empson's houses, while the latter was still languishing in the Tower. According to the formal grant made on 10 January 1510, the house was called 'La Maison Curiale' and boasted 'twelve gardens and orchards between the Thames and St Bride's gardens'. While Wolsey would, no doubt, have preferred the more splendid city residence at Walbrook, where Empson had lived next door to Dudley, the grant was nevertheless unmistakable evidence of his sovereign's growing favour, and now, at least, he would be able to boast the Bishop of Salisbury as his neighbour.

Furthermore, the dwelling itself was a handsome enough building of stone and brick, and although the bank of the Fleet, where it lay, had long since turned into a running sewer for London and beyond, its new owner would soon transform his new home into what Polydore Vergil termed 'a shrine of all pleasures'. In due course, Wolsey would throw up walls, build a great hall, add guest chambers for the increasing numbers who sought his influence, enlarge the kitchens, excavate vast cellars, spin grand staircases and fashion fine galleries. But equally importantly, the house was conveniently near to the king's palace at Bridewell and assisted Wolsey's access to the king – an increasingly important consideration, for, as Cavendish informs us, he now 'daily attended upon the king in court, being in his especial grace'.

Soon enough, the broader pleasures of domestic bliss would also be on offer, for in or around 1510 Wolsey took a mistress with whom he would enjoy a lasting relationship. Although the records are obscure, the woman concerned appears to have been the daughter of a certain Peter Lark, 'gentleman of Huntingdonshire'. It is known for sure, however, that in 1463 other members of the same Lark family were associated with the town of Thetford, not far from Ipswich, and that a man named Peter Lark was twice mayor of that town. Described as a farmer and grazier, he is almost certain to have been the grandfather of Joan Lark.

We know, too, that Joan's own father was probably an innkeeper at Thetford and that she had two brothers who entered the Church and obtained several benefices, thanks, in some part, to Wolsey's growing influence. One brother, Peter, would ultimately enter the service of Stephen Gardiner, Bishop of Winchester. But the other, Thomas, rose higher still to become surveyor of the king's works and later served as Wolsey's confessor. This particular individual was, then, clearly a man of some substance. According to no less a figure than Erasmus himself he was the most cultured and sincere of all the men he had known in England, while another observer, the Latin secretary to the king, even went so far as to suggest later that Lark was 'omnipotent' with Wolsey.

Joan Lark's connections were therefore sound enough by all accounts and the union itself was not, perhaps, entirely disreputable – even though it breached canon law and had been engineered, in all likelihood, by the brother who would become Wolsey's own confessor. The edict that priests should remain celibate, regardless of their functions or the character of their work, had never been wholeheartedly respected, of course, and in his failure to fulfil his obligation to chastity, Wolsey was neither better nor worse than many other high ecclesiastics of the Renaissance. Indeed, while the mealy-mouthed might talk of uncanonical unions that begat nephews and the more forthright spoke of bastards, an impartial observer could well be forgiven for thinking that, in Rome, any cardinal without a natural son lacked a stature of sorts.

If it was true that contemporary demands for reform of the Church included a return to celibacy and chastity at every level, it was equally the case that very few regarded sexual misconduct as the worst feature of the age. The visitation reports of English and Welsh dioceses and religious houses showed how widespread breaches of the seventh commandment actually were, and, much more often than not, such incontinence was conveniently forgiven by fines. Even Archbishop Warham himself was said by Erasmus to have had a wife who was openly displayed in the company of his friends. Was there not, in any case, less to deplore in a churchman who broke the rules of celibacy to keep a mistress and remained faithful to her, than in a layman who freely formed a string of liaisons outside marriage, as did Ferdinand of Aragon and successive kings of France, not to mention Henry VIII himself in years to come?

Equally, there is nothing to suggest that Wolsey was either disrespectful or dismissive of the woman in his life, or that she suffered in any way at his hand. On the contrary, Wolsey appears to have exercised an almost paternal care for Mistress Lark, and seems to have made no particular effort to hide her from sight, though her existence might easily have counted against him when he was still on the fringes of the council. The 'lusty Lark' was, for instance, well known to the poet and bitter critic of Wolsey, John Skelton, who, as it so happened, could no more live the life of a celibate priest than the man whom he delighted to bait.

All the evidence suggests, too, that Wolsey remained consistently generous to the Lark family, giving tokens of his good feeling from time to time and assisting the career of Thomas Lark wherever possible. It was no coincidence that Thomas was instituted to the rich living of Winwick in Lancashire, nor that he was entrusted with the education of the future Earl of Derby. Later, indeed, he would secure a royal chaplaincy and by the early 1520s he had become Master of Trinity Hall at Cambridge. He would even play a minor role in the Duke of Buckingham's downfall before returning to Wolsey's service and dying at Southwell in 1530.

All in all, then, Wolsey seems to have managed his sex life both moderately and discreetly. And even Skelton's rude remarks on the subject are surprisingly restrained in comparison to what he later wrote concerning other matters. In *Why come ye not to court?* Skelton complained that Wolsey 'foynes and he frygges' and claimed also that he 'spareth neither mayde ne wife'. But beyond this there is nothing worthy of note and one can only assume that any more specific charges of licentiousness would have been unconvincing. Even the most biting of satirists, after all, can only succeed if their observations have at least some semblance of conviction and plausibility.

Nor does Article 6 of the charges drawn up against Wolsey after his fall from power provide any really compelling evidence to support Skelton's claim. The article concerned accused him of 'blowing upon' the king with his 'perilous infective breath' after 'the foul and contagious disease of the great pox' had 'broken out upon him in divers places of his body'. Yet Wolsey would always vehemently deny all aspects of this charge, which had a particularly hollow ring even at the time. Moreover, nothing of his mistress, or even so much as a hint of sexual misbehaviour is to be found in any reports from the all-seeing and ever talkative foreign ambassadors who wallowed tirelessly in every grimy rumour of court life.

As far as we can tell, therefore, Wolsey remained more devoted to his concubine than many contemporary men were to their wives. Nor did Wolsey lightly discard Mistress Lark in later years when his own need for her had abated. When the time duly came he gave her in marriage, just as a father might, to George Legh of Adington, a wealthy landowner in the county of Cheshire, and the bride and groom went on, it seems, to enjoy both a happy and fruitful union, producing a son named Thomas, appropriately enough, and three daughters: Isabel, Margaret and Mary. Not only did Wolsey remain on cordial terms with Legh after the marriage had taken place, but, if his enemies are to be believed, he even contrived a convenient, though reprehensible, way of providing a generous dowry for the couple to enjoy.

Just prior to his fall, it seems, he had summoned Sir John Stanley, the illegitimate son of the former Bishop of Ely, and ordered him to give some of his lands to Legh as part of the planned dowry arrangement. When Stanley quite rightly refused to comply, Wolsey was said to have imprisoned him in the Fleet prison for a year until he gave in. In consequence, the unfortunate Stanley was said to have been so shaken that he became a monk in Westminster and died there soon afterwards.

True or otherwise, the tale captures that same mixture of loyalty, self-interest and moral elasticity that would come to characterise so much of what Wolsey stood for. And over the years ahead, he would demonstrate similar devotion to the two bastard children with whom Joan Lark had duly supplied him. A daughter, Dorothy, was born in 1512 and adopted by one John Clansey. But Wolsey's interest did not stop here, for she was eventually placed in Shaftesbury Nunnery, which had the reputation of being the finest 'finishing school' in England for daughters of the wealthy. She was also obviously well provided for in the years that followed, since she stayed in the house, faithful to her vows, until the place was finally dissolved by Thomas Cromwell, after which she was awarded a pension.

In the meantime, at some unknown date after Dorothy's birth, Wolsey had also fathered a son, whom he would always publicly acknowledge as his nephew. Given the name of Thomas Winter, the boy was placed with a family in Willesden and remained anonymous until 1521, when a lively correspondence began between his father and his tutor, Maurice Birchinshaw. Thinking back to his own prowess as a 'boy bachelor', Wolsey confessed at this time that he was frankly disappointed with his offspring's attainment. But though Birchinshaw apologised for the boy's 'speaking less Latin' than the father may have wanted, he nevertheless defended both himself and his pupil by claiming that the fault lay in the curriculum they were required to follow. Later, when Winter became ill from a fever near Trent in northern Italy, it was Erasmus himself who offered to help with the boy's schooling, though Wolsey for some reason declined the offer.

Plainly, however, Wolsey spared no effort in ensuring the best possible education for his son, for the boy was indeed educated at some of the highest seats of learning that Europe could boast, including Louvain, where he studied under the eminent humanist Thomas Lupset. We know, too, that he went on to study further at Poissy, Ferrara and Padua, as well as Paris, where, it seems, he lived magnificently, using his parentage to associate with the highest figures in the land. At this time, in fact, his frequent demands for money appear to have disturbed his father, who fell into the habit of asking any friend passing through the French capital to inquire after his son's condition.

If Wolsey spared no effort on Winter's education, he was no less diligent in his attempts to secure the boy's advancement within the Church. When in 1525 the king decided to bring his own bastard son, Henry Fitzroy, out of the shadows by creating him Duke of Richmond, Wolsey would quickly follow suit, and in consequence his boy was smothered with ecclesiastical honours. Having been granted in 1526 a coat of arms with a defiant bar sinister which closely resembled his father's, Master Winter, still in his early teens, soon became Dean of Wells, Provost of Beverley Abbey, Chancellor of Salisbury, an archdeacon of both York and Richmond, and a canon of Lincoln Cathedral and Southwell Abbey. He was also made rector of Rudby in Yorkshire and St Matthew's Church in his father's native Ipswich. Wolsey even seems at one point to have attempted to secure the bishopric of Durham for the boy, who had still not been ordained a deacon.

Irrespective of the fact that Thomas Winter was under the canonical age at which he was eligible to hold any of these offices, Wolsey managed to obtain all the necessary dispensations, not only for age, but also in connection with pluralism and non-residence. At one point, indeed, the English ambassador tactfully reminded him that it would also be necessary to obtain a further dispensation on account of his son's illegitimate birth and this, too, was granted. Ultimately, in a letter of 1528, Wolsey actually appealed to the king on behalf of Winter, whom he referred to as 'my poor scholar', in the hope that Durham might be granted to him 'when I should fortune to leave the same'.

Perhaps, though, Wolsey had made the mistake of many fathers who force-feed their offspring with privilege as a substitute for a more personal relationship. For all his father's efforts Winter would never achieve the heights earmarked for him. After Wolsey's death, Henry appointed him a chaplain, though he returned to Padua, where he lived wretchedly, toying with scholarly pursuits and lacking both clothes and money. The last we hear of him, therefore, is in 1532, shortly after his return from the Continent, when he wrote several pathetic letters to Thomas Cromwell describing his state of poverty and begging assistance. On one such occasion he pleaded for an immediate advance of £100, though whether his father's former servant obliged him is unknown. Awarded a few benefices of little value, he would ultimately beg to keep them. 'I am devoted to letters,' he told Cromwell ultimately, 'but desire to keep my preferments.'

However, if his son was apparently one of life's victims, Wolsey himself remained unstoppable, and never more so than in the early stages of the new reign. From the very moment that he had secured his place at Henry VIII's court, in fact, Wolsey continued to gather a plentiful random harvest of preferments and promotions. In April 1510, for example, he was granted a doctorate in divinity from Oxford University, which was a crucial prerequisite for further ecclesiastical advancement, although in Wolsey's case the qualification had been awarded purely by virtue of his position in the royal household and without any requirement for additional study. Then, surely enough, another string of clerical sinecures also fell into his lap. In July, he was appointed a canon of Hereford; in November, Vicar of Torrington in Devon; and in February 1511, the prebend of St George's Chapel, Windsor. Next year, Wolsey was made Dean of Hereford, only to resign the office when he was appointed a canon of York in January 1513 and Dean of York in February.

But, in the meantime, there had been much more significant advances. On 27 April 1510, for instance, Wolsey had been named registrar of the Most Noble Order of the Garter, a post which brought him as close as any commoner-turned-churchman could ever come to the most select and closed circle of the entire realm. Yet even this paled into insignificance beside his appointment to the Privy Council, which had already taken place in the early winter of 1509.

Wolsey's first known appearance as a councillor seems to have been on 20 November, when he countersigned, as the most junior member present, a warrant for the issue of a proclamation. And though it was not until the autumn of 1511 that he became a fixture in council proceedings, the almoner was also certainly present at the unusually important meeting on 21 June 1510 to consider the Duke of Buckingham's claim to become hereditary Constable of England. Thereafter councillors, nobles and ambassadors alike would all be discovering that the best way of presenting business to their sovereign was by way of Thomas Wolsey's mouth.

By May 1511, moreover, Wolsey had already become so confident of the king's support that he was fully prepared to bypass all established methods for giving legal effect to the royal will. Under normal circumstances the king would sign a bill or petition and pass it on to his secretary, who would, in turn, compose a letter under the king's signet to the Lord Privy Seal, keeping the bill signed by the king. The Lord Privy Seal would then write to the Lord Chancellor as Keeper of the Great Seal, holding the secretary's letter as his warrant, after which the Lord Chancellor would issue written instructions. On 26 May, however, Wolsey produced for the Chancellor a signed bill which had gone through none of this standard procedure. Even more significantly, the Chancellor duly accepted the bill purely by virtue of the fact that 'Dominus Wulcy' had given him the document at the king's command. To trample so casually on such a standard point of procedure was, of course, a high-handed act on any terms, and the fact that the Lord Chancellor accepted this action without question proved incontrovertibly just how close the almoner now stood to the king.

Nor was Wolsey any more inhibited when it came to expressing himself freely on personalities and affairs at court. One of his earliest extant letters was written on 30 September 1511 to tell Richard Fox that the chief noble about the king, Thomas Howard, Earl of Surrey, had met with a cool reception at court, after which 'he departed home again, and yet is not at court'. 'With a little help now,' Wolsey added, 'he might be utterly excluded; whereof in my poor judgement no little good might ensue.'

Naturally, Wolsey will have known well enough that there was no possibility of the Lord Treasurer being excluded from his apartments at court and the privilege of regular attendance on the king. But the almoner was clearly emerging as a man well skilled in handling people and playing on rivalries, and this was big talk, indeed, from the son of an Ipswich commoner, whose native county had long stood cap in hand before the Howards of Norfolk. Moreover, it is clear that divisions among England's elites were growing deeper and fuelling Wolsey's boldness by the day.

The root cause of these divisions is clear enough, for as Wolsey entered into the private conferences of the council he found all discussion centred on war. In reality, of course, there were the soundest reasons why England should not embroil herself in the affairs of the continent, for any French possessions gained in the previous century had been won at a time when France was riven by factions and ruled by a mad king. They had been won, too, at a time when England was guaranteed the allegiance of Burgundy and neutrality of Brittany; all these peculiar circumstances had long since disappeared.

Military developments, in their turn, also ensured that a new dismemberment of France was increasingly impractical. More than half a century had passed since England had been seriously engaged in a great foreign war, and there were now serious doubts about how any English force might fare against the famous French artillery and regular cavalry. Similarly, while France boasted a heavily armed *gendarmerie*, fully versed in modern pike tactics and recently reinforced by an elite corps of Albanian light cavalry, known as *estradiots*, who could swim their horses across deep streams and ride across hitherto unpassable mountains, English infantrymen were still armed with bills and bows.

At the same time, the best equipment was to be obtained from sources outside England. The finest artillery came from Flemish and German foundries, the keenest blades from Bilbao. And for the transport of heavy guns, there was no draught horse like the Flanders mare. Milan, meanwhile, remained incomparable for armour and Almain rivets were most cheaply purchased from Florence. The strongest anchors, in their turn, came from Biscay, the stoutest masts from Norway. Even bowstaves were now imported from Italy.

Yet if Henry VIII's wish to recover England's lost dominions across the Channel was utterly impractical, he remained determined to play a decisive role in European affairs at any cost. In effect, there were three ways for him to cut a dash in international power politics: marriage, treaty and conquest. But since he had no children and only one sister to deploy in the matrimonial horse-trading at which his father had proved so adept, his options were limited. And, in any case, the rush of war was so much more exhilarating.

It was no secret, of course, that England's new king had been reared on countless tales of derring-do and knightly honour, and the demands of chivalry and duty now seemed clear cut. On 14 May 1509, only a few weeks before Henry VIII's accession, the French king Louis XII had won a remarkable victory over the Republic of Venice at Agnadello, to become the master of northern Italy as far as the Mincio, thereby shattering the balance of power in Europe. 'In one day,' wrote Machiavelli in his *Discorsi*, 'the Venetians lost all that they had acquired during eight hundred years of strenuous effort.' The atrocities committed by the French troops – how they hunted men through the maize fields with bloodhounds, and spared neither age nor sex – also lost nothing in the telling by the Venetian ambassador, Badoer. Unless something were promptly done, it was said, the French king would make himself 'lord of Italy and monarch of the world'.

Nor did subsequent events do anything to cool Henry's growing war fever. He was, for example, earnestly encouraged in his martial ambitions by his father-in-law, King Ferdinand of Spain, who, through Catherine of Aragon, exercised a strong influence over him. England's natural ally, Burgundy, now the territory of the Holy Roman Emperor Maximilian, was also primed for war with France; and so, most of all, was Pope Julius II, who remained obsessed by the fact the French armies and puppet rulers had been in control of Milan for nearly twenty years. In April 1510, indeed, he lured the young king of England with the gift of a golden rose and by October of the next year Spain, the pope, the Empire and the Netherlands, as well as various Italian states were all poised for action as members of a Holy League. Scotland alone sided with its old French ally. In such circumstances, it was almost inconceivable that England could continue to remain uncommitted.

The opening phase of the reign therefore witnessed an ongoing struggle between the king and his supporters and those other councillors who opposed his belligerent stance. On the one hand, Henry's desire for conflict was being constantly fuelled by his close companions in the privy chamber such as Charles Brandon and Edward Neville, whose actual influence vastly outweighed their nominal authority. Then, too, there was Thomas Howard, Earl of Surrey, the thick-shouldered old warhorse who tramped northward from time to time to sharpen his sword against marauding Scots. Though hesitant at first, Howard had come to feel that national greatness, not to mention his own best interest, was most aptly nurtured by means of military force.

Ranged against these, however, was the peace 'party' on the council, made up mainly of ecclesiastics, the chief of whom was Richard Fox, who shared with the former king the belief that England's best interests lay in its physical and emotional isolation from the intrigues of foreign princes abroad. In his view, while the French ruler was the old and decrepit Louis XII, there was little cause for alarm. Meanwhile, if France was not to be an open enemy, it was best she should be an acknowledged friend. Among other advantages to be gleaned from the alliance were generous French pensions for English councillors, and a tribute to the king in respect of the Treaty of Étaples, two instalments of which were paid over at Calais in May and November 1511. Fox's trust, therefore, was in treaty – marital not martial – and in the early manoeuvrings Wolsey, his protégé, was with him, or so at least it seemed.

But there was more to Wolsey's dealings at this time than Fox himself (or any other for that matter) may have fully realised. According to the reports of Polydore Vergil, when Henry attended the council to preside over a debate on policy towards France, the majority of those who faced him were against the prospect of war. In the view of the Spanish envoy, Villaragut, meanwhile, these men were 'very different to the king, slow in concluding anything' and the cause of 'much disgust' to him. It is not difficult, therefore, to appreciate how in such difficult circumstances personality clashes began to occur between councillors. Indeed, rumours were soon rife.

One that reached Lord Darcy on the Scottish border spoke of a disgruntled Bishop Fox finding himself isolated by a new aristocratic clique, led by Howard and George Talbot, which was trying to draw the Duke of Buckingham and the Earl of Northumberland into an alliance against the ecclesiastical majority. Significantly, the originator of this rumour was none other than Thomas Wolsey. But much as he genuinely hated the waste and horror that warfare brought, Wolsey would not choose to go against the king's wishes for long. Besides which, there were the pleas of the pope and the unity of Christendom to consider. Soon enough, therefore, Fox would be both reluctantly and decisively deserted by the very chick that he himself had reared.

6

Mars Ascendant

When Parliament gathered on 4 February 1511, the call to arms was growing ever more insistent. On every side angry talk of Scottish outrages and fearful tales of French designs upon the Holy See abounded. The 'subtle, untrue and crafty imagination' of the King of Scots could, it was said, be tolerated no longer. Nor, it seemed, might any true-born Englishman further ignore the King of France's 'high and insatiable appetite' for conquest. Even England's merchants were all in favour of conflict, for if Venice were ruined or the Atlantic trade routes cut by French sea captains, their interests would be sorely compromised. So when the Master of the Rolls held forth at length upon 'the impiety of the French king', his message struck home with such force that two substantial war taxes were gladly granted, along with a third before the year was out.

There were other worried cries as well to stoke the general clamour for war. On the one hand, the Scottish navy had continued to grow alarmingly, while Brittany's union with France was spawning even graver concerns, since Breton sailors were thought to know every creek and landing place along the Cornish coast. With this in mind, justices, mayors and constables from Land's End to Plymouth were empowered to construct sturdy defences, by forced labour if necessary, while English archers were made to train with renewed vigour.

By contrast, when William Warham addressed MPs, taking justice and peace as his theme, there was the deepest irony in his choice of text and a collective deafness to his message that was every bit as profound. Try as he might, the archbishop could not have failed more roundly to convince his opponents that war was God's punishment for the sins of princes and their subjects.

The pope himself had, after all, already sanctified the forthcoming conflict in response to Louis XII's decision to convene a Church council at Pisa to depose him[And while Henry's father-in-law, Ferdinand of Aragon, was busy girding his realm for action in the papal cause, his daughter, Catherine, was no less resolutely set at her own task of steadily stirring her husband's conscience. Last but by no means least, there was also royal grief to tip the scales in favour of conflict. On New Year's Day, Queen Catherine had been safely delivered of a baby boy. Only seven weeks later, however, the infant prince was dead and, in the depths of his disappointment, the grief-stricken father sought solace in dreams of conquest.]

The whole press of circumstance therefore dictated that peace must end, and with the pope itching and the king aching for battle, what wise man would try to impede the juggernaut? This, then, was what Thomas Wolsey came to accept soon enough. And it was by means of such hard-edged realism that his rise would now be sealed once and for all.

Not altogether surprisingly, Wolsey's critics down the centuries have been particularly inclined to speak of ulterior motives at this point of his career. Some, for instance, have depicted a grasping, base-born schemer, all too ready to pander to his master's reckless inclinations. On this interpretation, Wolsey not only exploited his sovereign's ego for his own devious purposes, irrespective of the kingdom's interest, but also fatally undermined the standing of his patron and sponsor, Richard Fox, whose anti-war stance was reducing him to increasing impotence by 1511. Others, in their turn, have smelt a conniving rat, keen to protect the Holy See, in order to curry favour with Roman cardinals by cynically supporting Julius II's war plans.

Was it not inevitable, the argument runs, that such an unrivalled egotist would soon be considering the long-term possibilities for high ecclesiastical rank once he had fully harvested the gains to be had from royal service? And if Wolsey's rise so far had, indeed, only served to whet his appetite, might not further progress now require much less laudable talents than the ones that had carried him to his present positon? He had, of course, already displayed a keen eye for the main chance and a knack for divining the whims and prejudices of his superiors. Now, perhaps, it was also time for him to exhibit a set of elastic principles which might be stretched according to circumstance.

Nor are such claims entirely unfounded. For one of Wolsey's background, advancement and opportunism could never be mutually exclusive. Rather, they were flip sides of the same golden coin. And yet the full explanation of Wolsey's eventual transition from dove to hawk is neither so simple, nor so damning as his critics might suggest, for principle as well as pragmatism played its part in the whole process. Support for one's sovereign and the safeguarding of Holy Mother Church were, after all, noble ends in their own right, especially when the grand alliance against France, which the pope was intent upon forging, provided England with the best opportunity in years for conquest and glory. And would not the balance of power be shattered, to all Europe's detriment, if France were not squarely thwarted?

Naturally, there were moral dilemmas involved for any cleric advocating bloodshed. The eminent humanist John Colet continued to preach pacifism loudly and passionately at St Paul's Cross in London and would do so before Henry himself. Erasmus, too, was a consistently bitter opponent of war as an instrument of policy, having seen at close quarters the damage wrought by mercenaries in his native Netherlands. Yet Wolsey's favourite thinker was Thomas Aquinas, who left no doubt that just wars were not only permissible but even desirable under certain conditions. Besides which, Wolsey possessed no mean mind of his own and for one of his undoubted wit and wisdom, there were few, if any, ethical circles that could not be neatly squared on moral grounds.

Precisely when Wolsey abandoned the cause of peace is difficult to say, however. Certainly, the king's warlike inclinations long predated his almoner's appointment, and if Wolsey really was the unalloyed opportunist of legend, the main puzzle, perhaps, is why his conversion was not ultimately even swifter and more sweeping. He would, it should be remembered, continue to support his ecclesiastical colleagues against their noble adversaries until at least the autumn of 1511.

Moreover, any claim that Wolsey was simply hedging his bets during the intervening period is far from convincing, since he was priming Fox with information for some while after the bishop's star had begun to wane and at a time when the old man was increasingly absent from court. On 30 September, for instance, he wrote to Fox complaining of the attempts by the war party to squander the king's money on military expeditions, and of Surrey's son, the Lord Admiral Sir Edward Howard, who was inciting the king to wage war against the Scots. Around the same time, Wolsey also issued a plea to Fox that he return to court with all haste, which also seems to give the lie to any claims that he was bent on sidelining the elder statesman. By Howard's 'wanton means', Wolsey told Fox, 'His Grace spendeth much money and is more disposed to war than peace.' 'Your presence,' he concluded, 'shall be very necessary to repress this appetite.'

But if the royal almoner knew full well that war came at a cost, he alone of all the churchmen on the council was still prepared to urge Henry forward to a reckoning with France. And by the time that England formally entered into alliance with the pope at Windsor on 13 November 1511, there was no doubting Wolsey's wholehearted support for what lay ahead. The objective was simple. Henry for England, Ferdinand for Spain, and Maximilian for the rambling and comparatively impotent Holy Roman Empire would join forces with the blessing of Pope Julius II, so that 'the French king shall not nor may not attain unto his cruel purpose for to destroy all the country of Italy'.

The original plan for achieving this objective was simple, too – painfully so, as things transpired. An English army of poorly trained, untried men would be entrusted to the lacklustre and inexperienced generalship of Wolsey's former pupil and sponsor, the Marquess of Dorset, who was to join Spanish troops led by Ferdinand in person for an attack on Guienne. Then, in return for his army's efforts, Henry would receive Guienne as a prize before launching a second front upon Normandy, which he himself would lead. Naturally, such a fantastic scheme bore many of the hallmarks of the king's own devising. But Wolsey was already sufficiently prominent to be the object of public rumour and if common gossip could be relied upon, this was his war.

In fact, from the moment that the marquess set foot on the coast of Spain at San Sebastian on 7 June, the inadequacies in preparation were painfully obvious. The victuals were bad, there was no adequate provision of tents, and as the army of 10,000 men lay out under bushes, exposed to the drenching rain and parching heat of a particularly pestilential Spanish summer, the bonds of discipline were speedily loosened. To his great cost, Dorset had relied upon Spanish transport, which was never forthcoming as Ferdinand opted to subdue Navarre for his own ends rather than enter Guienne. And as the summer drew on, discontent increased in the English camp, for while Ferdinand was capturing stronghold after stronghold in Navarre, the English force lay idle and helpless before Bayonne.

Isolated and devoid of horse and adequate artillery, Dorset could not mount a single offensive against his French foe and when his officers did eventually take the initiative and bought hundreds of local pack animals at exorbitant prices, they became the laughing stock of both Basques and their own men, since the beasts were untrained and all but useless. In the meantime, Dorset's men died of dysentery and no doubt died disconsolate, since there was no beer. Predictably, it was not long before the soldiers of this ragtag, ill-led, ill-provisioned force were telling their officers that they would not abide after Christmas 'for no man'.

Furthermore, as the English army, broken and dejected, headed for home against its sovereign's express orders, the news at sea brought no more consolation. Sir Edward Howard, the Lord Admiral, had conveyed Dorset's force to its destination at the end of May before proceeding to raid the coast of Brittany with some success, capturing a total of sixty-six French hulks and merchantmen. But when Howard set out once more in the first week of August, the result was a catastrophe.

In the thick of battle with the French fleet, Henry's capital ship the *Regent*, commanded by his very own Thomas Knyvet, was successfully shackled to the French carrack the *Cordelière* when a death-or-glory French gunner fired his ship's powder store. Porzmoguer, the French captain, jumped into the sea in full armour and was drowned, while Knyvet then perished in identical fashion along with some 700 of his crew.

Under other circumstances, the stirring tale of two such noble vessels, locked in deadly embrace and sinking with their gallant crews in a consuming fury of smoke and fire, might well have delighted England's king. But, on this occasion at least, the reality of war seems to have struck him unusually painfully. Nor did Edward Howard's subsequent burning of twenty-seven French vessels and capture of five more, along with 800 prisoners, do anything to sweeten the bitter pill.

In the event, an almighty royal tantrum was the very least that might now have been anticipated, and, ironically enough, Henry did indeed force Dorset's disgraced commanders to beg forgiveness from the Spanish ambassador upon their knees. Yet, though officers and men might lay the blame for the unfolding fiasco at Wolsey's door, the almoner would emerge from the whole sorry episode not only unscathed but with considerably enhanced influence. In truth, the conduct of the campaign bore none of the classic hallmarks of his organisation and even the preliminary diplomatic manoeuvres suggest that the almoner had little, if any, influence upon either the direction or detail of decision-making. From first to last, in fact, Henry had been personally outwitted by Ferdinand in ways that Wolsey was always unlikely to have been.

As was well known by all with eyes to see, Ferdinand had only joined the Holy League for personal gain and thereafter deserted his allies as soon as Venice had satisfied his appetite. Moreover, when he subsequently offered Guienne to his English counterpart, he had cared not a jot about Henry's aspirations, which he considered wholly unrealistic. Instead, his sole interest had been to use the Marquess of Dorset's force as a distraction to the French, while he himself quietly consumed Navarre at leisure and thus gave his kingdom the whole length of the Pyrenean frontier. With hindsight, the ploy was as crude as it was predictable, and it was more than surprising that even one as impetuous as Henry did not see the potential pitfalls awaiting him. However, for Wolsey to have paid no mind to such possibilities would have been little short of incredible.

Equally, as Dorset's expedition unfolded in the field, Wolsey once again seems to have had little, if any, direct control of actual events. The art of war was invariably the hallowed preserve of the aristocratic warrior caste, which no cleric might freely encroach upon, and both the design and execution of military strategy were on this occasion, as always, firmly in noble hands. Besides which, Wolsey had not been a councillor nearly long enough to be handed management of such an enterprise.

If Frenchmen therefore believed, as they did, that the plan of invasion was his work, this was more a reflection on the almoner's growing reputation than firm proof of any real control over strategy on his part. Likewise, the fact that the correspondence from Spain was all addressed to him is more indicative of his expanding administrative responsibilities and evolving relationship with the king. Even foreign ambassadors as well as English councillors and nobles were now discovering that the best way of presenting business to their sovereign was by way of Thomas Wolsey's mouth. And, by 1512, none other than England's lone hero, Edward Howard, was writing to the almoner in person to thank him for interceding with the king on his behalf.

Throughout the campaign, in fact, Wolsey appears to have been using his special relationship with Henry mainly to echo the king's plans, to confirm his reading of events and to console him in defeat. And here for the first time there is a clear glimpse of the kind of bond that the precious almoner had now established with his sovereign. Far from suffering his master's wrath, Wolsey was clearly detached from any blame and content to act primarily as a sympathetic shoulder while Henry reeled under the weight of successive disappointments.

In a letter written to Fox on 26 August, for instance, Wolsey gave a detailed account of the loss of the *Regent* and described the king's reaction to the tragedy in a way that only someone on the most intimate terms with him possibly could have. Betraying a genuine sympathy for the distress of his young master, Wolsey implored Fox to 'keep these tidings secret to yourself', since 'there is no living man knoweth the same here but only the king and I'. 'To see how the king taketh the matter and behaveth himself,' he continued, 'ye would marvel and much allow his wise and constant manner. I have not on my faith seen the like.'

Clearly, this young, inexperienced monarch who was determined to appear so decisive and forceful amid the buzzing swarm of would-be heroes that surrounded him also needed an inner circle of companions who could meet the more private needs of his personality: people who could satisfy his spiritual pangs and intellectual aspirations; people, too, who could resolve his dilemmas or salve his wounded ego as the need arose. Significantly, all those admitted to the king's innermost circle were invariably some years older than he: old enough, that is, to counsel and console, but young enough, all the same, to do so unconditionally. Wolsey had joined this select band rapidly because he also offered his master the all-important quality of discretion. There were times, it seems, when Henry needed to be alone with himself in someone else's presence and it was Wolsey, perhaps more than any other, who supplied this need.

In the event, then, it had required just such a failure as the campaign of 1512 to provide Wolsey with his ultimate chance. Though sufficiently detached from military responsibility to avoid the brunt of blame, he was yet close enough to the centre of things to win the king's trust and affection in adversity. And in this respect he had gained especially richly from the news of blunders and reverses which reached the king's ears daily, for where others offered gloomy tidings and bankrupt schemes, the almoner offered consolation and hope. Therefore it was no coincidence when, in the early months of 1513, Wolsey was appointed Dean of St Stephen's, Westminster, and Dean of York to boot.

It was now, too, that Wolsey first began to feel the mounting tide of power surging through his person on a much broader front, for from this point onwards, a share in the direction of policy, as well as responsibility for its execution, became more and more of a reality. Indeed, there was even scope for a place at the council table senior to all but the king himself. Certainly, there would be a pressing need for better leadership henceforth, since in spite of his council's growing calls for peace, it was widely reported in London by November 1512 that both Henry and his queen were resolved upon a new campaign. As it transpired, then, the setbacks and crushing disappointments of the previous year had only reinforced their determination to prosecute the war with France more vigorously than ever.

If, however, the king had adopted his council's view, few could have blamed him. Not only had he incurred the burden of a costly expedition, only to find himself cheated by his ally, but the humiliation of France had already been squarely achieved in his absence, for after the loss of Navarre to Ferdinand, Louis XII had been driven out of Italy, and his Church council at Pisa laughed out of existence. Yet for England to have withdrawn from the war at this juncture would still have entailed the greatest loss of prestige. At the same time, Henry had received a generous grant from Parliament and the war fever among his subjects was still surprisingly high. To accept peace from the hands of the French would therefore look like nothing other than an abject confession of failure, as if it were only the victories of foreign allies that could rescue England from the consequences of her own military weakness. In his own mind, too, Henry had no doubt that he could and would deliver the military glory he craved in a second, grander campaign. And just as it was Wolsey who reinforced this conviction, so it would be Wolsey who provided his master with the means to pursue his dreams.

The smoothness of the hectic war preparations which occupied the subsequent weeks and months did indeed owe everything to the almoner, who was utterly tireless in arranging for supplies, troops and transport for France and for the defence of the Scottish border. Knowing full well that he would almost certainly be casually discarded once and for all if operations now continued as disastrously as they had begun, Wolsey realised with equal certainty that success at this critical moment could be his making. Therefore, his messengers continually raced back and forth from Southampton, Portsmouth and Dover to London, where he himself could be found at his 'lodgings' in the Palace of Westminster, which now became the teeming hive where ambassadors, admirals, generals, paymasters, pursers and men of all grades gathered.

One had to traverse three rooms, we are told by a foreign ambassador, before the inner closet could be reached where Wolsey beavered away. And any chatterers or dalliers who might eventually pierce this protective cordon were invariably given short shrift, for at this time more than ever the man at the centre of things was exasperated by any talk divorced from action. Such inaccessibility, of course, did nothing to increase the almoner's popularity. But though he was constantly surrounded by a raft of clerks and secretaries, he seems nonetheless to have demonstrated at every turn that characteristic impatience with creaking bureaucratic ways which invariably helped him to cut corners so conveniently and ensure that decisions were taken and implemented in a manner that suited a new kind of war.

This, after all, was now a conflict transformed from a religious crusade into a naked demonstration of national might and pride. Much to Henry's indignation, Ferdinand had professed himself to be outraged at English perfidy and was loud in rebuking his son-in-law for earlier letting his troops desert *en masse*. English soldiers were, complained Ferdinand, 'self-indulgent and idle, inconsistent and fickle, rash and quarrelsome and incapable of acting in concert with allies'. Even women now decried Henry's armies, it seemed. Margaret of Savoy, for instance, declared dismissively that Englishmen had 'so long abstained from war, they lack experience from disuse, and, as it is reported, they now be almost weary of it'.

Not only were English soldiers ill-led and ill-fed, they were also ill-armed – a fact of which Dr Knight, England's ambassador to Spain, was all too aware when he told Wolsey that of the 8,000 bowmen dispatched upon the ill-fated expedition of 1512 only 200 had been properly equipped. Therefore any army which left English shores would now have to be armed to the teeth and to this end Wolsey scoured all Europe for the necessary weaponry. In Italy especially, he drew up massive contracts for armour, thousands of suits being purchased through the agency of the great Florentine bankers, the Frescobaldi, and from Guydo Portinari and John Cavalcanti, merchants of Florence. From Germany, meanwhile, and still more often from towns in Flanders, such as Malines and Brussels, came a deluge of artillery pieces. 'Serpentines', weighing about 1,200lbs, brass curtals of some 3,000lbs and other smaller guns such as 'bombards' and 'falcons', as well as lightweight swivel guns known as 'murderers', all flowed into the ordnance stores at Calais.

Even so, neither Wolsey nor Henry were content that England should rely wholly upon foreign powers for arms and munitions. Bows and arrows, pikes and bills, lances and partisans were nowhere better made than in England and their production now increased apace. Gunpowder, too, was mainly produced in England, and enormous stores of it now accumulated in the Tower of London, at Southampton and at Calais.

But the time had also come for England to enter the budding technological age of warfare, and with this in mind Wolsey caused the first large-scale cannon foundries to be built on home soil. As a result, he became responsible, with typical love of scale, for the production of the largest guns ever cast: the twelve famed cannons, named for each of the twelve apostles, which, it was said, would speak with tongues of fire and preach in tones of thunder on Henry's new crusade. Predictably, they at once became a glowing symbol of national pride and a particular source of delight for Henry himself. Nothing, it seems, pleased the English king more than to extol their unrivalled destructive power in his letters to fellow sovereigns or his ministers abroad. And equally predictably, when one of these great monsters had, in due course, to be fished from a pond in France, it would be Wolsey who settled the payment.

To his credit, Wolsey had learnt, too, that any effective army must be full-bellied as well as suitably armed. The same eye for detail, the same capacity for attending to all aspects of a transaction, the same nose for a good deal were thus all evident in his purchase of victuals. Throughout the months of February, March and April 1513, stores of food were being steadily poured into Calais in anticipation of the time when England might have as many as 40,000 men operating across the Channel. Moreover, in ordering the slaughter of 25,000 oxen at the end of January, he insisted that only the finest beasts from Lincolnshire and the Netherlands be secured. And once the deed was done, he duly insisted on securing rebates for the hides and tallow.

Likewise, the cost of cauldrons for 'seething' the beef was submitted to Wolsey in person, along with the prices for bacon, biscuits, cheese, dry cod and ling, while on 9 April we also find the almoner giving direct instructions to John Rycroft, Sergeant of the Larder, that he procure 20,000 quarters of malt, 3,000 quarters of beans, and the same amount of oats, along with 100 lambs and fodder for the king's horses. But, in the meantime, he still found time to supervise the work of John Daunce, 'Treasurer of the War', who, among other things, was charged with the unenviable task of conveying the mass of provisions across the Channel. And the overall outcome was such a triumph of logistical skill that Brian Tuke, Clerk of the Signet, would report eventually how the soldiers were able to live in time of war 'far more cheaply than they lived at home in time of peace'.

Of necessity, too, Wolsey was no less anxious to trade in intelligence than he was to barter for rivets, rope, wagons or beef. Not only did he seek out spies who could betray the activities of the French, but he also appealed to farmers who knew the enemy's terrain and fishermen who were familiar with his coast. Likewise, he urged daily reports from English emissaries in the courts of Ferdinand and Maximilian, since allies who had betrayed once were likely to betray again. No snippet of information was overlooked, no detail ignored. Indeed, in his restless obsession with minutiae, Wolsey displayed what may look to many a modern observer like a genuinely neurotic streak, for this, it seems, was a man driven as much by fear of failure as by any passion to succeed.

Every last detail of activity was, in fact, drafted and overseen by him personally. At the slightest hint of confusion, he would take his barge down the Thames, stopping at every dock, encouraging, persuading and charming all manner of stores on their way. The armies of each command, their days of assembly and departure, the careful routing of the shuttles back and forth across the Channel, the tackle for ships, the cost of their pilots' coats, the weapons for war, the tents and the bedding were all meticulously provided for. Nor, of course, would Wolsey neglect the English soldier's seemingly unquenchable thirst for beer as well as glory, for brew houses were swiftly erected up and down the length of England, the largest being at Portsmouth. All in all, it was hardly surprising that Fox should express concerns about his protégé's health and pray God on his behalf that he be delivered out of his 'outrageous charge and labour'.

Yet Wolsey apparently remained more preoccupied with the health of those soldiers who would soon be risking life and limb on their sovereign's behalf. Among the mountain of brief notes that he generated around this time, there is, for instance, a memorandum that he wrote to help him remember 'the sickness that now is at Brest'. Clearly, even the ever-hovering hand of God in the form of the plague could not be allowed to knock him from his stride.

In the meantime, Wolsey was also at pains to guarantee that the broader medical needs of the men were well catered for, and he personally oversaw the appointment of those physicians and surgeons attached to the army. In his accounts there are references to a payment of £8 10s 6d to one John Westall 'towards his lechecraft and his wages', while another payment of £6 13s 4d is made to Robert Symson for 'healing certain men hurt on the sea'. In all, there were some eighty or ninety surgeons who travelled to France, a much greater number than had ever before accompanied an English force abroad. And though they were paid no more than archers or yeoman carters – only eightpence a day – their presence in such numbers is yet another testament to both the care and detail of the planning involved.

More significantly still, the scope of Wolsey's activity was already moving beyond that of chief procurer and facilitator, for now he even ventured to encroach, however tentatively, upon that most hallowed noble preserve: the conduct of the war itself. Though he would never dare to determine when or where the army fought, he could certainly determine its more general behaviour, and *The Statutes of War*, which he drew up at this time, confirm subtly but decisively just how far he had now risen in the ranks of the high and mighty.

In all 1,600 copies of the statutes were produced for officers by the king's printer, Richard Pynson, at a cost of £16 13s 4d. Their purpose was to set forth in fine detail the rules of war and they were to be read out formally to all soldiers at regular intervals. Once a week, in fact, officers were obliged to issue a comprehensive range of warnings to their soldiers. 'Murmurs or Grudges against the King or the Officers of his Host' were, for instance, to be strictly forbidden. There were stern injunctions, too, against such unknightly acts of warfare as sacrilege, robbery, pillage, violence towards civilians, the firing of houses etc., all of which were made punishable by death. And a further special ordinance barred soldiers from entering any house in which a woman was lying in childbed. Several others aimed at maintaining good order in the camp by preventing dicing, card-playing, and other games of chance. Finally, Wolsey even saw fit to encourage morale by stipulating that 'no man is to give reproach to another, because of the country he is of, that is to say, English, Northern, Welsh or Irish'.

But if Wolsey's plans might appear to have been proceeding well, there were also storm clouds and potentially heavy reverses to contend with. In the first place, the king's decision to rescue the Holy Father from the French had already stretched crown expenditure to some £111,445 in the third year of the reign. Now, though, as the price of meat more than doubled as a result of his purchases for the war effort and the price of bread also rose month on month, Wolsey contemplated expenditure amounting, possibly, to more than five times that amount. In the event, Parliament was still sufficiently under the king's spell to comply remarkably willingly with his requests, but in the country at large there were restive murmurings.

No man – or clergyman – of any means or property escaped Wolsey's financial probings and the valuations were carried out on the spot by the king's commissioners, who were armed with sweeping inquisitorial powers allowing them, if necessary, to question not only a man's neighbours, but even his servants. There was no way either to seek hope in evasion or bribery, for the roving taxmen were everywhere. True, the new depredations were entirely legal, but they hurt no less for that, and though the headless bodies of Empson and Dudley were long-since cold in the grave, there was already gossip enough in the great halls of the elite as well as in scattered towns and hamlets that their place was now being taken by the new priest at court. The need for military success therefore increased drastically, especially for Wolsey himself, who had no refuge beyond the fellowship and good favour of his sovereign.

Meanwhile, the continual flux of European politics raised growing doubts about the likelihood of any favourable outcome. In February 1513, Pope Julius died and was replaced by Leo X, whose artistic and dilettante temperament prevented him from being an energetic leader of the league created by his predecessor. Even so, the confederation against France was maintained, albeit with a change of partners from England's perspective, for in March the canny King of France made peace with Venice, seeing clearly that it was only through Venetian aid that he could hope to recover Milan.

In allying herself to Venice, however, France threw away once and for all any hope of friendship with the Holy Roman Emperor Maximilian, who now drew closer to the Holy League. Accordingly on 5 April 1513 the envoys of Leo, Ferdinand, Maximilian and Henry signed a treaty at Mechlin for the joint invasion of France, though the treaty was, in reality, anything but equitable. Maximilian, for instance, was to receive 100,000 crowns from England's seemingly bottomless purse, while two English armies were to be thrown into France. And in the meantime, unbeknown to Wolsey and his master, the Spanish king had far surpassed even his own high standards of skulduggery by signing a year's truce with his French enemy, a full four days before the solemn ceremony at Mechlin affirmed his allegiance to the league.

Scotland, too, was a nagging worry for the hard-pressed almoner. It was a time-honoured axiom of Anglo-Scottish relations that the Scots would always cross the border whenever England and France were at war, and in spite of the fact that Henry had married his sister Margaret to James IV, the match had done nothing to soothe the underlying hostility between the two countries. Moreover, a Scottish warden of the marches had already been murdered in a border feud and one of the assassins was now snugly sheltered south of the border.

To James's credit, however, he was still not overly forward in taking up arms against the Holy League. He had initially dispatched an ambassador to reconcile the pope and Louis, and had spoken enthusiastically of a crusade in a vain effort to re-channel the seething hostility between the two. Nevertheless, Lamotte, the French envoy, continued to flit to and fro between Paris and Edinburgh, pleading for a military alliance on grounds of staunch and ancient friendship, and James duly promised support not only against England but against any who should attack France. Accordingly, in July 1512, Scottish ships had taken thirteen English prizes.

Even now, however, open war was staved off, though the situation continued to hang more and more precariously in the balance. In March 1513 an English diplomat named Dr West was sent to Edinburgh in an effort to induce James to renew the perpetual peace with England. But the Scottish king was already pledged, and West was told in no uncertain terms that any such proposal could never be accepted so long as England's king was intent upon conflict with Scotland's ally.

The implications of all this for Wolsey's war planning could not have been more grave. Not only was a Scottish incursion in the north country during Henry's absence on campaign now guaranteed, but the problem of transporting England's army across to France became altogether more formidable. The English Channel presented its own special obstacles, of course. But now there might be Scottish fighting ships as well as the curse of ill winds to contend with.

Skirmishes between English and Scottish vessels were already common and in August 1511, the two sons of the Earl of Surrey, Lord Thomas and Sir Edward Howard, had become involved in a major battle with Andrew Barton, James IV's most famous sailor. In the ensuing fray, Barton was killed, his crews either slain or captured, and his two ships, the *Lion* and the *Jenny Perwin*, towed into the Thames and incorporated into the English navy. Yet though the victory was resounding the Scottish naval threat appeared to remain as ominous as ever, since James's capital ships remained intact and the Scots were wholly intent upon revenge.

In any case, an even greater English loss was soon to occur in a disastrous engagement with the French which threatened to undo at a stroke all Wolsey's most meticulous planning of the previous months. The year 1512 had been remarkable for the development of England's navy; in the course of merely twelve months, eight ships had been built and five purchased, while in the late winter every ship had been overhauled. 'Such a fleet,' wrote Sir Edward Howard to the king, 'was never seen in Christendom.' And on 10 April, twenty-four ships of the line, carrying 2,880 seamen and 4,650 soldiers left Plymouth harbour in the direction of Brest with a view to clearing the Channel of French shipping, so that the passage of the main English army across the Dover Straits might be conducted unmolested.

By the time that Howard arrived before the great French harbour, moreover, he could not have been more confident that his moment of ultimate glory had arrived. Fifteen French ships had already fled before the English approach and at least another fifty lay at anchor before him. 'Sir,' he wrote, 'we have them at the greatest advantage that ever man had. The first wind that ever cometh they shall have broken heads that all the world shall speak of it.' He had not, however, counted upon the skill of the French admiral of the Mediterranean, Prégent de Bidoux, who had been called home to organise the defence of the Channel against the English.

Prégent had, in fact, already fortified the harbour and laid hands upon no fewer than twenty-four huge hulks, which he intended to launch as fire-ships upon an English attack. He had also manned four galleys with convicts from the Angers jail and provided them with deadly basilisks, which were said to be able to sink a ship at one blow. When, therefore, on 4 April 1513, young Howard set out to attack the French galleys in their moorings, against the express advice of his senior captains, it was a desperate and foolhardy venture.

Arrow-shot and gunfire rained down from every side of the harbour, but it was not until Howard's force finally managed to grapple and board Prégent's galley that the main carnage occurred. As ill-luck would have it, the grappling cable which was fastened around the French capstan now became severed, leaving the English boarding party hopelessly cut off. And after a brave attempt to sell his life dearly, Howard was last seen casting into the sea his signature of office – a precious golden whistle – before being pushed overboard himself at the end of massed French pikes.

The loss of this renowned admiral on the eve of such a massive invasion was a withering blow by any standards, though what followed only served to demonstrate how even adversity of this kind might once again serve Thomas Wolsey's purposes. Alarmingly, the dead admiral was immediately replaced by his brother Thomas, who, along with his father, had already become an object of suspicion for Wolsey. Yet the new admiral was sure to have taken up his new post with furiously conflicting emotions. On the one hand, of course, the 40-year-old Thomas Howard was at last in a position to emerge from the long shadow of his dashing and ostentatious younger brother. There was, however, a striking similarity between his new responsibilities and the task that had been foisted upon him the previous autumn, when he had been asked to replace the Marquess of Dorset as commander of the ill-fated expedition in Spain.

Once more, he was being set the impossible task of rallying a hopelessly dispirited force and redeeming a desperate situation. Put simply, his mission at this point was to lick his men and ships into shape and bring them from Plymouth to Southampton, where in mid-June he would supposedly take on board a contingent led by Charles Brandon, Henry's soul mate in the tourney and hearty companion in the chase. Brandon was then to lead a diversionary attack on Brest while Henry and the main English host crossed the Channel farther east. Yet, in spite of its key role, Howard described the force that he now led as the 'worst ordered' and 'furthest out of rule' that he had ever seen.

Worse still, by mid-May the king was already growing restive. Thanks to Wolsey's ceaseless industry, everything was being brought to a pitch of readiness. The ships for the main invasion, including the newly built *Henri Grace à Dieu*, were lying in the Thames; the mighty 'Twelve Apostles' were freshly delivered from the foundry; the campaigning season was already well advanced. Impatiently, Wolsey now wrote to Richard Fox, stationed in Southampton, demanding to know when the fleet would be ready for inspection, though Fox's reply on 19 May gave no grounds for optimism. 'The whole army and their victuallers,' wrote the bishop, 'lie so far within the haven of Plymouth, that they cannot come out of it without a north-west wind and the wind hath been south-west continually three days past.'

By the time that Fox wrote, however, Howard was already on his way to London in a desperate effort to still those gossiping tongues which were condemning his inaction. Upon his arrival, neither the king nor Wolsey would deign to see him. For Henry to refuse an audience to one of his principal military officers was the clearest indication of just how far Howard's stock had fallen. And for Wolsey to follow suit was an equally clear indication of how high his own had risen. He might well claim with some justification that the intense pressure involved in final preparation gave him no time to spare. But for the son of the country's most influential noble to be treated in this way was an unprecedented snub. To have to go cap in hand to an upstart cleric was galling enough in its own right, but to be spurned in the process left a truly bitter taste. And the fact that the tone of Howard's correspondence with Wolsey was cringingly respectful throughout fooled no-one, including, of course, the almoner himself.

Nor would the head of the Howard house, the Earl of Surrey, be any less outraged by his own subsequent treatment at Wolsey's hand. For a soldier of his pedigree, the invasion of France was the ultimate challenge and pinnacle of achievement in its own right. But now, of course, with the death of his second son, it was also the perfect opportunity for revenge. Moreover, at the advanced age of 70 he was hardly likely to gain a second chance. Therefore, when Wolsey prevailed upon the king to send the ancient noble north to contain the Scots instead of across the Channel to deal a mortal blow to France, the magnitude of his disappointment can well be imagined.

To compound matters, Surrey was not even empowered to launch a heroic strike against the old foe, though James IV continued to talk of war more freely than ever. Instead, he was placed under strict instructions not to breach the existing treaty and merely to guard against invasion. Furthermore, to complete his frustration, these orders were capped by the news that Wolsey himself would accompany Henry to France at the head of two hundred of his own men. In the event, the old man's fury was every bit as great as his utter inability to forestall the almoner's plans.

Naturally enough, Wolsey had been fully alive to the political advantage accruing from Surrey's absence from the French expedition. In separating the belligerent earl from the king, his own views were subject to less argument and his voice more likely to be heard. Yet, as usual, there was also sound sense and solid principle underlying Wolsey's manoeuvrings. In many ways, this was indeed Surrey's longed-for war. But Wolsey was determined to contain it and limit the obvious risks attached to any escalation of the conflict. Once whetted by fresh battle, there was every possibility that Surrey might encourage and ultimately persuade Henry to press on further with more reckless adventures.

Henry, after all, still styled himself in the manner of his ancestors as King of England and France. Indeed, that title – empty as it was – was now bandied about more lavishly than ever at court, in the council chamber and in the country at large. Were Surrey to play on his sovereign's vanity, it was likely to lead to battle upon battle, grinding taxation and, in all likelihood, eventual military disaster that would make earlier reverses over the past year or so pale into insignificance. Would not a pretentious grab for the crown of France, which Surrey was bound to advocate, also dash entirely any future hopes of peace?

On the other hand, Surrey's knowledge of Scottish affairs was second to none and this, coupled with his impressive military record, made him the obvious choice to defend England from the real and present danger in the north. In 1497 he had repelled an attack on Norham Castle by James IV in support of the pretender, Perkin Warbeck, and followed up this success with a raid into Scotland itself to seize Ayton Castle. Furthermore, Surrey had also enjoyed diplomatic as well as martial success north of the border. In 1503, for instance, he had accompanied Princess Margaret for her wedding to James.

Despite their past battles the King of Scotland and Surrey appear to have got along splendidly as fellow chivalrous knights. Indeed, the aged noble was said to have returned south laden with gifts – much to the chagrin of Margaret herself, it might be added, since her new husband genuinely seemed to prefer Surrey's company to her own. Quite apart from being Wolsey's greatest rival, then, the head of the House of Howard was palpably the best-equipped general to meet the Scottish threat and, as such, the role now chosen for him made perfect sense from all perspectives but his own.

With England's defence in safe hands, Thomas Wolsey's carefully laid plans at last glided to completion in the spring of 1513. Ultimately, the defiant death of Sir Edward Howard had therefore proved a fillip to the king's cause. Indeed, even Wolsey himself could not have predicted its sharpening effect upon English minds. Until then, the war had been associated with heavy impositions, rising prices and back-breaking sacrifice as all available resources were diverted to the daunting challenge ahead. 'There is no business doing', a Venetian observer had lamented at one point. 'All are engaged in preparation for war,' he continued, 'and the chief trade is in military stores and equipment.'

After Edward Howard's death, however, the war assumed an altogether different meaning. No longer merely a cold commercial enterprise, it was transformed by degrees into a display of national pride and courage – a rediscovery and reaffirmation of England's epic past. It was one thing to stitch tents and brew beer day and night at Portsmouth, but quite another to avenge an English hero and reclaim the King of England's birthright in the process. Henry VIII's long-awaited war was now a stirring, colourful pageant in which brave Englishmen might at last emulate their red-blooded ancestors and carve their own names in history. And now it would begin for real.

7

To Tournay's Towered Walls

On 30 June 1513 the full scale of what Thomas Wolsey had achieved over the previous hectic months became apparent. The previous day had been unpleasant, with a gale from the north and continued rain towards evening. Far away over the frothing waters of the Channel the tents of the advance force of English soldiers already encamped outside Calais had been severely damaged. Indeed, so many poles had been smashed and guy-ropes broken that Richard Gibson, yeoman tailor in charge of tents, was hard put to find replacements. The new dawn, however, brought a transformation in the weather and by midday the waters off Dover teemed with ships, a fleet 'such as Neptune never saw before'.

Three- and four-masted warships, with huge emblazoned banners flying from their masts, now rode at anchor side by side, while swarms of rowboats bobbed among them, bringing aboard the last loads of bowstaves, flour and beer. The *Peter Pomegranet* and the *John Hopton* were both there, along with other heavy warships like *The Sovereign*, the *Trinity Sovereign*, the *Gabriel Royal* and the *Mary Rose*, all of which had been laid down since Wolsey's appointment. Loaded with some 12,000 infantry and 4,000 cavalry, not to mention 12,000 suits of armour and a train of artillery the like of which had never been transported by sea before, vessels great and small now heaved in eager anticipation of a prearranged signal from the royal flagship, the *Great Harry Imperial*.

It was, in fact, exactly one hundred years to the day since England's greatest hero, Henry V, had asserted his right to the French throne. Two years later, he had sailed to France to meet his enemy on a field sown with winter wheat near the village of Agincourt. And there his sickly men-at-arms and archers had resoundingly defeated the Frenchmen massed against them, slaughtering their foes until they lay in bloody heaps 'taller than a man's height', as one chronicler recorded with patriotic relish. Nor was Agincourt the last of Henry V's martial exploits, for he had added to the lustre of his name thereafter by conquering Normandy and winning the French throne itself. Finally, as if to gild his place in history once and for all, he had gone on to die at the tender age of 35, still a hero, leaving the dented helmet he wore in France to hang upon his tomb at Westminster; a symbol of renown for the young Henry VIII to dream upon.

Glory, fame and a place in history had, in fact, been the present king's passionate aim since the earliest days of his boyhood, and both his grandmother and tutors had helped make the conquest of France nothing less than a consuming fixation for him. Having been reared on stories of the Holy Grail and stirring tales of Lancelot, Galahad, Tristram and Percival, his later reading of Malory, Caxton and Froissart was all of English kings waging war on French soil. And though the social order of the Middle Ages was rapidly waning, he readily immersed himself in the chivalric code of selfless heroism which still held sway throughout the courts of Europe.

The king's fondness for the trappings of chivalry had also been steadily reinforced by his father, who created him Earl Marshal at the age of 3. Indeed, Henry VII's court had consciously imitated the Burgundian model, which interpreted honour in stridently martial terms. It was no accident, therefore, that a succession of English kings were portrayed at Richmond Palace 'like bold and valiant knights' rather than in the customary regal panoply. And it was no coincidence either that Henry VII's successor would always conduct his ceaseless quest for 'name, fame, honour and renown' in the shadow of these self-same warrior ancestors who had looked down upon him since childhood from the high walls of his Richmond home.

In due course, foreign visitors and courtiers alike would remark upon the young king's unstinting devotion to the joust and other military pursuits, and predicted that he 'would renew the name of Henry V'. But it was not enough to be 'the most valiant prince under heaven' in his own age. He was also determined to be 'the most goodliest prince that ever reigned over the realm of England'. And in this respect, as in almost every other, Henry felt his closest competitor to be the victor of Agincourt, whom he consciously took as a model.

Each was the son of a troubled usurper, seeking to identify the new dynasty with the nation by an aggressive foreign policy. Each, too, was a devout defender of the Church and enthusiastic advocate of naval power. And while Henry V showed altogether more personal courage on the battlefield, and certainly worked considerably harder at the less exciting administrative details of kingship, Henry VIII did not let these things deter him from an almost ritualistic imitation of his namesake. Predictably, his badge of war, the Lancastrian red rose, was borrowed straight from his predecessor and even the ideal end to the war he now planned looked back to his hero's unfulfilled quest. Only one uninformed Fleming and the blustering Duke of Bourbon would ever speak of crowning the second Tudor at Reims. By contrast, Henry VIII's own aim was always from first to last a coronation in Paris itself.

There was also, of course, the anti-French bile of Henry's subjects to fuel his ambitions. Englishmen were still renowned for their hatred of foreigners in general and this reputation was well deserved. In 1513, for instance, Londoners attacked the servants of the Venetian ambassadors in the streets after Venice had made peace with France. This was only a single example among many, for Englishmen regularly rioted against alien merchants, and when war finally came they would fall out just as readily with foreign mercenaries in their king's pay. English writers, in their turn, mocked the French as a nation of downtrodden and perfidious peasants, and a Spanish merchant was not exaggerating in the slightest when he noted gleefully around this time that 'the best word an Englishman can find to say of a Frenchman is "'French dog"'. It was hardly surprising, then, that before 1513 was out many French nobles would be surrendering to Netherlanders after the so-called 'Battle of the Spurs', because the English were once again killing Frenchmen rather than taking prisoners.

England's elites, too, were raring to wage war across the Channel. The prevailing view of the operation of fortune's wheel in history only reinforced the misconception that France had now had her day, especially since a fall would always accompany the kind of proud and greedy expansionism pursued by French kings since 1453. But, more importantly, while Henry's oldest councillors such as the Earl of Surrey had lived just long enough to remember the national agony at the loss of France, the headstrong young bucks who now featured so prominently at court had no notion whatsoever of the harsh realities of defeat.

On the contrary, to the knights at Henry's court who shaped his mental world, war meant nothing more than valorous deeds and triumphant tales. Like their royal master, they wallowed in those medieval romances of 'bold bawdry and open manslaughter' so beloved of earlier generations, and one of them, Lord Berners, 'a martial man, well seen in all military disciplines' who became master of the royal ordnance, translated Froissart's romantic account of the Hundred Years War at Henry's own request. He did so, he said, because of 'the great pleasure that my noble countrymen of England do take in reading the worthy and knightly deeds of their valiant ancestors'. Not long after, an anonymous Englishman went on to translate an Italian life of Henry V, hoping that the new king, seeing the 'virtuous manners and victorious conquests' of his namesake would be inspired to emulate them.

No-one, however, expected more of Henry VIII than he did of himself. Well before the first year of his reign was out, he had reinforced Calais, ordered general musters, commissioned new artillery, expanded and upgraded his father's small bodyguard of courtiers – the so-called 'King's Spears' – and initiated an expansion of the navy which would quintuple its forces by 1515. And he had made all the right warlike noises to lay down the scale of his intent, for from almost the very moment that he succeeded his father he was proclaiming his duty 'to seek fame by military skill'. 'He hoped,' it was said, 'to create such a fine opinion about his valour among all men that they could understand that his ambition was not merely to equal but to excel the glorious deeds of his ancestors.' And as the reign went forward it was this consuming dream that Thomas Wolsey tapped into and offered to turn into effortless reality.

Surely enough, then, when Henry finally took his leave of Queen Catherine at Dover Castle that fine summer's day in 1513, the scene could not have been better written or stage managed. Only three weeks earlier it had been reported that she meant to cross with him to France, despite being pregnant for the fourth time. Henry had insisted, however, that she remain behind to serve as regent in his absence, and now she played her womanly role to perfection. 'The king,' said Edward Hall, 'took leave of the Queen and the Ladies, which made such sorrow for the departing of their Lords and husbands that it was great dolor to behold.'

But while his wife whimpered touchingly, Henry stepped forth boldly to realise his destiny. Standing in the bow of his royal launch in gleaming German armour, he wore a polished steel headpiece lined with crimson satin and crowned with a rich coronal. And over his armour he had slipped the tunic of a crusading knight, a simple garment of white cloth fronted with a large red cross. With a jewelled brooch of St George on his crown, the cross of Christ on his heart and the arms of the pope festooned on his banners, the crusading king was therefore off to war at last.

As the great ship which bore him weighed anchor and slowly moved out of Dover harbour, accompanied by the whole fleet, Henry continued to stand on deck, a prominent object in the eyes of his loyal subjects cheering enthusiastically on the quay. Among them, with heavy and envious heart, stood old Thomas Howard. Thomas Wolsey, meanwhile, with his personal retinue of

200 men safely stowed, faced the beckoning horizon and rejoiced, for the time being at least, in the stiffening breeze which carried him forward.

In the event, the crossing to Calais passed without incident, for, in spite of Sir Edward Howard's death both French and Scottish admirals alike accepted that a fleet of this size was effectively unstoppable. Indeed, the king and his ships enjoyed a 'goodly passage', even though, according to Edward Hall, the wind had veered somewhat to the west during the passage and carried them eventually to the coast of Picardy, 'open upon St John's Road', a longish way off course. In consequence, the fleet made its landfall west of Calais, which had the incidental effect of terrifying the inhabitants of Boulogne, who concluded that a direct assault was about to be made upon them.

Nevertheless, after a great deal of trumpet blowing and firing of cannon, which will have excited Henry no less than it frayed the nerves of his French foes, the fleet turned eastwards to its intended haven, and as they neared Calais the English ships continued to fire salvo after salvo until they were joyfully answered by the harbour's own artillery. So great, indeed, was the din that the thunder of the guns could be plainly heard at Dover 22 miles away, prompting John Taylor, who witnessed the episode, to declare that there was 'such firing of guns from the ships and from the towers of the fortifications you would have thought the world was coming to an end'. All the same, by seven o'clock – about an hour and a half before sunset – the guns had finally fallen silent for Henry's first meeting with the Deputy of Calais, Sir Gilbert Talbot, 'and all other nobles and gentlemen of the town and country'.

No doubt, Talbot, who had held the post of deputy for three years, was mightily relieved at the safe arrival of his royal master and the last of the invasion troops, for he had been under particularly severe strain in recent months. Only a few weeks earlier, in fact, his health had apparently broken under the unremitting pressure and he had taken to his bed for a fortnight. His own explanation was that he had served the king so diligently that he had forgotten to serve God. The real cause of his indisposition, however, had not a little to do with the increasingly onerous whims of the king's almoner.

Though Talbot had, for instance, managed easily enough to lay in the tun of wine that Wolsey had ordered for his own use in Calais, none of the special black 'gown cloth' which he also requested was available locally. Yet every wish of this rising star, whose demanding presence was becoming ever more prominent, would have to be met, irrespective of the time and effort involved. In consequence, messengers were sent to St Omer and Bruges in search of the cloth before the governor was eventually able to report with considerable relief that the precious material had been dispatched to Wolsey in England.

Now that the almoner was landed in France, however, he was most concerned initially with the successful completion of the mammoth logistical task that had occupied him so fully in recent weeks and months. Therefore, along with Charles Brandon, who had recently been created Lord Lisle and marshal of the army, Wolsey now supervised the unloading of the ships. Alert to every detail, the man whose signature lay on literally thousands of orders, receipts and authorisations watched the sailors leading ashore the oxen and mules and great Flanders mares that were to pull the carts and ordnance. And in the process he ensured that not a chest, barrel or box loaded in Dover would fail to emerge from the ships' holds in Calais.

The 'house of timber', contained in fourteen wagons, which was to be the king's lodging on campaign, was duly accounted for, along with the fourteen fine horses 'with housings of the richest cloth of gold and crimson velvet with silver bells of great value' that Henry had seen fit to bring with him. Likewise, Wolsey also oversaw the unloading of his master's garments, items in which he had a special personal interest, since he had even chosen 'the shade of the colour of the satin for the king's doublet'. Nor was this surprising, for one of the man's many gifts was his unerring attention to those flourishes that displayed his sovereign to the best possible effect.

In spite of his many duties, however, Wolsey still seems to have found sufficient time to pose and posture on his own account, for he featured prominently in the grand ceremonial entry into Calais which now occurred amid much noise and spectacle. First inside the walls were members of the king's own household, followed by the retinue of England's only duke, the Duke of Buckingham. But following close behind Buckingham's banner, third in line and before both Fox and Ruthall, came Wolsey.

Further back came the Earl of Northumberland, who brought with him not only an imposing noble pedigree, but all the creature comforts and necessities befitting a man of his substance, including a feather bed and mattress for his pavilion, with cushions of silk and worsted hangings, a close carriage with seven horses, two chariots each with eight horses, four carts each with seven horses, not to mention a steward, a chamberlain, a gentleman usher of the chamber, a master of the horse, carvers and cupbearers, a herald and a pursuivant. That so august a figure should follow Wolsey on such a momentous occasion was perhaps the fullest confirmation yet of the almoner's new status.

More significantly still, in the procession which followed Wolsey not only rode high but in close attendance upon the king. As became his station, and no doubt, too, as a ploy to emphasise his Christ-like humility, he wore, we are told, a plain cassock and rode a mule rather than a richly caparisoned horse. And before long, the glittering cavalcade had moved from the quay, across the garden lying between the harbour and the town, known as Paradise, where nine-pins, dice and other gambling games of the day were customarily played, and on to the Lantern Gate, the main entrance to the fortress.

Moreover, as Henry treated the inhabitants of Calais to their first full taste of his might and colour, they responded with precisely the kind of ardour that he craved. Indeed, the importance of the scenes which Henry now witnessed and had savoured throughout the day leading up to them cannot be overestimated, for not only did they represent the crowning achievement of his life so far, they helped determine what would become the prime objective of his reign and the main benchmark by which he came to measure his own ultimate success. Marital adventures would punctuate the years ahead, of course. Religious experiment would also be a recurring theme. But by and large these things offered vexation rather than fulfilment, and to a man such as Henry the prospect of conquest was always infinitely preferable. Playing with marriage could not, after all, compare to playing at soldiers, while religious dabbling was a long and winding process offering no decisive outcome of the kind that could be gained in a single morning on the field of battle. Moreover, if glory abroad and universal adulation at home were indeed the guiding lights of his existence, then any man who might furnish him with both – or even the illusion of them – would automatically secure a leading place in his intimate circle.

Certainly, Henry bore his subjects' homage well that midsummer day in 1513. With 'amiable visage' and 'princely countenance' he gratefully accepted the noisy admiration of the many men and women crowding at the overhanging windows along his path. And he was no less gracious when offered the plaudits of 'the Mayor and Merchants of the Staple, well apparelled', who greeted him in front of the Staple Hall. When the time came, though, he also moved with more solemn intent, for as proceedings reached their climax he adopted a new role: that of the Christian crusader and guardian of his Mother Church.

In this final phase of the procession, even Wolsey would have to forsake his mule, for only the king and his sword-bearer were to remain mounted. Led by the Garter King of Arms and other heralds in brilliant uniforms, Henry finally arrived at the great western entrance of the Church of St Nicholas, which he entered just as the day was waning. There he offered thanks for the safe passage of both himself and his armies across the perilous seas and dedicated the coming conflict against the sacrilegious insolence of Louis XII to the Almighty and His Church. Kneeling before the high altar with his almoner close by, he heard Mass and a triumphant *Te Deum* before finally retiring in high spirits to the Staple Inn, which was to be his lodging throughout his stay in Calais.

That night, however, neither the king nor Wolsey slept undisturbed, for about eleven o'clock there was a commotion in the camp outside the wall which led to the sounding of the alarm in the town. An enemy agent had, it seems, succeeded in obtaining a job with Wolsey's victuallers and led a force of about 300 Frenchmen from the neighbouring coastal towns of Wissant and Boulogne with the objective of passing Fort Risban, which guarded the harbour, and then destroying the supply tents pitched between the town and the encamped army. As luck would have it, the watch was well kept and the attackers were driven off by a company of English archers who waded into the sea to repel them.

But though Henry himself had hastened to the battlements to witness the commotion and returned to bed excited and satisfied after hearing Richard Gibson's account of the affair, Wolsey's response will almost certainly have been much more pensive, for though he had no more experience of war than his master, he had more imagination and far more to lose. This, after all, was no longer merely a war of inventories, bills and receipts. Now it was a war of deadly intent and real destruction; one, indeed, in which so much of his recent effort might well have disappeared in smoke overnight.

By contrast there was altogether less drama during the days that followed. For the next three weeks Henry's army idled in Calais, while he himself spent much of his time in ceremonial processions to Mass and showy displays of his prowess with the longbow. But if it seemed at this time that the King of England was more concerned with parading than invading, Wolsey played no small part in ensuring that business of state was not altogether neglected by his master. Accordingly, Henry was still encouraged to meet with his council regularly and to read and sign a steady stream of papers.

At Wolsey's instigation the king met ambassadors of all descriptions. On the day after his arrival, for instance, he received representatives of the emperor and Margaret of Savoy in the dining-chamber of the Staple Inn, and in the same week he ratified an agreement about the plan of campaign with the emperor before the high altar of St Mary's. There was also time to meet with envoys from Ghent and Bruges, who offered supplies to the invading army, on condition that the soldiers refrain from unfriendly acts towards their territories, to which Henry readily agreed. A few days later the Spanish ambassador, too, called on Henry, though in light of his master's previous machinations his reception is certain to have been cool.

Henry did not leave Calais with his army until 21 July, which meant that three weeks of high summer – the best part of the campaigning season – were largely wasted. It meant, too, that for a considerable period the English forces were divided, with the Earl of Shrewsbury's advance force, which had left Calais on 13 June, already besieging the fortress of Thérouanne.

Nor was Henry's departure auspicious when it finally came. In the first place, the rain normal to campaigns in Flanders and Picardy had begun to close in and the soldiers found themselves mustering in fog. Moreover, as they were doing so, a stampede occurred among the cavalry, in the course of which Sir Henry Marney, captain of the king's guard, had his leg broken and a number of other gentleman were injured. As one chronicler recorded, 'it was long ere ever the army might be set in order according to the bill devised by the council' and, in the event, the stampede was serious enough to upset the entire departure plan. At the same time, Richard Fox was unfortunate enough to be kicked by a mule, leaving the elderly bishop unable to either 'sit or stand' for days. To make matters even worse, it then rained heavily throughout the first afternoon and when darkness fell the troops had covered no more than 3 miles. To cap all, the tents, which had already suffered from the weather, particularly in the heavy storm of 4 July, were further damaged and began to leak.

Even Wolsey is likely to have suffered some serious discomfort that first night as the army endeavoured to take its rest somewhere between the townships of Fréthun and Old Coquelles on its muddy way to the fortress of Thérouanne. Naturally enough, he enjoyed special treatment and his lot will certainly have been preferable to that of the common soldiers huddled in their thousands under the open skies beneath dripping bushes and windswept trees. His tent, which was known as the Inflamed House, occupied more than 1,700 square feet – about half as much again as the records show for Charles Brandon, second-in-command of the whole army. And he enjoyed other creature comforts, too, not the least of which was that most prized of status symbols, his own indoor toilet or 'stool place', a facility provided for only four other members of the king's retinue: the captain of the yeoman of the guard, the treasurer at war, the lord chamberlain and the master of the horse.

But the sixteenth-century tent was much more vulnerable to the elements than its present-day counterpart, and in spite of the fact that virtually all of those on the 1513 expedition were custom-made for the task, Richard Gibson's accounts prove that a good deal of modification and repair was needed as the campaign unfolded, which suggests that the original designs left more than a little to be desired. Some occupants also seem to have suffered from the cold as well as the damp, for in several cases walls were doubled and extra partitions had to be added. On Wolsey's first real night of campaigning, then, the warm fires and oak panelled walls of St Bride's may well have seemed a particularly distant prospect.

Nevertheless, the almoner's solution to discomfort and dreary thoughts was, as always, feverish activity and from the time that the invading force dragged its weary way from Calais, he stood ready to perform any and every chore which might smooth the king's path to his imagined destiny. Naturally, he was constantly by Henry's side, acting as confidential adviser and universal minister, especially in diplomatic negotiations with the allies, where he exercised a general administrative control over anything and everything: so much so, indeed, that one of the Holy Roman Emperor's emissaries, Philippe de Bregilles, who eventually met Wolsey before Thérouanne, complained of him as 'an obstinate man who rules everything': an epithet which has stuck to him particularly doggedly down the years.

Certainly, Wolsey was obstinate enough in his refusal to sacrifice his master's interests merely to suit the game of his imperial ally. But if he did indeed rule 'everything', this remained truer of the humdrum detail of the campaign than it did for matters of high policy. Throughout the entire campaign Wolsey was still primarily fixer, provider and clerk-in-chief – managing the army's financial arrangements, controlling the supply of every kind of military store and dispatching messengers at all hours to do the king's bidding – while sustaining, in the process, his additional personal role as captain of 200 fighting men.

Not least, Wolsey was responsible with the high marshal for correcting any error in the line of march, which was no small task with such a sizeable force strung out over some 2 or 3 miles along the narrow French roads of the day. At the head of the column, some way behind the high marshal, under-marshal and a body of 'valiant soldiers', rode Henry with his attendants and pages, his spears and 600 guardsmen, his clerks, secretaries, heralds and pursuivants, his physicians and surgeons. The king's personal bowyer and fletcher rode near him, too, as did his trumpeters and minstrels and the thirty-five artificers who forged his armour and kept it and his weapons in good repair.

Next came the 250 officers and servants of his stable, the members of his chapel and the grooms and menials of his household, nearly 1,000 strong, while directly behind them trundled the great guns, each pulled by teams of a dozen or more oxen or heavy draft horses. Still further back, a small army of 1,200 accompanied the ordnance: gunners and blacksmiths, miners and pioneers, masons, armourers, trench-makers and carpenters, along with 'toile setters' to raise the tents.

Then, last of all, came the great nobles and royal favourites, each with their individual retinues: the Duke of Buckingham with his 500 men, William Compton with his 600, and grandest of all, Charles Brandon, Lord Lisle, with 1,500 archers, billmen and armoured knights. It was with this last group, along with Fox and Ruthall, that Wolsey mainly travelled. And it was from here, too, that Wolsey eased the passage of this lumbering force whose pace was constantly limited by both the absence of maps and the painfully sluggish progress of its slowest element, the artillery.

Wolsey was also, of course, a first-hand witness to all the memorable incidents of the campaign and this, in itself, will have played no small part in further cementing the uniquely personal place he came to occupy in the king's favour. Having been with his royal master through thick and thin – the arduous days of marching, the niggling frustrations and discomforts, as well as the dizzy highs of victory – Wolsey would see the king in a more intimate light than even he had hitherto enjoyed and confirm, at the same time, his own credentials as a man of the king's own heart.

The king may well have had his almoner with him when, on that first wretched night of their march out from Calais, he rallied his rain-drenched men. Having read, no doubt, of how in similar adverse circumstances Henry V had ridden round his camp encouraging his men, Henry VIII now did the same, it seems. Through most of the night, as the storm raged on, the king rode in full armour from one miserable cluster of men to another, calling out to them that better luck was sure to follow. 'Now that we have suffered in the beginning,' he told them, 'fortune promises us better things, God willing.'

Wolsey will also have been on hand when the king learnt occasionally of those ugly setbacks which characterise even the most successful of military campaigns. Some five days or so into the march, for example, a party of French soldiers attacked an English contingent carrying supplies from Calais to the main English force. The raiders captured 150 English wagons and also killed some 300 of the English force accompanying them, with the rest fleeing to a nearby castle. Then, after another skirmish near Ardres, the French gathered up all the enemy corpses they could find and mutilated their faces beyond recognition.

There seems little doubt either that Wolsey witnessed the king's 'bad fright' at Tournehem, where, according to the *Histoire de Bon Chevalier*, the English narrowly escaped attack from 1,200 men-at-arms. Having dismounted and taken shelter in the midst of 4,000 *Landsknechte*, whom Henry regarded as better fighters than his countrymen, he was only saved, it seems, by the indecision of the French commander, de Piennes, who refused to charge against the English, in spite of the fact that they had no cavalry to defend themselves at that particular time.

Throughout the 1513 expedition, therefore, Wolsey will have seen war at close range and from all angles – the drab and the dreary, the arduous, the mundane, the stirring, the beastly and the nerve-jangling. Furthermore, with every passing day he will have been able to share more and more fully in his master's campfire tales, not merely as a rapt listener, but as a direct participant in the unfolding events. He will certainly have been present, for instance, when 'an affray in which many were killed on both sides' took place between English and German soldiers in the king's pay at the camp near Aire-Sur-Lys. The flashpoint occurred, it seems, when mutinous Germans seized some artillery pieces and turned them on Henry and his staff, at which point some English archers, 'greatly fumed with this matter', loosed a number of arrows in their king's defence. It was only, in fact, the prompt intervention of senior officers that prevented a much more disastrous conflict.

Less dramatically, Wolsey would also ensure that the queen was kept fully informed throughout the whole campaign, for while Henry was busy with his armies even the most commonplace husbandly civility was too much for him. The king had written to his wife while he was in Calais, but it was simply about a minor business matter raised by the Bishop of Winchester, and the letter was addressed to her in her capacity as regent rather than wife. It was Wolsey, however, who remembered that Queen Catherine was entering the last months of her pregnancy and had begged for frequent letters, as she was without any other comfort in Henry's absence. And now, obviously recognising Wolsey's influence as an intercessor with the king, Catherine sent him a steady stream of correspondence, which he caringly reciprocated.

Although preoccupied with the imminent campaign against the Scots, she worried constantly, it seems, about all aspects of her husband's welfare, including his tendency to catch cold. Then, in mid-August, she wrote to Wolsey expressing her thankfulness that Henry had safely accomplished his intention to besiege Thérouanne, and saying that she trusted to God 'it shall be so continued that ever the king shall have the best on his enemies with as great honour as ever king had'. She added, too, that she had been very troubled to think that Henry was so near to the action, but now thanked God for Wolsey's assurance 'of the good heed that the king taketh of himself to avoid all manner [of] dangers' and begged him to do everything in his power to keep the king safe. In truth, though, she need not have worried unduly, for the council had already agreed that the king should watch all military operations from a safe distance, particularly in the solitary battle of the expedition, which was only a few days away.

The siege of Thérouanne had already been running for some weeks when Henry's army arrived before its walls on 1 August, but it would take a further fortnight before the English king at last achieved the military victory he craved so ardently. Helped by persistent storms, the defenders of Thérouanne were holding out so stalwartly that the French army besieging the nearby imperial town of Hesdin had not even bothered to send relief troops in force. Instead, they dispatched only raiding parties, which, much to Henry's consternation, had seized two of his great guns and sunk one of them in a deep pond.

But on 16 August, the English would have their revenge when the French commander, Vendôme, decided to try to draw the English away from Thérouanne and sent two companies of knights towards the town. According to one account, Vendôme's force was accidentally intercepted and the English charged, sending one body of French horsemen back into the others and causing wholesale panic. Within minutes the whole French host was galloping back madly across the fields whence they had come, shedding their standards and lances and even the bardings of their horses. In all, nine standards were taken, along with a fortune in forfeited arms and accoutrements, while more than a hundred notable prisoners were seized for ransom, including none other than the legendary Chevalier Bayard. And though a French eyewitness would report later that Henry might have routed the whole French army, had he re-formed his horsemen for a fresh charge, the glory accruing was unquestionably very great. Men would indeed speak of the so-called 'Battle of the Spurs' for years to come, and they would credit Henry VIII with the outcome.

Yet Wolsey, too, would have ample opportunity to bathe in the warm glow of the further victories that came Henry's way over the remaining weeks of that summer. Thérouanne itself capitulated on 22 August and became the first town to be taken by the English in France since the capture of Guienne in 1453. Then even more glorious news followed from home after the Scots were comprehensively crushed at Flodden on 7 September. Their king, James IV, vain and over-confident, had wasted every advantage over his foes and finally seen his men squeezed into an ever-tightening circle until they had torn the shoes from their feet to clench their toes more firmly in the blood-soaked hillside on which they made their stand. In the end, both they and their leader had fallen, leaving Scotland with a nation of broken families and a king only one year, five months and ten days old. Such was the scale of the victory that Queen Catherine described it in a letter to Wolsey as 'a matter so marvellous that it seemeth to be of God's doing alone'.

Finally came the fall of Tournai, 'the wealthiest city in all Flanders, and the most populous of any on this side of Paris', wrote Brian Tuke, Clerk of the Signet. With its thick double walls and ninety-five towers, this 'great, handsome and powerful' stronghold – the so-called 'Unsullied Maiden' – which held the key to Picardy became Henry's on 24 September. And in Tournai's fall, Thomas Wolsey once again displayed his thoroughness. Preparing for a long and strenuous siege, he had not been content to trust the army of his king to canvas. Instead, he had ordered the building of an immense number of wooden huts; enough, it seems, to shelter the entire English contingent of some 35,000 men. There were so many, we are told, that they covered a space around the walls of Tournai as extensive as the area covered by the town itself, which boasted 80,000 inhabitants.

Perhaps it was only fitting, then, that when Henry finally took possession of his finest prize after the tame surrender of the French garrison, his almoner should feature so prominently in all aspects of what followed. Indeed, while the banners of victory were still being hung out and the king himself was preparing to ride at the head of his army through the city's St Fontaine gate, Wolsey had already organised the terms of the surrender and was now calling upon the inhabitants to kneel before their new ruler.

In the ensuing procession, the king, wearing a full suit of richly decorated armour, rode a magnificent barded courser, as his henchmen carried his weapons before him. His nobles and heralds, in their turn, paraded their finest outfits before a large crowd of townspeople who managed with some encouragement from the attendant soldiers to raise a few dutiful shouts of '*Vive le Roi*'. And as though to mark such a portentous occasion, the heavens, we are told, revealed in the clear light of day a 'clear sun, a pale moon, and a bright star'. Meanwhile, in a pavilion of gold and purple, it was Wolsey himself who celebrated the Mass of victory.

8

Author of Peace

When, with the onset of winter in 1513, Henry VIII's conquering heroes returned in glory to their homeland, the bonfires and burbling fountains of wine which greeted them were largely misplaced. It was, in fact, the Emperor Maximilian who had been the main beneficiary of English efforts, since the capture of two French fortress towns not only made the borders of the Holy Roman Empire more secure, but also temporarily distracted France from engaging the imperial armies in Italy. So when one English ambassador generously compared his own sovereign to the heroic Athenian King Codrus, who was too preoccupied with the welfare of his neighbours to remember his own, the underlying implication was clear enough.

But this was not the only folly of Henry's French adventure, for though he now hastened to Richmond to lay the keys of both captured towns at his wife's feet, even the military prowess of his army remained largely unproven. Throughout the entire campaign the aged, sickly and careworn King of France had hidden away at Amiens and resigned himself to offering only the feeblest of resistance to his English foe. Tournai, for instance, had been no more than grudgingly fortified, while the town's strategic importance was, in any case, largely neutralised by the encircling territories of the Netherlands. And in spite of the predictable glut of stirring warriors' tales now circulating, Thérouanne had, in its turn, been sorely under-defended and lightly lost by mischance. Certainly, English claims that 3,000 Frenchmen had fallen at the Battle of the Spurs appear to have been wildly exaggerated.

More significantly still, Henry's tinsel victories in France had placed a grievous strain on his kingdom's finances. Ironically, one of his last acts before leaving England was to order that the jewel house in the Tower of London be made more secure, and with this in mind, he had instigated the urgent construction of an unbreachable brick wall and the installation of reinforced bars on all windows. Mighty doors were also put in place along with specially devised 'hanglocks' and keys. Yet by the time he returned from his adventures across the Channel there was little left to guard.

The Venetian Lorenzo Pasqualigo was only one among many who marvelled at the king's extravagance in war. The sums spent by Henry on 'artillery and camp furniture' alone, he told his brothers, would fill a well of gold, while his countryman, Antonio Bavarino, reported to his business colleagues at home that Henry had taken with him fourteen wagons laden with gold and four with silver coin: 'facts which sound like tales of romance but are nevertheless true'. In total, the military expenses between 1511 and 1513 now stood at some £922,000, and Tournai, in its turn, would cost a further £230,000 to fortify, notwithstanding the fact that when the French retrieved it in 1518, they would do so for well under half that sum. When all was over, therefore, the treasure in jewels and plate that had been Henry VII's hard-earned legacy to his son was largely spent, and to no lasting purpose.

Yet, if nothing else, Henry's war had at least won him in the short-term the fame he craved so desperately and the consequences of this for the gifted priest who had made everything possible cannot be overestimated. Now, with every conceivable assistance from Wolsey himself, news of the King of England's victories in France spread like wildfire, and not just in his own land. Indeed, largely as a result of his almoner's efforts, men to whom the English king had once been only a shadowy figure of small repute now spoke glowingly of how he had won the day at the Battle of the Spurs and returned to Guinegate after the capture of Thérouanne, eagerly awaiting a personal challenge to do battle for the town. All were learning, too, how he had walked for hours in the open at the siege of Tournai, heedless of French cannon fire.

In the meantime Henry was also being widely depicted as an avid champion of papal interests and the Christian faith itself. Leo X, for example, did not hesitate to reward him with a cap and sword for his broader efforts on behalf of the Holy See, while an Italian poem on the capture of Thérouanne singled him out for special admiration on the grounds that he had spared the town's churches. 'Let all other Christian princes take example by this unconquered king,' wrote one observer, 'and be prepared to pour out wealth and blood as he has done in defence of the Church, to gain both from God and man the same reward for their labour.'

Astrologers, in their turn, confidently foretold that the Turkish tyrant was next in line to be tamed by the all-conquering King of England, while Henry's image as the ultimate Christian warrior was neatly embroidered with further tales of mercy for his vanquished foes. He had, it seems, shown uncommon charity to French prisoners, allowing some to ransom themselves for a token payment and subsidising the ransoms of others from his own pocket. To the captured Duc de Longueville – a noble of the highest rank – he had given a gown of cloth of gold, and thereafter forced him, despite his humble protestations, to dine at the royal table. And though Henry had shown himself a fearful adversary, declaring through his Garter King of Arms to the citizens of Tournai that if they did not yield he would 'put them and their city to sword, fire and blood', it was said, nevertheless, that he eventually treated the conquered population with uncommon leniency.

Finally, thanks in no small part to Wolsey's *Statutes of War*, the behaviour of Henry's soldiers was also widely represented as yet another minor wonder of the campaign. Though the English artillery at Thérouanne had destroyed a large house – possibly a convent or *béguinage* – killing 'many dozen fair young women', the soldiers themselves had, it was said, avoided any manner of pillage, robbery and sacrilege. Camp followers, on the other hand, had been outlawed and the 'marvellous fair, well fed and clean washen' girls of the region went unmolested. For good measure, it was also said that English soldiers neither swore profanely nor failed to recite Our Lady's rosary daily. If, therefore, Henry VIII had not yet actually won the French crown like his idol Henry V, his campaign had none of the brutality of his predecessor's. Besides which, he had won his victories at a younger age and earlier in the reign. Who could say, then, what glory his next campaign might bring?

Nor was there ever the slightest shadow of doubt in Henry's mind that he would soon be at war again. Indeed, even before the autumn mists of Flanders and Picardy were behind him, he had assured Pope Leo of his resolve to return as quickly as possible with a larger army to resume his conquest. And, surely enough, after a bout of measles or smallpox in early 1514, he would soon be rising from his bed, 'fierce against France'.

As Wolsey had already discovered, however, success in war was also predicated upon careful play at peace, when occasion required. The business of conquest was, after all, expensive, and the winter months lay ahead. Furthermore, there was also the very real possibility that the French might rally, if caution were not applied. In consequence, it was only sensible to bide a while and hope that stronger links might be forged with those who could offer the promise of even greater glory to come.

By now the fulcrum of future control in Europe was already the Holy Roman Emperor's grandson, Charles. Earnest and reserved beyond his 13 years, the simple pleasures of youth had wholly bypassed this Habsburg prince and he now carried the burdens of impending power squarely on his narrow shoulders. He was heir to the imperial throne and, more importantly, also heir to the richer holdings of the Spanish crown through his other grandfather, Ferdinand. Through this latter link, moreover, he was also nephew to Henry VIII's own wife. And if any further proof were needed of the gangling boy's emergence as the dominant force in the dynastic politics of the day, he had already inherited Flanders and the Netherlands, which were ruled on his behalf for the time being by his other aunt, Margaret of Savoy, daughter of the emperor.

On 12 September, therefore – even before Tournai was taken – Henry had made solemn entry into Lille to court his Habsburg friends. Wearing his jewelled crown and a doublet of cloth of silver, he was greeted by young girls bearing sceptres and garlands of flowers, along with outlaws and penitents, holding, as was the custom, white rods betokening their pleas for pardon. From the city gate, throughout the crowded streets and alleys, down to the palace itself, torches and banners were hung, while at every corner pageants portrayed victorious scenes from both the Old and New Testaments. And in the courtyard of the royal palace itself stood a great ox, a personal present from the Emperor Maximilian himself.

A few weeks later the Habsburgs duly descended upon the newly captured city of Tournai to return the visit. And there, away from the jousting, feasting and amorous attentions of Henry's closest friend, Charles Brandon, Margaret of Savoy duly confirmed the marriage of her nephew Charles to the Princess Mary, younger sister to the King of England – a union which far exceeded in potential even those achieved by the late Henry VII, and one, in turn, which also brought with it the tantalising prospect of a further assault on France. This new treaty, signed against France in the name of peace, was duly ratified on 17 October and set the marriage date for 15 May of the following year.

It was small wonder, then, that Henry had returned to England in the highest of spirits, puffed up as much with gratitude to his trusty almoner as he was with restless thoughts of his next foray across the Channel. In November, Parliament granted him the grand sum of £160,000, part of which was immediately earmarked for the hire of a contingent of Swiss mercenaries. Then, at Candlemas, there was a glittering investiture in the great hall of Lambeth Palace to honour the men who had commanded the victorious forces in France and Scotland. While Lord Treasurer Surrey regained the family dukedom of Norfolk, his son Thomas, the Lord Admiral, was created Earl of

Surrey, and Charles Brandon, marshal of the army in France, was created Duke of Suffolk. Though the doors were strictly manned, the hall was nevertheless heaving with spectators, and among those present were the captive Duc de Longueville, 'captain of the 100 gentlemen of the French king's house', and, naturally enough, Thomas Wolsey.

It was not long either before Wolsey himself received his richest crop of rewards to date, beginning with has appointment as Bishop of Lincoln in March 1514. The previous incumbent, William Smith, was a protégé of Lady Margaret Beaufort, who had held the post for eighteen years. But he had been employed intermittently on various embassies and had effectively dropped out of public life early in the century. Thereafter, he had devoted his energies, as well as the considerable wealth of his benefice, to various charitable causes.

Smith's death had occurred in the very first week of January and the vacant bishopric seems to have been bestowed upon Wolsey immediately, since Erasmus heard of the promotion on 4 January and the papal letter confirming it was dated 6 February, four days after the investiture of the dukes of Norfolk and Suffolk at Lambeth. However, the bull appointing Wolsey in his place was granted only reluctantly by Leo X, who was as keen to discourage the needless accumulation of benefices as he was to prevent the accelerated advancement of his clergy. Moreover, the objections in this particular case were especially obvious, since Wolsey's ecclesiastical privileges and responsibilities would subsequently extend to nearly every corner of England.

Nevertheless, Leo's dilemma was real enough, for Henry was adamant that the promotion should be granted, and with the see of Lincoln vacant, it was difficult to see how the English king's wishes could be refused. Leo was, after all, far too shrewd to stir royal tempers without good cause – especially when the monarch involved had been instrumental in curbing French designs on Italy. Therefore, notwithstanding the decree of the Lateran Council of 1512 against pluralism, Wolsey was eventually permitted to hold both Lincoln and Tournai, with which Henry had unofficially rewarded him after its capture, though he was no longer able to retain his post as almoner. Ultimately, he would be consecrated in the chapel of Lambeth Palace on 26 March by Archbishop Warham, assisted by Fitzjames of London and, appropriately enough, Fox of Winchester, who had been so instrumental in encouraging his early rise at court.

In the event, the evolving relationship between Bishop Fox and his former protégé was further proof of just how rapidly the latter had completed his ascent. Back in September 1511 Wolsey had still been little more than a useful go-between for his previous master – Fox's eyes and ears at court. 'Yesterday at mass,' Wolsey informed his patron routinely, 'I broke with the king on this matter and showed him how much honour and also furtherance of all his affairs in time to come should ensue to him.' Eight months later, the bishop was still being fed with information, but now acknowledged that the messenger's activities had grown considerably in scale and importance. 'I require you,' he informed Wolsey, 'though I know well ye have no leisure to write me news yourself, make Brian Tuke [Clerk of the Signet and Wolsey's secretary] by your information write me soon.'

By June 1513, however, Fox was assuming a blatantly apologetic, even deferential, tone to his former assistant. Explaining that his slowness in replying to Wolsey's letters was because of delays in the post, he assured the royal almoner that he had risen from his bed in the middle of the night to respond. And by April 1514 Fox's wishes had, it seems, become wholly subservient to those of the younger man. Dispatching some documents to Wolsey, he wrote: 'I pray you look upon them and advise me as ye shall see cause.' Even more significantly, Fox was no longer addressing his former assistant as 'Brother Master Almoner', but as 'My singular good lord'.

By this time, then, Wolsey's ascent had achieved a momentum all of its own, for not only was Lincoln the largest diocese in all England, it was also one of the richest to boot. Encompassing the counties of Northampton, Rutland, Leicester, Cambridge, Huntingdon, Bedford and Buckingham, as well as Lincoln itself, it brought its incumbent an annual income of £896 19s. And since it also included Oxford within its boundaries, Wolsey would now have a special role to play in the affairs of his former university.

Yet fortune, it seems, has a curious habit of favouring the already fortunate, and even before he could be enthroned in his new office, the new Bishop of Lincoln had been gifted the even grander prize of the archbishopric of York. As absentee Dean of York since February 1513 Wolsey had been content to leave the administration of the cathedral church to Thomas Dalby, the Archdeacon of Richmond, while he himself focused feverishly upon preparation for the impending campaign in France. Furthermore, he had previously asked the Bishop of Worcester, Silvestro Gigli, to serve as his agent in Rome with a view to managing relations with the existing Cardinal Archbishop of York, Christopher Bainbridge, who was serving there as English ambassador.

Wolsey's luck was far from exhausted, however, for Bainbridge did not live long afterwards, and when news of his death arrived in England in the summer of 1514 his would-be replacement had little difficulty in raising the necessary funds to secure the archbishopric for himself. Thanks to Bishop Gigli's shrewdness and speed of action, Wolsey was able to borrow, on the security of his predecessor's estate, some £3,400 from Italian bankers to meet the heavy expenses in Rome connected with his promotion. And on 18 August he also arranged a further bond of £2,000 involving Antonio de Vivaldis of Genoa and two London merchants: one W. Botry, a mercer, and Thomas Raymond, grocer.

But while the customary greasing of palms was duly completed, sinister rumours about the manner of Bainbridge's death were beginning to circulate. It seems that Bainbridge had, in fact, died from poisoning on 14 July after caning an obscure steward in his household for disobedience. The servant concerned was a priest by the name of Rinaldo di Modena, who had then proceeded to take revenge upon the cardinal. However, Wolsey's agent, Gigli, was also believed by some to be implicated in the affair, possibly at the behest of Wolsey himself, and the repercussions were considerable.

Without doubt, Bainbridge had been involved at the time of his death in a series of intrigues in Rome which might, in any case, have endangered him, but his enmity for Wolsey and Gigli was well known. He had, for instance, called the latter a traitor and told King Henry in no uncertain terms that his fellow cardinals were amazed how 'such an infamed person' should be employed by the English government, adding that Wolsey's agents in York were systematically harassing his own. Indeed, he had even asked the pope to dispatch him to England as a papal legate *a latere,* so that he could stand there as the premier voice of the Church and, in the process, curb the hasty advancement of the king's favourite minister, which was already causing grave concern in some circles.

It was in these circumstances, then, that Bainbridge met his mysterious end, and though few lamented his passing, the whole unsavoury business would cause Wolsey untold trouble. Ultimately, the claim that the poisoning had been carried out by di Modena was first related to Wolsey by Richard Pace, who by now had become his secretary. According to Pace, the guilty priest had confessed to his crime under torture, after which the pieces of his quartered body were hung at the four gates of Rome. But the accused had also claimed, it seems, that he had been paid to commit the murder by none other than the Bishop of Worcester. After the long inquests and discussion that followed, Pace wrote to Wolsey:

> As for the poisoning of my late Lord Cardinal, it hath been in the hands of the greatest learned men in Rome, and determined by the most part of them, that my said Lord was poisoned in such a manner as is comprised in the confession of him that did it [...] I may not write herein that [which] I do know.

But while Gigli eventually established his innocence by branding his accuser a madman, an ominous shadow of innuendo would continue to hang over Wolsey. And even though Renaissance Rome, as epitomised by Borgia morals and methods, remained wholly unknown territory for him, this did not prevent the Bainbridge episode from serving as the most fertile ground yet for Wolsey's rumour-mongering enemies, who were growing in number around this time as never before. Certainly, it was widely mooted in Rome itself that the poison had been 'sent from England by some prelate there, being enemy unto my said Lord', who 'procured the same to be ministered unto him by his cook'.

Nevertheless, by September Wolsey had also been formally confirmed as Bishop of Tournai by the pope, though here too this particular promotion would carry with it its own fair share of vexation. On the one hand, the English representative on the spot, Richard Sampson, would face countless wearisome negotiations to thwart the efforts of the rival French bishop elect, Louis Galliard – the exasperating effect of which upon Wolsey was apparent in his correspondence. 'Ye need not doubt thereof,' Wolsey told Sampson in his grandest style, 'the Pope would not offend me for one thousand such as the [French bishop] elect is …'. 'I would not have you muse upon the moon,' he continued imperiously, 'but to go straightly and wisely to my matters.'

More worryingly still, Wolsey's appointment to a French bishopric rankled deeply with those whose suspicions of France never waned. And there were many in England, like the new Duke of Norfolk, who considered that the only good business across the Channel was done on horseback with lance in hand. Wolsey's bishopric of Tournai demanded, after all, wholehearted English commitment to the holding and protection of the city, and when a chief minister of the government was tied in this way to a personal involvement across the Channel, his conduct of government might well be compromised.

But beyond the jealousy surrounding his giddy promotion, there was also Wolsey's apparent hold over the king's affections for his enemies to seize upon. Henry, it was widely believed, divided his attentions between Wolsey and the new Duke of Suffolk to the extent 'that all things passed at the will of these two obstinate men'. Nor was it especially surprising that at this stage of their careers, at least, both men should be 'friends' and give each other what mutual support they could. Each, after all, was forceful and charismatic in his own distinctive way: Wolsey with his self-confident charm and stiletto intellect, Brandon with his own particular type of animal magnetism. And both were considered upstarts in the eyes of the old nobility, especially by the Howards, whose administrative influence in their traditional power base of East Anglia had been seriously challenged by Brandon's elevation to the dukedom of Suffolk in 1514.

Predictably, therefore, every means was used to darken the reputations of both men and before long there were even rumours of occult forces at work. Together, it was said, Wolsey and Brandon 'meddled with the devil and by his puissance kept their master subject'. Wolsey, in particular, became the object of much suspicion in this regard, and it was soon being suggested at court that he possessed a magic ring and had a familiar demon in his service. According to one creeping whisper, he had, it seems, calculated the king's horoscope, then 'made by craft of necromancy graven imagery [...] wherewith he bewitched the king's mind and made the king to dote upon him more than ever he did on any lady or gentleman'. Even the hard-boiled Duke of Norfolk would believe himself before long to be 'sore vexed with a spirit' sent to him by the archbishop.

Yet the extent to which Wolsey in particular had by now ingratiated himself with the king might well have tested even the devil's ingenuity. Indeed, the elements themselves seemed to assist the royal favourite when, in April 1512, fire gutted Westminster Palace, destroying all the royal and domestic apartments as well as the kitchens. In fact, only Westminster Hall, the renowned Painted Chamber and the adjoining offices, including Star Chamber, where the Council occasionally met, were spared and this was of the greatest significance, for it meant that while the work of government could continue, there was nevertheless no room there for the royal court. Consequently, Wolsey was left largely to his own ends at the very centre of government, while the king resided at Greenwich, the nearest palace with sufficient accommodation for his entourage.

Such an arrangement was not without its risks, of course, for others who had the king's ear on a daily basis might well upset the plans that Wolsey was hatching throughout laborious days and often sleepless nights. By this time, too, Wolsey's reputation as a man of influence was also burdening him with a wider range of professional services, which, though lucrative, further sapped his precious resources of time. As early as 11 June 1513, for instance, he received a substantial annuity from Lady Margaret Pole for advice he had given her on money matters. Nevertheless, the opportunities arising from his isolation at Westminster still far outweighed any dangers, for Wolsey was now free to occupy the high ground in the execution of government policy and to establish an unparalleled reputation for industry and efficiency in his master's service.

There was no doubt either about the considerable effort that Wolsey was always capable of expending on state business. George Cavendish tells, for instance, of one particular occasion when his master rose at about four o'clock in the morning to write letters:

Commanding one of his chaplains to prepare him to mass, insomuch that his said chaplain stood revested until four of the clock at afternoon; all of which season my lord never rose once to piss, nor yet to eat any meat, but continually wrote his letters with his own hands, having all that time his nightcap and keverchief on his head.

Moreover, any threat that he might somehow be marginalised by his own preoccupation with the minutiae of government or the myriad of other commitments weighing in upon him was soon neutralised by an elaborate routine of communication with the king which was put into place without delay. Written and oral messages, for instance, passed back and forth between king and minister every day and both men kept sufficient couriers and horses on hand to ensure contact at all times and over any distance. With such an arrangement in operation, the king could satisfy his ego on all counts, confident in the knowledge that government was his, yet free to enjoy his pleasures unencumbered.

At the same time, when Henry was at Greenwich, Wolsey would almost always travel there once a week for a face-to-face meeting. Indeed, the regular ritual of Wolsey's passage to Greenwich became a popular spectacle for Londoners of all kinds. Every Sunday the archbishop left York Place in a brightly coloured and gilded barge attended by a large, liveried retinue. Travelling downstream to Paul's Stairs or Queenhithe, he would be met by horses waiting to convey the party in solemn procession through the city. And once below the bridge and its treacherous rapids Wolsey then boarded another barge for the final stage of the journey to Greenwich.

It was at these meetings in particular that the minister would continue to impress his personality upon the young ruler. With such diligence it was hardly surprising that Wolsey had already won so much influence with a king who, of his own admission, found writing 'somewhat tedious and painful'. Pope Leo, for instance, who had good intelligence at the English court, would be contending before long that Wolsey had Henry so much under his influence that the king would even sign state papers without knowing their actual content. So long, then, as the fun-loving, easily distracted king could be convinced that he was served by the cleverest chief minister in Christendom and duly persuaded that he, rather than the minister, was the real instigator of the policies pursued in his name, all would be well.

But it was at these meetings, too, throughout the early months of 1514, that Wolsey laid the groundwork for his most remarkable diplomatic feat to date: the negotiation of a 'perpetual peace' with none other than England's ancient enemy. The much-vaunted coalition against France, upon which Henry had set his heart in 1513, was never to materialise. In the first place, both Henry and Wolsey were soon aware from disturbing reports sent by English ambassadors in

Spain and the Netherlands that Ferdinand and Maximilian were already deeply embroiled in treacherous negotiations with the French king. Ferdinand, for example, had made a truce with France at precisely that moment when his co-operation would have been most valuable, and was now plotting a match between Renée, Louis's second daughter, and his namesake and grandson, Ferdinand. To compound matters, Pope Leo was apparently as anxious for peace as his predecessor had been for war, and both Henry and Wolsey were bound, as always, to follow the papal line: the king in hope of some form of official recognition by the pontiff; Wolsey, perhaps, as much out of loyalty to his sovereign's wishes.

But strange though Wolsey's subsequent machinations might now appear, they were wholly in keeping with the topsy-turvy world of Renaissance diplomacy. Indeed, it is to his credit that as soon as the suspicion of Spanish and imperial treachery became fact, he was ready at once with an alternative plan, which not only protected England's security, but also undercut her two-faced allies deliciously. Any other policy, after all, was likely to have left the realm faced with a potentially disastrous war that threatened to combine her former allies with her old enemy. The timing, too, was nothing short of exquisite, for in January 1514 the gouty, pock-marked and flux-ridden King of France, bent and withered by his fifty-two dissolute years, became a widower.

Now, for the right price, wounds of long standing could be painlessly healed. All that was needed, it seemed, was sufficient imagination on Wolsey's behalf and the sacrifice of a suitable bride – young, virgin and beautiful – on the altar of marital revulsion. In the event, it was Henry's elder sister, Margaret, the Dowager Queen of Scots who was first dangled before King Louis, but more than a little unappetisingly, it seems, since she was by reputation dowdy and matronly. Furthermore, her reputation for wilfulness made the asking price even more unrealistic. In all, the French were expected to cough up some 1.5 million gold crowns, along with the towns of Thérouanne, Boulogne and St Quentin. Not altogether surprisingly, therefore, Louis was only prepared ultimately to settle for Henry's younger sister, Mary, the 18-year-old beauty who was described by various court reports as 'the most attractive woman ever seen'.

This particular option carried complications all of its own, however, since the princess' departure to a foreign land and odious husband would also remove her from Charles Brandon, the hulking, spade-bearded, bosom companion of the king whom she had long yearned to marry. Yet the arguments that Henry and Wolsey now rained upon her finally prevailed. If, after all, the Holy Roman Emperor was offering his grandson, Charles, in marriage to a princess of France, could she stand to be jilted before the eyes of all Europe? And even if, moreover, her father had raised Brandon as one of his own and kept him in his household as long as Mary could remember, had she not always known that marriage with him was never a remote possibility? In the same way that her sister, Margaret, had wed the philandering king of far-off Scotland for the security of her realm, so Mary must now cease her weeping and cursing, and face her own duty bravely across the Channel. Besides which, Henry was finally prepared, it seems, to sweeten his sister further by promising with typical recklessness, that she would at last be allowed to marry the man of her choosing in the event of Louis's untimely demise.

So it was that a peace treaty between England and France was duly signed at St Germain-en-Laye on 9 July 1514 and on the thirtieth day of the same month, in a carefully rehearsed ceremony at the royal manor of Wanstead, conducted in the presence of Wolsey and the dukes of Norfolk and Suffolk, Mary duly repudiated her contract of marriage with Charles, heir to both Spain and the Holy Roman Empire. Although ably assisted by Fox and working through the Duc de Longueville as intermediary, there is no doubt that Wolsey took full control of the preceding diplomatic exchanges, and, in doing so, he had held out for hard terms. Eventually, the French king would offer to pay half of Mary's expenses for her travel, her entourage and the marriage ceremony itself. To this he added the jointure of lands given to his late queen, Anne of Brittany, along with the promise that, should he die, his 'nymph from heaven' might keep all the jointure and 'all the jewels which the queens of France have used to enjoy after their husband's death'.

Such was the speed of Wolsey's negotiations, moreover, that Mary's proxy marriage had actually been completed at Greenwich by mid-August. And in addition to providing for the marriage itself, the treaty also secured a range of other measures that were highly beneficial to English interests. After much haggling, Henry was, for example, to receive from Louis an annual pension, as well as the prompt payment of the arrears of the pension under the terms of the Treaty of Étaples, which had been signed during the last reign. There was also to be a restoration of the ancient privileges of English merchants, as well as guarantees against the Scottish invasion of England, which included a promise from Louis to keep the troublesome John Stewart, Duke of Albany, in France.

There was no denying, of course, that the sacrifice of Thérouanne for Tournai struck deeply in many an English heart. Thérouanne was, after all, nearer to Calais and, therefore, both easier and cheaper to defend. Nor, of course, was the connection with Wolsey overlooked by his enemies and the rumour soon went round that he had personally persuaded the king to keep the place as 'a trophy of his victories'. But whether the rumour was true or not was largely unimportant.

What mattered more was that such talk was generally believed, for peace of any kind with France was never something to be savoured by Englishmen. And what mattered most of all was that the wholly unforgiving Duke of Norfolk seems to have believed it, for he would never allow Wolsey to forget that this treaty was of his making.

Even so, for the short while it lasted, the peace would redound greatly to Wolsey's credit and his support was now sought more and more by people who plainly appreciated the weight of influence at his disposal. The Dutch scholar Erasmus, seeking support and patronage as always, sent a copy of his translation of Plutarch's *De Unitate* and admitted to Wolsey that he hesitated 'to approach so great a man with so petty a gift'. The Earl of Arundel, on the other hand, dispatched 'a morsel of venison' from a deer killed in his own park to grace Wolsey's table, while Sir Henry Vaughan offered 'a Normandy cloth to make sheets for your servants'. And that great Plantagenet figure, Lady Margaret Pole, soon to be restored to the family title as Countess of Salisbury, even granted Wolsey an annuity of 100 marks for his counsel and aid. Cambridge University, too, saw fit to elect him its Chancellor, though he stood aside graciously in favour of its most distinguished representative, Bishop John Fisher of Rochester.

By the late summer of 1514, then, Thomas Wolsey was no longer a coming young man, tipped for high office in the murky medium term. Instead, he had arrived with a deafening fanfare and was poised for greatness in the blinding light of here and now. Twelve months earlier it would have been inconceivable that the former royal almoner should control the direction of his country's diplomacy. Not least of all, it would have represented an outright slight on the other monarchs of Europe who negotiated only through high-ranking dignitaries. But Henry would later assure the pope that no-one had 'laboured and sweated' more to bring about the diplomatic revolution in European politics than his own Archbishop of York. Nor was Wolsey himself backward in acknowledging his own achievement. 'I,' he told the Venetian ambassador in no uncertain terms, 'was the author of the peace.'

9

Thomas Cardinalis

Long before Christopher Bainbridge's sinister death on 14 July 1514, Henry VIII had been all too keenly aware of England's paltry representation in the College of Cardinals. Bainbridge himself had been appointed Ambassador Extraordinary to the Papal Court in 1509 and Cardinal of St Praxedis in March 1511, but thereafter cut a lone path in the corridors of the Roman curia. Moreover, not since John Morton's death in 1500 had a cardinal been resident in England, and this injustice could not be tolerated indefinitely. Henry was, of course, a devoted son of the Church, who had readily committed himself to the pope's cause in both peace and war, and without a richly bedecked prince of the Holy See to decorate his court, it could never be complete.

Thomas Wolsey, on the other hand, was no less alert to the greater opportunities that might accrue in the longer term, if the kingdom were to acquire such a senior churchman. Knowing full well that the word 'cardinal' is derived from the Latin term for a hinge, he could see all too clearly what doors might open ultimately for Henry, not to mention the chosen man himself. And as early as 1511 – when false rumours reached England that Pope Julius was at death's door – Wolsey was said to have talked earnestly to his master at Mass and 'shewed unto his Grace how much honour and also furtherance of all his affairs in time to come should ensue to him if that by his commendation some Cardinal might attain to be Pope'.

But while it is far from certain that the king's master strategist had himself in mind for the papacy at this or indeed any other time, the possibility of a cardinal's hat was still undoubtedly a tempting enough prize in its own right. As a cardinal, Wolsey would, for example, automatically become a member of the governing body of the Church, with a direct influence upon the election of any future pontiff. He would also occupy a fitting platform from which to speak with kings and play their arbiter, while acting as a conspicuous representative of the Church in England, with power both to control its affairs and reform its abuses. Significantly, almost all the monks and friars resident within the realm – with the meagre exception of some half dozen or so religious houses – would at once be brought under his control, including those of Archbishop Warham's Canterbury.

On 7 February 1514, therefore – only one day after the pope had agreed to his consecration as Bishop of Lincoln – Wolsey dispatched the papal revenue collector, Polydore Vergil, on a secret mission to Rome. Ostensibly the purpose of this trip was to allow Vergil to revisit his old home and kiss the feet of the new pontiff Leo X, since he was now 44 years old and had been permanently resident in England for the previous twelve years. The Italian's real mission, however, was of altogether more significance, for he was instructed to engage in subtle intrigue on Wolsey's behalf to secure for him the highest prize that the Holy Father could bestow upon any member of his clergy.

The aim, moreover, was not merely to achieve election to the cardinalate, but also to attain the additional office of legate *a latere* in one fell swoop. Such papal legates were usually men of the broadest experience and highest reputation who were dispatched to distant foreign countries with full papal powers at times when the most delicate political negotiations were in progress. They were sent, therefore, on special occasions for specific reasons and returned to Rome at the earliest possible opportunity, since the whole essence of their mission was that they had come direct from the pope himself.

Pope Leo had, it should be remembered, already considered the possibility of assigning such a role to Christopher Bainbridge before his death. And not without good reason, since Bainbridge was a man of considerable reputation who had earlier shown his mettle by leading a successful military expedition against Ferrara, which he besieged at Julius II's specific request. But during the spring and early summer of 1514 Wolsey had expressed staunch opposition to the proposal on a number of grounds. In the first place, he argued, Bainbridge had been the English ambassador to the pope for so long that he could not be received as legate *a latere* 'without suspicion'. Besides which, the circumstances in England were not sufficiently exceptional to justify such an appointment.

Yet, in spite of these earlier reservations, Wolsey now had no hesitation in seeking the very same post for himself; ultimately, as it transpired, for life. If successful, he would immediately gain precedence over Archbishop Warham, primate of all England, who himself enjoyed only the rank of *legatus natus* – a largely nominal title giving him purely disciplinary responsibilities within the confines of his own province. As a legate *a latere*, however, Wolsey would also be empowered to issue dispensations of all kinds, to absolve wrongdoers from excommunications and other sentences, to make appointments to benefices, to grant degrees, to make bastards legitimate and even, under certain circumstances, to sell off ecclesiastical lands. More significantly still, he would be able to grow richer than ever, since the exercise of these powers was guaranteed to produce a steady flow of fees.

But this was not all, for the true audacity of Wolsey's suggestion lay in the fact that unlike previous legates, he was a resident subject of the king, an Englishman living in England and working there permanently. If, therefore, his appointment were granted, it would in effect involve handing papal power not only to Wolsey himself, but also to the king whom he served.

The full nature of Vergil's journey is only revealed in the letter he wrote to Wolsey in May, after his arrival in Rome. Firstly, he had been instructed to call upon Cardinal Adriano Castellesi, a man whom Wolsey had recommended for the papacy in 1511 at the time when Julius II's death seemed imminent. But although Julius had actually lived two more years before being succeeded by Leo X, Vergil was nevertheless to refresh Castellesi's mind of events not long past, and, if Castellesi showed himself duly grateful, the subject of Wolsey's own election to the College of Cardinals was to be broached. In the meantime, not a word was to be said, and the affair managed in such a way as to make the pope's eventual offer seem wholly spontaneous, 'as,' remarked Vergil to Wolsey, 'your reverend lordship told me it was to be done'. Indeed, if Vergil can be trusted, it would seem that Henry himself did not know of the proposal at this time.

Wolsey had not, however, simply trusted to the efforts of Vergil on his behalf. It was better, after all, to exercise pressure by means of a pincer movement and to this end he had also routed his request through none other than Silvestro Gigli, the Bishop of Worcester. Indeed, Gigli was, it seems, already pressing the pope to make Wolsey legate *a latere* for life. Such a move required what can only be considered the most remarkable nerve, but it would prove yet another example of Wolsey's extraordinary political nous and uncanny knack for timing.

England was, after all, in the words of one former pope, 'our storehouse of delights, a very inexhaustible well'. 'And where much abounds,' continued this particular Holy Father, 'much can be extorted from many.' Nevertheless, the English Church was restive and could well be drawn closer to Rome by a masterful papal representative in permanent residence. There was, too, the possibility of political tit-for-tat. Leo might, for instance, be given – as he himself suggested – some credit in the text of the marriage contract between Mary and Louis XII for suggesting the match in the first place. If Wolsey could manage this, along with a few other amendments in the draft Anglo-French treaty, which Leo kindly listed, it would, wrote Gigli in August, bind his holiness to grant the legation, if not for life, at least for successive periods of years.

Crucially, too, another major bar to Wolsey's advance had been conveniently excised by Bainbridge's unexpected demise. At least for the time being, there was now no Archbishop of York, no rival claimant for the post of legate *a latere*, and no English-born ambassador at the papal court. Nor, eventually, was there any doubting the King of England's personal enthusiasm for the promotion, though it was Wolsey himself who drafted an appropriate letter for royal signature on 12 August. Wolsey's merits, the letter to Rome pointed out, 'are such that the king can do nothing of the least importance without him and esteems him among the dearest friends'. Therefore, the message concluded, 'our most secret councillor' should be made a cardinal 'with all the honours held by the late Cardinal of York'.

Until this point, then, Wolsey's plans were proceeding with typical smoothness and precision. As early as April it was being reported by Polydore Vergil that Pope Leo was keen to offer his support to one who held such influence with the king. Leo was also promising, it seems, to give the appearance of a spontaneous election, just as Wolsey had hoped, and by August money was already being forwarded to purchase the necessary votes. Nevertheless, Leo remained determined not to be hurried, and concerns about Wolsey's forwardness and ambition doubtless underlay much of his caution.

There was still the murder of Bainbridge to consider, too. The papal master of ceremonies at the time, de Grassis, wrote that:

> Men say an English cardinal ought not to be created lightly, because the English behave themselves so insolently in their dignity, as was shown in the case of Cardinal Bainbridge, just dead. [...] Moreover, as Wolsey is the intimate friend of the king, he will not be content with the cardinalate alone, but, as is the custom for those barbarians, will wish to have the office of legate over all England.

Ultimately, then, the frustrated applicant would have to wait upon the Holy Father for nigh on a year before he was finally granted his cardinal's hat, and even then he was temporarily denied the additional title of legate *a latere*.

Meanwhile there were other pressing matters at hand. Not least, there was the swift unravelling of the Anglo-French peace treaty to consider. Everything, of course, had been premised on the marriage of Louis XII to the Princess Mary, which had certainly begun auspiciously enough, since the French king was from all accounts overcome with sensual delight in his new bride. Such was Louis's determination to charm her, indeed, that upon their first meeting at Abbeville he had somewhat ludicrously chosen to attempt to hide his all-too-apparent years by donning the garb of a young man. Nor did he hide his gratitude towards the one who had done most to ease his passage into marital bliss. Wolsey was therefore sent a mule, 'the best in the world', for his troubles and told that the French ambassador in Rome had been instructed 'to no further meddle against you' regarding the bishopric of Tournai.

Certainly, in material terms at least, Louis was as generous a husband as any might be. He spoke of taking his English wife to Venice, a place she had always wanted to see, and showered her at the same time with magnificent jewels. Before she left England, for example, he had sent her a matchless diamond 'as large and as broad as a full-sized finger', known as the Mirror of Naples. With its pendant pearl, the size of a pigeon's egg, the jewel was estimated at 60,000 crowns in value. And there were others nearly as splendid, including table diamonds, another 'marvellous great pointed diamond' worth 10,000 marks and a ruby 2.5in long.

But Louis's initial enthusiasm for his spouse was soon dampened by suspicion of her servants and intolerance towards her ways. Reports from across the Channel told how he loved to observe the French custom of dining at eight in the morning and going to bed at six in the evening, while it better suited his young queen to dine at noon, and remain awake till midnight. It was not long, too, before Louis dismissed Mary's English ladies on the grounds that they came between husband and wife. Ultimately, she was even deprived of her favourite English sheepdog. Much worse still, on New Year's Day 1515 Louis died. Only eighty-five days after his marriage the lifeless body of the French king was lying in state in the great hall of Tournelles, and with him lay the grand alliance with England that Wolsey had forged so boldly.

It was the Duke of Norfolk who first accompanied Mary to France for her wedding and the princess had resented his presence from the first. Norfolk had opposed the marriage throughout, not least because of the triumph it represented for Wolsey, and it was to the duke that Mary ascribed the ease with which her husband had dismissed her favourite attendants. By contrast, she never once doubted that Wolsey was her real friend at court, the one man besides her brother who realised how painful a duty it was for her to go through with her marriage to the old roué Louis. 'Would God my Lord of York had come with me in the room of my Lord Norfolk,' she wrote to Henry, 'for then I am sure I should have been left much more at my heart's ease now.'

There would certainly be reason enough for the princess to be heavy-hearted as events unfolded over the coming weeks. In the first place, there were the unwelcome attentions of Louis's successor for her to parry as best she could. Upon becoming king at the tender age of 20 the bold, dashing and incorrigibly over-sexed Francis, Duc d'Angoulême, had immediately married Louis's elder daughter, Claude, though this marriage to his cousin did not prevent the new king from at once propositioning her dead father's former wife into the bargain. And even after Mary had apparently escaped his lecherous clutches by fleeing to Cluny, she was not left in peace, for now she was harassed with other offers of marriage involving a motley assortment of French peers and even, at one point, the Emperor Maximilian. But if the former queen's own lot was fraught enough, she would soon initiate a desperate tangle of events that would require all of Wolsey's considerable skill to unravel and smooth.

Not surprisingly, the arrival of a new king upon the French throne had made the dispatch of an English embassy across the Channel a matter of the utmost urgency. In the first place, protocol required that Francis be congratulated, however hypocritically, upon his succession. But more importantly still, it was necessary to forestall by all possible means any plans for the remarriage of Henry's sister that the French might be currently hatching. In the first frantic days after Louis's death, Wolsey had already written to Mary, informing her that 'to the effusion of my blood and the spending of my goods', he would never forsake or leave her and warning her that 'if any motion of marriage or other offer of fortune' be made to her, she should 'in no wise give hearing to the same'.

There was also the issue of the now defunct treaty with France for Wolsey to consider. Would Mary, for instance, be allowed to keep her dower lands and their revenues? And equally importantly, there was the particularly delicate question of the 'jewels, precious stones, plate, apparel, and other things that her Grace brought with her, as also of the charge of traduction [transportation], which the French king received for the value of 200,000 crowns'. With typical sharpness, in fact, Mary had lost little time in pledging her jewels and plate to her brother, though this, in itself, was no cast-iron guarantee of their safe return.

The need for an English mission to France was, then, clear enough and it was through Wolsey's agency that Charles Brandon, Duke of Suffolk, was duly dispatched across the Channel in the company of that seasoned diplomat Nicholas West. By any reckoning, however, the selection of Brandon as England's envoy was nothing less than extraordinary, for his personal ambition was known to one and all, and Mary's deep feelings for him were already the subject of barely suppressed court gossip.

Predictably, amid her tear-stained letters to her brother and desperate entreaties to Wolsey, came reminders from Mary of the promise that had been made to her by Henry upon her departure for France. And as the French spies about her proved increasingly obtrusive and the malicious dangling of foreign marriages grew more persistent, so the nearness of her long-sought loved one presented her with an unrivalled opportunity to make good that promise, even though the duke himself seemed to be in no position to comply; prior to his departure towards the end of January 1515, he had been made to promise on oath in front of both the king and Wolsey at Eltham that he would make no attempt to marry his pining sweetheart.

Events would soon outpace Brandon, however, for, prior to his arrival, Mary had already told Francis that she and her brother's favourite boon companion had made a pledge to marry one another that they were determined to keep. Moreover, largely to spite Henry, who continued to regard his sister as a valuable marriage counter in the game of international diplomacy, Francis now discarded his own schemes and encouraged the match wholeheartedly. Indeed, during a private audience with Brandon, the French king teased him with coming to carry off the Queen Dowager, and when the Englishman denied it, he was told that Mary herself had said as much. As Brandon confided to Wolsey afterwards, Francis had made him blush by relating details of his relationship with Mary, 'which I knew no man alive could tell but she'.

As it transpired, the duke's resistance was not long in crumbling. Though he hedged by telling Mary that he must get Henry's written approval before proceeding with the match, none of this had the slightest effect on his ardent admirer and he was no less befuddled by his lady's arguments than blinded by the bitterness of her tears. 'Sire, I never saw a woman so weep', he wrote to Henry. But it was when she risked all by telling him that he must wed her immediately or 'look never to this day to have the proffer again' that he finally broke. 'And so,' he confessed, 'she and I was married.' Furthermore, knowing that any clandestine wedding ceremony could be easily set aside, the couple had proceeded to put matters beyond recall, for as Brandon now confided to Wolsey in secret: 'To be plain with you, I have married her heartily and lain with her, insomuch [as] I fear me that she [may] be with child.'

The scale of the ensuing outrage cannot be overemphasised. Henry, for his part, was said to have taken the news 'grievously and displeasantly' and his reaction was hardly surprising, for while Mary's irresponsible behaviour might be put down to womanly hysteria, Brandon's lack of self-control and apparent betrayal of long friendship was much harder still to forgive. Henry would not have believed that his old friend would break his promise in this way 'had he been torn with horses', he told Wolsey. Furthermore, the couple had not only betrayed and embarrassed him, but also cost him a good deal of money into the bargain, since Francis had been given the legal right to confiscate Mary's dowry, not to mention the gifts she had been given by Louis, including the much coveted Mirror of Naples. To cap it all, Brandon still owed Henry the £3,000 he had borrowed to pay for his mission to the French court.

Nevertheless, the king's displeasure was mild by comparison to the reaction of his council, who, with the sole exception of Wolsey, called for Brandon's imprisonment or execution. For a gentleman's son to marry the king's sister was outrageous, even if he had recently been made a duke. And the French, meanwhile, were equally angry that their former queen had disgraced herself thus. It was said that Brandon did not dare to walk the streets of Paris for fear of the mob. All in all, then, it was hardly surprising that when the floundering bridegroom turned to Wolsey for help, he would be told in no uncertain terms that he had put himself 'in the greatest danger that ever man was in'.

Wolsey, too, had good reason to be furious with the newlywed couple. Not least, he was rightly annoyed that the brilliant political alliance he had forged with France had been sacrificed so impetuously and selfishly. But he also knew that he himself might well be compromised in the ensuing scandal. The Howards and their allies on the council were producing evidence that Brandon was in league with Francis and if they gained the upper hand they would not hesitate to implicate his confidant. Furthermore, Wolsey had been put in the unenviable position of having to break the news to Henry and face the royal wrath in person. Under the circumstances, Wolsey could not resist his own rebuke to the couple who now so earnestly threw themselves on his aid. 'Cursed be the blind affection and counsel that have brought ye to [this]', he scolded. 'Such sudden and ill-advised dealing shall have sudden repentance.'

Curiously, too, Wolsey made a direct reference in the same letter to Brandon's humble origins, reminding him of his dependence upon the king for his rank and emphasising that 'ye hath failed to him which hath brought you up of low degree to be of this great honour'. The sign of the importance of this point in Wolsey's thinking may be seen from the fact that the words 'low degree' were inserted in the place of 'nothing'; the only editing in the entire letter.

Yet, in spite of his stern admonitions, Wolsey's response to the couple's entreaties was to assure them eventually of his support and he promised that he would use all his power to bring the matter to 'a successful conclusion'. Brandon was, after all, Wolsey's single possible challenger for the king's affection and, as such, it made perfect sense to have him beholden. He was also, for the time being at least, still a valuable bulwark against the Howards and their cronies. Wolsey insisted, therefore, that he was the duke's 'firm friend' and seems even to have relished the chance to outwit and wound the jealous and disapproving members of the court and council who were now baying for blood on every side. Should the king be persuaded by these hostile elements not to allow the couple to return as man and wife, he told Brandon, 'all men here, except his grace and myself, would be right glad'.

All the same, Wolsey's position as a go-between in a royal family quarrel was an awkward one, which called for juggling of the most skilful kind. He would have to communicate with the disgraced couple without leaving any shadow of doubt that his loyalty lay unequivocally with the king. He would also have to gauge the king's priorities with his usual skill and this he seems to have done to perfection. In the event, he continued to draft letters of petition for Brandon and Mary to sign and also sent the pair money to 'make friends'. Nor did he fail to take as well as receive, for, in the meantime, Brandon was finally able to secure the bishopric of Tournai for his would-be saviour.

Ultimately, though negotiations dragged on and tempers grew warm, Wolsey correctly realised that Henry's main concerns were financial rather than moral. Therefore, in a letter to Brandon, he revealed that the king had spoken to him in private after a meeting of the council and bade him 'use all effort to obtain from Francis Mary's gold plate and jewels' without which neither the duke nor his bride could 'obtain license to return'. At the same time, Wolsey also assured Brandon that 'the hope that the king hath to obtain the said plate and jewels is the thing that most stayeth his grace constantly to assent that ye should marry his sister'.

After due wrangling, moreover, the issue of Mary's jewels and jointure was indeed settled amicably, and this seems to have swung the king once and for all to the side of reconciliation, though neither his gains nor the warmth of his response were in any sense glowing. Mary's gift of the Mirror of Naples to her brother was, for example, received in silence, while most of the other jewellery and gold and silver plate remained on the other side of the Channel as property of the future queens of France. In fact, when the dust had finally settled, she brought home only twenty-two diamonds, sixteen pearls, one ruby and a large emerald, though she did, all importantly, retain her jointure, together with the payment of 200,000 gold crowns.

With this news Henry seems to have mellowed sufficiently to agree to the couple's return, for in early May, after waiting several days at Calais for permission, Brandon and Mary finally embarked for England. It was only at

Calais, perhaps, that Brandon and Mary came face to face with the full extent of their unpopularity. Forced to barricade their lodging against a screaming mob, their fears did not begin to subside until they reached Dover, where they were greeted by a smiling Wolsey and conveyed to Henry, who met them with open arms at Barking on 13 May.

This initial response from the king was, of course, typically curious, for after undisguised fury he now seemed more than keen to advertise his unbounded delight at the return of his sister and her husband, and was soon insisting that a second grander marriage ceremony should be arranged at Greenwich. Ultimately, the happy event occurred in Grey Friars Church, and Henry accepted the compliment graciously when the couple named their first child after him, after which he even equipped them with extensive lands and estates in East Anglia as a token of his renewed esteem.

But, as so often, Henry's joy and bounty were deceptive, for, in the meantime, apparently at Wolsey's suggestion, the couple themselves were forced to pay a crippling fine of £24,000 in annual instalments. And though the sum was never paid in full, the king continued to look for these payments, complaining loudly when they were overdue, and then conspicuously squandering the money once it had been received. Each year some was poured into the eager hands of Queen Catherine's waiting maids, while more was distributed to his minions to play with at cards. It was money, he told them, paid in token of his domination of France.

Brandon, meanwhile, was temporarily eclipsed – not only financially, but politically as well. Once described as 'scarcely inferior to the king himself', he now spent much of his time away from London. 'He has ceased to reside at the court,' it was soon noted, 'secluding himself on account of the accusations prevalent in great courts, where favour does not always remain stable.' And, in the process, Brandon's absence from the centre was to remove one more political check on Wolsey's influence with the king – at least for the time being, since the duke would harbour a gnawing grievance over all of fourteen years until, at last, the chance for revenge presented itself.

Presently, however, Wolsey was once more preoccupied with his ongoing quest for a cardinal's hat. In July 1515, he grew tired of waiting for what he considered an overdue honour and wrote to Pope Leo to press his case. From his own perspective, or so he declared, the cardinalate was merely one more means of binding the king ever closer to the pope, and since the King of England had consistently proved himself to be a friend of the papacy, it was only fitting that his request should not be refused. Nor, as Wolsey was quick to point out, should the dangers entailed by refusal be overlooked. If, after all, the King of England were to forsake the pope, Leo would be 'in greater danger on this day two year than ever was Pope Julius'.

Yet in spite of further letters in the same menacing tone, it was ultimately none other than Francis I who unwittingly persuaded the pope, against his better judgement, to act at last. Just as the Brandon affair was reaching its climax another Anglo-French peace treaty was once again being carved out of thin air by an English delegation consisting of Wolsey, the Duke of Norfolk and the Bishop of Winchester. Signed eventually on 5 April, the Treaty of Paris provided for mutual defence against invasion and was supposed to last the lifetime of both kings. It also called for the release of prisoners, forbade either country to harbour dissidents and permitted free passage for Venetian and Florentine merchants to both England and France. But though it gushed with the usual platitudes concerning peace and wellbeing, the agreement predictably guaranteed nothing.

Surely enough, after the customary short-lived hypocritical lull, news reached England in July that the King of France had turned himself towards the unfinished task of conquest in Italy. Equipped with a massive army, he had set out to regain Milan and left Pope Leo with no choice but to bind the English king to him by any means possible – a state of affairs which Wolsey himself did not hesitate to play upon in a letter to Silvestro Gigli:

> If by your politic handling the pope can be induced shortly to make me a cardinal, ye shall singularly content and please the king; for I cannot emphasise how desirous the king is to have me advanced to the said honour, to the intent that not only men might perceive how much the pope favoureth the king and such as he entirely loveth, but also that thereby I shall be the more able to do his Grace service.

In the event, however, Wolsey's potent mix of threats, promises and subterfuge proved largely redundant, for shortly before Francis's crushing victory over the Venetian army and the hitherto undefeated Swiss mercenaries at the Battle of Marignano, Leo proved only too willing to withdraw his last objections. And even though the rank of legate would be denied the new cardinal for the time being, the full scale of the pope's capitulation was undeniable. Indeed, on 10 September, as a mark of special favour and contrary to all normal protocol, Wolsey's name was submitted for election to the cardinalate entirely on its own.

Ten days later, the Venetian ambassador to England, Sebastiano Giustiniani, was reporting that 'a king's courier has arrived here from Rome, having been dispatched with the news that the Right Reverend of York has been created

Cardinal at the suit of this most serene king who with might and main is intent upon aggrandising him'. He was quick to add, too, that he himself was keen to keep the new cardinal 'on the most friendly terms, both by reason of his extreme influence with the king, and also because he is of a very active and assiduous mind in matters of business'.

Nor was the Venetian the only one to appreciate the significance of Wolsey's elevation, for letters of praise and congratulation, as well as gifts and commendations, now poured in from all directions. Erasmus, for example, interrupted his translation of the New Testament to call Wolsey his 'sheet anchor', while Bishop Tunstall sent a present of a clock, along with a herald to advise upon how to set it. The Abbot of Winchcombe, in his turn, was even more unashamedly effusive. 'The mother that bore you,' he wrote, 'has reason to rejoice but not less so than your alma mater, Oxford, that gave you to God.' And the cardinal's old university would, indeed, celebrate its distinguished son's achievements most warmly by ordering 'that whosoever preaches at Oxford or London henceforth shall mention Wolsey's name in the bidding prayer'.

Bishop Fox, on the other hand, was more inclined to offer good sense and warned his former protégé not to imitate his predecessor in avarice, pride and anger. But there were also broader ramifications, of course, to which others seem to have been fully alive. It was Silvestro Gigli, in fact, who had selected the title of 'St Cecilia Beyond the Tiber' for Wolsey's cardinalate, and he had not found the choice an easy one to make. But now he wrote to tell Wolsey that the title was actually most apt, 'as many popes had proceeded from it'.

Meanwhile, as news of his great event continued to resound, the cardinal himself was planning his forthcoming installation with his usual eye for fine detail. He was, it seems, especially anxious that he should have a cardinal's habit and hat by the time that Parliament opened on 3 November and, with this in mind, he had already written to Gigli in Rome to make the necessary arrangements. 'Send to me,' he requested, 'two or three hoods of such pattern and colour as cardinals be wont to wear there and also one paper of caps larger and shallower than those were which your lordship lately sent to me; with two kirtles (tunics) and other like garments.' And though cardinals like himself, who had not yet achieved the rank of legate *a latere*, most often wore violet, he would also ask for bolts of silk, damask and taffeta in scarlet, which was properly the papal colour.

Ultimately, the delayed arrival of Wolsey's hat from Rome would become a source of considerable frustration for him. Along with the ring which all cardinals wore, his hat was the most visible symbol of his newfound eminence and he fretted about its absence excessively. Writing to Gigli, for instance, he mentioned how 'the King's Grace marvelleth that the pope delayeth so long the sending of the red hat to me, seeing how tenderly, instantly, and often his grace hath written to his holiness'. In response, Gigli confessed that he could not imagine what had caused the delay, but promised that he would do his best to expedite matters. Yet six more weeks would pass before the hat was finally sent on its way along with a ring 'of more than usual value' and a plenary indulgence for all those present at the installation ceremony. And it was not until early November that the treasured object, with its heavy red tassels, arrived at Dover.

Predictably, no effort was spared in making the most of the occasion, in spite of the fact that Cardinal Gambara, the papal protonotary accompanying the hat 'seemed to all men to be a person of slight estimation' who had little sense of style or proper decorum. Indeed, according to some reports, Gambara arrived in Dover carrying the hat in nothing more than a servant's bag and was intending to push on to London like an ordinary courtier before Wolsey intercepted him and, in the words of William Tyndale, 'clothed the ruffian in rich array and sent him back to Dover again' to be offered a symbolic welcome by the gentlemen of Kent.

This, however, was only the beginning of the pageantry, for Wolsey had made sure that on its way to London the hat would be conveyed 'with such triumph as though the greatest prince of Christendom had come into the realm'. At Blackheath, for example, an imposing deputation of temporal and spiritual peers, including the Bishop of Lincoln and the Earl of Essex, paid due reverence, while in the City of London the lord mayor, sheriffs and aldermen, along with the members of the livery companies and guilds, were all on hand to make their obeisance as the precious hat made its final journey to the high altar of Westminster Abbey to await its wearer. There, Tyndale informs us, tapers were set about it 'so that the greatest duke in the land must curtsie thereto; yea, and to his [Wolsey's] empty seat, he being away'.

It was at Westminster, on Sunday, 18 November, that England's new cardinal was finally consecrated in a ceremony that was characteristically grand. There had been no difficulty in ensuring the attendance of the kingdom's great and mighty, since meetings of Parliament and Convocation were already in process, and it was Warham himself who, after presiding at an unusually elaborate high Mass, placed the hat at last upon his rival's head. Throughout the whole spectacle, moreover, Warham had been assisted by the two Irish archbishops of Armagh and Dublin, eight mitred abbots and eight senior bishops, including John Fisher of Rochester, who acted as crosier during the mass. It was, thought George Cavendish, more like 'the coronation of a mighty prince or king' than any other ceremony.

Only the sermon of John Colet, Dean of St Paul's, struck a less adulatory note. Avoiding his favourite themes of peace and war, he described how the order of cardinals reflected the order of the seraphim in the heavens and must, like the seraphim, be consumed continually by love of the Trinity. To emphasise the point, Colet then went on to point out that a cardinal's scarlet robe was intended to be nothing less than a symbol of his burning love, a love that must extend to righteous protection of both rich and poor alike. Furthermore, Colet continued, a cardinal must remember that, like his heavenly Master, he came not to be ministered unto, but to minister, since 'whosover shall exalt himself shall be abased, and he that shall humble himself shall be exalted'.

But if Colet's words were intended to instruct Wolsey, they only served, in effect, to emphasise the irony of what followed, for though it was Warham who set the hat upon the cardinal's head, there was no doubting where seniority now lay. Indeed, as the procession made its way solemnly down the nave of the cathedral, Cardinal Wolsey was preceded by two crosses, while Warham had no cross carried before him at all. And in an age which made the symbolic affirmation of status an obsession, there could be no doubting the significance of this fact. Indeed, in no ceremony from this time forth, public or private, would any cross ever be carried before another clergyman when Wolsey was present.

Naturally enough, the same unmistakable message was reinforced both by the passage back to York Place and the junketing that followed. Eighteen temporal peers, headed by the dukes of Norfolk and Suffolk, formed the cardinal's personal escort and for the subsequent celebrations all the chief clergy of the English Church were on hand in Wolsey's newly built banqueting hall, along with the king himself, Catherine his queen and his sister Mary. Sumptuous tapestries and pictures covered every chamber and corridor, we are told, and 'a great feast was kept as to such a high and honourable creation belongeth'. It was, from all accounts, a uniquely splendid spectacle for one who was rapidly becoming a uniquely splendid spectacle of a man.

10

Pillar of Church and State

Little more than a month was to pass after Wolsey's installation as cardinal before he found himself immersed in those troubled waters of Church–State relations, which were ultimately to consume him. Throughout the autumn of 1515 a prolonged debate over the rights of the clergy had been raging ever more vehemently, and the lavish arrangements accompanying his promotion had been intended in no small part to distract public attention from the Church's current predicament. England's new cardinal was, it seems, a firm believer that where reason could not prevail, awe and gravity might suffice, and with this in mind he had hoped that a massive display of ecclesiastical power in England, vested in his own person, might serve to stifle the baying anticlericalism of the laity, which was now reaching a rowdy crescendo in every alehouse and market place of the capital. This, after all, was not the last time that he would resort to a show of magnificence in an attempt to quell insolent resistance. Nor, incidentally, was it the last time that such a ploy would fail.

The question before both Parliament and Convocation – the question, indeed, on everyone's mind – concerned the rights of the clergy to immunity from secular courts, and it had been raised in the starkest possible form by the case of Richard Hunne, a captious merchant tailor of suspect religious views, who had met his death in mysterious circumstances in the Bishop of London's custody on 14 December 1514. Hunne had first fallen foul of the ecclesiastical authorities two years earlier after the death of his son, when the local parish priest, Thomas Dryffeld, demanded the infant's bearing-sheet as a burial fee.

The real flashpoint came, however, after Dryffeld's claim was upheld in a clerical court, whereupon the outraged father responded with what proved to be a truly explosive counter-charge of '*praemunire*' in the Court of King's Bench.

The term *praemunire*, which was inextricably linked to the notoriously controversial Statute of Praemunire of 1393, had long been guaranteed to excite the most intense antagonism between both laity and clergy, and especially among the latter. For the statute made it illegal for any ecclesiastical court to impinge upon matters properly falling within the authority of royal justices, and laid down strict penalties for any offender. In practice, the resulting definition of legal impropriety on the Church's part was so loose that it had served ever since as a convenient tool of abuse by the state whenever occasion demanded.

Not surprisingly, then, the English clergy were especially sensitive to Hunne's insolence and none more so than the no-nonsense Bishop of London, Richard Fitzjames, who subsequently sent his own men to imprison Hunne in the Lollards' Tower of St Paul's Cathedral on suspicion of heresy. And when Hunne was found hanged in his cell after a preliminary hearing in the bishop's court, and Fitzjames's vicar-general, William Horsey, was later indicted by a coroner's court to stand trial for murder, the scene was set for a clash of truly seismic proportions.

It was at this point – as a text of the inquest, with subsequent scurrilous additions, was circulated in the capital – that Fitzjames first turned to Wolsey rather than Archbishop Warham in the hope that he might be better able to enlist the support of the king against the swelling anticlerical tide, which now threatened to engulf the Church. It would be futile, said the bishop, to expect a London jury to act justly, 'so set were they on heretical depravity'. And in any case, he continued, the trial of Horsey by a secular court would serve as a dangerous concession to the anticlerical bile of the Church's enemies. 'Help our infirmities, blessed father,' begged Fitzjames, as though Wolsey were the Pope himself, 'and we shall be bound to you forever.'

Yet Wolsey knew all too well that intervention in this particular hornet's nest was not to be undertaken lightly. The special privileges accorded to the clergy in criminal cases had long plagued the Church in England and the groundswell of bitterness made even the king reluctant to become involved. Furthermore, Parliament had already affirmed its determination to take the ecclesiastical courts in hand by laying down a statute in 1512 which denied immunity from royal justice 'to all those clergy who murdered people in their own homes, in hallowed places or on the king's highway'. Though the statute was of limited significance in practice, its potential as a precedent for further incursions upon the independent status of the clergy was manifest.

Sensibly enough, then, Wolsey sought to maintain a judicious silence on the whole issue while his quest for the cardinalate unfolded in the intervening months, but by the time that his cardinal's hat was firmly on his head, such sober detachment was no longer an option. In February 1515, for instance, the Church had assumed the offensive when the Abbot of Winchcombe chose to preach at St Paul's Cross against Parliament's statute of 1512. Then, five days later, the House of Lords poured further oil on the fire by rejecting the self-same statute, and as MPs stood firm in their insistence that the offending measure should remain law, the king himself now saw fit to enter the action.

Henry's solution was to summon the learned men of the realm to debate the matter before him, and with this in mind he appointed Dr Henry Standish, warden of London's Franciscan Friars and one of his favourite court preachers, to defend the principle that no papal decree could overrule the established practice of English laws. But though Standish appears to have won at least a moral victory in what followed, the meeting recessed without resolution and, during the subsequent pause, Fitzjames once again blundered grievously by accusing him of heresy.

Predictably, the Franciscan turned to Henry for succour and the king did not – indeed could not – fail to help him on this occasion. Once again the contending parties were called before the king at the Abbey of the Blackfriars in London, but by this point the whole balance of forces had, it seems, shifted decisively against the ecclesiastical authorities. Now even the House of Lords urged the king to stand upon his coronation oath, maintaining his temporal jurisdiction and shielding Standish 'from the malice of the clergy'. Henry also sought the advice of Dr John Veysey, Dean of the Chapel Royal, who was firmly convinced that the jurisdiction of the secular authorities over the clergy was of ancient tradition in England. When, therefore, the bishops renewed their cry of heresy against Standish, the king's justices left them in no doubt that all who stood against him would be subject to the dreaded charge of *praemunire*.

This, then, was the situation confronting Wolsey when he became cardinal, and though the situation was hardly of his making it was once again he rather than Warham who was called upon to represent his fellow clergy at the spectacular climbdown, which was now stage-managed before Henry at Baynard's Castle towards the end of November 1515. Kneeling in submission before his royal master, Wolsey's first act as a prince of the Church was to beg pardon on behalf of the clergy who, he said, owed their advancement to Henry alone and had never therefore intended to encroach upon the royal prerogative.

Wolsey also knew, however, that his words were for the consumption of his brother clergy as well as his sovereign and he continued to maintain, therefore, that the principle of bringing clergy into secular courts 'seems contrary to the laws of God and the liberties of the Holy Church, the which he [...] and all the prelates [...] are bound by their oath to maintain'. He then even went as far as to suggest that Henry might let the whole question be referred to the pope in Rome. But what might have sounded like a stalwart defence of the clergy's independence resulted – just as Wolsey intended it to – in diplomatic fudge and compromise, and in spite of outcries from Fox and Warham, the last word, as always, was left to the king:

> It seems to us that Dr Standish and others of his spiritual counsel have answered you on all counts [...] By the ordinance and sufferance of God we are king of England and kings of England in time past have never had any superior but God only. Wherefore know you well that we will maintain the right of our Crown and of our temporal jurisdiction as well in this point as in all others, in as ample wise as any of our progenitors have done before us.

Clearly, the decision would not be referred to Rome, and Standish for his part was to be spared the rigours that Convocation were holding in store for him. Horsey, meanwhile, was kept under house arrest for a few months before making a token appearance at the Court of King's Bench and being allowed to plead 'not guilty'. Moreover, by the time that the whole case had been neatly defused once and for all, Wolsey himself, not coincidentally perhaps, had already been entrusted with the highest legal rank in the land.

It was on Christmas Eve 1515 that the Archbishop of York succeeded Archbishop Warham of Canterbury as Lord Chancellor, and although rumour had it that Warham's resignation was forced by his successor, the whispers were unfounded. The older man had, it is true, expected greater deference to his long experience and was doubtless resentful of Wolsey's appointment to the cardinalate. There was also, it seems, a personal edge to this resentment. Indeed, when Warham finally retired from the council, he would charge Henry 'not to suffer the servant to be greater than the master'. But the passage of time had made the ageing cleric increasingly inflexible and bad-tempered, and he argued with even the gentlest of people, including Queen Catherine. In fact, he had few or no friends and it was now time for him to go, with or without Wolsey's assistance.

Some observers, like Thomas More, were generous in their explanation of Warham's departure. In a letter to Erasmus, More noted that:

After some years of strenuous effort to secure his liberty, [the archbishop] has at last been allowed to resign the office of Chancellor and, having secured the privacy he has so long desired, is now enjoying the delights of leisure among his books and the memories of a most successful administration.

But if, at the age of 65, Warham may well have been keen to forsake his labours, it is equally certain that Henry was just as happy to be rid of him. There was a yawning generation gap between the king and the old archbishop, and the latter's grumpy sobriety must surely have served as an uncomfortable reminder to Henry of his father's stern-faced style. To add to his unpopularity, of course, Warham had also consistently disapproved of his king's more adventurous foreign policy. Nor, for that matter, had he proved sufficiently pliant in the ecclesiastical controversies of 1514 and 1515.

In contrast to the proceedings earlier in the month at Westminster Abbey which had accompanied the bestowal of his cardinal's hat, Wolsey's receipt of the Great Seal was accomplished with minimal fuss. Upon his resignation, Warham had placed in the hands of the king a small 'bag of white leather five times sealed by the archbishop's signet', which Henry then opened. Removing the Seal, without which no business of government could be done, he then replaced it in its wrapping before re-sealing it with the signet of Thomas Cardinal of York. Finally, in the presence of the Duke of Suffolk, the Archbishop of Canterbury and the papal protonotary, the king placed the Seal in the hands of its new guardian. Thus, 'in a small and lofty chamber near the chamber of Parliament', Wolsey became the Lord Chancellor of England. That evening after the singing of vespers at Eltham Palace, he took his oath of office in a private ceremony involving the king and the Master of the Rolls.

In truth, Wolsey had already long been in a position of primacy. In the preceding March, for instance, Erasmus had described him as omnipotent. But now there could be no possible remnant of doubt that, in the words of Sebastiano Giustiniani, 'he really seems to have the management of the whole of this kingdom'. Indeed, the Venetian envoy, who had an audience with Wolsey within the week, was soon declaring that 'in point of fact, for authority he may be styled *ipse rex*'. He also observed that 'all state affairs likewise are managed by him, let their nature be what it may'.

Nor, of course, was Wolsey any less diligent than ever in the execution of these affairs. 'He alone,' wrote Giustiniani, 'transacts the same business as that which occupies all the magistracies, offices and councils of Venice.' And the common view, it seems, was that Wolsey's ambition remained every bit as boundless as his stamina, for, if we are to believe a letter of Andreas Ammonius to Erasmus, there was even tittle-tattle circulating in London early in 1516 that 'after urgent entreaty' Wolsey, been appointed Archbishop of Canterbury.

But though this last office would always elude him, Wolsey was nevertheless in a unique position of authority, enjoying unrivalled dominance in both Church and State. Certainly, with the Duke of Suffolk reduced to impotence after his ill-considered marriage and the Duke of Norfolk, likewise, prowling his distant estates in disillusionment and disgust, there was no layman on hand to rein in the mighty cardinal. Norfolk, though still Lord Treasurer, had needed little encouragement to return to East Anglia after he had escorted Princess Mary to France on her ill-fated marriage mission. Restored to the dukedom of Norfolk after his crushing victory over the Scots at Flodden, he did not underrate Wolsey, but rather feared his ambition. The duke's son, on the other hand, who would succeed him as Lord Treasurer in 1522 and as head of the Howard household two years later, would eventually become loudly outspoken in his opposition. For the time being, however, the Howard clan and their cronies were, to a man, left with no choice but to lie low in the political shadows, while Wolsey continued to bask in the dazzling blaze of royal favour.

In the meantime, the old guard on the king's council, represented by the likes of Sir Edward Poynings and Sir Thomas Lovell, were already history's men. In effect, they were reluctant to cling to power while the youthful king looked more and more to the cardinal's guidance. Only a few years earlier Lovell had apparently 'exercised extreme authority', but now, with Wolsey's inexorable rise, he seemed to the Venetian ambassador 'to have withdrawn himself and interferes but little in the government, so that the whole direction of affairs rests (to the dissatisfaction of everybody) with the Right Reverend Cardinal'.

Nor, with Warham's tame departure, was there anyone on the clerical side who might seriously challenge, or even so much as ruffle, Wolsey. Richard Fox had resigned as Lord Privy Seal and his replacement, Thomas Ruthall, had already been swiftly overtaken by Wolsey, even though he once seemed destined for an illustrious career when he became the king's secretary at the turn of the century and a privy councillor in 1504. Though he had been appointed Bishop of Durham the month before Wolsey became Dean of Lincoln, it was certainly clear to Fox among others that the advantage lay all with his former protégé.

In fact, Wolsey, who was invariably an impeccable judge of all men's limitations except his own, considered Ruthall suitable to work as his principal assistant, which the bishop did both ably and loyally until his death in 1523. And such was the depth of Ruthall's devotion to his new master that during the lengthy discussions on the growth of French power conducted at York Place in mid-1516 his fawning subservience seems to have seriously wearied the Venetian envoy, Giustiniani. So exhausted was the Italian 'with this long and laborious negotiation at which the Right Reverend Bishop of Durham assisted likewise, singing treble to the cardinal's bass' that he had by the end of proceedings, or so he claimed, 'no appetite for supper'.

But if Wolsey really was free for the time being from all challengers, this made him neither complacent nor remiss in attempting to rise to the considerable challenges of his new office. Certainly, as Lord Chancellor he had his limitations. Authoritarian in style, his primary aim was to preserve the status quo, and though, as a benevolent despot, he sought to preserve the internal harmony of the kingdom by fair judgements, he had no blueprint for administrative reform of either the law itself or the creaking machinery of state, and no vision of a new social code. Likewise, Parliament played no significant role in Wolsey's model of government. In his view, it was essentially no more than a menial body existing for the sole purpose of passively proffering revenue upon royal request. Indeed, he would visit it only once in his fourteen years of power – in 1523 – and only then with a view to curbing the free expression of its views.

Meanwhile, Wolsey's role as head of the English judiciary, sitting in his own court in Westminster Hall, was certainly not aided by his lack of formal legal training. Unlike many churchmen of similar rank, he had not even taken a degree in canon or civil law. Instead, it was the broader symbolic status of the Lord Chancellorship as the greatest administrative and political office under the crown that really captured Wolsey's imagination. The Chancellor was head of the oldest department of state, the dominant figure on the king's council and his main spokesman in Parliament. In effect, he was the king's principal minister – a shaper-and-doer-in-chief – and it was this that gave Wolsey what he most desired: the status to negotiate on equal terms with emperors, popes and princes.

Nevertheless, Wolsey quickly found his feet as a judge and his performance was soon receiving rich praise. In the view of Bishop Nicholas West of Ely, for instance, there had never been a fairer or more effective Lord Chancellor 'within memory of man', and from early on Wolsey's zeal for swift and impartial justice was also being highly commended by both Sebastiano Giustiniani and Thomas More. The Venetian noted that he had 'the reputation of being very just'. 'He favours the people exceedingly,' said Giustiniani, 'and especially the poor, hearing their suits and seeking to dispatch them instantly. He also makes the lawyers plead gratis for all paupers.' More, meanwhile, declared that no chancellor of England ever acted with greater impartiality or exhibited a more comprehensive knowledge of the law.

Indeed, as someone who had no formal training, Wolsey's impact upon equity law in the Court of Chancery was, in the short term at least, little short of extraordinary. Curiously, perhaps, his lack of legal expertise may even have been a crucial element of his success, for he was a layman's hero rather than a judge's judge, having more concern for clear-cut considerations of right and wrong than legal niceties. In this regard, he seems to have appreciated the significance of Chancery as a 'court of the king's conscience' more clearly than any of his predecessors and he expanded the volume of litigation passing through it considerably, partly because litigants preferred pleadings before Wolsey in Chancery than proceeding through common law, and also because the Lord Chancellor was often inclined to remove cases into Chancery from other courts by means of writs and injunctions.

However, it was this last tendency which was soon arousing the antagonism of a formidable swarm of common lawyers deeply resentful at the incursions of a disrespectful amateur upon their sacred preserve. Naturally, Wolsey's reputation for arrogance and love of display counted against him, too, in the creaking corridors of the Inns of Court, and the fact that he seems to have ordered the close confinement of one of the Middle Temple's most distinguished brethren, Sir Amyas Paulet, out of nothing more than personal animosity, would be forgotten no more lightly than his many insulting remarks about common law judges. Most seriously of all, Wolsey's vigorous extension of the Court of Chancery's jurisdiction would ultimately serve to destabilise the whole delicate balance between the common law courts of King's Bench, Common Pleas and Exchequer, which had been developing steadily over the previous half-century.

It was not only the legal profession that the Lord Chancellor would seriously provoke. With the king's active encouragement, he now reintroduced and extended Henry VII's policy of clipping the wings of all manner of 'overmighty' subjects. There seems little doubt, in fact, that the creation of a more just society and the extension of the king's peace to all subjects were issues that Wolsey himself cared deeply about. The ability of the rich and powerful to exploit their inferiors and, on occasion, to wage damaging local feuds had still not been entirely eradicated and, with this in mind, he made it a personal mission to step up considerably the judicial activity of the council in the Court of Star Chamber.

In fact, the new Lord Chancellor was determined to demonstrate beyond all shadow of doubt that wrongdoers of whatever rank must learn 'the new law of the Star Chamber which, God willing, they shall have indifferently ministered to them according to their deserts'. Those who believed they had suffered in local courts at the hands of perjured witnesses or intimidated juries were therefore now encouraged to come forward, although it still took considerable boldness to stand up to the leaders of shire society, and not a little persistence, since the process was almost invariably slow.

Nevertheless, the chronicler Edward Hall noted the immediate change that Wolsey effected in this area, for besides prosecuting perjurors, 'he punished also lords, knights, and men of all sorts for riots, bearing and maintenance [of arms] in their countries, that the poor men lived quietly, so that no man durst bear for fear of imprisonment'. In 1516, the Earl of Northumberland was sent to the Fleet Prison and other peers were also heavily fined for keeping armed retainers. And even though it would take more than a decade to do it, the Leicestershire landowner Sir Richard Sacheverell, was another particularly shameless offender eventually brought to heel. It had been said in his locality that newly sworn jurors were openly and regularly intimidated by him, for whenever summoned to answer for his misdemeanours 'he cometh with such a company that he ruleth the whole [assize] court'.

Nor did the Lord Chancellor always wait for complaints to filter through to Westminster, for in 1516, when the king's sister Margaret visited him as Queen of Scotland, Wolsey was swift to deal with members of the council who dared to attend a formal reception in the company of retainers wearing livery other than their sovereign's. Such a display of independence could not be tolerated and, in launching a full-scale inquiry into the whole question of illegal retaining, Wolsey was, as always, fully prepared to incur the nobility's largely unjustified accusation that he was acting mainly out of jealousy towards his betters. Not for the last time, Sir Richard Sacheverell was one of the offenders, but several grander figures were now caught up in the Star Chamber spotlight, including lords Hastings and Bergavenny, and even Wolsey's former pupil, the Marquess of Dorset.

But if insubordination from the elites was disconcerting to the king, then riot from below was no less so, and in the spring of 1517 the Lord Chancellor was given the perfect opportunity to prove that he could deal every bit as effectively with a popular outburst of the most dangerous kind. For, while it may have been largely predictable with hindsight, the so-called 'Evil May Day' rising would prove to be one of those genuinely shocking occurrences which demonstrated all too acutely how tenuous the grip of even Henry VIII's government's might become in time of crisis.

The apprentices of the capital's craft guilds had long envied the prosperity of foreign communities, and for some time agitators had been stirring widespread fears of unemployment through foreign competition. One day in April 1516, for instance, bills were posted upon the door of St Paul's Cathedral, as well as at the church of All Hallows in Barking, to the effect that the king himself had been lending money to Florentine merchants who were then using it to trade at advantage over their English competitors. And such was Henry's concern at malicious gossip of this kind that he subsequently ordered an enquiry to be made in every ward of the City, so that the handwriting of all apprentices could be checked. Even so, the sullen antipathy of the London mob now turned to a much more direct form of action.

For the particular purpose of an anti-foreign crusade, no gathering could have been more fitting than the motley crowd of merchants and shopkeepers, apprentices and bargees, who, during the Easter or Whitsuntide holidays, crowded round the pulpit of St Mary Spitall, at which time the sermons were also preached before the mayor and aldermen of the city. So it was that on Tuesday of Easter week 1517, a canon of St Mary's by the name of Dr Beale saw fit to lay the blame for the increase in the capital's poverty squarely upon the shoulders of grasping aliens. God had given England to Englishmen, he fumed in the old familiar manner, and 'as birds would defend their nest, so ought Englishmen to cherish and defend themselves and to hurt and grieve aliens for the common weal'.

A few days later, on 28 April, Beale was taken at his word when some foreigners were buffeted in the streets and thrown into a canal. But, though arrests were made by order of the mayor, a rumour soon spread that on May Day the whole of the capital would rise and all foreigners be slain. Wolsey, meanwhile, sent for the mayor and an order was given that on the eve of the fatal day every Londoner should stay indoors between the hours of nine o'clock in the evening and seven the following morning.

Nevertheless, as a certain Alderman Munday was attempting to enforce the order in Cheapside, an angry crowd of watermen and apprentices, carters and priests, drawn from every quarter of the city began to run amok. The jails were forced open and even Newgate was forced to yield up those men who had already been imprisoned for the patriotic cause. Thus reinforced, the crowd proceeded to surge through St Nicholas' shambles towards the liberty of St Martin's-le-Grand – one of the principal resorts of London's foreign colony – where none other than Thomas More, then serving as under-sheriff of London, tried to reason with them.

As the uneasy parley was unfolding, however, the foreign inhabitants of the threatened buildings chose to seize the initiative with a volley of stones and other missiles, at which point the fury of the rioters finally span out of control. Sacking and plundering as they went, they first wrought vengeance upon St Martin's and then steamed off to loot the foreigners of Cornhill and Whitechapel. In the process, the king's French secretary, Meautis, barely escaped with his life, though the Italian merchants, by contrast, were too well armed to be pillaged with impunity.

Ultimately it was largely due to Wolsey's personal influence that the forces of order finally rallied. Doubtless in recognition of his own unpopularity, he had initially strengthened his residence at York Place with men and ordnance before arranging for the Lieutenant of the Tower to shoot some rounds of artillery into the crowded streets. In the meantime, he also alerted the Earl of Shrewsbury to be ready with reinforcements while the Howards, leading some 1,300 troops, restored order.

In the event the apprentices, who were ready enough to loot a foreigner's house or bludgeon a peaceful Flemish merchant, were disinclined to come to close quarters with trained soldiers and those who were able to do so made good their escape. Thirteen, however, were eventually tried upon a far-fetched charge of high treason, and for some time afterwards the city gates would be gruesomely decorated with their quartered remains.

As for the rest, they would swiftly take part in a remarkable display of clemency, which was deliberately staged by Wolsey in Westminster Hall. Some 341 prisoners in all, complete with halters around their neck, were duly brought before Henry, his wife and his sister Mary, to witness Wolsey's prostrate appeal for mercy on their behalf, which was theatricallly rejected in the first instance. At this point, however, a 'spontaneous' appeal for mercy appears to have been taken up by all present, after which the king generously conceded. When Wolsey then conveyed the news to the prisoners, urging them to obey the laws in future and to ensure that all strangers were well treated henceforth, they were said to have torn off their halters and tossed them to the rafters, overjoyed.

'It was,' said Giustiniani's secretary, 'a very fine spectacle and well arranged.' And so it was, for in carefully crafting the whole scene, Wolsey was continuing to establish himself as one of the first great political propagandists. He had already projected his master throughout Europe as knight-errant and conquering hero, and now, by masterful improvisation, he had presented the king to his own people as both awesome enforcer of justice and fount of Christian mercy. Indeed, Wolsey was already well on the way to creating what would become one of the first and most enduring personality cults of its kind.

In the aftermath of such a publicity triumph, it was unsurprising, perhaps, that the Lord Chancellor himself had little doubt about his merits in maintaining law and order. Only three months after the 'Evil May Day' riots, in fact, he told his sovereign plainly that the realm 'was never in such peace nor tranquillity; for all this summer I have had neither riot, felony, nor forcible entry, but that your laws be in every place indifferently maintained without leaning of any manner'.

It was true, he admitted, that there had been an affray between a royal official by the name of Pygot and the servants of Sir Andrew Windsor about a wardship in which a man had been slain, yet 'I trust the next term,' he added, 'to learn them the law of the Star Chamber, that they shall ware how from henceforth they shall redress their matter with their hands'. A few months later, Wolsey was writing to Rome in even prouder terms. 'Never,' he declared, 'was the kingdom in greater harmony and repose than now; such is the effort of my administration of justice and equity.'

Such was his devotion to 'justice' and 'equity' through the courts of Star Chamber and Chancery that the commonwealth was indeed secured for the time being against all challenges. But his heavy-handed methods were nevertheless making him influential enemies among the great landowners who increasingly despised him, and there was, in the words of one contemporary, soon to be 'a great snarling at court'. Furthermore, while Wolsey was defending his king and country from lawlessness and disorder, his own Mother Church was being left to fend too much for herself.

There seems, in truth, no compelling reason to assume that Wolsey did not take his appointment as cardinal very seriously. On 2 June, for instance, he told the Venetian ambassador with all apparent sincerity that 'we would prefer not being honoured with the dignity rather than do what is unworthy of it'. Nor are there strong grounds to doubt that he would have favoured a more comprehensive reformation of the Church in England, if time and circumstance had allowed. Richard Fox, for example, was wholly convinced that his former protégé was planning 'a more entire reform of the ecclesiastical hierarchy of the English people than I could have expected or ever hoped to see completed or even so much as attempted in this age'. And the venerable bishop did not doubt either that Wolsey would deliver success, 'for I am sure, after frequent experience, that whatever your Grace may design or undertake, as it will be wisely concerted, even so will it be accomplished prudently and resolutely without difficulty or delay'. Certainly, in all his petitions for promotion, Wolsey's avowed aim was always to amend the Church in the face of its enemies.

Yet the obstacles facing the Cardinal of York were formidable. In the first place, there was the stubborn presence of Archbishop Warham to deal with. Though by now politically neutered, he remained nevertheless primate of all England, and this was yet one more reason why Wolsey would need the full papal powers that could only be his if he were to become, at last, a legate *a latere*. Only with this authority, it seems, could he seriously contemplate any sweeping programme of ecclesiastical reform, for though he now technically outranked the archbishop within the Church hierarchy, the office of cardinal, as it stood, gave him dignity rather than power and signified in reality no more than a tenuous umbilical connection with Rome. Not only was his distance from the Holy City considerable, but his persistent refusal to become involved in the machinations of the Roman consistory further reinforced the impression that, though he enjoyed the trappings to the full, Wolsey was, in essence, a cardinal in name only.

In spite of its nominal status, Wolsey's own archbishopric of York was, after all, little more than a country cousin within the English Church as a whole. It was, on the one hand, far from London and gave him supervision of only three dioceses. But other smaller details also served to emphasise the gulf in influence between York and the senior province of Canterbury. The Archbishop of Canterbury, for instance, resided at Lambeth Palace, in close proximity to the king and his court. As such, he dwelt at the heart of a thriving community of some 5,000 people, centred upon the court itself and the Benedictine Abbey of Westminster. The Archbishop of York, by contrast, officially resided upon his visits to London in either the cramped and shabby gloom of York Palace, as it was originally known, or in a much humbler dwelling still, far down the river at Battersea. And though Wolsey would soon thoroughly overhaul York Palace and rename it York Place, he knew full well that this would do nothing of itself to gain him the primacy he now desired.

All depended, therefore, upon Wolsey's appointment as legate. Yet Rome's ongoing antipathy towards him is amply reflected in the reports of Juan Manuel, the imperial ambassador at Rome. 'The statesmen in Rome,' wrote Manuel, 'are persuaded that the cardinal will do what is most lucrative for himself', and the ambassador made it clear, too, that the pope, like so many other contemporaries, remained convinced of Wolsey's hold over his master. The Holy Father, said Manuel, had told him in no uncertain terms that 'the cardinal, who is the governor of the King of England, is a very strange person and makes the king run hither and thither just as he likes'. On another occasion, Manuel revealed the pope's feelings even more starkly, but recognised at the same time that the Holy Father was unable to halt the progress of the man he so disliked:

> Although there is no man on the face of the earth whom His Holiness detests so heartily as the cardinal, he will be constituted legate, if the pope is given to understand that in no other way can he get out of the difficulties in which he is placed.

The difficulties to which the ambassador referred concerned Pope Leo's fresh summons for a crusade against the Turks, and they would indeed prove insurmountable. On 16 March 1517, Leo had announced a five-year truce between the European powers, and to raise finance for the great armies which were intended to sweep the infidel from North Africa, the Middle East and the Balkans, he duly dispatched legates to the leading sovereigns whom he intended to wage war in the great Christian cause. But when Cardinal Lorenzo Campeggio set out from Rome to London on 15 April, his mission was not welcomed by King Henry, who commented ominously that 'it was not the custom of this realm to admit legates *a latere*'. On the contrary, the king maintained, it was most unusual for a foreign authority to exercise legatine authority in England, and especially so when his own chief minister was already a cardinal archbishop. Spurred on by Wolsey, Henry then laid down a series of conditions before Campeggio would be allowed to arrive, and in consequence the hapless, gout-ridden Italian was left to kick his heels in Calais for the best part of two months before the necessary assurances were delivered from the Vatican.

In particular, it was demanded that Wolsey should himself be granted the rank of legate *a latere*, and that Cardinal Hadrian, one of Wolsey's most persistent critics, should, with papal consent, be deprived of the bishopric of Bath and Wells. Therefore, only after consent had been squeezed out on both accounts was Campeggio finally allowed to land on Rye beach, ill at ease, deflated and windswept by the stiff sea breeze that had finally brought him over.

Nevertheless, the Italian was eventually accorded a suitably magnificent reception when he reached London. There were, of course, the usual pealing bells and salvoes of artillery from the Tower, along with the predictable deputations of the great and mighty. And if the chronicler Edward Hall is to be trusted, the papal envoy had been specially equipped by Wolsey with twelve mules bearing empty coffers covered in scarlet, so that the common people might believe he was bringing treasure. Upon reaching Cheapside, however, it seems that the unsuspecting onlookers were mightily amused when one of the mules turned restive and upset the chests, 'out of which,' said Hall, 'tumbled old hose, broken shoes, bread, meat and eggs, with much vile baggage'.

Even so, like the old trooper he undoubtedly was, Campeggio appears to have maintained his composure well enough in face of the torrent of jeers and was treated for his trouble to a stirring Latin oration from Thomas More before proceeding on his way. He had already travelled from Dover in the midst of a cavalcade of some 500 riders and his final passage to St Paul's was duly impressive, except, perhaps, for the absence of Wolsey, his co-legate, and the king himself, who were said to have been kept away from these ceremonies by fear of plague.

Thereafter, Campeggio was lodged at Bath Place and kept waiting some days before he was finally granted an audience with the king at Greenwich, where the events of real significance unfolded. Here, in the palace's great hall, observers noticed that while Campeggio's seat was raised three steps above the floor, Wolsey's own increasingly ample frame was perched in an imposing gilt chair at more than double that height. Likewise, it was no coincidence that while the king stood for Wolsey's speech, both he and his principal minister remained seated for Campeggio's. Throughout the remainder of his stay, too, Campeggio was continually made to feel inferior to his English counterpart. Indeed, it was noted by one observer that 'less respect for the papal see could hardly have been shown'.

To compound matters, the formal audience yielded nothing of substance for the pope. Even Henry, devoted Catholic though he was, needed no prompting to see the folly of Leo's grandiose plan, and England was in any case far too remote from the Turkish menace to stand to gain from combating it directly. When Henry heard of Maximilian's offer to assume the role of commander-in-chief, he laughed out loud at the suggestion and proceeded to observe that the Venetians should be more fearful of the King of France than any Turkish sultan. Wolsey, meanwhile, was equally disinclined to further a papal crusade in any way, especially by means of English participation. He had gained his prize and this of itself was enough.

Similarly, the sweeping tide of religious reform that had been so eagerly anticipated in some quarters was never forthcoming. Though Wolsey threatened, exhorted and cajoled the monastic orders to reform, and stressed his intention to tend to the matter personally, he had neither the time nor the tenacity to deliver. Preoccupied by the press of state affairs, he also faced a formidable array of vested interests that were determined to block any and all incursions upon their cosy privileges. Most obviously, the monastic institutions ranged against him had numbers, wealth and power on their side. There were over 800 of them in England as a whole, and in Gloucestershire alone ninety held an average of 65,000 acres of land apiece. There was also the political power of the abbots to consider, for twenty-seven of the heads of great religious houses had seats in the House of Lords.

So when, in 1518, Wolsey finally began his inspection of England's monasteries, it was not altogether surprising that the only one to be visited that year was the royal Abbey of Westminster, which stood near enough to his residence at York Place that it involved no need for a lengthy absence from court. Moreover, the abbey itself was the safest of bets, for though he was prepared to investigate the monks 'with considerable rigour', the ones at Westminster, as Wolsey well knew, enjoyed the highest repute. It was true, of course, that the abbey enjoyed considerable wealth, with its lands stretching far out into what today are Hyde Park, Pimlico and Covent Garden, but all the same there was no risk of either decadence or malpractice. In effect, the legate's visit to Westminster amounted to little more than a token gesture – a show of paternal authority over the abbot and his monks and a sop to those who expected greater things.

When Wolsey turned his attention to the Augustinians the following year, he confined himself to purely didactic details, instructing them that all monks should be present at services, especially matins and Mass, and urging that their offices should be said neither too slowly nor too quickly. There was also, it is true, a suggestion that the education of his holy brethren should conform with the intellectual standards already in place at Oxford and Cambridge. But the bulk of Wolsey's efforts seem, nevertheless, to have been expended upon telling the heirs of St Augustine how to sing:

> And with all ecclesiastics, and especially religious, that method of singing is divinely appointed which is not intended to gratify the ears of those present by the levity of its rhythm, nor to court the approval of worldlings by the multiplicity of its notes. But that which is plainsong raises the minds of the singers and the hearts of the hearers to heavenly things.

Plainsong, therefore, it had to be.

The equally bland content of the provisions that Wolsey drew up for improvements in his own province of York also demonstrates the comparative modesty of his plans for parish clergy. Playing the safe option once again, he contented himself mainly with reinforcing the enactments of his predecessors, and where he initiated ideas of his own, he thought very much in terms of tried and trusted formulae. Four times in the year every priest with care of souls was to explain 'in the vulgar tongue and without any subtlety of fantastic turning about of words', the fourteen Articles of Faith, the Ten Commandments of the Law, the two evangelical precepts of charity, the seven works of mercy, the seven deadly sins, the seven opposing virtues, and the seven sacraments of grace. There were also certain decrees for the safeguarding of churches as places of prayer and forgiveness, while clergy were urged to be different in dress and deportment from the laity and forbidden to attend unlawful spectacles, 'especially duels, tournaments and sports in which blood might be shed'.

More damagingly, Wolsey would never countenance partnership with other church leaders. Upon discovering that Warham had called his suffragans to hold a council of their own at Lambeth for the 'reformation of enormities', he wrote patronisingly to his fellow archbishop, expressing his astonishment 'that you should enterprise the said reformation to the express derogation of the said dignity of the See Apostolic and otherwise than the law will suffer you without mine advice, consent and knowledge'. At the same time, he was quick to subvert his rival when the king issued writs both to him and to Warham to summon their clergy to meet at St Paul's in London. Almost before the ink was dry on the king's instructions, Wolsey was insisting that any assembly must be held under his auspices, and when the proposed meeting did finally occur, it was no coincidence that the Archbishop of Canterbury was overridden or that the final location was the Abbey of Westminster, which was exempt from his jurisdiction.

Moreover, just as Wolsey would consistently distrust Warham, so the notion of ecclesiastical reform through synods, convocation or any other kind of clerical assembly remained essentially alien to him. When, for example, in 1519 he finally summoned a legatine council to examine the state of the Church, his approach was merely to assemble a few handpicked bishops at his residence and deal with them as his lieutenants. So, all in all, it was not altogether surprising that Warham's secretary was by that time already referring to Wolsey as 'this great tyrant'. Undoubtedly, no member of the English episcopacy seemed entirely safe from attack by the cardinal, for even Warham, whose longevity was yet another source of irritation to Wolsey, was threatened with *praemunire* and the Bishop of Coventry and Lichfield charged with treason. John Stokesley, meanwhile, who, like the young Wolsey, was an almoner destined for high office within the Church, was sent to prison.

Nor, for that matter, was Wolsey any more inclined to respect the proper procedures of the ecclesiastical courts than he had those of the common law as Chancellor. Indeed, as legate he created legatine courts that superseded in authority all the other courts of the Church, and this, too, would have momentous consequences, for in doing so, he succeeded in making interference from 'Rome' increasingly distasteful to certain sections of the English clergy.

By the time that Wolsey was finally made legate for life by Pope Clement VII in January 1524, he had in any case grown weary of the task of ecclesiastical reform. It was true that during the years ahead he would set about the dissolution of twenty-nine decayed monasteries and three nunneries with the help of John Allen and a certain Thomas Cromwell. But the promise of significant reallocation of funds to education was never forthcoming. Heresy, too, was given desultory, albeit humane, treatment. When, for instance, an Oxford organist named Taverner was brought before Wolsey for hiding heretical books under his bed, the wretched man was, it seems, excused on the grounds that he was a musician.

As legate *a latere*, then, Wolsey remained at best a reformer by memorandum. But worst of all, perhaps, his own reputation for personal corruption seemed to epitomise those very abuses that anticlerical writers seized upon so readily. In his scathing *Practice of Prelates*, William Tyndale dubbed him 'Wolfsee [...] this wily wolf, I say, and raging sea, and shipwreck of England'. He was, said Tyndale, prone to 'all manner of voluptuousness' and 'utterly appointed to semble and dissemble, to have one thing in the heart and another in the mouth'. 'One cross,' said Polydore Vergil elsewhere, 'is insufficient to atone for his sins.'

Though some of Wolsey's excesses were by no means entirely untypical, the damage they did is therefore impossible to ignore. Indeed, he came to epitomise, however rightly or wrongly, all the features of ecclesiastical life that were themselves most in need of reform. Fifteen years after his appointment as Archbishop of York, he had visited that city only once. In the meantime, however, he had proceeded to accumulate yet another string of ecclesiastical posts, which he could not possibly hope to administer effectively in person. Becoming, in turn, Bishop of Durham and then Winchester, he also controlled the sees of Worcester and Salisbury, and farmed out three other bishoprics, earning £1,000 per annum from the proceeds. For good measure, he derived a considerable income from the probate of wills and was also appointed abbot of both St Albans and Salisbury, though he had taken no monastic vows of any kind. All the while, therefore, that the pope's very own representative in England was exhorting his clergy to modesty, charity and self-sacrifice, he himself was leading the life of a prince.

11

'Glorious Peacock'

Throughout his fourteen long years as Lord Chancellor, Thomas Wolsey would be guided in his conduct by two principles above all others. On the one hand, he would always believe that to govern was to dominate. Supremely confident of his own ability, he felt neither the need to delegate nor the inclination to consult. At the same time, however, he was equally convinced that high office could never be exercised effectively unless it was duly reinforced by continual displays of pomp and splendour. On neither account would Wolsey ever compromise. And in consequence no subject of the crown in the whole course of English history ever left so deep an impression of power, magnificence and conceit upon his contemporaries.

'The Cardinal of York,' wrote the papal nuncio, Francesco Chieregato, in 1517, 'by reason of his excellent qualities governs everything alone [...] so that foreign envoys fancy themselves negotiating not with a cardinal but with another king.' Two years later Giustiniani was remarking that Wolsey 'is in very great repute, seven times greater than if he were pope'. Yet to others the most striking thing about the Lord Chancellor was always his inordinate vanity. In the opinion of Marino Sanuto, for example, he remained 'the proudest prelate that ever breathed' and even that most loyal of servants George Cavendish would be unable to deny ultimately that his master was 'the haughtiest man in all his proceedings that then lived'.

Certainly, Wolsey seems to have relished any and every opportunity to affirm his status and in doing so he was always more than willing to exploit the elaborate manners and conventions of the day. His passage to Star Chamber on Mondays, Tuesdays and Thursdays, for instance, and to the Court of Chancery on Wednesdays, Fridays and Saturdays involved him in a characteristically theatrical spectacle. After saying his daily office in the company of his chaplain, attending to routine business and hearing two Masses in his privy closet, he was usually ready to set out by eight o'clock in the morning. And the glittering train of nobles and gentlemen that invariably accompanied him on his short journey to Westminster Hall left no doubt at all about the importance of either the man or his office.

At the head of the solemn procession, two great crosses of silver were always held on high before him – the first symbolising the power of a papal legate, the second representing the office of archbishop – while the two heavy pillars of state followed close behind, along with the Lord Chancellor's own sergeant-at-arms and a bare-headed page, specially chosen for his exceptional beauty, who carried the Great Seal of England in a silk purse. Then came Wolsey himself, astride a scarlet-clad mule, with four footmen shouldering gilt poleaxes and either a peer or a gentleman usher reverently bearing his cardinal's hat. Meanwhile, as the whole party made its stately way through crowds of suitably awed onlookers, other gentlemen ushers were at hand to clear the path. 'On, my lords and masters!' the cry went up. 'Make Way for my Lord's Grace the Cardinal Legate of York, Lord High Chancellor of this realm!'

In all other respects, too, Wolsey preened and paraded himself in a manner and on a scale that rivalled even his master's renowned extravagance. It comes as no surprise at all that at the time of his death he still owed just over £1,690 to the court jeweller, Robert Amadas. And though almost none of his possessions survive today, the inventories which describe them leave no doubt as to their splendour, range and value. We hear, among other things, of an exquisite salt cellar decorated 'with scallop shells, antics in the feet, and a boy with a serpent on the cover', as well as six candlesticks, made at Bruges and weighing 297oz, all of which were embossed 'with leopards' heads and cardinals' hats'. Elsewhere, there is mention of a portable sundial made by the German astronomer Nicholas Kratzer, along with countless other items which seem to proclaim their owner's love of novelty and ostentation no less loudly.

Even in death it was Wolsey's intention to glorify himself like no other. Long before his end actually came he had already commissioned the distinguished Florentine sculptor Benedetto da Rovezzano to design his final resting place. Described by one contemporary as 'a more costly mausoleum than any royal or papal monument', it was intended quite unashamedly to surpass the tomb that Torrigiano had recently fashioned for Henry VII and his wife at Westminster

Abbey. Indeed, Rovezzano is known to have asserted with total confidence that his own construction would be at least three times as magnificent.

But if it seemed to many that the cardinal had been utterly beguiled by such 'manifest tokens of vainglory', the truth was rather more complex. 'Outward esteem to a great man,' ran the contemporary proverb, 'is as a skin to a fruit, which though a thin cover, preserveth it', and though Wolsey undoubtedly carried this particular notion to unheard-of extremes the fact remains that no-one who breathed the air of Henry VIII's court could ever have thought otherwise. Conspicuous consumption had, after all, always been a wholly natural means of commanding respect, both for oneself as well as the superior one happened to represent. And now it was also viewed increasingly as the surest possible defence against the kind of social emulation that all contemporaries viewed with such suspicion.

There was, then, nothing inherently offensive in Wolsey's decision to dress only in 'fine crimson taffeta, or crimson satin engrained', to trim his shoes with pearls or to buy his hats only from France, where they were enhanced with a brilliant scarlet dye unobtainable in England. He was equally at liberty, if he so desired, to wear sable scarves around his neck, to adorn his bedstead with gilt cardinal's hats, or to emblazon his servants' scarlet livery with the initials 'T.C.' for *Thomas Cardinalis*. And if his cross-bearers were chosen specifically for their height and beauty or his master chef 'went daily in damask, satin or velvet with a chain of gold about his neck', this, too, could be borne equitably enough by most who witnessed it.

For his part, Wolsey seems to have seen no inconsistency between his own behaviour and the frequent attacks that he launched upon the immorality of others. He did not flinch, for instance, in waging sharp campaigns against dicing and gambling in the country at large or rooting out indecency at court. His conscience was equally clear, too, when he roundly condemned the pilfering and destruction which invariably accompanied royal visits to the houses of nobles and gentlemen. And when one particularly audacious critic spoke out against Wolsey's own love of excess, he was typically unfazed. 'How think ye,' he responded, 'were it better for me, being in the honour and dignity that I am, to coin my pillars and poleaxes and give the money to five or six beggars? Do you not reckon this commonwealth better than five or six beggars?'

Nor, for that matter, did Wolsey hesitate to discourage men from aping their betters, even though his own humble origins were known to all. When he did so, moreover, there was little, if any, disapproval among those who might well have been counted upon to protest. Not a single eyebrow seems to have been raised in 1515, for instance, when he devised an Act of Apparel to combat the prevalence at court of what has been described elsewhere as 'socially subversive over-dressing'. Though the king might wear whatever he pleased and could licence the wearing of any attire by those he chose, Wolsey now ordained that no man under the rank of duke should wear any cloth of gold, while those under the rank of earl were forbidden to wear sables.

Any indignation would be just as muted two years later, when he was behind the only known English proclamation to regulate the consumption of food in accordance with social rank. Henceforth, laymen and clerics with an annual income of at least £40 per year or goods to the value of £500 were to be allowed no more than three courses at a meal, with special exceptions for weddings and additional exemptions in respect of 'potages', i.e. soups, and 'brawn and other entrails'. Noblemen, Lord Mayors and Knights of the Garter, on the other hand, were to be granted six dishes under normal circumstances, while cardinals were to be permitted nine.

Even some of the more jarring aspects of Wolsey's behaviour were not without precedent or parallel. Archbishop Warham, as we have seen, took little trouble to conceal his own mistress from visitors to his home, and both he and Cardinal Morton before him had sought to profit substantially by exploiting probate fees. Outside England, meanwhile, Wolsey's pluralism looks pale beside the two bishoprics, four archbishoprics and twenty-seven abbacies held by Cardinal Tournon in Italy, and no income that Wolsey ever derived from any of his ecclesiastical offices could match the revenues that cardinals Mendoza or Cisneros drew from the Archbishopric of Toledo. Similarly, in terms of lust and pride, Wolsey was by no means the biggest shark in the ecclesiastical ocean. Cardinal David Beaton's score of eight bastards in Scotland speaks for itself as does the unbending demand made by Cardinal Matthaus Lang of the Holy Roman Empire that he be permitted to bear a sword whenever he chose and remain seated in the presence of the pope.

However, when it came to blatant self-advertisement and excess England's cardinal eventually came to outshine each and every one of his competitors and, in doing so, he would ultimately stretch convention to breaking-point. At state banquets Wolsey now dined at the royal table, from which even the highest nobles in the land were excluded, and though in the earliest days of his rule a new ambassador might be entertained at his side, it would not be long before the cardinal was being served separately with special meats reserved for him alone. Much more provocatively still, nobles rapidly became little more than accessories to Wolsey's daily rituals. Dukes, for instance, now found themselves holding bowls and offering towels as he washed his hands at table, while earls bowed down before him to tie the latchet of his shoes. Likewise, young peers taken into his household as wards were expected to jump dutifully to his every instruction.

'In all things the Chancellor was honoured like the King's person and sat always at his right hand', wrote du Bellay, the French ambassador. 'In all places where the King's arms were put up,' he continued, 'the Chancellor's appeared alongside of them, so that in every honour the Sovereign and his minister were equal.' Before long, the University of Oxford's habit of addressing Wolsey as 'Your Majesty' was also taking on a new significance and in due course money would even be coined with the cardinal's hat upon it. At the same time, neither peers of the realm nor foreign envoys could be assured of an appointment with the Lord Chancellor except through his secretary and, even then, rarely before the fourth time of asking. Indeed, Lord Dacre's messenger was said to have waited all of five months in London before receiving an answer to a pressing petition.

Most obviously of all, there was Wolsey's income to consider. His revenues from the archbishopric of York alone brought him some 14,000 ducats annually and in 1519 Giustiniani would estimate his total annual income at three times this figure. However, even this huge sum would be considerably enhanced over the years by his steady acquisition of further ecclesiastical posts. On 17 December 1521, for instance, he became Abbot of St Albans, the richest monastery in the land, and this was followed by the prestigious bishoprics of Durham in March 1523 and Winchester in October 1528.

Wolsey's total profits from legal fees, including legatine jurisdiction, can only be guessed, but his income from the Court of Chancery is known to have been yielding some 5,000 ducats shortly after his appointment, and the fact that he would claim a shilling in the pound on the value of all wills that he handled leaves no doubt that this source of income alone would have yielded many thousands. Ultimately, he would also enjoy a rich crop of pensions, including one from the French which ran to some 25,000 crowns 'without the extras, of which not one penny is owing'.

Giustiniani had no hesitation, then, in claiming that 'wherever Wolsey was, he always had a sideboard of plate worth 25,000 ducats'. And when the Venetian ambassador Marco Antonio Venier visited him at the height of his glory, he would estimate the worth of the Cardinal of York's gold and silver plate to be £150,000. Such, indeed, was Wolsey's wealth that the question inevitably arises of whether he was even richer than the king himself. There is no doubt, for instance, that his regular New Year's gifts, which were reckoned at 15,000 ducats, exceeded the king's in value. And while royal revenues were undoubtedly greater than Wolsey's, royal expenses included those of national government, which suggests that, at the height of his power, the cardinal may well have boasted a larger disposable income than his sovereign.

Nor should it be forgotten that countless gifts, unsolicited and otherwise, also came Wolsey's way. Just before Giustiniani left London, for instance, he was engaged in delicate negotiations involving the grant of a licence to import Candian wines into England, and Wolsey had no apparent hesitation in letting the ambassador know that he could be better induced to lighten the appropriate customs duties if the businesslike Signory of Venice made the right gesture of friendship. Should the gift of some 'Damascene carpets' be made, said Giustiniani, he felt sure that the cardinal would comply. 'To discuss the matter further until the cardinal receives his 100 carpets would,' he added, 'be idle.'

Nowhere, however, were Wolsey's raw wealth and appetite for magnificence more apparent than in the majestic scale and adornment of his dwellings. Certainly, the Archbishop of York's official London residence, York Place, had seen better days when Wolsey came to occupy it in 1514. Standing on the site now occupied by the modern Banqueting House in Whitehall, some of its buildings had first been erected towards the end of the thirteenth century and during the years in which Wolsey's predecessor, Cardinal Bainbridge, had been living in Rome, very little money had been spent on either maintenance or improvement. So when Wolsey acquired it after Bainbridge's death its surveyor, James Bettes, was keen to recommend what amounted, even so, to a comparatively modest programme of repairs and refurbishment.

To his great and pleasant surprise, however, Bettes was soon to discover that the new occupant of 'York Palace', as it was called at the time, was not a man for half-measures, particularly when his own status and comfort were involved, and an extensive schedule of rebuilding was initiated at once. The result was one of the finest houses devised by an English subject since Humphrey Duke of Gloucester had erected 'Bella Court' at Greenwich. And in the process, Archbishop Warham's Lambeth Place, which had itself been renovated by Cardinal Morton during the previous reign, would be almost wholly overshadowed.

The man appointed to supervise construction was Henry Redmayne, master mason of Westminster Abbey, and the list of his assistants reads like a who's who of the finest English craftsmen of the day. The master carpenter, Richard Russell, and Thomas Stockton, the king's chief joiner, were both involved, along with Bernard Flower, the king's glazier, and John Burwell, the king's sergeant plumber. At the same time, a host of Cambridge craftsmen, who had been employed at the colleges there, were also enlisted and, before long, red bricks made in Battersea kilns were being delivered to Westminster by barge for a new hall and kitchens. Appropriately enough for a *bon viveur* of Wolsey's distinction, vast wine cellars were also installed, the full scale of which was only discovered during the renovation of the modern Treasury Building in the early 1960s.

Predictably, Wolsey pressed ahead with characteristic energy, so that by July 1516 the work was sufficiently advanced for the king to be entertained there. Nor is there any question of the lavish expenditure entailed by the whole project. Two months after his appointment to the province of York, Wolsey had borrowed £3,500, and in his first year as archbishop he spent the massive sum of £1,250 on ensuring that his new home was suitable for his needs. A new set of 'water stairs' was built leading on to the Thames, along with a fine new chapel, equipped with an outer and inner vestry, and by 1516 the household accounts were referring to an armoury, a gallery, a dining chamber and a cloister. Ultimately, the building would also incorporate an area of some 1,600 square yards of reclaimed river upon which part of an eastward-facing long gallery, measuring some 200ft, was constructed. And extensive alterations were carried out to the grounds as well, for although Wolsey was not given to physical exertion, he does seem to have been fond of gardens and particularly orchards.

Last but not least, there were also, it seems, at least two libraries, though, sadly, their contents will never be known. Curiously there is virtually no information at all either on what Wolsey read, or even the books that were on his shelves in any of his houses. No relevant catalogues remain, and only four surviving books have been closely associated with him in any way: Aelfric's *First Book of Homilies*; another text entitled *Nova Legenda Angliae*; and both a gospel-book and epistle-book, neither of which possess particular significance in their own right.

But the crowning glory of York Place was, in any case, the Great Chamber, where Wolsey received high-ranking petitioners and staged his most lavish entertainments, the menus of which provoked foreigners to conclude that gluttony was a national vice amongst the English. Though the precise details of its design and decoration are unknown, the extent to which it was intended to affirm and overawe is beyond doubt. One of its many outstanding features, for instance, was a stunning array of gold and silver plate, the pick of which was a series of huge vases, purchased no doubt from the Goldsmiths' Company of London with which Wolsey always maintained the closest links. Likewise, access to the chamber was specifically arranged to humble any visitor fortunate enough to be welcomed into the presence of the great man himself. 'One traverses eight rooms before reaching his audience chamber,' recorded Giustiniani, 'and they are all hung with tapestry which is changed once a week.'

Even the king himself marvelled at the splendour of York Place. Not only did its marvellously central location make it an object of particular envy for him, it was also much more up-to-date than any of his own palaces, with the partial exception of Richmond. Westminster Palace, as we have seen, was largely destroyed in April 1512, and Henry had been forced thereafter to make more and more use of Baynard's Castle as well as his quarters in the Tower of London, both of which were inordinately cramped. Moreover, even though Wolsey now transferred his partially completed house at Bridewell to the king's use and personally supervised its transformation into a royal residence, the resulting palace was still a comparatively modest construction, leaving the king to rely increasingly upon Greenwich.

Yet, though it now became the custom increasingly to talk about the 'absence of the court' whenever Wolsey was away from the capital, his London residence was not without its limitations. The existing site was a comparatively confined one, already much built upon, and surrounding property was both expensive to purchase and difficult to come by. To ease the problem Henry would grant Wolsey a plot of land between King Street and the Thames in 1519, and the following year Wolsey also managed to buy from a certain William Lytton the remainder of a 24-year lease on five tenements and their gardens, stretching between King Street and the Thames on the south side.

Even so, the area involved was never sufficient to allow building on a truly grand scale, and for this reason the accommodation on offer for ambassadors as well as for the royal family was never extensive. Indeed, there is no record of any overnight stay by the king or any evidence of more than two or three royal visits in total. Ultimately, therefore, York Place would remain essentially Wolsey's working town house – his residence during the legal term and the place at which, from time to time, he would stage the obligatory extravaganza or two. The home of his dreams lay elsewhere.

As it happened, the site for that ideal dwelling had already been identified at around the very time that James Bettes was being instructed to press ahead with the renovation of York Place. Within five months of becoming archbishop Wolsey had acquired from the Prior of St John of Jerusalem and the Knights Hospitallers a ninety-nine year lease for the manor of Hampton, which lay 20 miles to the south-west of London on the highest bank of the Thames south of the city. Away from the hazards and vexations of the capital, but still within a few hours reach of it by boat, and only a day's ride from Windsor, it seemed an ideal location for a home which would reflect his ambitions and outshine in every detail the rival dwellings of his fellow councillors.

In choosing this site Wolsey was, it seems, seeking rather more than a convenient and suitably splendid country seat. Even before his appointment as Lord Chancellor, he was already growing more and more impatient with the nagging throng of importunate suitors who were always around about him. And this jealousy of his personal space was not something that he ever appears to have lost. When, for instance, Sir Thomas Allen tried to bring Wolsey letters from the Earl of Shrewsbury, he found him so inaccessible that he wrote to the earl to express his frustration in no uncertain terms. 'I had rather your lordship had sent me to Rome,' complained Allen, 'than to deliver him letters and bring answers to the same.' Nor, it seems, was this an isolated example of the value that Wolsey was always to attach to occasional periods of solitude, for Allen ended his letter by observing that 'when he walks in the park he will suffer no suitor to come nigh unto him; but commands him away as far as a man will shoot an arrow'. From now onwards, then, Wolsey looked forward to that blissful time when he could have eight sturdy oarsmen carry him off to Hampton Court and away from everything other than the king's own business.

But hand-in-hand with Wolsey's search for a place of escape went other deeper concerns – not least of all about his health. According to one of his sternest critics, William Tyndale, he was a man of 'bodily strength to do and suffer great things'. Yet his constitution was always fragile. There is no question, for instance, that he regularly over-indulged an already gargantuan appetite for food, especially after a dispensation had freed him from the stern requirements of abstinence and fasting imposed by the Church upon lesser mortals. But he was also undoubtedly a worrier – so much so that around the time of his election to the cardinalate, Giustiniani caught a memorable glimpse of him deep in thought, his features troubled and his forehead furrowed in 'mental perturbation' as he gnawed distractedly at his cane.

Perhaps it was because of his worrisome nature that Wolsey continually drove himself too hard. So punishing, indeed, was his regular schedule that even his self-centred master would eventually warn him of its potential toll. On one occasion, having thanked him for the 'great pain and labour that you do daily take in my business and matters', Henry urged him 'to take some pastime and comfort, to the intent that you may the longer endure to serve us, for always pain cannot be endured'. But in this one respect, at least, Wolsey seems to have ignored the king's advice consistently, though if illness struck him – as it frequently did – he was never inclined to ascribe it to overwork. When, for instance, he became sick in 1521 after obviously pushing himself to the limit on government business, he would attribute his indisposition to the 'unwholesome air of Calais'.

Long before this, however, Wolsey had been prone to recurrent attacks of ague and quinsy and it was already being reported that he was suffering from a kidney stone, which may account for the colic of which he often complained. Furthermore, as his health deteriorated he began to display a marked fondness for taking all kinds of preventative medicines – so much so that even the king, who was, if anything, even more obsessed with concoctions of every description, expressed his disapproval. In 1519, for instance, Henry urged Thomas More to write to assure 'my own good cardinal' that if he continued to forgo the frequent taking of medicines, he would not 'fail of health'.

In the meantime, Wolsey had also developed a morbid concern about the dangers of contagious disease. Whenever he travelled through the streets of the capital, for instance, he now always held to his nose an orange stuffed with vinegar and olives to combat the 'pestilential airs'. At Bridewell, moreover, the stink and polluted water of the stagnant Fleet river almost certainly contributed to the onset of those bouts of dysentery which would trouble him regularly and carry him ultimately to his grave. 'For some days past,' recorded Giustiniani on one occasion, 'the Cardinal of York has been indisposed, and he is much reduced by dysentery; owing to which I have been unable to visit him, as he received no one.' And York Place, in its turn, proved little better, for the crowds who followed him there also fouled the rushes underfoot and flooded the sewers, leaving him with 'the rheum and catarrh'.

Above all, of course, there was the dreaded 'sweating sickness' for Wolsey to dwell upon. This deadly disease, which usually visited the capital around November each year, tended to run its course in only a few hours. Beginning suddenly with a high fever, palpitations and rapid pulse, the victim soon exhibited breathing difficulties and a copious, general sweating. One contemporary physician, Dr John Caius, captured all too vividly the reasons why 'the sweat' was so thoroughly dreaded, saying of its victims:

As I found them, so it took them; some in sleep, some in wake, some in mirth, some in care, some fasting and some full, some busy and some idle; and in one house sometime three, sometime five; sometime all; of the which if the half in every town escaped it was thought a great favour.

And though Wolsey invariably kept his post in Westminster when 'the sweat' appeared, while the king himself fled for refuge at Windsor Castle or far-off Hunsdon Manor in Hertfordshire, he sometimes did so at great personal cost. The Lord Chancellor's earliest encounter with 'the sweat' seems to have occurred in June 1517, when he was so ill that 'his life was despaired of and for many days neither the grandees nor other members of the privy council, who are wont to be so assiduous, went near him'. But if this was his first enforced break in the royal service since 1512, it would not be his last. Indeed, following a brief convalescence, he appears to have suffered four more attacks in August alone when the same outbreak carried off many of his household 'and not merely his under-attendants, but some of the principal ones'. Such was his relief, in fact, at his truly remarkable survival that in September he undertook a pilgrimage to the shrine of the Virgin Mary at Walsingham in Norfolk.

It comes as no surprise, therefore, that the purchase and design of Wolsey's finest home should have been so directly influenced by matters pertaining to his health. Without doubt, Wolsey seems to have exhibited an almost unhealthy obsession about hygiene from the moment that Hampton Court was conceived and the fresh water supply of Coombe Springs, not far from Hampton itself, was a key consideration in his choice of site. That the same springs were also deemed to be particularly beneficial for sufferers with kidney stones was clearly another factor. There is, indeed, a tale that prior to the purchase of his greatest house, Wolsey engaged a team of physicians, aided by learned doctors from Padua, to visit a range of possible sites for a suburban residence and that at the end of their tour they pronounced Hampton to be by far the healthiest site they had visited: a place of 'extraordinary salubrity'.

The aim was that fresh water should be collected in standpipes on Coombe Hill before being conveyed in a double set of strong leaden pipes running over a distance of 3 miles through Surbiton and Kingston and passing under both the Hogsmead river – a tributary of the Thames – and the Thames itself at Kingston. In all, more than 250 tons of lead were likely to have been needed for the task and, for good measure, Wolsey also ordered the construction of brick sewers some 3ft thick and 5ft high to run from the palace to the Thames, arrangements which were certainly not paralleled at the king's own residence in Westminster, and ones which would not, in fact, be superseded at Hampton Court until 1871.

But while the arrangements below ground were impressive, the building above would be nothing short of stunning. Though the original plans appear to have been drawn up by Ellis Smith, the architect mainly responsible for the palace's eventual design was once more Henry Redmayne, who was ably assisted this time by William Reynolds, the same master mason who had finally completed the tower at Wolsey's Magdalen College. Most of the timberwork, meanwhile, was prepared under the direction of the master carpenter, Humphrey Cook. And at every stage of development, Wolsey appears to have acted as any earnest bourgeois might, showing a daily interest in the minutiae of construction – the terracing, gardening and drainage, the colour of brick, the pleasing architectural effects, and, not least of all, the avoidance of damp.

Yet again, the same frantic energy was in evidence and by the spring of 1515 a veritable army of workmen had descended upon the place. Even before summer arrived a moat had been dug and, just as importantly, the obligatory Tudor herb garden was planted with parsley, thyme, caraway and coriander for medicinal as well as culinary purposes. At the same time, building materials also converged on Hampton from all directions: stone from Reigate and Barnet, timber from Reading and Weybridge, lime from Ruislip and red bricks baked in nearby kilns by Richard Reculver, costing 3s per thousand. To speed matters further, Wolsey also installed a crane on the site and, as a result, the erection of the house itself seems to have been executed with remarkable rapidity, for by May glaziers had already been employed to put in the 65ft run of windows, which extended down both sides of the gallery.

Sadly, the precise layout of Wolsey's buildings cannot be determined with total accuracy, due to the extensive alterations made by Henry VIII after he acquired the palace. To complicate matters further, Henry would also use the same materials and, indeed, the same craftsmen, headed by Redmayne, while additional changes were also made during the reign of William III. But if Wolsey's Hampton Court retains many mysteries, there can never be any doubt that it was built on the grandest possible scale. And when it is remembered that the man who conceived it was not yet Lord Chancellor, let alone a cardinal, there can be no doubting either his inestimable ambition or his soaring self-confidence.

In all, the palace covered nearly 8 acres and contained almost 1,000 rooms. The First Court, for example, which greeted visitors upon their arrival, measured an imposing 167ft by 142ft. Three sides of its quadrangle housed long, narrow galleries that contained some of the palace's 280 chambers for guests, most of them so-called 'double lodgings', consisting of one large chamber, and a smaller one for attendants. 'There were,' said the Venetian Count Mario Savorgnano, 'two hundred and four score beds, the furniture to most of them being silk, and all for the entertainment of strangers only.' The beds themselves, meanwhile, were often filled with flowers 'for the delectation sake unto the eye and the odoriferous savours unto the nose'. And there were innovations, too. In all the principal apartments of the palace, for instance, there were baths and toilet facilities, and not only was the area of glass at Wolsey's palace much greater than usual, the windows themselves were glazed and no longer closed only with a shutter.

Each gallery, it seems, stood two stories high, with windows ranged equally at every level, while the fourth side of the court, although bricked and stoned in the manner of the others, discarded the regularity of design. Here the elevation of the façade gave way to a third storey, which, in turn, gave way to turrets before the whole then lifted to a central clock tower, rising to some 80ft. Beyond the quadrangle stood two smaller courts, each with its own smaller yards, galleries, chapels, bedrooms and offices.

For the purpose of embellishing the exterior Wolsey became the first man in England to employ distinguished artists and sculptors from Italy, and in doing so he began to establish a reputation as a patron of the arts which would ultimately outstrip even that of his master. The Florentine Giovanni da Maiano, for example, came to work at Hampton in 1521 to make a series of terracotta roundels depicting the heads of Roman emperors and costing, we are told, £2 6s 8d each. At the same time, Maiano also made panels of the 'Histories of Hercules' for the oriel windows of the great gateway, which were eventually replaced by the king's beasts when the palace became Henry's. Yet the finest terracotta work of all to be commissioned by Wolsey was perhaps the panel with his arms over the gateway of the clock tower, showing the cardinal's hat, his archiepiscopal crosses and legatine pillars, with two exquisite nude *putti* as supporters of the shield.

Naturally enough, Wolsey did not stint on the interior of his showpiece either. His favourite colours were byse – a fierce light blue – and gold, and these seem to have dominated. Some walls, in fact, were hung with cloth of gold, cloth of silver and gold tissue, while others were embellished with linen fold oak panels or painted in oil with scenes from Christ's life, including the Nativity and Passion. Ceilings, in their turn, were decorated with running meanders, scrollwork, ornamental bas-relief, vaulting of moulded wood, bosses of leaves and, of course, cardinal's hats. But most impressive of all were the magnificent galleries about which Wolsey loved to stroll. Described by Mario Savorgnano as 'long porticoes, without chambers, with windows on each side, looking on gardens or rivers', these galleries would set a fashion to be followed by nearly every great house in England for the next century.

Savorgnano also referred with equal admiration to the 'hangings of wonderful value' which were displayed in Hampton Court's various chambers. On one particular occasion, Wolsey ordered 132 pieces of tapestry for the clock tower alone. The majority depicted biblical stories, including those of Jacob, David, Solomon, Samson, the prodigal son and the Virgin Mary. But some featured classical tales involving Pluto, Paris, Priam, Hercules and Jason, and one portrayed Hannibal. Others took as their themes the Pilgrimage of Life and the Romance of the Rose, and there were also allegorical scenes dealing with Love, Chastity, Eternity, Time and Death. Appropriately enough, Fame and Fortune figured too.

Wolsey's agents scoured the markets of Flanders, France, Italy and Venice for all kinds of rich art, and the purchase of beautiful objects now became a lifelong passion, which is just as likely to have sprung from a genuine love of beautiful things as from any mere love of display or wish to acquire for acquisition's sake. It comes as no surprise, therefore, that oriental wools rather than straw covered the floors of Hampton Court's main rooms or that fine gold and silver objects, purchased either abroad or from the goldsmiths of London, should have been on display everywhere.

But it was probably the sheer size of Wolsey's regular household at Hampton Court that demonstrates the full grandeur of his lifestyle most vividly. More than 400 staff were in attendance at any one time, and the simple task of feeding them was the most formidable logistical task in its own right. As well as two master kitchens, therefore, Wolsey also maintained a third smaller one for his own table, and all were serviced by a master cook, two other chief cooks and six further assistant cooks, along with a scrambling horde of other helpers, many of whom were children. Then there was the spicery with its yeoman; the pastry room with two further cooks and two paste layers; the scullery with four scullions, a yeoman and two grooms; the larder with a yeoman groom; the buttery with two yeomen and two grooms; the ewery with more yeomen and grooms; as well as the cellar, chandlery, bakehouse and wafery, all with their own specialist staff.

The day-to-day management of the main hall, meanwhile, was overseen by the steward, the treasurer and the controller, and here, at tables where the places were assigned according to rank, the main body of Wolsey's staff dined. By now, too, Wolsey had his own almoner who, at the very lowest table of all, duly dispensed food and drink to paupers. To assist with the infinitely elaborate dining arrangements, therefore, a buzzing horde of waiters and gentlemen waiters, gentlemen cupbearers, carvers and servers were kept in a state of perpetual motion. And to keep order among the crowds of visitors to the hall as well as in the corridors outside, there was a chamberlain and twelve gentlemen ushers on constant watch.

Eventually, a total of sixteen physicians, or 'leeches', would also be retained at Hampton Court - including from 1523 a renowned Venetian by the name of Agostino degli Agostini — along with a tutor who instructed the wards in Wolsey's charge, such as Edward Stanley, third Earl of Derby. The stables, too, had their own master, aided by a farrier, a yeoman of the stirrup and a horde of grooms for the hundred horses kept for general use, as well as the six grey and white mules that Wolsey himself rode. Likewise, there was the master of the wardrobe and his staff of twenty to assist with sleeping arrangements, plus the staffs of the laundry and the woodyard, as well as the grooms and porters of the gate. The so-called 'yeoman of the barge', in his turn, attended to transport arrangements to and from the capital, and somewhat surprisingly, perhaps, for a churchman there was also a tent-keeper and an armourer in permanent residence, as well as a personal herald.

The chapel was a prominent feature of all Wolsey's households and the one at Hampton Court was particularly large, boasting a complement of fifty-four persons in all. Supervised by a dean and subdean, it included a reader of the gospels, a singing priest for the epistles and two grooms of the vestry, who saw to the chapel's ornaments and vestments. A team of chaplains was also employed to say daily Mass for the cardinal in his closet, though on feast days Wolsey would, it seems, say Mass in person 'after the manner of the Pope himself' with 'not only bishops and abbots serving him therein, but even dukes and earls giving him water and the towel'.

Last but not least, of course, there was Wolsey's famous choir, consisting of twelve boys and sixteen men, which was the envy even of the king. On one occasion, indeed, Wolsey saw fit to devise a singing competition between the king's chapel royal and his own Hampton Court choir, requiring each to sight-read in turn the same composition. Remarkably, even Henry himself acknowledged that Wolsey's choir 'more surely handled' the piece, after which Wolsey wisely took the hint and arranged for one of his best choristers to be transferred to the chapel royal, where Mr Pigot, the king's choirmaster, became, according to Richard Pace, most enthusiastic about the new arrival, 'not only for his sure and cleanly singing, but also for his good and crafty descant'.

To describe Wolsey's household as a hive of furious activity is, then, to err wholly on the side of understatement, and though Hampton Court had first been purchased with isolation in mind, it was partly to escape the clamour of this bustling microcosm that Wolsey eventually found himself wishing to acquire a number of other properties. He had already purchased a small residence at Kingston-on Thames, while Hampton was being built, but in 1519 he would persuade Bishop Fox to allow him to reside from time to time at his house 2 miles away in Esher. Fox, in fact, seems to have been more than happy to oblige, offering it as 'a cell to Hampton Court' and praying God that Wolsey be sent 'as much good health, pleasure and comfort in it as I would wish myself to have'. In due course, when Wolsey succeeded Fox as Bishop of Winchester, he became outright owner of the house.

Wolsey would also take a personal interest in two of the manor houses belonging to the Abbey of St Albans, once he had become its titular abbot. Of these, Tittenhanger in Bedfordshire proved much too far from London for him to visit very often, though the other – the manor of the More near

Rickmansworth in Hertfordshire – became a favourite retreat from the capital and was even considered by du Bellay, the French ambassador, to be preferable to Hampton Court.

But however keen Wolsey might sometimes have been to escape the relentless press of affairs, it was never a practical option for long. Nor, realistically, could it ever have been, for from the very moment that he came to occupy pride of place at the royal council table, Wolsey's workload was bound to increase exponentially. In next to no time, his own considerable talents had highlighted all too clearly the shortcomings of those around him. And as the man most able to deliver he was called upon, both by his master and his own pride, to deliver more and more. Regularly, therefore, he worked over state papers in the quiet of his private chambers from four o'clock in the morning until past midnight, awakening his secretaries at all hours and causing a never-ending trickle of tired pages to make their weary way along candlelit corridors with news of urgent dispatches.

If anything, Wolsey's purchase of Hampton Court actually increased his need to surround himself with officials. Almost at once, the place was teeming with its very own army of auditors, surveyors and doctors of law, all of whom were primarily concerned with drafting leases, checking accounts and preparing litigation, often in connection with the new property. And once Wolsey was Lord Chancellor he would also have no choice but to attach numerous Chancery officials to his household, including the Clerk of the Crown, who attested all letters and writs issued under the Great Seal, and the Clerk of the Hanaper, who looked after the fees of the Chancery Court.

Above all, though, it was diplomatic business which ensured most decisively that Hampton Court could never serve as the haven of peaceful withdrawal that Wolsey seems to have been wishing for initially. Since his master's priorities lay abroad, so too did his, and since Europe never rested, the same was equally true for him. For this reason, two principal secretaries would always be kept on hand at Hampton to assist with the constant flow of foreign correspondence that arrived there. In all cases the individuals concerned, such as Richard Pace, Brian Tuke, William Knight and Stephen Gardiner, were assistants of the highest ability and all would ultimately rise high in the king's service. But the role of these men was always to execute Wolsey's wishes rather than share the burden of decision-making or substantially shorten the hours of his toil. And before Hampton Court's foundations had barely begun to settle, new and momentous events across the Channel were ensuring that even secretaries of their calibre would be unable to ease the relentless pressure weighing in upon their master.

This time, however, it was not only the ambition of his own king that disrupted Wolsey's sleep, but also that of France's new ruler, for the so-called 'perpetual peace' had proven all too soon to be nothing of the kind. As 1515 unfolded, in fact, French armies were proving unstoppable in Italy and the entire balance of power that England depended upon so completely was on the verge of collapse. If, then, Hampton Court were ever to attain its full splendour under its present owner, it would be up to him to salvage what he could from the wreckage abroad, and continue thereafter to satisfy his master's restless ambition for the foreseeable future.

12

'Arbiter of Christendom'

While the walls of Hampton Court were continuing to rise so grandly in the late summer of 1515, the crumbling edifice of England's peace with France was already bound for demolition. Not only had the French victory over the pope's Swiss mercenaries at Marignano in early September given Francis I the opening success of his reign, it had also presented him with the greatest military triumph in living memory. In a battle lasting two days and part of a night, those same Frenchmen who had quailed and run at the sight of English forces outside Thérouanne less than two years earlier now defeated the best fighters in the whole of Europe. They had done so, moreover, in the kind of gory combat that made Henry's first campaign across the Channel seem little more than a summer outing. 'For two thousand years,' Francis wrote to his mother, 'there has not been so grand or so hard a battle.' And to gall his English counterpart further, the French king had been in the thick of the fighting throughout.

Such was the stunning scale of events in Italy that on 11 October, almost a whole month after the battle, Wolsey was still pretending not to believe the news. Henry, meanwhile, was even more dazed by what had taken place. Both Francis and his mother had written directly to inform him of the victory, but he had dismissed the letters as forgeries and ultimately it was only the arrival of the French envoy, Bapaume, which confirmed the English king's worst fears. Predictably, the letters and reports which Bapaume brought with him did not bring Henry 'any great pleasure', for it seemed, said the Frenchman, 'as if tears would have burst from his eyes, so red were they from the pain he suffered in hearing and understanding the good news and prosperity of my master'.

Wolsey's eventual reaction was, however, altogether more controlled and calculating. When officially informed of Francis's triumph, he was said to have told Bapaume that he greeted the glad tidings 'as much as if they had been the king's his master, by reason of the alliance and friendship between them'. And having 'laid his hand on his breast', he gave his firm assurances that his own sovereign had not been entertaining any thought of endangering 'the peace and amity' existing between the two kingdoms. Needless to say, such hollow professions of friendship fooled no-one.

Nor could they conceal the seriousness of England's predicament, for the warning signs had been clear for all to see throughout the preceding weeks and months. As the French war machine cranked into gear under its new leader, Wolsey had sounded the usual threats. He told an assembly of Venetian diplomats:

> Be assured that should the King of France show signs of valuing the friendship of our King, he will never violate the confederation and his faith [...] Should the said King choose, on the other hand, to maltreat English subjects, and appear not to hold his Majesty in account, his [Henry's] power is such, that he will know how to avenge himself; for I tell you, Sir Ambassadors, that we have ships here in readiness, and in eight days could place sixty thousand men on the soil of France; so we are able to thwart any of his projects at our pleasure.

On this occasion, however, both Wolsey and his master were more concerned with striking poses than inflicting blows. Indeed, their sole hope now rested on the fond belief that the greed of Emperor Maximilian might somehow be turned to advantage. Chiefly through the English agent on the spot, the ever reliable and cautious Richard Pace, money was therefore steadily released to Maximilian for the purchase of mercenaries. But so avaricious and duplicitous were the emperor and his ministers that even Pace was stretched to breaking point. In dealing with 'such people', he finally declared, 'Christ himself should with difficulty obtain anything without money'. And though, against all odds, the funds were eventually gathered to mount a challenge against the French, the imperial troops remained unpaid and ultimately turned and ran.

To compound matters, the French had also played a cunning hand in Scotland, which not only distracted attention from their manoeuvres in Italy, but also genuinely threatened England with war against her northern neighbour. Henry's sister Margaret, had, in fact, already tested her brother's affection to the limit by giving herself to the 19-year-old Earl of Angus after the death of her husband, James IV, at Flodden Field. More importantly, however, in throwing herself at an unworthy youth she had completely lost whatever slim affection the native Scots may have felt for her in the first place.

Not surprisingly, then, the French lost no time in loosing that renowned hothead and Anglophobe the Duke of Albany upon his sworn enemies, and before long he had rallied the disaffected Scottish chieftains, secured the infant King James V and ousted Margaret from any vestige of influence. In the aftermath of this calamity, Margaret had fled south into her brother's protection. But this was far from the end of the matter, for she was heavily pregnant and the hard riding over wild countryside caused her to give birth prematurely. Though the child survived, the queen herself became so sick that she was unable to travel on to London, taking shelter instead at the border castle of Thomas Lord Dacre. And there, for the moment, she rested in pathetic and fevered state, surrounded by the fine gowns and presents her brother had sent on to her in the vain hope that her return to England might not be construed as the total embarrassment it undoubtedly was.

From some perspectives, of course, the French victory at Marignano was merely the final sorry chapter in a long and sorry tale, but this is not to minimise England's impotence in its aftermath. Certainly, it would not be easy to revive any kind of anti-French alliance. King Ferdinand, for instance, remained as unreliable as ever and after his death in January 1516 – from 'hunting and hawking to the last in fair weather or foul, and following more the counsel of his friends than his physicians' – the prospects of Spanish assistance remained as remote as ever. Indeed, the 15-year-old grandson who succeeded him as King Charles I before later becoming the Holy Roman Emperor Charles V was for the first few years of his reign wholly under the influence of his pro-French council in the Netherlands, where he remained. The English envoys who were now sent to Brussels to ply him with baits of money and friendship were consequently wasting their time, and it would not be long before Charles was speaking more and more frequently of marriage between himself and the 4-year-old French Princess Renée.

Nor were England's alternatives any more favourable. Charles's other grandfather, Maximilian, was, in theory at least, somewhat more ready to oppose France, but the world had already come to know beyond all shadow of doubt that 'the said Emperor doth so oftentimes change his mind as the weathercock doth change his turn'. And his susceptibility to bribery remained undeniable. 'He is always dunning for money', the pope said of him, while Machiavelli observed that if all the leaves on all the trees of Italy had been converted into ducats for his use, they would not have been sufficient to his needs. Venice, on the other hand, was still at loggerheads with him and hastened to support Francis's armies as soon as they advanced into Italy. Likewise, Pope Leo X, wholly lacking his predecessor's stomach for a fight, rushed to make peace with the conqueror.

For the Duke of Albany and his French sponsors, therefore, there were English threats and curses, but little else besides. 'Believe me,' said Wolsey, after passionately recounting the story of Queen Margaret's humiliation to the council, 'his majesty and the kingdom will not brook such an outrage.' And by October, Venetian ambassadors were, indeed, talking of England's mounting preparation for war. Ships in the Thames were being steadily armed and stocked with military supplies, while Henry, it seems, was being encouraged to play the role of would-be warrior to his heart's content. At the launch of his great five-masted warship, the *Henry Grace à Dieu*, for instance, he brandished his golden admiral's whistle in boyish high spirits and 'dressed galley-fashion, with a vest of gold brocade reaching to the middle of his thigh'.

Unlike the king, however, Wolsey was far more concerned on this occasion with conserving money rather than launching heady schemes for conquest abroad. By any standards, the expenditure of the last three years had been truly enormous, and, to make matters worse, less than half the sum voted by parliament in 1514 had ever been collected. Accordingly, when MPs gathered once again in November 1516 they granted two subsidies to make good the shortfall, but nothing else. And the sums involved were, in any case, intended more for national defence than for further indulgence of the king's ego across the Channel.

Under such circumstances, then, Wolsey certainly had good reason to keep the peace. Francis was, after all, still a nominal ally and nothing in his recent actions actually constituted a breach of his country's existing treaty with England. Even the help he had given to Albany had been granted in strict conformity with current treaties between France and Scotland, which were known to exist by all concerned. But the King of France had been altogether too successful and by December 1516 he was genuinely threatening the balance of power in Europe after winning eight Swiss cantons over to his side. More importantly still, he had been too dismissive of Henry and in consequence Wolsey was now left with little choice but to opt for a policy which would prove to be every bit as ineffective as it was crooked.

The plan itself was simple enough. While Henry maintained a show of open friendship with Francis, the hapless Richard Pace was to be dispatched to Zurich to hire Swiss troops with English gold, in the hope that the Holy Roman Emperor might thereby be able to prevent the remaining Swiss cantons from falling under French control. Once again, a vast treasure was placed at Pace's disposal, though Wolsey issued the strictest instructions that no money was to be shown until the emperor and his advisers had proven their word. 'Ascending little by little, and not in anywise passing or exceeding the said sum of four thousand nobles by year,' Wolsey informed Pace, 'ye by your wisdom and discretion shall satisfy and content them with as little sum as ye conveniently may.'

But haggling with Maximilian, especially on his own territory, was like ploughing the desert or sowing the sea, and in this case the whole empty exercise would prove not only vain but life-threatening, too. As always, Pace, it seems, 'did the king's business admirably without expending money'. And it was even more to his credit that, in doing so, he also 'disturbed all the attempts of the French, who lavished large amounts of their own'. But in return for his efforts, Pace was made to suffer the full brunt of Maximilian's 'hospitality' – so much so that he barely lived to tell the whole frustrating tale. Verbal abuse, capricious threats of banishment and frequent house arrest all came Pace's way, in fact, before he eventually became the target of an unsuccessful attempt at murder by poisoning.

In the meantime, while Pace was eating insults and dodging death on the continent, Wolsey was meeting with mounting frustration of his own and, in the process, finding himself less and less able to contain his anger. His fits of temper were already familiar enough to those close to him. But now they began to flare with increasing frequency and unprecedented violence. More worryingly still, they were sometimes directed at individuals of real substance who would not be treated to such outbursts lightly.

On one occasion, for instance, Wolsey became so 'wrath and excited, that he did not seem in his right mind'. The trigger was an interview with Matthias Schinner, Cardinal of Sion, who had been travelling throughout Italy, Switzerland, Germany and the Netherlands instigating resistance to the French with English money. What had actually passed at the meeting is unknown, but in its wake Wolsey was so incensed that he suddenly demanded the presence of the imperial ambassador once more, regardless of the fact that 'it was already night and the hour inconvenient'. Nor can there be any doubt about the kind of reception that awaited the hapless diplomat, for Wolsey was said to have been 'in such a state of perturbation' afterwards that he would not grant an audience with the Venetian ambassador for a number of days.

Only a few weeks later, moreover, another high-profile victim was to feel, quite literally, the full force of Wolsey's frustration. On this occasion it was the papal nuncio Francesco Chieregato who would be told in 'fierce and rude language' to reveal what he had written to the King of France. And this time Wolsey also 'laid hands on him', threatening that 'unless he told by fair means', he would be 'put to the rack'. Needless to say, such gross mistreatment of a papal official scandalised many a foreign capital. Yet it reflected, too, the overwhelming pressure and frustration that Wolsey was experiencing on an almost daily basis.

Now, as a finishing touch, Maximilian's military expedition against the French, which had been subsidised so lavishly by England's treasury, failed in the strangest and most abject manner possible. At the head of 30,000 Swiss and German freebooters, the emperor had swept down over the Brenner Pass and by late March was within striking distance of the ill-provisioned French garrison in Milan. But just as the prize beckoned for the imperial forces, their leader slipped away by night and withdrew to Verona. Whether he had been bribed by Francis or whether, as he claimed, his nerve had suddenly left him at the prospect of fierce resistance is hard to say. Wolsey, however, was in little doubt of Maximilian's double-dealing. 'The Emperor,' he recorded drily, 'doth play on both hands, using the nature of a participle, which taketh *partem a nomine et partem a verbo* [part from a noun and part from a verb].' But guilt and grammar aside, the fact remained that England was now as vulnerable as ever with no real prospect of improvement in sight.

Even the ongoing struggle between London and Paris for the goodwill of the new King of Spain brought no better news. Indeed, on 13 August 1516, Charles agreed to the Treaty of Noyon by which he consented to marry Princess Louise, the 1-year-old daughter of the French king, in return for which Francis abandoned his claim upon Naples. In October, meanwhile, Maximilian formally renounced French gold and committed himself to a league with England before brazenly joining the French and Spanish two months later in return for 200,000 ducats. In all, the English had paid the emperor some 1.5 million crowns of their own for nothing more than his masterful cynicism. 'You, my grandson,' he told Charles, 'are going to trick the French and I the English', and in this particular respect, at least, he had proven true to his word.

But if Wolsey had played a weak hand badly on this occasion, he had already proven in 1514 that he could rapidly turn defeat to advantage, and now he would do so more stunningly than ever. His rescuer this time was, arguably, the most unlikely of all, for while Western Europe was tearing itself in pieces over a small Italian duchy, the Turkish sultan Selim I had been advancing his Ottoman Empire with gigantic strides. In 1516 alone, he conquered Northern Mesopotamia from the Persians, beat the Mamelukes at Aleppo, and annexed Syria. The following year he would win Egypt in a single battle and obtain from the last caliphs of the Abbasid line the surrender of supreme religious authority over Islam. In other words, he had become the greatest political figure in the world, and now his conquering energies were turning westward towards Hungary and Rhodes.

In March 1517, therefore, Leo X issued a papal bull imposing a five-year truce upon the whole of Christendom, and called for a combined expedition against the Turk, involving all Catholic monarchs. Almost at once, Maximilian, Francis and Charles pledged their allegiance, and, by April, England, too, had lent her nominal support. Accordingly, the door was also neatly opened for Wolsey to conduct negotiations of his own with France, which steadily ripened throughout the summer. By October, indeed, representatives from Francis duly appeared in England, and in order to counter Charles's suspicions, two English envoys were at the same time sent to Spain with a view to playing down the significance of the French visit. Not surprisingly, all negotiations were handled in such secrecy that Thomas More was inclined to believe 'that the king himself scarcely knows in what state matters are'.

But with characteristic panache and ingenuity, Wolsey was already looking beyond amity with France and conceiving of something altogether grander than his Holy Father's scheme – nothing less, in fact, than a 'universal peace' within Europe, with none other than himself as the sole architect in the name of his sovereign lord, Henry. As an essential preliminary, Francis would have to be appeased over the loss of Tournai, which still rankled with all Frenchmen. But the King of France was willing to buy and Henry willing to sell in return for an annual pension of £15,000, while Wolsey, in his turn, was more than willing to surrender his claim to the bishopric for a round sum of £12,000. The matter of Scotland was also taken in hand with the French agreeing that the Duke of Albany, who had returned home on a visit in June 1517, should be kept there. To cement the peace once and for all, Henry's 2-year-old daughter, Mary, was to be betrothed to the dauphin. And as a means of dispelling the mutual suspicion which might undermine peace in the longer term it was also agreed, at Wolsey's very specific urging, that Francis and Henry should from this point onwards meet one another regularly.

It was around this fragile accord with France, then, that the whole grandiose plan for a Europe-wide peace was to be constructed. As early as January 1518 Wolsey had drafted the main outline of his scheme, and with the help of the Archbishop of Paris, who had travelled to London in secret, he soon made sufficient progress to write to Pope Leo, Maximilian and Charles for their help in securing a permanent truce. With sufficient moral pressure, it seemed, the unimaginable could indeed become a reality: Habsurg-Valois rivalry might, against all odds, be terminated once and for all, leaving Italy free at last from invaders, and allowing Rome to regain her former authority.

Naturally enough, the sealing of this 'universal peace' was of such significance that it would have to be marked with fitting celebrations, and the pomp and junketing that accompanied the initial Anglo-French component of the treaty was quite without parallel. In late September the largest French embassy ever to enter England arrived in London. Some 600 horsemen in all, along with another seventy mules, made their way through crowded streets amid brilliant banners, beating drums and fanfares. The English, not wishing to be outdone, sent the Earl of Surrey accompanied by the same number of riders to lead the procession alongside Bonnivet, High Admiral of France. A smaller delegation, meanwhile, sailed down to Greenwich to be welcomed by Henry and Wolsey in person.

But it was not until Sunday, 2 October that events were to reach their fitting climax, for on that day England and France formally committed themselves to maintain their part of the cardinal's multilateral peace. They did so, appropriately enough, at the high altar of St Paul's Cathedral, following a Mass which Wolsey himself celebrated with a splendour that was said to have defied exaggeration. Assisted, as always, by abbots and bishops as well as priests, Wolsey not only held centre stage but appeared to own it, and it was no coincidence that the feast which followed was held at his very own York Place.

Giustiniani leaves no doubt either about the splendour in store for all those lucky enough to have been present. The whole banqueting hall was, it seems, so sumptuously decorated that the Italian fancied himself 'in the tower of Chosroes, where that monarch caused divine honour to be paid to him'. All involved were served with 'countless dishes of confections and other delicacies', and 'after gratifying their palates', we are told, the guests also 'gratified their eyes and hands'. Feasting was followed by music, masques and dancing, and 'large bowls, filled with ducats and dice, were placed on the tables for such as liked to gamble' before dancing recommenced until midnight. It was, said Giustiniani, an event 'the like of which, I fancy, was never given by Cleopatra or Caligula'.

Two days later, proxy marriage celebrations between the infant Princess Mary and the dauphin occurred at Greenwich, and on the following day Wolsey, Henry and Bonnivet concluded all outstanding business in private, while Campeggio, the papal legate, was left to wait outside in the corridor. Most important of all, it was now finally settled that Henry and Francis should meet each other near Calais at the earliest convenient opportunity.

Before many weeks had passed the remaining powers – Spain, the Holy Roman Empire and the papacy, along with Venice and a number of other Italian states – had all signed Wolsey's treaty and in due course Portugal and Denmark, plus another eleven principalities, would also follow suit. Under the treaty's terms any state that became the victim of aggression was to appeal to the other signatories, who would issue a collective request for any invading power to withdraw its troops. If, after a month, the aggressor remained resolute, all were to declare war in a conflict that was to increase in intensity by stages. No state, moreover, could forbid the passage through its territory of any army coming to the aid of a country in danger and there were also strict clauses forbidding the hire of Swiss mercenaries.

The scheme's boldness was undeniable, and arguably only someone of Wolsey's limitless imagination and energy – not to mention audacity – could ever have fashioned it. Only in Rome was the cardinal's plan greeted with outright cynicism. There, predictably, it was regarded with jealousy and seen as nothing less than a crude hijacking of the pope's own proposal. It was noted, too, how papal hopes for a crusade had been conveniently downgraded in Wolsey's agreement. But most of all the treaty was seen as a sign of possible things to come. 'From it,' commented Cardinal Giulio de Medici, 'we can tell what the Holy See and the Pope have to expect from the English chancellor.'

Elsewhere, however, the praise flowed freely. Giustiniani, 'knowing the cardinal to be greedy of glory and covetous of praise,' told Wolsey that he would win immortal fame by his actions, 'for whereas the pope had laboured to effect a quinquennial truce, his lordship had made a perpetual peace; and whereas such a union of the Christian powers was usually concluded at Rome, this confederacy had been concluded in England'. Old Bishop Fox, meanwhile, was especially delighted at his former pupil's achievement. 'I doubt not,' he informed Wolsey on 30 October:

> that there be some *invide et malivoli obtrectatores* [envious and malevolent detractors]; but undoubtedly, my lord God continuing it, it shall be the best deed that ever was done for the realm of England; and after the King's Highness, the laud and praise shall be to you a perpetual memory.

But, as usual, the most effusive praise of all seems to have flowed from the pen of Erasmus, who saw Wolsey's efforts as the final fulfilment of Christian enlightenment. Seven years earlier, when Julius II had formed the Holy League with Spain and Venice to defend the unity of the Church by expelling France from northern Italy, the Dutch scholar had deplored the coming bloodshed. 'I was dreaming of an age that really was golden and isles that were truly blessed,' he wrote from London, 'and then I woke up [...] when that Julian trumpet sounded all the world to arms.' Now, however, Erasmus's dreams seemed at last to have become a reality. 'I see a truly golden age coming,' he told Wolsey in 1518, 'if that mind of yours should persist with some number of our rulers. He, under whose auspices they are made, will reward your most holy efforts; and eloquence, alike in Latin and in Greek, will celebrate with eternal monuments your heart, for to help the human race.'

All had been achieved, moreover, in the face of the most formidable obstacles. There was deeply entrenched distrust and bigotry to contend with on both sides of the Channel; French children were still reared on stories about the Hundred Years War, when English 'no-goods with tails' had ravaged their lands, while many' Englishmen remained convinced that French peasants were so backward that they walked barefoot and drank only water. Nor was English hostility confined to their Gallic counterparts, it seems, for at the height of negotiations one of Wolsey's countrymen wrote to declare in no uncertain terms how 'it is a true saying that the Germans are tipplers, the French unchaste, the Spaniards thieves, the Scots perfidious, the Danes bloodthirsty'.

At the same time, Wolsey's reluctance to delegate encumbered him with a mountain of petty chores. On the one hand, as he struggled with the intricacies of the balance of power in Europe, there were the preparations for Queen Margaret's return to Scotland to attend to, as well as the careful arrangement of her affairs once she was there. The issue of passports and letters of safe conduct to all attending dignitaries was also overseen by Wolsey in person, along with the responsibilities he had recently acquired from Pope Leo as an apostolic collector of funds for the building of St Peter's in Rome. Harassed as well by the ongoing clashes between town and gown at Oxford, he still found time, nevertheless, to attend to the ponds and palings about the park at Hampton Court and, last but not least, to intervene in a case of horse theft involving the Marquess of Dorset.

However, if Wolsey's latest venture was nothing short of mind-boggling in terms of its ambition and the effort it entailed, its real benefits were to prove minimal and the optical illusion of English influence that it created woefully short-lived. Martin Luther had already sown the seeds of religious turmoil in Europe the year before, and predictably the projected crusade upon which Wolsey's scheme was supposedly premised never materialised. Syria and Egypt would remain under Turkish control for another three and a half centuries, and while the sovereigns of Europe were collecting tithes from their clergy for a holy war waged in the name of brotherly concord, the Emperor Maximilian was achieving his final flourish by dying with typical inconvenience on 19 January 1519. Thereby, he would plunge Europe into a succession struggle for his crown, which shattered at a single stroke the whole balance of power that had been established at such pains only four months earlier.

[The resulting election for a new Holy Roman Emperor marked the beginning of what would become an interminable struggle for hegemony in Europe between France and the Empire. Charles of Spain, bolstered by his blood relationship with the dead emperor, pressed ahead with his claim confidently, while Francis I was supported in his candidature by the pope and, like Charles, lavished exorbitant sums of money on sweeteners and outright bribes. Even Henry VIII proved as willing as ever to lash out money that England could ill afford, in order to press his own tepid claims, though Wolsey secretly shared the opinion of Richard Pace, who was duly rushed into action yet again on his sovereign's behalf. 'Here,' said Pace of the imperial crown, 'is the most dearest merchandise that ever was sold; and after mine opinion, it shall be the worst that ever was bought, to him that shall obtain it.'

The outcome, however, was always a foregone conclusion, since Germans would never tolerate an English ruler, let alone a French one, and on 28 June 1519 Charles of Spain was duly elected King of the Romans. As it transpired, the whole tawdry contest had paralysed the German government and would, in the longer term not only destroy any last hopes of concerted action against the Ottoman Empire, but directly presage the downfall of Rhodes and the Turkish annihilation of Hungarian forces at the Battle of Mohács. Ultimately it would also bring the newly invigorated forces of the Holy Roman Empire sweeping into Italy as conquerors in their own right.

With his 'universal peace' therefore reduced almost at once to the status of a dead man walking, Wolsey once again fell back upon pomp, spectacle and sleight-of-hand to maintain at least the myth of English mastery. Nor, of course, did he have much option, since the abandonment of lost causes that were dear to his master's heart was unlikely, even now, to be a healthy option. In effect, the only alternative was to direct all energy towards the meeting between Henry and Francis, which had been agreed earlier in London, and to ensure that it should take the form of the most dazzling spectacle possible. If, Wolsey reasoned, a truly unparalleled chivalric extravaganza could now be staged, it would appeal to Henry's most deeply held romantic sentiments while placing him, ostensibly at least, at the very centre of European affairs. Moreover, by advertising the King of England's friendship with France in the most vivid way possible, there was also the tantalising prospect that the new Holy Roman Emperor might himself be forced into offering an alternative alliance on even better terms.

Throughout the closing months of 1519, therefore, Wolsey began the colossal task of arranging a meeting between the Kings of England and France at the place just outside Calais that would become known to posterity as the Field of Cloth of Gold. It was intended that the event should be staged the following summer, and this meant that there was no time to lose. As events unfolded, therefore, Wolsey was in almost continual communication with Francis himself, as well as his mother, Louise of Savoy. And he lost no opportunity to charm as well as cajole, for when a new French prince was born, he at once dispatched a christening gift of £100 for the nurse, the four rockers of the royal crib, and the gentlewomen of the queen's chamber. The French, in their turn, also played the friendship game with some aplomb, for Francis duly named his son Henry, while the Grand Master of France told Wolsey directly that 'it had not been seen or heard of one man being a cardinal to be in so great esteem, trust and reputation of both the Kings of England and France as your grace is'.

Predictably, however, there were also niggling causes of delay and frustration for Wolsey to overcome in his tireless efforts 'to bind the two majesties together in a knot of perdurable amity'. The young Englishmen who had been sent on embassy to the court of Francis, for example, were soon said to be ill from 'the haunting of harlots', while the French Queen Claude proved 'very sickly' during her latest confinement. Much more fundamentally, there was also the question of where exactly the projected meeting would take place, which was made especially thorny by the time-honoured principle that an inferior prince was always obliged to visit the superior rather than vice versa. Not surprisingly, therefore, Wolsey wanted the event to take place at Guisnes within the English Pale of Calais, while the French suggested Ardres, some 10 miles away on their own territory.

Yet by December a compromise had been reached and in January the French king gave Wolsey full authority to proceed to the detailed planning of what would now become not only a political conference, but also a grand tournament, a festival of arts and, not least of all, a perfect opportunity for a series of state banquets that would surpass any staged hitherto. Everything about the event, in fact, was specifically designed to conjure up a long-vanished chivalric past that still captivated and titillated the rulers and elites of the day. It was said, for instance, that every knight of the Christian world would be invited to run at the tilt and show his prowess with sword and lance – something that was especially likely to tickle the interest of Francis and, above all, Henry.

Wolsey, too, was eager for his share of the limelight. Indeed, it was suggested by Polydore Vergil that he 'longed like a peacock to display his many-adorned tail, that is, to exhibit his special appearance, in the land of France'. Twelve chaplains, fifty gentlemen and 237 servants were to travel with him, in comparison to the 140 men apiece allocated to the two dukes that would be making the journey and the mere 70 allowed for Archbishop Warham. But more than this, the cardinal would be at the centre of events: wining, dining, easing, dealing, confiding, advising, posing and charming as occasion required.

Certainly, Wolsey was in his element as the preparations forged ahead in the early spring of 1520 with all the intensity and thoroughness of the military campaign that he had organised seven years earlier. In a characteristic fit of enthusiasm Francis had once told Henry that he was determined to meet him, even if he came with no more than a page and a lackey, but as the proposal hardened into reality, both monarchs soon sought to outstrip the other in terms of the grandness of their plans. This, after all, was as much a contest as a reconciliation – an unprecedented opportunity to flaunt, assert and confirm the superiority of one realm and its prince over another.

Ultimately some 5,172 Englishmen and women would now be transported across the Channel before the end of May with all their requirements for a full month. The king's immense entourage eventually numbered 3,997 persons on its own, including the Archbishop of Canterbury and five bishops, two dukes, one marquess, ten earls and twenty barons, not to mention 200 members of his household guard. And whatever Wolsey's achievements as a diplomat, no one can fairly deny him his rightful place as the greatest picnic-planner in history on the basis of what he now organised. In all, provisions costing £8,831 and a further £1,568 for wine and beer were duly assembled at Calais, and every last culinary detail was personally overseen by him, from the ordering of 700 conger eels, 2,014 sheep, 26 dozen heron and a bushel of mustard, right down to the purchase of cream for the king's cakes at a price of £1 0s 10d.

At the same time a countless number of other details, great and small, all came under Wolsey's personal supervision. The most meticulous attention was given to the task of safely transporting 2,865 horses across the Channel, including the particularly hefty Neapolitan breed which English knights preferred for jousting. The steel mill at Greenwich was to be dismantled and set up at Guisnes castle, which the English had decided to use as their base. And Wolsey also arranged for the erection of a suitably splendid palace of brick and timber to serve as the king's temporary lodging during his stay.

In the event, the additional plan for a banqueting house was abandoned in favour of a vast highly ornate tent. However, the palace itself, which was distinguished by the amount of glass in it, would still include three chambers for the king on the first floor, the largest of which was more spacious than the White Hall at Westminster. Measuring 124ft in length, 42ft in width and 27ft in height, it was adjoined by an 80ft dining room and withdrawing room covering some 1,620 square feet. Each chamber, meanwhile, was to be hung with cloth of gold, embroidered with pearls and fine jewels, emblazoned with Tudor roses and portcullises and lit by a thousand candles. And, in the courtyard outside, streams of malmsey and claret, free for all, would flow from a fountain bearing statues of Cupid and Bacchus.

Even Leonardo da Vinci himself, according to one Italian, could not have surpassed the design of the palace, while another, not without some justification, compared it to the fairytale palaces of Ariosto's *Orlando Furioso*. The state apartments would be equipped with Turkish carpets, chairs of estate and gold and silver plate brought across from Greenwich and Richmond by the Lord Chamberlain's men. For the chapel, meanwhile, bejewelled vestments, canopies and chalices were to be transported specially from Westminster Abbey. Such, indeed, was the scale of effort involved that England virtually emptied its shores of carpenters, builders, masons, glaziers and artists as preparations reached a climax in late April and May.

While the king was cosseted in unprecedented luxury, the needs of those close to him were not forgotten either. Queen Catherine would be lodged in her own separate apartments within the palace, while the Duchess of Suffolk, as Dowager Queen of France, was assigned quarters next to her. Henry's chief courtiers were also allocated rooms in Guisnes Castle itself, while the rest were to stay in the encampment of nearly 400 tents that Richard Gibson, master of the king's hales, tents and pavilions, intended to erect in the neighbouring fields.

Wolsey, naturally, was accorded his own suite next to the king's, and it was no coincidence that his coat of arms was made to feature particularly prominently amid the vast array of heraldic displays which could eventually be seen everywhere at the site. Appropriately enough, the arms themselves recalled his East Anglian origins through the sable shield and cross engrailed of the fourteenth-century Ufford earls of Suffolk and the azure leopards' faces of their successors to the titles, the de la Poles. His cardinalate, on the other hand, was depicted by means of Leo X's purple lion, and there was room too for the choughs that the College of Arms believed to have been the arms born by Thomas Becket, whom Wolsey had adopted as his patron. As supporters, there were dragons holding aloft pillars, the symbol of his legatine authority.

If showmanship and attention to detail were any measure of a servant's worth, Wolsey would truly surpass all contenders by his efforts across the Channel in the summer of 1520. And it was only fitting, perhaps, that when the waiting was over and the mighty English horde had finally made its way across the Channel on the final day of May, Wolsey should be the first to sally forth towards the French camp to arrange the time and place for the two sovereigns to meet in person. Accompanied by more attendants than the dukes of Suffolk and

Buckingham and the Archbishop of Canterbury combined, his retinue caused the greatest possible stir.

Fifty mounted gentlemen in crimson velvet preceded him, with fifty ushers bearing gold maces 'as large as a man's head'. His standing gold cross with its jewelled crucifix was also borne before him, and the richly trapped mule upon which he inevitably rode was surrounded by dozens of lackeys wearing his insignia. Behind him, there then rode a clutch of bishops and other churchmen, including the Grand Prior of the Knights of St John of Jerusalem, along with 100 mounted archers of the king's guard – their bows bent and at the ready – who brought up the rear.

Moreover, when Henry and Francis finally met in person forty-eight hours later on Corpus Christi day, Wolsey stage-managed every detail of the event with comparable skill. At the sound of a cannon shot from Guisnes Castle, both men left their respective camps late in the afternoon and made for two artificial hillocks built at opposite entrances to the 'Golden Valley' at which their rendezvous was to occur. In preparation, a little pavilion had been erected at the exact centre of the valley, where the first conversation between the two rulers was due to take place. But before they entered, arm-in-arm and accompanied only by Wolsey and the French admiral Bonnivet, each king abandoned his retinue and rode alone towards the other in full view of the thousands of spectators crowding the surrounding ridges. Nor did the ensuing climax disappoint. Indeed, the lavish display of feigned affection, which stunned all onlookers, caused one Italian eyewitness to swear that Henry and Francis proceeded to throw their arms around each other more than thirty times.

There followed three weeks of feasting, jousting, carolling and carousing during which the myth of friendship and concord was played out with tireless energy by all concerned. Francis gave banquets for Henry's knights, Henry for Francis's knights. Queen Catherine and Queen Claude also lavished splendid banquets upon one another, while their two husbands dined together in a hall lined with pink brocade. Likewise, Francis entertained Catherine and Henry Claude, just as Wolsey himself entertained Francis's mother, Louise of Savoy. According to one account, an inexhaustible supply of dishes was served at each of these banquets, though another commentator noted drily that the guests of honour did nothing but converse on one occasion, having eaten before they came.

In the meantime, the craftsmen of the weapons forge worked furiously as the knights of both countries broke hundreds of lances and fought valiantly at the barriers. Francis himself 'shivered spears like reeds,' it was said, 'and never missed a stroke', while Henry lived up to his reputation as an expert jouster, tiring six horses in rapid succession one day, 'laughing the whole time, being in truth very merry, and remaining in the lists for upwards of two hours'. Rather less conveniently, Francis experienced an unexpected defeat at the hands of an English knight named Weston Brown, suffering a slight wound and momentary humiliation in the process, though any loss of face was soon made good when the French king threw his English counterpart to the ground in an impromptu wrestling contest, albeit one with potentially explosive consequences. Even so, both men eventually emerged with their egos intact, since each was said to have surpassed himself in various forms of mock combat, dealing blows 'with such force that the fire sprang out of their armour'.

Yet for all its splendour and hearty back-slappery, and all the undying promises of Anglo-French friendship that it generated, the Field of Cloth of Gold amounted to little more than an unrivalled exercise in empty posturing. Shortly before the sails of Henry's ships billowed in the breeze that carried them over to Calais, Wolsey had already organised a visit to England by the new ruler of the Holy Roman Empire, only six days earlier. And though this meeting at Canterbury was consistent, in theory at least, with the principles of 'universal peace', the implication was clear enough – particularly as Charles had been trying to abort plans for the Field of Cloth of Gold since April and would in no way consent to a personal meeting with Francis.

Meanwhile, Wolsey's firm professions of commitment to Anglo-French reconciliation had served as a most convenient means of increasing the emperor's inclination to ply him with patronage. As planning for the meeting with Francis went forward Charles had been in frequent correspondence with the cardinal, and in February wrote to thank him personally for his efforts in maintaining peace and for arranging a meeting with Henry. In order to secure Wolsey's continuing good offices, moreover, Charles also offered him the bishopric of Pace and its substantial incomes, as well as a pension of 7,000 ducats. More importantly still, before his departure from Dover Charles had promised Wolsey his support whenever the next papal vacancy occurred, and won, in return, the guarantee of a further meeting with Henry as soon as events at the Field of Cloth of Gold had been concluded.

Even before Wolsey and Henry had set off for Calais on the last day of May, then, the long-term prospects for peace with France were already ebbing. In truth, it was always going to require more than a few weeks of mealy-mouthed cavorting across the Channel for Henry to shed his deep-seated antipathy to France and craving for her crown. Nor is this something that Wolsey can ever seriously have doubted. He was certainly no lover of war and remained keen to play the peacemaker whenever opportunity allowed, especially if such an opportunity might be used to further the illusion of his master's central importance to European affairs. But now he was driven more and more uneasily by the king's ambition, and now, more ominously still, he was increasingly a hostage to it, feeding it by whatever methods he could, in order to prevent it from consuming him.

Pomp and panache, after all, could only be used to camouflage painful realities for so long. Indeed, from most perspectives the entire spectacle at the Field of Cloth of Gold merely reflected the cardinal's unbending determination to satisfy his sovereign's weakness for an extravagant show at which he could be the star performer. And surely enough, as soon as the English camp at Guisnes had been dismantled, both Henry and Wolsey were hastening to Gravelines to consult with Charles once more. Within a day of this initial rendezvous, moreover, all three were making their way back to Calais, where Sir Edward Belknap, General Surveyor of the Crown Lands, had constructed a huge wooden hall, lit by 'a thousand torches and other lights of wax' and topped by a vast canvas roof depicting the heavens. It was here that the serious business of negotiation was to begin, and here, too, that the hollow overtures to France of recent weeks were finally given the lie.

For while the French king had done his best to gain admittance to this subsequent meeting, even hinting that he required no elaborate accommodation and would come instead as a member of Henry's entourage, the resulting snub was anything but subtle. Two French noblewomen, the Lady Vendôme and her daughter-in-law, gained access to Calais on business and a few French nobles attended the masquerade ball subsequently given for the emperor by his English counterpart. But this was as close as any French subject got to the conference itself, since the game at hand, as all could plainly see, was a double one. Uppermost in the ensuing discussions was the question of marriage between Henry's daughter Mary and her cousin the emperor, notwithstanding the child's existing betrothal to the dauphin. And while it would take another year for firm agreement to ensue, the die was already well and truly cast. The 'defensive' alliance made only a month or so earlier at Canterbury during Charles's recent visit was duly confirmed, and arrangements set in place for a further meeting the following year. Nor was the French king long in looking to his own interests. For he too was swiftly hatching war, this time in Navarre: a war which, by 1522, Henry would have joined as Charles's ally. In a world of clockwork diplomacy, where subterfuge, suspicion and tawdry self-interest were the norm, how could things have ever been otherwise?

13

'Butcher's Cur'

When Henry VIII returned from his celebrated encounter with Francis I in the high summer of 1520, flushed with the illusion of success and brimming with false confidence of greater things to come, the position of his chief minister may well have seemed more secure than ever. To all outward appearances he had brought lasting peace to Europe and laid the balance of power at his master's feet. 'Christendom owes much to you', the Archbishop of Sens informed Wolsey on 13 July, precisely one week after Leonardo Lerodan, the Doge of Venice, had sent a similar note of hearty congratulation. Both Francis I and Charles V had also heaped their warmest messages of flattery, friendship and great promise upon the cardinal's shoulders, and now their English counterpart was equally prepared, it seems, to recognise his minister's crowning achievement. Success of any kind, after all, could always be guaranteed to show the King of England at his generous best, and never more so than when his own personal glory was involved. Accordingly, Wolsey was graciously granted the canonry of the Collegiate Church of St Mary and St George at Windsor Castle.

Yet fame and fortune are fickle playmates, and Wolsey's plans were as fragile as they were ambitious. The French for their part would prove slow in reducing their fortifications at Ardres, and it was not long either before they were once more shaping to invade Italy. In the event, the projected alliance between England, the Empire and the pope would also swiftly falter as Charles temporised over his projected marriage to the Princess Mary, and the sickly Leo X sought shelter from the French invader by promptly arranging a private treaty with him.

The emperor's attitude was 'far discrepant from the overtures made us at Calais and by his ambassadors in England', Wolsey was to inform Bishop Tunstall, the English ambassador to Charles. 'We marvel at the sudden change.'

Nor was this the sum of Wolsey's mounting problems. For Henry himself was now no longer a callow prince in need of a mentor. On the contrary, he was a rampant, calculating adult in search of both a miracle-worker and ready-made scapegoat, and any impression that he was under his minister's thumb could not have been more deceptive. Apart from the cardinal's weekly visits to Greenwich when the king was in residence there, the amount of direct contact between the two men had always been surprisingly limited, and the king and his minister were generally more likely to meet for public worship or at the banqueting table than for private discussions. As such, the possibility that Wolsey's primacy might be undermined in his absence was ever present, and whether the dangerous art of deferential manipulation that he had practised so deftly for so long could, in any case, be conducted indefinitely was far from certain. Indeed, those who saw Wolsey as some kind of ubiquitous master-puppeteer were wholly deceived. While the shark basked and his needs were tended continually, the cardinal could be sure of rich pickings. But success in this case bred ever greater hunger, and the fear that Wolsey's primacy might be undermined by new favourites or scheming enemies was already beginning to nag him with growing urgency.

So when Henry headed for a prolonged spree of hunting in Berkshire upon his return to England, it was perhaps small wonder that his chief minister sought solace and repose in pious pilgrimage to the shrine of the Virgin at Walsingham. For the last year his health had been increasingly fragile, and though he had overcome his body's creeping rebellion by a potent mixture of raw willpower, ego and adrenalin, springing mainly, no doubt, from a pulsing fear of failure, the longer-term consequences for his constitution were predictable. Throughout his forlorn attempts to secure the imperial crown for his master he had been grievously stricken with the 'murr', an intense swelling of the mucous membrane that meant he could 'not hold up his head'. During the spring, moreover, continual bouts of dysentery and diarrhoea had threatened indefinite postponement of the all-important meeting between the French and English kings. It was under these circumstances that the foundering cardinal had finally been granted a papal dispensation to eat meat during Lent. But his commitments neither paused nor slackened. And if the vultures were not quite circling at this point, they were nevertheless hatching all the while – and hatching, it must be said, on all fronts.

In May 1519 it had been necessary for Wolsey to stage a minor purge of the Privy Chamber after a troublesome clique of young courtiers, led by Nicholas

Carew and that one-eyed, swashbuckling 'Vicar of Hell' Francis Bryan had caused general offence by their boisterous behaviour and forwardness with the king. They had returned, it seems, from a stay in France 'all French in eating, drinking and apparel, and in French vices and brags, so that all the estates of England were by them laughed at'. Even more provocatively, they were too 'familiar and homely' with their sovereign, observed the chronicler Edward Hall, 'and played such light touches with him that they forgot themselves'. But though these 'minions' were actually of limited political significance in their own right, they were still considered by many to have 'enjoyed very great authority in the kingdom'. Indeed, the French ambassador, who relied in part on information from compatriots held hostage at the English court, was convinced that Wolsey was behind the dismissal of the minions for fear that they might use their influence against him. And while their removal in the first instance was neither fussy nor troublesome, they nevertheless exposed a lightness and potential inconstancy on their master's part, which could not be altogether ignored. For it was widely mooted that they had been 'the very soul of the king'; and in little more than a year they would be back, both aggrieved and unchastened.

Albeit with the best of intentions, Wolsey had also alienated influential sections of the landed elite by his bold, if misguided, attacks upon one of the most widely resented causes of social injustice at that time. The 'enclosing' of land to facilitate large-scale sheep farming was responsible, or so it was believed, for widespread depopulation of villages and hamlets, as well as food shortages, inflation and vagrancy, and although a law of 1515 had required that land enclosed for pasture should be restored to cultivation within a year, there was every indication that it would remain a dead letter unless vigorous administrative measures were taken for its enforcement. Accordingly, Wolsey appointed commissions of enquiry in both 1517 and 1518, and followed them by a decree ordering that all enclosures, hedges and ditches made in the past thirty-two years should be abolished.

In consequence, some 264 powerful men across the country, including Bishop Richard Fox, now found themselves arraigned before the Court of Chancery to defend their actions under a law of which many were genuinely ignorant. In the main, they were the very people upon whose shoulders the chief burden of local administration lay, and they were quick to assume that Wolsey's primary motive was not so much the 'good of the common weal' as a cheap desire to court the general populace at their expense. Nor, ironically, did the vaunted architect of sweeping agrarian reform actually succeed in achieving his ends. 'There was never thing done in England more for the commonwealth than to redress these enormous decays of towns and making of enclosures', wrote

John Longland, Bishop of Lincoln, in 1528. Yet he implored the cardinal to visit the countryside to witness the shocking scale of the ruined hamlets, forsaken ploughs and grinding poverty that still remained. In the event, Wolsey had been distracted by other problems and failed to create adequate machinery for helping those husbandmen, labourers and landless vagrants who were most in need. As so often, he had started without finishing, and in doing so he stirred a hornet's nest, for ultimately, at the time of his fall, it would be claimed quite rightly that he had acted *ultra vires* in carrying out the limited provisions of 1515 and seeking 'to execute the statute of enclosing'.

This, however, was only one aspect of Wolsey's much broader unpopularity. While religious zealots now depicted him as little less than the Whore of Babylon incarnate – an all-corrupting influence who flouted Christ's teaching at every level and flagrantly encouraged his fellow churchmen to abuse their vows of chastity – even the pope, it seems, was his enemy. There was 'no man,' it was reported, 'on the face of this earth that his Holiness so much detested'. Merchants, meanwhile, were inclined to twist the knife further by accusing him of profiting from loans to foreigners out of the royal treasury. Nor, for that matter, were the humbler folk, whose cause he claimed to champion, any more inclined to warm to the cardinal's efforts. Instead, they railed against his lofty pretensions and damned the baseness of his origins and motives. Rumours originating at court that 'he was the king's bawd, showing him what women were most wholesome, and best of complexions' were soon being savoured in the capital's grimier quarters, and it was no coincidence that the rioting apprentices of Evil May Day had threatened to kill the upstart favourite of their king. 'Almost all men hated him and disdained him', recorded Edward Hall, and many were both predicting and praying for his ruin. A brewer, so Wolsey's own spies reported, had claimed to 'see by prophecy that a great man being bishop, should ride upon a high horse and should have as great a fall as ever had man'. Elsewhere, a certain Thomas Gyldon was predicting in 1520 that 'within this two year the said cardinal would have the shamefullest fall that ever chanced in England'. If so, added Gyldon, he would give £100 from his own purse to see that time come soon.

Of far greater long-term significance, however, were the personal polemics launched against Wolsey by a series of vindictive literary assassins who berated his 'brazen insolence' and crafted a venomous template, which moulded both popular and scholarly perceptions for centuries to come. Few were more influential in this regard than the Italian Polydore Vergil, who had arrived in England in 1502 as a papal tax collector and soon obtained a series of ecclesiastical preferments, including the prebend of Oxgate in St Paul's, which brought him into the thick of affairs. More significantly still, as a humanist scholar whose *Adagia* and *De inventoribus rerum* had earned him a significant literary reputation, he had been invited by Henry VII to write a detailed history of England from earliest times. And though it was not revised for publication until long after Wolsey's death, it was this same history that eventually became the source of so much hostility towards its by then defenceless victim.

The scalding sentiments expressed by Vergil were, however, firmly founded in a personal grievance dating back to the year 1514, when he had been dispatched to Rome by Wolsey to support his quest for the cardinalate. At that time, while the Italian was away on his errand, he had been overlooked for promotion and the result was a chain of events culminating in simmering enmity. For when Vergil discovered his 'betrayal' by the very man whose cause he had been faithfully attempting to assist, he indiscreetly penned his complaints to his master, Cardinal Adrian of the papal curia. Worse still, his letter, written in 1515, reflected badly not only on Wolsey but upon the king himself, and after its interception the guilty cleric found himself confined for a spell to the bleak hospitality of the Tower. Nor would a swift pardon, after what amounted to an almost blasphemously abject apology on his behalf, reconcile the slighted Italian. For when in the later years of Henry VIII's reign he finally came to pen Book XXVII of his *Anglica Historia*, covering the years 1513 to 1537, he gave full vent to his residing hatred.

While all the earlier books of Vergil's history display a refreshingly critical attitude to the interpretation of events, earning him a rightful reputation as one of the first 'modern' historians, he could not, it seems, restrain his personal grudges when besmirching the man who had once imprisoned him. On the contrary, in one purple passage after another, Wolsey was blasted, damned and derided as a man thoroughly corrupted by vanity and self-interest. 'The enjoyment of such an abundance of good fortune,' observed Vergil, 'is to be reckoned most praiseworthy if it is showered upon sober, moderate and self-controlled men, who are not proud in their power, nor are made arrogant with their money, nor vaunt themselves in other fortunate circumstances.' Yet none of these characteristics applied, it seems, to Wolsey, 'who acquiring so many offices at almost the same time, became so proud that he considered himself the peer of Kings'. 'Nothing,' we are told, 'so much pleased him as worldly vanity, in comparison with which he held true glory of small worth.' And the 'odious' prelate was not only arrogant, it seems, but incompetent and dishonest to boot – a man 'unique in his irresponsibility', 'headlong and erratic in all his judgements', and one whose 'habit of untruthfulness went far beyond the bounds of diplomatic necessity'. 'Nothing,' Vergil concluded, 'was more old-established in Wolsey (indeed from his youth onwards) than lying, which is the mark of a shameless man.'

The verdict was harsh, to say the least, but the mud stuck, and from the time that Vergil's book was published in 1555 the die was irrevocably cast – firmly reinforced, it must be said, by a merciless deluge of vitriol hailing down upon Wolsey from all points of the literary compass throughout the 1520s. On the one hand, there was the biting handiwork of Alexander Barclay for the cardinal to contend with. This particular Benedictine monk first achieved fame in 1509 for his translation of Sebastian Brant's *Das Narrenschiff* or 'Ship of Fools', but in enjoying the patronage of the Duke of Norfolk, whom he praised as 'the flower of chivalry', he did not miss the opportunity in his first eclogue on the miseries and manners of courtiers to take a passing stab at Wolsey as well as Bishop Fox. And while the former was sufficiently forgiving to employ him in writing decorative mottoes and epigrams for the pavilions at Field of Cloth of Gold, Barclay could not curb his 'opprobrious and blasphemous words' in the longer term. By 1528, indeed, Wolsey's spies would locate him in Lutheran Germany, hobnobbing with William Tyndale and denouncing the cardinal as a tyrant.

Then there were personal criticisms emanating from the pulpit, which Wolsey also treated with commendable restraint. In this case the main offender was Robert Barnes, prior of the Augustinian monastery of Barnwell in Cambridge, who spent almost his entire adult life venting his evangelical spleen against any powerful symbol of ecclesiastical corruption conveniently to hand. During a scathing sermon delivered on Christmas Eve 1525, Barnes saw fit to contrast the simplicity of Christ's nativity with the pomp of cardinals and bishops, calling upon them to spend their money on alms for the poor rather than ostentatious display. Nor, predictably, could he forgo a direct gibe at Wolsey that made an official inquiry into his remarks inevitable. 'He wears a pair of red gloves – I should have said bloody gloves', Barnes had declaimed from the pulpit.

Yet when Wolsey heard the friar's case personally in London, he displayed considerable forbearance, even after the accused gave no hint of retreat. Indeed, when Barnes remained recalcitrant over the issue of Wolsey's wealth by boldly dismissing the claim that symbols of rank were necessary 'to maintain the commonwealth', the cardinal appeared amused by his response, commending his sharpness, and suggesting that he make an informal submission on the spot in order to avoid the stress and more serious consequences of trial by episcopal court. When Barnes declined, Wolsey calmly wished him luck, though the ultimate reward for such generosity was further recalcitrance and deceit. For, after doing public penance for heresy, the guilty party nevertheless proceeded to escape house arrest at Northampton, leaving an impudent 'farewell' letter to the cardinal who thereafter swore that he would recapture him even if it cost him 'a great deal of money'.

Perhaps it was partly as a result of such ingratitude that Wolsey was not always so generous to his detractors thereafter. Certainly, a farce produced for the Christmas festivities at Gray's Inn in 1526 by a young lawyer named Simon Fish seems at first sight to have provoked a decidedly sensitive response. Taking as its theme the weighty proposition that 'Lord Governance was ruled by Dissipation and Negligence, by whose misdemeanour and evil order Lady Public Weal was put from Governance', there could be no doubting the authors' target, and Fish's decision to act the part of the cardinal in person, aping his pomp and worldliness, did not help matters. But the summary imprisonment of John Rouse and Thomas Moyle, two of the actors, and Fish's enforced flight to Europe struck some as excessive. No doubt savouring the opportunity to sound the voice of reason while his rival smarted, Archbishop Warham, for instance, confessed himself 'sorry that such a matter should be taken in earnest', even though Rouse and his friend were released before long.

Yet in this case, too, Wolsey's ire was not entirely misplaced, especially when it is recalled that Fish, like Alexander Barclay, was soon in residence in Lutheran Germany with William Tyndale and producing his notorious *Supplication of Beggars*, which openly denounced the pope himself as a 'cruel and devilish bloodsupper drunken in the blood of saints and martyrs of Christ'. By the latter part of the 1520s, moreover, the continent was the base for at least two other bitter critics of the cardinal, both of whom were apostate friars. William Roy, for his part, had assisted Fish with the Gray's Inn farce and first met Tyndale in the Netherlands, where he served as his amanuensis in the publication of his English translation of the New Testament. But in 1526 he had gone on to produce a rhyming dialogue of his own, entitled *Rede me and be not Wroth*, which attacked the persecutors of the Lutherans, and specifically compared Wolsey to Pontius Pilate, who found no fault in Jesus but nevertheless acquiesced in his persecution. More significantly still, Roy also encouraged his collaborator, the Greenwich Franciscan Jerome Barlow to write the far more vituperative *Burial of the Mass* (1528), which rang with furious references to 'the vyle bochers sonne' and 'the mastif Curre bred in Ypswitch towne', who, 'more like a god celestial than any creature mortal', preens and parades himself 'with worldly pomp incredible'.

The tone was relentless and, notwithstanding the work's considerable literary demerits, it clearly hit home. For Wolsey was sufficiently furious to dispatch two friars to the continent in a vain attempt to track down the author. But while Barlow's raging satire was as violent as anything else produced at the time, its immediate and longer-term significance was merely powder puff by comparison with the impact of John Skelton, the first, most famous, most skilful and most influential of all Wolsey's critics in print. Sponsored by men and women of high influence and further energised by the bitter pill of his own financial loss and rough treatment at the cardinal's hands, Skelton was a former tutor to Henry VIII who had been lauded as a poet and man of letters by both Lady Margaret Beaufort and Erasmus before swapping the glitter of the Tudor court for the altogether more humdrum obscurity of life in a Norfolk rectory. In 1512, however, his temporary exile from the centre of events came to a sudden and decisive halt when he was appointed poet laureate in succession to the blind French cleric Bernard André. And the results of his return were little short of electrifying, as his eccentric flare for self-advertisement and blatant provocation reached shocking heights.

Predictably, within a year of his return, Wolsey had become the sitting target for Skelton's barbs – just as he would remain over the next decade – and before long the poet's verses about the 'greasy genealogy' of the 'bragging butcher' who 'carrieth a king in his sleeve' were being secretly but widely circulated, nowhere more so than at the court itself. The allusions to Wolsey in Skelton's only play, *Magnificence*, which was probably written in 1516, were actually comparatively mild. In this case the writer focused mainly upon the squandering of the king's wealth by a costly and misconceived foreign policy, and to a lesser extent upon the impact of Wolsey's wars upon the reputation and safety of Englishmen across the Channel. But if none of this was quite the stuff of mortal scandal, *Colyn Cloute*, written in 1521, was altogether another matter – a bitterly trenchant attack upon the corruption of the Church, containing, into the bargain, a number of scarcely veiled references to Wolsey astride his mule in imitation of Christ's humility, yet 'with all gold betrapped', 'richly and warm bewrapped' while 'neighbours die for meat'. And as the poet jangled on, the references to Wolsey's 'high and lordly looks', 'so puffed with pride', became even more pointed, with the cardinal ruling 'both king and kaiser' and great lords forced to 'crouch and kneel before him'.

Yet Skelton's well had by no means run dry. For in autumn of the same year he penned *Speke Parrot*, in which Wolsey was scathingly dismissed as someone 'so bold and so bragging', 'so lordly of his looks and so disdainly' that he merited only disgust. 'So fat a maggot, bred of a flesh fly', railed Skelton. Never was there 'such a filthy gorgon, nor such an epicure'. And while other critics like Barlow would highlight Wolsey's impact upon Church and State in general, Skelton now targeted, above all, the cardinal's apparent readiness to detract from the king's own majesty. Indeed, it was this that made the subsequent *Why Come Ye Not to Courte?* both so effective and so damaging. Written in either 1522 or 1523, the poem satirised the opulence of Wolsey's lifestyle and influence over foreign princes and ambassadors, as well as his control both of canon and common law, all of which far exceeded the king's. But this, once again, was merely part of the picture, for only by 'sorcery or such other loselry', the poet contended, might we fully understand how the king was 'so far blinded' by his 'darling'. 'The great peers of the realm,' we are told, 'dare not look out at doors for dread of the mastiff cur', and his appointment as papal legate, which for Skelton was merely a 'title of pride', had only served to make him more insufferable than ever. Moreover, the same self-interest, arrogance and incompetence also applied to his administration of the law as Lord Chancellor, where in the 'Chamber of Stars, all matters there he mars'. Ultimately, therefore, the choice confronting Wolsey was simple. He must, concluded Skelton, face a headlong fall no less dramatic than Lucifer's or mend his ways at once and 'pill the people no more'.

Clearly the steady, stinging stream of such invective was not something that Wolsey could altogether ignore. The irony, however, was that the poet remained effectively untouchable throughout. Before his attacks gathered momentum, Skelton had taken the wise precaution of securing a residence within the sanctuary of Westminster, a lodging on the south side of the great belfry, costing him the tidy sum of £50 a year. Much more importantly, however, he had acquired the keen support of the Howard faction, led by the second Duke of Norfolk, who like his son after him, quickly realised that his position as Lord Treasurer and the king's foremost general was being progressively undermined by the upstart cardinal's influence. As all knew, the Howards stood for everything that Wolsey lacked – nobility of birth, tradition and feudal exclusiveness – and they had into the bargain an arrogance of blood that matched his own earthier self-confidence. In due course even old Norfolk's daughter-in-law, the Countess of Surrey, would also become a keen advocate of Skelton's verses, and with patrons like these, the poet could well afford his boldness.

Wolsey had little choice, therefore, but to approach the task of silencing him with considerable circumspection. In the event, he would opt to wait, watch, endure and pretend to ignore until his critic began to exhaust both his repertoire and his novelty. If, moreover, the poet could not be intimidated, he might well be 'softened' by other means, and even won over in due course by appropriate enticements, to the extent perhaps that his undoubted talents might actually be used in his former victim's favour. In the meantime the long-suffering cardinal could also take some solace from the fact that the offending verses were still circulating only in manuscript form and were not to be printed for years to come. Nor, of course, did Wolsey forget that the king was still the fulcrum of his political universe and that he, for the present, remained wholly unmoved by Skelton's gibes. As such, the bitter scorn of Skelton might yet be scorned itself.

By 1523 the strain of sanctuary life – not to mention the high rent it entailed in Skelton's case – was assuredly taking its toll upon the poet's stamina. Indeed, within a year of penning *Why Come Ye Not to Courte?* Skelton was ready for an astonishing accommodation with the man he had lambasted so gleefully for more than half a decade. He had, after all, vented his spleen so fully that there was little more to say, and when Wolsey offered gifts and patronage he duly succumbed – not only suddenly but completely, unreservedly and abjectly so. Before long, in *The Merrie Tales*, Skelton would depict himself kneeling to beg forgiveness and beseeching his newfound patron 'to let me lie down and wallow, for I can kneel no longer'. And this was not the only work in which Skelton ate his words and swallowed his pride. In *A Replication Against Certain Young Scholars Abjured of Late*, he excelled himself. Addressing Wolsey in a Latin dedication 'as the most honourable, most mighty, and by far the most reverend father in Christ', he proceeded to pledge his 'humble allegiance' to this 'great and magnificent Chief of Priests' and 'most equitable moderator of all justice'. Not only had the poet's principled stand against clerical decadence therefore evaporated entirely, it had done so at the warming touch of Wolsey's own generosity.

Yet as Skelton's venom waned, his former target's problems were still only beginning, since another altogether more potent card was already emerging in the Howard pack. In 1520, in a temporary wooden chapel built in a single night but splendidly decorated with twenty-four enormous gold candlesticks and golden images of the twelve apostles, Wolsey had concluded proceedings at the Field of Cloth of Gold by singing high and solemn Mass before the monarchs of England and France. Attended by two other cardinals, two legates, four archbishops and ten bishops, he presided with customary grandeur. The air, we are told, was 'perfumed with incense and flowers' and the altar, fittingly enough, was hung with finest gold tissue. At that point, the most powerful nobles of two mighty realms were no more than kneeling spectators, and even their respective kings and queens were inclined for the time being to concede centre stage to the man who had made their meeting possible.

Yet this most solemn of occasions was not without a dash of the most exquisite irony. For behind the French queen knelt one of her attendants, a lively, sparkling, coquettish figure, with long black hair and captivating eyes, who, contrary to the sombre fashion of that time, allowed her hair, interlaced with jewels, to flow alluringly down her back. Since her arrival at the French court as a raw and earnest adolescent, this young Englishwoman had listened, watched and blossomed and was now no longer a naive newcomer to either the world of high politics or, for that matter, the seamier side of human affairs in general. Nor was she quite the supine maid of her early youth. On the contrary, she was both sharp-witted and assertive, and as the second Duke of Norfolk's granddaughter she had connections to match her ambition. Her name was Anne Boleyn, and although it would still be more than a year before she took up residence at the English court, the foundations for her later impact upon both Henry, his wife and his cardinal had already been well and truly laid elsewhere.

By contrast, the current Queen of England had long seemed plain amid the court's young beauties. Notwithstanding her glowing complexion, flowing flaxen hair and 'lively and gracious disposition', a supercilious Venetian once described Catherine of Aragon as 'rather ugly than otherwise'. And though her piety and loyalty were exemplary, she lacked both magnetism and panache. In kneeling to pray, she invariably denied herself the comfort of a cushion, and after hearing matins at midnight, she would often rise again for Mass at five, dressing hurriedly and reproaching her maids for trying to waste too much time on her appearance. But, in spite of fasting on Fridays and Saturdays, she was prone to portliness. And while she recited the Office of the Virgin daily and read the lives of the saints to her ladies after dinner, she remained neither truly vivacious nor wholly at ease with the more trivial fripperies of court life. In brief, she was dependable rather than exciting, stolid and somehow rather dull; a cushion in times past for her husband's wounded ego, though one that he, too, might now be tempted to discard under the right circumstances.

On 31 January 1510 a stillborn daughter had dashed the king's high hopes, but by autumn of that year the royal nursery had once again been fitted out in expectation of the arrival of a new prince. Fresh hangings were ordered for the birthing chamber, along with a royal bearing pane sewn in purple velvet, and when the proud midwife finally took her place in church after a successful delivery she wore a gold chain worth £10, the gift of the joyous and grateful father. In the banquets and pageantry that followed, King Henry exceeded even his usual extravagance, and at the Richmond tournament which crowned the celebrations, he posed with typical bravado as 'Sir Loyal Heart'. But the same keeper of the great wardrobe who had dutifully made ready the nursery was soon arranging the baby prince's hearse. For while the junketing proceeded, the 'New Year's Boy', Henry Duke of Cornwall, had weakened and by February was dead.

The child lived less than two months, but two sons that followed not long afterwards fared even more dismally. One was either stillborn or died just after birth in 1513, while his eagerly awaited successor was born both prematurely

The old Grammar Hall of Magdalen College, Oxford, which served as the college's school from 1480 until 1928. It was here that Wolsey studied and later taught.

The Church of St Mary at Limington became Wolsey's first parish after his departure from Oxford. Presented to him by Thomas Grey, 1st Marquess of Dorset 'in reward for his diligence', this quiet parish in a remote part of the kingdom soon became a launching pad to higher office.

Anno ᚼ o ꜱ 29 octobꜛ imago henzirh vii franciꜩᵹ zege illuſtriſſim oꜛdinata p hermanu̅ ꜛnuck ꝓo zegie ... ... aiuerium ·

Wolsey's status and influence at court before the reign of Henry VIII is often underestimated. After his appointment as royal chaplain in 1507, he became a valued servant of Henry VII during the king's declining years, when Sir Richard Empson and Edmund Dudley were powerful figures that any ambitious newcomer needed to watch warily.

Richard Fox (c. 1448–1528) was a prominent English bishop, who, as Lord Privy Seal, was instrumental in assisting Wolsey's rise to influence.

Wolsey's expertise in the area of foreign policy made him especially valuable to Henry VIII, though his early encounters with the king's father-in-law Ferdinand II of Aragon were to result in frustration and disappointment.

This portrait by Jacques Le Boucq, produced in 1567, offers an unusually favourable image of the cardinal. In spite of his later corpulence and contemporary references to his facial disfigurement by the pox, the Venetian ambassador Sebastiano Giustiniani described Wolsey as 'very handsome'.

An administrator of exceptional energy and talent, Wolsey drew up proposals for reform and retrenchment at court, which eventually bore fruit in 1526 as the so-called 'Eltham Ordinances'.

After serious misgivings Pope Leo X finally appointed Wolsey to the cardinalate in 1515.

This painting by Lucas van Leyden is not what it first appears. Far from being an innocent depiction of card players, its actual concern is the conduct of secret diplomatic negotiations at the highest level. Emperor Charles V sits opposite Cardinal Wolsey as an alliance is forged against the King of France. The woman in the centre appears be Margaret of Austria, sister of Charles and regent of the Netherlands.

The Battle of Pavia in February 1525 resulted in Charles V's capture of Francis I and prompted a headlong rush by Henry VIII to seize the French crown. When Parliament refused to raise the necessary taxation, however, Wolsey was forced to devise the Amicable Grant and in doing so encountered a tidal wave of hostility.

Illustration from George Cavendish's biography of Wolsey, depicting the cardinal's downfall. Here Wolsey surrenders the Great Seal of England to his enemies, the Dukes of Norfolk and Suffolk, in October 1529.

Of all Wolsey's enemies, Thomas Howard, 3rd Duke of Norfolk, was the most persistent and formidable. The uncle of Anne Boleyn, Howard was instrumental in leading the alliance of nobles that orchestrated the cardinal's downfall in 1529.

and died the following year. As such, the arrival of a healthy baby girl in February 1516 proved something of an anti-climax. For although the queen's physician, Ferdinand de Vittoria, was paid handsomely for his patient's success in bearing a spindly daughter who, instead of dying, would bawl and kick her way into healthy infancy, the king's ego was hinging increasingly upon the prompt arrival of a lusty male heir. Catherine was clearly not barren, so was the deficiency his? There was also the comparatively unlikely prospect of a return to the disorders of the previous century to drive his fixation, not to mention diplomatic considerations to fuel his yearning. With a son at his disposal, Henry might well arrange a match with the daughter of almost any European ruler he chose, demanding a large dowry and military alliance into the bargain.

Yet there were other, darker stirrings in Henry's mind, which even his chief minister and closest confidant could never stifle. His marriage to Catherine was whispered by some, after all, to be soiled by incest and murder. Theologians, as Henry well knew, had long questioned his union with his brother's widow, and, to compound matters, the marriage was arguably a match made in blood after the execution of the Earl of Warwick in 1499. If so, was not the shadow of God's justice already hanging over Henry and his hopes for male offspring? Furthermore, there were even those, it seems, who said as much. Some while later the Duke of Buckingham's chancellor would allege that his master had bemoaned the earl's death and suggested that God was exacting punishment for it 'by not suffering the king's issue to prosper'. Clearly the implications were profound, and if, ultimately, there proved no alternative other than to terminate such an accursed union, the grimier and more sordid details could, of course, be conveniently consigned by the king to the magical hands of his ever-compliant cardinal.

As early as 1514 a rumour substantial enough to make its way to Rome had been circulated to the effect that 'the King of England means to repudiate his present wife, the daughter of the King of Spain and his brother's widow, because he is unable to have children by her'. The report, produced by a Venetian writing from Rome, suggested that Henry planned to marry a daughter of the French Duke of Bourbon, and added that he intended 'to annul his marriage and will obtain what he wants from the Pope'. Nor were such whispers implausible even at that time. Catherine's father had already tricked and betrayed her husband on at least two occasions, and the marriage itself had taken place amid a thicket of doubts and uncertainties. Archbishop Warham had opposed it in the council, Henry VII had temporised awkwardly and the pope himself had hesitated in granting a dispensation. When asked for his assistance, he had warned that this was a 'great matter', which even he might not be competent to resolve.

But by 1518 Catherine had been pregnant five times, and much, perhaps everything, therefore depended upon the outcome of her next and last pregnancy in that year. Richard Pace recorded the king's delight the night he returned to Woodstock from a prolonged royal progress 'and the queen did meet with his grace at his chamber door, and showed unto him, for his welcome home, her belly something great, declaring openly that she was quick with child'. At once, Wolsey was officially informed and plans laid for the queen's pregnancy to be marked by the singing of a solemn *Te Deum* at St Paul's. The queen's chief physician, meanwhile, assumed a new and even greater importance than ever. By now Dr de Vittoria's wife had already been brought over from Spain at some considerable cost, in order to ensure his comfort. But from this point onwards he became an object of outright reverence whose every report was hung upon with unwavering interest and whose every request was met without demur.

In a secret letter written to Wolsey at this time, the king confided his hopes plainly. He trusted that Catherine was indeed carrying a live child, he told his chief minister, and stressed his determination that she should come to no harm. For her sake, he claimed, he would not return to London, 'because about this time is partly of her dangerous times, and because of that I would remove her as little as I may now'. Not altogether surprisingly, however, the king's excitement was guarded, for he had been disappointed too often not to restrain his optimism. Nevertheless, his last child had lived and this one showed signs of life. Nothing was certain, as Henry fully acknowledged, and all was in God's hands. Yet God might well bring to fruition that which he had begun, and the queen's condition, the letter concluded, 'was a thing wherein I have great hope and likelihood'.

In the event, all such hopes would prove vain. For the child, a girl, was dead within a week of her birth on 10 November and the consequences were profound. In the first place, the king now indulged his unfaithfulness more and more overtly. As early as 1510, in fact, Henry seems to have coped with the disappointment of his stillborn daughter by toying with Anne Stafford, sister of the Duke of Buckingham, and in the final months of 1514 there were rumours of another affair. This time the whispers involved Jane Popincourt, a French maid-of-honour to Catherine of Aragon, who eventually returned to Paris in 1516 with a personal reward from her royal suitor of £100. But now there was 'Bessie' Blount, a relative of Lord Mountjoy, who, by her 'goodly pastimes,' wrote the chronicler Edward Hall, 'won the king's heart'. In the late summer of 1518, just as Catherine of Aragon's pregnancy was approaching its unhappy climax, she had become the king's mistress. And by the time that Henry was informing Wolsey of his heartfelt, but ultimately futile, hopes for a child by his wife, Mistress Blount was herself full-bellied with the king's bastard.

The cruel irony involved will not, of course, have been lost upon the cardinal, who appears at this stage to have adopted a characteristically pragmatic attitude to his master's infidelities. The bastard boy was duly christened Henry Fitzroy, in acknowledgement of his royal paternity, and assigned a princely household comparable to that of his legitimate half-sister, Mary. Shortly after the birth, moreover, Wolsey became the boy's proud godfather, and in due course he would appoint him High Steward of the Bishopric of Durham and High Steward of the Liberties of the Archbishop of York. He may even have been instrumental in the decision to make Henry Fitzroy nominal head of the Council of the North in 1525, by which time the boy had become Duke of Richmond and Somerset. For, despite the documents and instructions 'signed with the gracious hand of the King's highness', almost all the senior figures appointed to supervise northern affairs in the boy's name had prior links to the cardinal. Only his treasurer, Sir Godfrey Foljambe; the vice-chamberlain, Richard Page; and the cofferer, Sir George Lawson, have been expressly identified as his father's men. And it was no coincidence, perhaps, that in March 1529 Henry VIII's illegitimate son was fully prepared to acknowledge his debt to the cardinal 'to whose favour and goodness no creature living is more bound than I'.

Nor was Wolsey unduly perturbed when Bessie Blount made way in the king's affection for a potentially more menacing mistress, the eldest daughter of Thomas Boleyn. Mistress Blount herself was finally awarded manors in Lincoln and York, and married to one of Wolsey's own retainers, Gilbert Talboys, whose father, it seems, was a madman in the cardinal's custody who had once been a soldier in Henry's armies. In arranging matters, Wolsey made no attempt either to discourage Blount's departure or bar the progress of the king's new lover. Making, at the very least, a virtue out of necessity, he realised no doubt the impossibility of thwarting his master's fancy and the potential danger involved in any attempt to do so. Besides which, the political influence of a royal lover was likely to be limited at a time when the king's marriage, in law if not in practice, was still apparently secure. Indeed, the prospect of steady extra-marital release might well be the best possible means of guaranteeing its prolongation.

Of Mary Boleyn Carey herself surprisingly little is known. Older than her more famous sibling Anne, she had become the wife of William Carey, one of the king's favourites, in 1520, and thereafter satisfied her sovereign's sexual needs over several years with her husband's full knowledge and complicity. A royal ship was subsequently named after her, but neither she nor her husband received rich rewards for their efforts and by the mid-1520s the elder Boleyn girl had become a spent force in Henry's affections. In the meantime, her impact upon court politics had been minimal and her significance for Wolsey negligible. On this occasion, therefore, the impact of the king's frustration with his wife's infertility had proven comparatively harmless for all concerned.

Yet the ramifications of Queen Catherine's ineffectual womb were not confined to her husband's sexual indiscretions with pretty playthings like Mary Boleyn, and these further shockwaves were to prove of the profoundest significance for Wolsey himself, since Henry now began to combine his growing sense of inadequacy and injustice with personal insecurity and fears for the succession, all of which would embroil his chief minister in the most reprehensible and damaging episode of his career to date. In playing loyal servant to his master and indulging royal whims whenever necessary, Wolsey had actually increased not only the force and frequency of these fancies, but also the impression that he would both do and achieve whatever was required of him. And as a result he was now forced to prosecute and destroy the most powerful noble in England, with consequences for his own reputation that would not only resound across Europe but haunt him till his death.

In the same year that the Field of Cloth of Gold appeared to place Henry VIII at the apogee of his influence, he confided to his chief minister a grating suspicion of the men of power around him. 'I would you should make good watch,' he wrote, 'on the Duke of Suffolk, on the Duke of Buckingham, on my lord of Northumberland, on my lord of Derby, on my lord of Wiltshire and on others you think suspect', adding that the reasons for his distrust were so secret that they were to be known by 'none other than you and I'. Henry Percy, fifth Earl of Northumberland, who had fought at the Battle of the Spurs, had already been imprisoned by Wolsey in 1516, and although the Earl of Derby was a comparative nonentity at court, the ambition of Wiltshire may well explain his own inclusion on the list. The shadow over the Duke of Suffolk, on the other hand, was almost certainly closely connected to his scandalous marriage to the king's younger sister, even though a reconciliation of sorts had taken place subsequently. But it was Edward Stafford, Duke of Buckingham, Lord High Steward and Lord High Constable of England – a hot-tempered man inclined to 'rail and misuse himself in words' – who had been selected as the primary target and carefully earmarked as scapegoat, sacrificial lamb and abiding example to his peers of the royal will in action.

Descended from Thomas of Woodstock, sixth son of Edward III, and Katherine Woodville, sister of Edward IV's wife Elizabeth, Stafford was a man of genuinely regal credentials; a prince in all but name whose family links extended far and wide throughout the highest ranks of the English nobility. Not only was his wife a Percy, but his children had been married to great advantage. Henry Stafford, the eldest son, had married a Pole, while two of the duke's daughters were joined in their turn to a Howard and a Neville respectively. And if the king may never have warmed to Buckingham thoroughly, he nevertheless had little choice but to treat him as an intimate member of his inner circle, relying on him as a soldier and stern governor of his lordship on the French border. In consequence, the two men were frequently in each other's company on the tiltyard, in the chase and on the tennis court, and the duke's prominence at Henry's coronation was even more striking proof of his exceptional position.

Rank and regal lineage, in this case, also went hand-in-hand with unrivalled wealth. Indeed, with his great castle at Thornbury in Gloucestershire and his fine residence at Penshurst in Kent, not to mention his liveried retainers and a rent roll that was easily the most valuable in all England, Edward Stafford seemed a lingering survival from an older feudal age. Both superstitious and devout, he had, in youth, showered largesse on West Country churches, particularly in Somerset, and duly honed the keenest possible sense of his 'natural' rights and obligations as a leading magnate. To everyone except his own tenants, to whom he sometimes appeared unsympathetic, even tyrannical, he was also popular: a would-be 'man's man', proudly outspoken and outspokenly proud, who lived life to the aristocratic full and exuded a bluff, no-nonsense bonhomie that was characteristic of his class.

Buckingham's spending habits say much about him. His wardrobe inventory, for instance, confirms his opulent tastes: one gown of white damask cloth of gold lined in crimson velvet is listed alongside another 'laid with silver and gilt, and a girdle of green riband silk, with a great knot thereto'. In all, the duke's wardrobe list included fourteen gowns, twelve doublets and jackets, nine pairs of hose and eighteen pairs of shoes. But his gambling debts are, perhaps, more revealing still. 'Lost to my Lord of Suffolk since coming to the king, £51' and to the same 'at shooting, £31', we learn from his accounts. 'Lost at dice to my Lord of Suffolk and the Frenchman, £76 1s 4d', the same accounts continue, with further losses 'to my brother of Wiltshire and Lord Montague, £40' and a further loss 'at dice to my Lord Montague at Syssiter, £15'. Clearly, this was a man who disdained caution. And just as surely, this was a man destined to be one of life's losers in an altogether more crucial respect.

Buckingham had, in fact, already caused a stir early in the reign when he interfered too boldly in the king's affair with his sister, Anne. After being rescued from early widowhood by her second husband, George Hastings, Earl of Huntingdon, she had gone on to become one of Queen Catherine's favourites before attracting the king himself. It was William Compton, Henry's former page and groom of the bedchamber, who acted as his master's go-between and, in this capacity, Compton made a habit of visiting Anne's quarters to arrange discreet liaisons. When the outraged duke learned of Compton's visits, however, he confronted his quarry in his sister's room and 'severely reproached him in many and very hard words', whereupon the king, to his boundless indignation, was duly informed. The abuse which followed was delivered to Buckingham in person and the king's display of temper continued until the offender left the palace in some disgrace. But he appears to have left in high dudgeon, too, for in spite of the king's anger, the wayward sister was nevertheless packed off to a convent some 60 miles away. If, then, Buckingham could not quite face down his sovereign, he was at least determined to stand his ground when his own prerogatives were clear-cut. And the duke was also prepared to dice with danger in other ways, for his pride and rashness, as well as his readiness to pose as the figurehead of the aristocratic interest in politics, appeared to confirm a threat to the succession.

No-one, of course, was more apt to offend Buckingham's acute sense of *noblesse oblige* than the upstart Wolsey, who seemed to epitomise the current threat to an entire political culture that had stood unchallenged for so long. Indeed, the duke took no pains to conceal his disdain as he cultivated a sulphurous campaign of petty insults and stinging, but measured, provocation. Polydore Vergil tells us, for instance, that Buckingham poked fun at the Field of Cloth of Gold, that 'conference of trivialities' and 'spectacle of foolish speeches'. Other chroniclers report that on one particularly notable occasion he had been holding a ewer of water for the king to wash his hands when Wolsey had the effrontery to dip his own hands after the king had finished. Outraged at such presumption, the duke then appears to have deliberately 'shed the water' upon the cardinal's shoes, at which Wolsey is said to have warned the aggressor that he would 'sit upon his skirts'. Nevertheless, Buckingham was determined to have the last word and when he appeared at court the next day, he did so without the skirts of his doublet. Asked by the king why he appeared at court dressed so eccentrically, he replied that he was resolved to frustrate Wolsey's malice towards him.

Such, then, was the measure of the 'fumes and displeasures' between England's proudest nobleman and the realm's haughtiest churchman. For all their visibility they were plainly, by and large, the stuff of peevish banter rather than mortal enmity, and when Buckingham's end came, it was the king and not his cardinal who willed it. But if Henry gave the order, it would fall to Wolsey to lay the snare and spring the trap. By now, in any case, the king and his minister were too closely identified for one to be insulted without the other, and to this extent the strident duke was already paving his path to the scaffold. When blue-blooded bluster therefore gave way to poisonous rumours about Buckingham's designs upon the throne itself, there could be only one outcome. Certainly, Wolsey did nothing either to muffle or dismiss the whispers, and in due course he would spin a false perspective on events for consumption abroad. Yet, if the method of securing Buckingham's downfall had the cardinal's indelible mark upon it, he remained neither instigator nor willing executioner.

The source of the fatal rumour was Charles Knyvet, the duke's former surveyor, who had recently entered the king's service with high hopes of advancement, and when Knyvet proffered sensational evidence of a matter that 'toucheth the king indeed', Wolsey did not hesitate to question him. Thereafter Robert Gilbert, the duke's chancellor, and his chaplain, John Delacourt, also turned informers, and after Buckingham had been summoned to Windsor, so sick with fear that at breakfast 'his meat would not down', he found himself fighting vainly for his life. On his fateful journey in his splendidly upholstered barge, he had landed at Wolsey's palace only to be told, as he came up the water steps, that the cardinal was indisposed. 'Well,' said Buckingham, with a feigned display of his former bravado, 'yet will I drink of my lord's wine or I pass.' So it was that a gentleman of Wolsey's household conducted the duke, with formal but gloomy courtesy, to the cellar. When, however, the duke perceived 'that no cheer to him was made', it was said that he 'changed colour' and returned to his barge.

The charges against the accused were duly delivered in May 1521 by a London jury, which included the Lord Mayor Sir Robert Brudenell and Sir Thomas Boleyn. It was claimed that in 1511 the duke had 'imagined and compassed the death of the king' and a year later had presumed to send his chaplain to consult with Father Nicholas Hopkins, a Carthusian monk at Hinton Charterhouse, who 'pretended to have knowledge of future events'. The result was a message to the duke that he should 'obtain the love of the community', since before long 'he should have all'. In 1513, the same monk had also, it seems, let it be known that 'the king would have no male issue from his body' and the following February the duke himself had blundered by carelessly discussing the possibility of his own succession to the throne. A number of treasonable questions were then put before Father Hopkins by Buckingham in April 1516 and for his trouble the clairvoyant monk received an annuity of £6 for a tun of wine, along with a further £3 for himself. Buckingham's accounts for 1519 had, moreover, revealed another payment of 100s to his 'ghostly father' at Hinton.

The duke's personal hostility towards Wolsey also featured in the indictment. According to the evidence of Robert Gilbert, Buckingham considered him an idolater, 'taking counsel of the spirit how he might continue to have the king's favour', and there was mention, too, of how Buckingham had helped fuel gossip that the cardinal had encouraged the king's vices, advising him on the most comely choice of mistresses. To compound matters, he had complained in Gilbert's hearing how he himself 'had done as good service as any man and was not rewarded, and that the king gave offices and fees to boys rather than to noblemen'. In this last connection, furthermore, he had suggested that the nobles should 'break their minds', since few were contented with being 'so unkindly handled'.

But Buckingham had been dabbling, we are told, in even more dangerous waters. He had foolishly broadcast, for example, that 'all the king's father did was wrong'. Worse still, he had allegedly gathered and armed fighting men, ostensibly in the name of the king but actually with a view to overthrowing him, and he had purchased considerable amounts of cloth of gold and silver and silks with which to bribe the king's guards and ensure their support when the moment of action came. In short, he had either placed himself or been conveniently stranded by others in a position of utter hopelessness. The peers assembled to hear his case at Westminster Hall were all rightly terrified of the king and though Wolsey was not present, he had prepared the king's case more than adequately to underpin the inevitable. 'Sir Edward, Duke of Buckingham,' intoned the Clerk of the Council, 'hold up thy hand! Thou art indicted of high treason', and Buckingham's response was unavailing. 'It is false and untrue,' he retorted, 'and conspired and forged to bring me to my death.' Nor, if reactions to his conviction are any guide, was his response far from the mark, since even that dyed-in-the-wool cynic, the Duke of Norfolk, was said to have broken down as he delivered sentence.

In the meantime, lords Bergavenny and Montague had also been implicated, but Wolsey was a good friend to each of them, and whether through genuine clemency or the judicious turning of a blind eye, both were spared. Indeed, once they had made the necessary submission, duly denounced the prime target, and given some gifts of land and money to the king and his cardinal, the erring lords were not only pardoned, but set free and allowed to keep their remaining estates. It was sound politics and good business to boot, just like the other practical outcome of Buckingham's execution. For the duke's lands in twenty-four counties of England and Wales, as well as his houses in London and Calais, were neatly seized by the Crown.

Significantly, however, the aftermath of the trial would prove an unusually sombre affair. Buckingham's death, wrote the Venetian ambassador, was 'universally lamented by all London' and there appears to have been little of the jeering contempt usually reserved for a convicted traitor. As he was rowed back to the Tower through the summer sunshine in his own barge, the duke had refused to sit on the splendid cushions and carpets, which were still, for the time being, at his disposal. 'When I went to Westminster,' he reflected, 'I was Duke of Buckingham; now I am but Edward Bohun, the most caitiff in the world.' At that time, in fact, he was anticipating the most excruciating of deaths, though four days after his condemnation the king graciously consented to spare him the ordeal of castration and seeing his bowels burnt before his eyes. Instead, on 17 May 1521, he was merely decapitated.

The king, in fact, had not been fit to enjoy the spectacle. Instead, he was confined to bed with a high fever and chills, fussed over by his physicians and unable to eat. Furthermore, it was left to Wolsey to draft the letters of consolation, which the king was required by custom to send to the widow and son of the condemned man. 'The letters I sent you today to be signed,' Wolsey reminded his master, 'are only letters of consolation and credence to the wife of the late Duke of Buckingham and his son Lord Stafford […] if, however, you think them not convenient to pass, I remit that to you.' It was a return to the routine of business, if, indeed, the trial and execution had ever represented a major departure in the first place.

However, Polydore Vergil's subsequent claim that Wolsey felt no remorse at 'devouring the beautiful swan' seems harsh. Certainly, he had good reason to be relieved at Buckingham's demise and had at no stage interceded with the king. But pleas on the duke's behalf were likely to have been no less dangerous than futile, for, as Wolsey well knew, the king was both implacable when roused and easily exasperated by well-intentioned councillors. Besides which, the king's perceived interest was at stake, and in cultivating this interest his chief minister was never less than unflinching.

Nor, for that matter, are Polydore's other claims any more intrinsically trustworthy. From the start of his account, the Italian has the cardinal 'flaming with hatred and lusting to sate it' with Stafford blood, and in these circumstances, we are told, he 'induced the king to consider the duke as someone to fear and, at length, as someone to be rid of'. Yet Vergil himself suggested that Buckingham fell 'because he had coveted the crown' and we have already seen that the initial alarm was raised by Henry. Wolsey would, it is true, later tell the French ambassador Antoine Duprat that the duke had fallen, because he had intrigued against his policy. But this chance remark is entirely consistent with the impulsive boasting to which Wolsey was always prone and may well have been intended to re-emphasise the pro-French slant of the policy concerned. Besides which, the spoils of the Stafford inheritance not retained by the Crown went chiefly to men that Wolsey trusted little more than the victim himself – namely, Norfolk and Suffolk.

Yet the mud once again stuck. Abroad, Buckingham's execution seems at first to have aroused considerable excitement, for both Charles V and Francis I believed that rebellion had broken out and competed to win the King of England's goodwill by offering him troops to assist in its suppression. In response, Wolsey hastened to assure them that the situation was entirely in hand, that Buckingham was Henry's only disloyal nobleman, and that Bergavenny and Montague had been foolish rather than wicked. But if the chief minister managed to smooth the ground once more for his king, the damage to his own reputation would be permanent. At home, the noble interest would continue to seethe in private, and throughout Europe, too, the 'obvious' conclusion would be drawn and relished. The Duke of Buckingham had been an enemy of the cardinal, had spoken openly of his contempt and baited him at every opportunity. Now this same duke was dead, and though he had been the greatest magnate in all England, he was cut down no less ruthlessly, his goods attainted and the very office of Lord High Constable of England, to which he had been appointed at the time of the current king's coronation, abolished as a token of the extinction of his line and memory. 'A butcher's cur,' quipped the Holy Roman Emperor, 'has slain the finest buck in England.'

14

Neither Glory nor Gain

Less than three months after Buckingham's execution, Thomas Wolsey was deeply embroiled in what was, to all appearances, the most subtle and cynical of all his diplomatic manoeuvres. Though it came as no surprise to anyone except possibly the King of England, the 'universal peace' had proven short-lived. A border incident on the southern frontier of the Netherlands involving Francis I's client, Robert de la Marck, had brought an imperial army crashing into Sedan to spark a general conflagration. And when Francis sent troops of his own, complaining that the Holy Roman Emperor had engineered an invasion, Charles appealed to England for support under the agreement of 1518 – a move swiftly replicated by his French counterpart. In the event, all Europe now stood on the brink of a war which would rage, with only brief intervals of peace, for nearly forty years. It was a conflict, moreover, which erupted at the very time that Christendom was mortally threatened from without by the looming menace of the Turks and from within by the rampantly aggressive cancer of Lutheran heresy. In such circumstances, there was neither margin for error nor scope for faint-heartedness. And it was in these truly forbidding conditions that Thomas Wolsey was called upon by his insatiable royal master to weave his familiar magic.

With typically inflated delusions of his kingdom's stature and influence, Henry proposed that Wolsey should arbitrate the current dispute and determine the true aggressor. In view of his recent meetings with the cardinal at Canterbury,

Gravelines and Calais, Charles V was predictably the more willing of the disputants to take up the offer, knowing full well that the English, in spite of their teasing dalliance with the French, were keen for an imperial alliance. The King of France, on the other hand, had initially achieved military ascendancy by overrunning Navarre and reaching the gates of Pamplona. With a successful army in train and his subjects primed for war, a postponement of hostilities therefore offered little attraction, particularly when the arbiter of any prospective conference was wily Wolsey. For if the cardinal was a genuine supporter of peace in principle, he was nevertheless in practice an advocate of opportunism and self-interest: his master's, his kingdom's and his own. From such a standpoint, 'universal' peace – just like the balance of power designed to achieve it – was never more than an ideal and transient objective, and if lasting harmony could not be achieved, then discord, as Wolsey fully understood, must be exploited accordingly.

Yet if Francis I, like all other participants in the diplomatic merry-go-round at that time, had little or no real faith in abstract principles or the platitudes and pious posturing that went with them, he, too, was soon feeling the full force of circumstance and bending, ostensibly, to the proposal of his English counterpart. For by the summer of 1521 the French king's earlier successes in ruffling his enemies had ground to an undignified halt and he found himself with no other choice than to play the game of reason, fairness and reconciliation. French ambassadors and their imperial counterparts would therefore meet at Calais under Wolsey's supervision and wait upon his wisdom. Both sides, moreover, were to provide written assurances that they would bow to the cardinal's judgement and guarantee that they would not be reconciled to each other until he had pronounced his verdict. By this means, the myth of English primacy, so beloved by England's king and so crucial to Wolsey's wellbeing, would be maintained.

As might be expected, the cardinal's journey to Calais in the summer of 1521 was in character with the usual pomp and display that accompanied his movements; only more so, perhaps, in view of the importance of his mission. Passing through London with the Great Seal of England borne before him, he was accompanied by Sir Thomas Boleyn and an impressive throng of gentlemen, knights and nobles. A sum of £2,400 had been spent on clothing his retinue in finest velvet, and he had also been lent the king's most accomplished trumpeter. And when he reached his destination on 2 August after a stormy Channel crossing, he was ready, once again, to assume the elevated role ordained for him by the vagaries of the international balance of power. Of the two alternative options available to him, the choice was now clear. The safe path involved neutrality and the offer of support to the highest bidder. The bolder one, however, held out the prospect of infinitely greater rewards, and it was this approach, predictably, that Wolsey selected. It entailed nothing less than a permanent imperial alliance, sealed by the betrothal of Princess Mary to the Emperor Charles, with a view to crushing France once and for all. The groundwork for such a plan had already been completed during the conferences of 1520, and it had been further reinforced by a secret meeting with imperial ambassadors which occurred at Windsor Castle on 5 June.

Not only, Wolsey reasoned, would England's ancient enemy be subdued by such means, but the increasingly pressing issue of the succession might also be solved at one and the same time. With every passing month it had seemed increasingly improbable that Queen Catherine would ever conceive, and as the king's vexation mounted, a convenient and, if possible, profitable solution was much needed. Under the terms of the 1518 treaty, of course, Princess Mary remained betrothed to the dauphin, which now raised the increasing likelihood that England itself might pass to French control, if no suitable male heir was begotten by Henry. Although less than ideal, the alternative prospect of the emperor as long-term ruler of England was therefore infinitely preferable, not least because it held out considerable possibilities for Henry during his own lifetime. If, after all, a joint Anglo-imperial attack were to subjugate France, might not the King of England be able to rule at last over most of those lands belonging to his vanquished enemy? Once Charles had annexed Guienne and Languedoc and absorbed the provinces of the old Duchy of Burgundy around Dijon, which had been lost by his predecessors in 1482, the remaining French territory could be ruled by Henry until they eventually reverted to Mary and Charles when his life was over.

It was a plan on the grandest possible scale – one wholly in keeping with Wolsey's most sweeping and ingenious designs, and in keeping, too, with his master's most feverish imaginings. In the meantime, however, the cardinal was at liberty to pose and posture at Calais to his heart's delight, pouring forth tokens of wisdom and listening with rapt attention to the solemn orations delivered at his feet by suppliant ambassadors from either side. And like the canny schoolmaster he once had been, the 'arbiter of Christendom' duly proceeded to tickle the expectations of his audience in a finely crafted spectacle of unparalleled irony. On the one hand stood France, boasting some 14 million subjects, and on the other the Holy Roman Empire, a rambling, hotchpotch edifice, but nevertheless controlling some 16 million more. Meanwhile, at the Olympian summit sat the imperious figure of Thomas Wolsey, scion of an artful Ipswich businessman, and Lord Chancellor of a kingdom on the damp and misty fringes of Europe, holding no more than 3.5 million souls at most. And all the while that he lectured, exhorted, frowned and admonished, the outcome of the entire sham was effectively a foregone conclusion.

Yet if Wolsey's masterstroke were to attain its ambitious goals, the façade of sincerity and fair play would need to be maintained at all costs. Ably assisted by the bishops of London and Durham, as well as Thomas More, the cardinal finally opened proceedings on 7 August after a lengthy wrangle between the French and imperial delegates over precedence and seating arrangements. On the very same day, however, the emperor requested him to hasten to Bruges in order to seal the terms of their secret agreement. Private negotiations with the imperial ambassador Gattinara were in fact already underway, focusing mainly upon the details of Princess Mary's marriage to Charles, and in particular the issue of compensation for England's inevitable loss of French payments both for Tournai and the earlier nuptial agreement with the dauphin. But the emperor now offered to press ahead in person and the offer was too good to refuse. He had promised Wolsey upon his arrival in Calais that 'I will show you the bottom of my heart'. Now, however, he went for broke, abandoning protocol and addressing his correspondent as an equal. 'You and I will do more in a day,' Charles told the English minister, 'than my ambassadors will do in a month.'

The primary question, of course, was how such a meeting might be rendered acceptable to the French. But Wolsey was nothing if not inventive when it came to the intricate art of subtle deception, and the ruse that he now concocted was made all the more satisfying by its simplicity. Gattinara, it seems, was to announce at the opening session that he had been sent to the conference only to announce the emperor's refusal to negotiate as long as French troops were in occupation of Navarre. Whereupon the imperial ambassador would stage a dramatic exit, leaving Wolsey to express his dismay and announce his readiness to save the negotiations by pleading with the emperor in person. The French king, predictably, was suspicious, but it was left to his chancellor Antoine Duprat to convince him of the cardinal's good faith. Clearly, the actor in Wolsey had worked its effect on even this most seasoned of political creatures, and Duprat's letter of reassurance to his sovereign on 8 August provided the cardinal with precisely the green light he desired.

Yet Wolsey had still not milked his moment of primacy to the limit, for when Spinelly, the English agent in Bruges, stressed the impatience with which Charles was awaiting their meeting, the cardinal showed no inclination to rush. On the contrary, he was determined to travel every bit as slowly as the dignity of a papal legate required, and thereby impress the world with both his status and his impartiality. Indeed, he did not leave Calais until 12 August – a whole day after the latest date stipulated by Charles for his arrival in Bruges – and took a further three days over the journey, finally reaching his destination on the evening of 14 August. As a final flourish, he even left the emperor waiting at the city gates for all of ninety minutes, in the company of his whole court, before finally making a suitably resplendent entry. Riding his mule in the company of 1,050 English horsemen decked in finest red satin, he could not have made a brasher or more compelling statement of self-confidence or personal style. For this short while, after all, he was undeniably pre-eminent. He knew it. He would show it. And while the opportunity lasted he would savour it.

Upon meeting the emperor Wolsey did not dismount, but merely raised his hat before Charles did likewise and embraced the cardinal, from saddle to saddle, as an equal. Indeed, Wolsey's only apparent concession to etiquette was to accord his royal partner the place of honour on the right as they rode side by side through the packed crowds and banners lining the streets. To be thus escorted to the very door of his lodgings by the Holy Roman Emperor was a wholly unprecedented honour and the fact that this hospitality was extended to the representative of a foreign ruler leaves no doubt about the potency of Wolsey's current position. The next day, moreover, Charles and the cardinal shared the same kneeling-desk under the emperor's canopy of state while hearing Mass at the cathedral.

Just how far Wolsey was driven on such occasions by personal pride remains debatable, however. Certainly, a curious incident during his stay at Bruges throws interesting light on his own rationale for appearing at times to ape or even demean his betters. When approached by the representatives of King Christian II of Denmark, who also happened to be visiting Charles at this time, Wolsey seems to have caused general consternation by deigning to suggest that if Christian requested a meeting, it should occur in his own apartments rather than the king's. When, moreover, this potential humiliation was firmly rejected by the Danes, Wolsey then suggested that he would pass through the garden of the palace assigned to Christian on his way to the emperor. If the king happened to be present, they could talk together, and this indeed is what took place, though Wolsey soon broke off the discussion, citing the urgency of his impending meeting with Charles. And this was not all, for Wolsey also suggested that the unfinished business might still be concluded the following morning in his own rooms. When Christian actually complied the next day and their discussion was ended, Wolsey finally had the temerity to accompany him only as far as the bottom of the stairs – a breach of etiquette guaranteed to intensify the cardinal's already pungent reputation. Yet when he told Henry of the incident, the cardinal insisted that he had treated his honoured guest in this way only to emphasise the King of England's own prestige.

In all discussions with Charles, meanwhile, there was tough and exhausting bargaining. The emperor, Wolsey informed Henry, was behaving 'coldly and discreetly', 'pondering and regarding' his proposals with great care and forcing him to negotiate 'sometimes with sharp winds, sometime in pleasant manner'. At one point Charles had visited Wolsey's lodgings 'familiarly' in the company of his aunt, the Archduchess Margaret of Austria, who was taking a prominent role in proceedings. And the cardinal had, it seems, duly charmed her into what would prove a lasting friendship, telling her how he regarded her as a second 'mother', though she was in fact a few years younger than him. But 'my lady had demanded', he wrote, that England 'make the declaration against France at once', and the strength of her insistence on this point demonstrated all too aptly that, while an Anglo-imperial alliance had been agreed in principle more than a year before, the devil nevertheless remained in the detail.

There was intensive haggling, too, over the size of Princess Mary's dowry, which Charles set at a million ducats, but Wolsey managed to whittle down to £80,000 in spite of numerous threats and much ill-feeling. And the underlying tension was magnified, of course, by the stakes involved. Such, indeed, was the gravity of proceedings that negotiations were suspended for three days while Wolsey lay panic-stricken in bed, suspecting that he had been poisoned by the emperor's cook. Even Charles had feared for his life when a small bladder filled with hair and foul-smelling powders was discovered in a platter of meat, though the mixture was later found to be nothing more dangerous than a stray love potion. Yet after two weeks of energetic wrangling, the crucial secret treaty was eventually agreed in principle. Embodying the long-sought military alliance against France and the marriage of Charles to Princess Mary on the most generous terms that her father could have wished for, it appeared another personal triumph for the weary cardinal who had conjured it from thin air.

Wolsey's tribulations were far from done, however. Initially, of course, there were the suspicions of the French to deal with upon his return to Calais. Leaving Bruges on 26 August, he once again set a leisurely pace, taking four days to resume his talks with Chancellor Duprat, by which time rumours of his agreement with the Holy Roman Empire were already circulating widely. Francis's spies in England were also reporting mounting preparations for war, and English students in Paris were said to be heading for home in increasing numbers. But Wolsey succeeded in quelling Duprat's fears with consummate skill. The build-up of armaments across the Channel, he reassured the French delegation, was a routine measure for national self-defence, and his account of events in Bruges was delivered with equally earnest insincerity. He had convinced the emperor, he said, that Henry would never allow him to conquer

Milan and he had spurned a large sum of money, accepting instead only two small bars of silver, which he had been impelled to accept out of nothing more than courtesy.

Once more, it seems, the deception worked perfectly. 'We have thanked him very much for the goodwill which we see more and more he bears towards you,' the French delegation informed Francis on 8 September, 'and we asked him to continue it, and said that you would not be ungrateful to him.' Three days later, moreover, Duprat dined alone with Wolsey in the cardinal's private apartments, where he was told, in strict confidence, of secret intelligence concerning the emperor's military preparations in Italy, Flanders and Navarre. It was also made quite clear to the French chancellor that, in spite of the considerable anti-French sentiments in England, both Wolsey and Henry were totally committed to friendship. Indeed, Wolsey added, any subterfuge on his part in Bruges would have lost him the favour of his master forever. All, it seems, was honesty, honour and fair play, and on the strength of such assurances, the French not only took the cardinal at his word, but agreed to allow corn supplies into Calais, which had been disrupted by the ongoing conflict on the border with the Netherlands.

In the meantime, however, the terms of the Bruges agreement had created growing divisions in the imperial camp, so much so that the Archduchess Margaret, who had played such a prominent role in negotiations, was soon writing to Wolsey in the deepest anguish. 'For long enough I had good hope, but now I am in despair', she informed him. 'The emperor has a will of his own and councillors who strengthen him in it.' She then went on to relate how Charles was adamant that Wolsey's demands were 'unreasonable and affect my honour'. He was convinced, moreover, that he would have no difficulty in finding a bride other than Mary. Wolsey 'cannot sell me his princess so dearly', the archduchess had heard him declare. But in her distress, she also confessed her continuing faith in the man to whom she was writing and, in doing so, left little doubt about the kind of personal magnetism that Wolsey was capable of exerting even among the highest and mightiest. 'I would dearly love to have two hours' talk with the cardinal to set all right again', she confided at the end of her letter.

Even so, the military aspects of the agreement had troublesome implications of their own for Wolsey. While an Anglo-imperial assault on France was always his objective, the timing remained a crucial issue since Charles's wish for swift action did not suit English needs. From Wolsey's point of view, the summer of 1523 was the earliest acceptable date, and upon his return to Calais, therefore, he found himself in the curious position of trying to work once more as peacemaker, in order to manufacture a temporary truce between France and the

Empire before the main business of war to the limit could conveniently begin. In doing so he could keep his options open, countering discontented rumblings among the imperial delegation, while maintaining both his own and his master's reputation as would-be peacemakers.

Yet claims that Wolsey was indeed sincere in his quest for peace, and that the secret Bruges agreement was nothing more than a fallback position in the event of the talks at Calais failing, remain largely unconvincing. For good reason, of course, Wolsey maintained his appeals for 'unity, peace and concord' throughout, and may even perhaps have partially believed his own mythology. In the thick of his latest negotiations, for example, he had composed a moving appeal to the Queen Mother of France and later wrote with equal conviction of his frustration with both sides as they blocked his initiatives. 'The more towardly disposition I find in the French party,' he complained, 'the more sticking and difficulty be showed' by the other side. Even after the talks at Calais had finally been abandoned, for that matter, he continued to express his frustration that the earnest quest for a settlement had proved fruitless. 'I have as effectually laboured [for peace] by all the politic ways and means to me possible as ever I did any cause in my life', he declared. But Wolsey's desire for compromise amounted, in this case at least, to nothing more than the quest for a temporary truce: a short-lived postponement of hostilities that would give England its much-needed breathing space before the dogs of war were finally loosed.

For Wolsey the dove was also Wolsey the realist. He had not hesitated, for example, to pass on authentic military intelligence to Gattinara once the talks at Calais resumed. And when fifty of the emperor's soldiers made a successful raid on the fortress of Ardres, he had urged the head of the imperial delegation to ensure that the walls should be demolished or the town burned before any withdrawal occurred. Nor would he hesitate to seal the provisional agreement made at Bruges when, on 16 November, the emperor finally ordered Gattinara to break off negotiations in Calais after the imperial capture of Tournai and Milan. In truth, therefore, the resulting treaty was precisely what he had been intending all along, just as he had hoped for the postponement of the 'enterprise' against France until March 1523, whereupon each side would contribute 'a land army of 40,000 horse and foot, as well as a fleet to harry the coast'. It was not, in any really thoroughgoing sense, an act of treachery devised by a cynical hypocrite. Rather it was a product of logic, realism and the unyielding imperatives of sixteenth-century statecraft: the uncomfortable result, in some senses, of a master's ambition on the one hand and his servant's understandable desire for political, perhaps even physical, survival on the other. Yet when Wolsey sailed for England on 28 November there was still unmistakable irony. For on the very same day, Francis instructed his envoys in Calais to remind the cardinal of his great affection for him and of his satisfaction that the marriage treaty between the dauphin and Princess Mary remained intact.

By this time, however, the intolerable pace of Wolsey's labours – not to mention the hidden burden of his unremitting personal anxieties – had once again taken their toll upon his health. So long as he was away from court there were many who might take advantage of his absence, and as the pressure of work and the late summer climate of Bruges bore down upon him, even the king urged him to 'set apart all business'. He had made no secret of his distress. 'I have been so tempested in mind,' he told Henry, 'by the untowardness of the chancellors and orators on every side, putting so many difficulties and obstacles to condescend to any reasonable conditions of truce and abstinence of war, that night nor day I could have neither quietness nor rest.' And now he faced a tempest of a more literal kind, since his journey home required fifteen storm-tossed hours to cover the 22 miles between Dover and Calais.

Yet the warmth of the welcome was at least some consolation. Indeed, Wolsey's master expressed unabashed satisfaction at the outcome of his efforts. Already imagining himself, no doubt, at the head of a victorious parade through Paris, Henry was on the verge of gaining an imperial son-in-law at relatively small cost and had lost virtually nothing from his break with France. Expressing his delight through his secretary, Richard Pace, the king 'thanked God that he had such a chaplain by whose wisdom, fidelity and labour he could obtain greater acquisitions than all his progenitors were able to accomplish with all their numerous wars and battles'. As if this were not praise enough, Henry then directed the secretary to write to Wolsey once more, conveying this time his 'most hearty thanks for the great pains and labours sustained in the bringing of his affairs to such conclusion and end, as most redoundeth to his honour and surety, saying that everything in effect is finished according to his desire'.

Nor, albeit with a little prompting from the cardinal himself, did the king proffer merely words of thanks, for the Abbot of St Albans, one of the greatest monasteries in England, had died during Wolsey's absence, and the latter now encouraged Pace to stir the king's gratitude further. A message was therefore dispatched by Wolsey to the secretary, who conveyed it in turn to Henry. Pace, it seems, finally found the king just as he was 'ready to go out shooting', but he nevertheless commanded the messenger 'to go down with him by his secret way into the park', where the letter was duly read. 'By God!', declared Henry, 'my lord cardinal hath sustained many charges in this his voyage and expended £10,000', which, added Pace, 'I did affirm and show his grace of good congruence, he oweth you some recompense.' Whereupon, it seems, 'his grace answered that he would rather give unto you the abbey of St Albans than to any monk'.

Within a month of Wolsey's return, however, an altogether greater prize loomed before him, for on 1 December Pope Leo X graciously expired, leaving vacant the stewardship of Holy Mother Church herself. Ostensibly, of course, the prospect of donning the papal tiara was an irresistible temptation, especially for one who openly looked upon Rome as the hub of both his own and his king's affairs, and Wolsey's fitness for it was acknowledged in many quarters. He had been personally assured at various times of the support that both Francis and Charles V controlled in the Roman curia, and a man of his undoubted pride could only have glowed with deepest satisfaction when Margaret of Austria quipped that she looked forward to becoming the 'mother' of her holy 'father' in the Vatican. The cardinal's phenomenal rise seemed to indicate, too, that the highest ecclesiastical office of all was little more than the obvious next step – the logical culmination of his breakneck journey from royal almoner to papal legate, and the obvious resting place for the exercise of his vigorous intelligence. Impatient with lesser minds, Wolsey took a scornful delight, of course, in bringing his intellect to bear on any knot of problems before cutting through to a solution that frequently dumbfounded his peers. 'His chief study, yea, and all his felicity and inward joy,' one contemporary wrote, 'hath ever been to exercise that angel's wit of his.' Infinitely forceful and disciplined, admirers and enemies alike trembled under his scrutiny. Yet when occasion demanded, he was also capable of 'rare and unheard of affability' – a 'man for all seasons' in his own right, perhaps. Was this not therefore an ideal candidate for the papal throne? Even his vices – his ostentation, his worldliness, his grandiloquent vanity – might have suggested as much.

At this particular time, however, the successor to St Peter's seat faced the most unenviable of tasks. Since Martin Luther launched his Protestant onslaught in 1517, the situation had gone from bad to worse. Men of itchy conscience had flocked to his cause and only four years after this restless Augustinian friar had proclaimed his ninety-five defiant reasons for condemning Roman superstition, he found himself at Wörms outfacing the emperor in person. By then, he had already been excommunicated and his books burnt, though this did not prevent the spread of his three great tracts – *On the Liberty of a Christian Man*, *Address to the Nobility of the German Nation*, and *On the Babylonian Captivity of the Church of God* – in which he directly attacked the pope and the organisation he headed. Together, these works were to cast sheet lightning throughout Christendom and by mid-December 1520 the rampant German friar had brazenly burned the pope's bull of excommunication before a cheering crowd in Wittenberg.

Wolsey himself had staged a ritual incineration of Luther's books, amid great ceremony, at St Paul's Cross in London on 12 May 1521 – though not before he had extracted from the pope an extension of his appointment as legate *a latere*, without which, he claimed, he might not have sufficient authority. Travelling in state to the cathedral, England's premier cleric had walked to the altar under a golden canopy borne over him by four doctors of divinity, before proceeding outside once more to face a crowd of some 30,000 spectators. Seated on a raised platform and flanked by Archbishop Warham, the papal nuncio, the imperial ambassador and Cuthbert Tunstall, he then heard Bishop John Fisher preach a powerful sermon, acknowledging Luther's learning, but denouncing him for his pride – the sin of Lucifer – which had sown such deep divisions. Whereupon the offending books were duly turned to ash and a decree issued, condemning their author as a heretic and forbidding the reading of his works.

That summer Wolsey also took up the king's own personal cause against Luther, drafting the dedicatory epistle of Henry's *In Defence of the Seven Sacraments* to the pope, while leaving any advice on the content to the likes of More and Fisher. Always more comfortable with politics than theology, he likewise eased the way in Rome for the pope's acceptance of the book and the eventual decision to reward Henry with the title 'Defender of the Faith'. A copy of the king's attack on Luther, superbly bound in a bejewelled gold cover, was duly dispatched to John Clerk, the English agent in Rome, and presented to Pope Leo: a gesture which eventually allowed Wolsey to present the king with the papal bull confirming his new title in February 1522, amid blaring 'shalmes and saggebuttes' and fulsome compliments to the royal recipient, 'so formed and figured in shape and stature, with force and pulchritude, which signifieth the pleasure of our Lord God wrought in your noble grace'.

Yet neither Luther nor his contagion abated. Before long, indeed, he had lashed out at Wolsey in person, 'that monster, the Cardinal of York, the public detestation of God and man, the plague of your Majesty's kingdom'. And Luther's onslaught was by no means the only trial facing any prospective pontiff. Throughout his long illness, for instance, Pope Leo had not dared to hunt in the Roman Campagna without a heavy escort, for fear of capture or assassination, and he had been equally disturbed by the possibility that the emperor might employ Luther for political advantage. At Wörms, after all, Charles had actually met 'the one who would not be well received even in hell' and then allowed him to take up residence with Duke Frederick of Saxony. To compound matters, there was also the ongoing war in Europe to set the pontiff's nerves on end. The Vatican had no wealth and no army to speak of, and Rome was under constant threat of sack from both French and imperial armies. In such baleful circumstances, a papal throne and electric chair had little, it seems, to distinguish them.

Wolsey had more personal reasons for avoiding the universal Church's most glittering post. Not least, his keen good sense left him in little doubt that his chances of election were, at best, slender. For anything could happen in a conclave, even with the apparent good offices of the Holy Roman Emperor himself in his favour. Within the Roman curia, too, he faced predators every bit as ravenous as he, just as his predecessor, Cardinal Bainbridge, had discovered to his cost. Rather curiously for someone whose name is synonymous with ambition and intrigue, Wolsey had actually remained remarkably detached from the deadly labyrinthine struggles within that body. He had, for that matter, never even visited the Holy City and made no attempt to establish a personal following by encouraging the election of sympathetic figures to the cardinalate. Indeed, the only cardinal with whom he was personally acquainted at all was Lorenzo Campeggio, whom he had nonchalantly upstaged and embarrassed on both his previous visits to England.

But Wolsey's neglect of his own best interests at Rome went even further and made him the type of colleague that more coolly calculating Italian operators found particularly hard to fathom. While other cardinals were in continual contact with the pope for no other reason than to advertise their energy and subservience, Leo X was frequently indignant that his English lieutenant made so little effort to communicate with him. Equally remarkable in its own way was Wolsey's failure to collect the revenues of the Church of St Cecilia to which he was entitled: a particularly strange oversight for one with his preference for milking ecclesiastical offices to the full. Such neglect may even suggest a certain disdain on behalf of a man who had more than enough sway in his homeland and more than enough personal wealth to sustain his position there. For, as Wolsey now appreciated, what one did not need was as superfluous as what one could not have. And what one could not control was best discarded for what one could. England, the English court and England's king were Wolsey's natural domain. Rome, by contrast, was a far-off, alien and inhospitable realm: a place of competition, danger and, ironically, comparative weakness. Like the king on a chessboard, in fact, the pope had limited scope for movement in a game that developed round him rather than through him – a crucial fact which England's lone cardinal had already grasped to the full.

Why, then, did Wolsey nevertheless find himself embroiled in a contest for an office that he had little genuine interest in obtaining and even less real chance of actually winning? The answer, as so often, lay in the whims and wilfulness of his royal master. Soon after news of the pope's death reached England,

Charles's ambassador, the Bishop of Elna, dined at Richmond with both Henry and Wolsey. 'As to the person to be chosen for the papacy,' he informed the emperor soon after, 'the king is fully inclined and resolved in favour of the most reverend cardinal of York' and 'is desirous, more than I can express that your Majesty should concur in this opinion.' Wolsey, on the other hand, 'assured the king in my presence, with the most solemn oaths and protestations, that he had no intention to accept this election, unless his master and your Majesty should consider that in so doing he could best promote the welfare and honour of both of you'. Nor, in all likelihood, was this comment any lame manifestation of mock modesty or sham devotion to duty. On the contrary, it captured the essence of Wolsey's current predicament all too accurately. For he found himself at this point thrust into reluctant action by the momentum of his own previous successes – an outright hostage now, not so much to his own ambition as to that of his master.

Before long, Henry was freely declaring that the election 'should not be lost for want of 100,000 ducats', while his bound and tongue-tied cardinal was left to play the part of willing participant, bearing himself as 'cheerful as if he had been elected pope' already. The king, it seems, was captivated at once by the realisation that there had been no English-born pope since Nicholas Breakspear became Adrian IV in 1154. Quite apart from any potential political advantages, Wolsey's election would therefore greatly redound to Henry's personal credit. And Henry was never inclined to look askance at what seemed to him a racing certainty. The emperor had, after all, written to assure him that 'Wolsey's prudence, doctrine, integrity, experience and other virtues and good habits make him eminently worthy to hold this see', adding that he would use every possible means to achieve this end, including, if necessary, 'the army which I have in Italy, which is not small'.

The foot-dragging prospective pontiff was therefore at the centre of an unwelcome, unwarranted and wholly unrealistic scheme to satisfy his master's ego, which had, in turn, been stirred by a cynical imperial ruse, worthy of his own well-practised gift for subterfuge and deception. With all the informal flattery of a skilled practitioner in his own right, the emperor had written to Wolsey in person at the outset of the charade. 'I suppose you have heard of the death of the pope', he observed casually. 'You remember the conversation we formerly had, and I shall gladly do what I can for you.' In all the many letters of Charles to his ambassador in Rome, however, there is subsequently only one instruction to canvass support for Wolsey's election, and this undated letter was almost certainly written much too late to affect the outcome. Throughout the autumn, moreover, the emperor had been receiving letters from his ambassador in London, which were highly critical of Wolsey. Only Margaret of Austria seems to have remained faithful to her friend. But the fact that she was informing Wolsey in mid-December of her ongoing efforts with the emperor to procure his 'exaltation' is hardly suggestive of any firm commitment on her nephew's part.

In these unpropitious circumstances, then, the King of England duly dispatched Richard Pace to Rome, where he was instructed to work closely with John Clerk to secure Wolsey's election. But while Henry claimed to have sent his secretary 'as if he had sent his very heart', Pace arrived too late in any case to affect the outcome. Even messengers riding 'in post' would take at least a fortnight to cover the distance from London to Rome, but the College of Cardinals was anxious to proceed as rapidly as possible, in order to minimise outside pressure. Despite the protests of ambassadors, therefore, they had fixed the beginning of the conclave for 26 December, and though they had been urged thereafter to wait until at least 6 January, so that the full feast of Christmas might be completed, there was no inclination on their part to allow orders from either Charles or Henry to get through in time. In the event, a token postponement of only forty-eight hours was granted before the conclave duly settled to its business.

By this time Rome was ominously tense, teeming with soldiers and guns, buzzing with suspicion, and awash with fears for the worst. Nor was public interest in the name of the new incumbent merely a matter of piety, for it was established by long custom that the successful candidate, who could never return to his own house after selection, should have it ransacked and pillaged by his new subjects. Among the thirty-nine cardinals immured in the Sistine Chapel, meanwhile, 'there could not,' it was rumoured, 'be so much hatred among so many devils in hell'. Cardinal Campeggio and his colleague the Cardinal of Sion were, it seems, prepared to lobby for Wolsey, but there were concerns about the Englishman's arrogance. There were comments, too, about his comparative youth, for the best kind of pope was not expected to live too long. All, in fact, was secrecy, speculation and flux – the only certainty, perhaps, that the new incumbent of the Vatican would be even poorer than most of his immediate predecessors. For Pope Leo, the great Medici art patron and rebuilder of St Peter's, had not only emptied the papal coffers, but run up mighty debts.

In the event, the conclave was painful and prolonged. Intimidated by the 500 Swiss guards who were thought to favour the candidacy of Giulio de Medici, the careworn cardinals conducted their deliberations with neither zest nor relish. When they demanded that the doors of the Sistine Chapel be opened, because of the filth, their request was refused, and on the sixth day, as an incentive to reach a prompt decision, they found their 'meat diminished', notwithstanding the fact that one sickly cardinal had already been carried out almost dead. As tension rose, moreover, so too did the level of intrigue and scale of speculation. 'Here,' wrote Pace, 'is the greatest freedom in saying evil […] and in all languages – this is Roman liberty!' And when false news of Cardinal Farnese's election spread like wildfire among the avid crowds outside, his house was swiftly plundered for long tradition's sake.

Yet it would require fourteen days of turbulence until the deadlock was eventually broken. For when it became clear that none of the more likely contenders could achieve the necessary majority, the final choice fell upon an ageing Dutch pedant who had the advantage of being both decrepit and '*muerto de miedo del Collegio*' or 'deadly afraid of the College of Cardinals'. Adrian Florentius of Utrecht, former Bishop of Tortosa and tutor to Charles V, therefore became Pope Adrian VI, and if his election had indeed been inspired by the Holy Ghost, nothing could have demonstrated more aptly how curious the workings of providence may prove. 'The schoolmaster of the emperor,' Francis I noted drily, 'has been elected Pope', and his elevation was greeted with whistling and shouts of derision by the angry crowd that surrounded the cardinals as they left their meeting in fear of their lives. Ultimately, the new pontiff would take eight months to arrive in Rome and in the meantime the Florentine traders who had swarmed into the city at Leo X's accession swiftly vanished as banks closed and artists migrated. Moreover, like any sensible outsider to the Roman imbroglio, Adrian had never wanted the post and, not altogether surprisingly, he lived for only a further ten months. 'Here,' ran his epitaph, 'lies Adrian VI, whose greatest misfortune was that he became Pope.'

Wolsey, meanwhile, had watched the unfolding spectacle with alert, but largely detached, interest. A curious letter in which he offered to pay for imperial troops to march on Rome to seize control of the conclave makes sense only as a threat to confound French intrigues. And John Clerk, it seems, was merely fooled into believing that Wolsey had actually fallen only three votes short of success on the fourth scrutiny. For the English candidate's total support is never likely to have exceeded more than six cardinals, all of whom appear to have voted in the fifth and final count. Giulio de Medici, it is true, claimed to have spoken on his behalf, though this tallies ill with disparaging remarks he had made three years earlier, and Cardinal Petrucci confided to Pace that support for Wolsey was always limited, since the majority of electors felt that 'he would never come to Rome'. Nor, as a letter from John Clerk implies, was this last suspicion entirely misplaced, for Clerk's comments leave little doubt about his correspondent's continuing half-heartedness:

I did not greatly labour before their entry into the conclave because your
Grace at my departing showed me precisely that you would never meddle
therewith. And on my faith were it not for the king's persuasions I should
stand yet in great doubt whether your Grace would accept it or no.

Not only was Wolsey therefore unperturbed by his defeat, he was soon
enjoying compensation of a much more welcome kind. The emperor, who had
previously been so ready to dangle hollow promises before him, now proffered
solid gold instead: a pension of 2,500 ducats a year, no less, from the revenues
of vacant Spanish bishoprics. On 20 March, moreover, Charles wrote to Wolsey
commending him for his efforts. He addressed Wolsey as '*Lieutenant Général
d'Angleterre*' and spared no praise in his efforts to ensure that the papal election
should be swiftly forgotten. 'I have found by experience,' he observed, 'that the
common affairs of England and myself succeed best wherever you are.' In a
postscript, written in his own hand, the Holy Roman Emperor then 'begged' the
cardinal 'to continue your good efforts, of the value of which I am fully sensible'.
The implication, plainly, was that Charles was as anxious as ever to come to grips
with the French. But, like his grandfather before him, his treasury was empty and
his soldiers stood on the brink of mutiny. Irksome as it was, England – and her
cardinal – would therefore have to be courted, however temporarily.

Only one week later Wolsey was informing the king that Charles had
unexpectedly advanced the date of his projected visit, and now 'desired to
keep Easter in England'. Yet Wolsey also retained his imperious composure and
counselled delay. The emperor's request, he told Henry, was simply to force his
hand in declaring war against France. Besides which, they would both have to
'labour in Holy Week if the change were agreed', which 'were not convenient
for princes, nor for meaner personages'. Clearly, if playing 'hard to get' were
an art form, Wolsey was among its most accomplished masters. Yet his feigned
attempts at sincerity and peacemaking were by now wearing thin. Certainly, his
requests urging the French king to come to England at the same time as the
emperor fooled no-one, least of all Francis himself. Resigning himself to the
forthcoming conflict, the King of France is said to have opened his heart at last.
'I looked for this a great while ago,' he remarked, 'for since the cardinal was at
Bruges I looked for no other.'

When, moreover, Charles V finally crossed the Channel on 22 May 1522,
the crudely anti-Gallic pageantry was much in prominence. A play by William
Cornish of the Chapel Royal openly ridiculed Francis and his alliances, and
Wolsey the peacemaker now found himself berating his former French allies
who must be 'exterminated' if peace were to dawn once more in Europe.

Extolling the King of England's claim to the French throne, he boasted how Henry 'would assuredly oust' its present incumbent. And on Whitsunday, Wolsey duly celebrated high Mass at St Paul's before the emperor and his courtiers, though they were said to be 'sore disdained' that two dukes, two earls and two barons served him at the altar. No fewer than twenty bishops were also in attendance upon the man whom de Salino sardonically referred to as 'the pope who is the cardinal'.

Wolsey had featured prominently from the very moment that Charles set foot in England. And unlike the first visit, which had been comparatively informal, no expense or effort was spared as the full red-blooded glory of war now beckoned at last. It was Wolsey rather than Henry who greeted the young emperor at Dover and together they embraced before riding in each other's company to the castle, though in a typically juvenile ploy, the King of England then pretended to arrive on impulse – 'that it might appear to the Emperor that his coming was of his own mind and affection' – whereafter he proceeded to show his guest the pride of the English fleet. In all, 1,000 people had arrived with Charles and they rode in splendour by Canterbury, Rochester, Gravesend and Greenwich to London, where lavish heraldic decorations and fantastic hangings and spring garlands lined the route. Waiting, too, was a fond greeting from Queen Catherine, the emperor's aunt, though the court was so short of beds that extra ones were brought from both Richmond and the Tower.

The subsequent junketing paid due dividends, at least from the emperor's viewpoint. And when Charles eventually concluded his visit at Windsor Castle by solemnising the treaty agreed at Bruges, it was fitting that he went by way of Hampton Court, since Wolsey had most surely been the architect of that covenant. It was fitting, too, that both Charles and Henry earnestly agreed to submit themselves to Wolsey's jurisdiction in the event of any breach of faith. As legate *a latere*, he was to excommunicate the offending party. Yet this last clause was supposedly mere formality, for when all arrangements were complete, the two rulers received the Holy Sacrament together and swore upon the four evangelists faithfully to observe the league contracted between them. To all appearances, it was a league born of undying friendship, caringly wrapped in the softness of a cardinal's cloak. And thus equipped, Charles duly departed from Southampton with his Spanish fleet, laden with gifts, loaded with promises and near to sinking with English money.

The war that followed, however, proved no more glorious or gainful than the papal election that had preceded it. It began in July with a preliminary expedition led by the Earl of Surrey to an area of France already ravaged by drought and pestilence, and this time, unlike the expedition of 1513, Wolsey assumed responsibility for military strategy. On 9 September he instructed Surrey to defer, wherever necessary, to imperial generals and focus his energies upon inflicting as much summary damage as he might, in order to provoke the enemy into battle. The earl was not, however, to besiege any fortification that could not be captured within a maximum of fifteen days.

The result was a campaign of particular degradation and inhumanity even by the fragile moral standards of the day. Morlaix in the Cherbourg peninsula was burnt, Brest was harried and by August Surrey was ravaging Artois and the Boulonnais, destroying towns, villages and farms, apparently at random. Around Lottinghen the English army burned everything over an area of 40 square miles, though the object of provoking a pitched battle proved signally unsuccessful. Instead, the French commander confined his activity largely to protests about the foulness of his enemy's tactics. Writing to Surrey, the Duke of Vendôme left him in no doubt about his deplorable campaign, though English prisoners returning from Montreuil reported that their captors were laying the blame for the devastation squarely on Wolsey's own shoulders.

Nor were their claims entirely unwarranted. By the middle of September the invaders had penetrated more than 50 miles of French territory and were laying waste to the countryside around Dorlance, before turning north-west to besiege Hesdin. Even imperial commanders, fearing reprisals in the border regions of the Netherlands, were now increasingly restive about the scale of destruction and urged that the siege be lifted. The autumn rain had recently set in, there was talk of desertion and Wolsey's original orders had in any case forbidden the conduct of prolonged sieges. Yet when Surrey subsequently sought the cardinal's advice, he was told in no uncertain terms to continue operations until the end of October, just as Henry had promised Charles originally. Once more, of course, Wolsey found himself bound to his master's coat-tails. But whether responsibility can be shifted quite so conveniently on this particular occasion is far from certain. A no-win, indeed no-point, adventure – one, moreover, that was patently counter-productive from most perspectives – was something that even Henry might have been persuaded to abandon with minimal finesse.

Plainly, a failed first sally into the unfamiliar realm of military strategy was not something that Wolsey was prepared to accept lightly, though ultimately the choice to stay or leave would not be his to make. For, as hungry men and animals sank ever deeper in the autumn mud and the emperor's commanders trudged home to their bases in the Netherlands, Surrey wisely followed suit. After informing Wolsey of the 'universal poverty' he was now leaving behind, as well as the 'great fear of this army' that was its legacy to the French peasants who had suffered under its yoke, he withdrew to Calais on 16 October. It was hardly the triumph that the cardinal might have hoped for and to add further gall to an already bitter cocktail, even the army's provisions had been lacking from the outset. Beef, bread, salt fish, wood and, above all, beer had been in short supply from the very time that the army had first set foot in Calais. And, as if for good measure, a Scottish force of 4,000 men under the Duke of Albany had meanwhile descended menacingly upon Carlisle before succumbing to dissent and divisions among its leaders and settling for a truce that left the King of England, as one might expect, rather more than mildly vexed.

It was money, however, that now came to preoccupy Wolsey increasingly, since the major onslaught on France under the Duke of Suffolk was planned for the following year, and there was already sullen resentment about the cost. In March 1522, three months before Surrey had set out on his vicious jaunt, commissioners had been sent out into every shire to ascertain the value of land, houses and valuables, and the City had been fleeced for a loan of £20,000. But this was not the end of matters, for soon after, a property tax dressed up as a loan was also proposed and firmly rejected by the wealthy London merchants who had already dipped into their pockets too deeply for their notoriously parsimonious liking. It had been scarcely two months since their previous loan, 'whereby,' they informed Wolsey, 'the city is bare of money'. They were equally concerned, it seems, by the snooping of Wolsey's commissioners into their financial affairs, and, under the circumstances, there seemed little choice but to concede to their request that they should make their own declarations.

However, any tactical moderation of demands could not be long sustained, since the estimates for the campaign of 1523 made the costs for the previous year seem insignificant. Suffolk's army was to consist of 26,000 English infantry, 4,000 'Almain' troops costing sixpence a day, and 8,000 horsemen at 8 florins per month. With the added cost of provisions, wagons, 'carriage of ordnance', sea transport, defence of the Scottish border and sundry other items, the total cost was reckoned at £372,404. As such, there could be no alternative to summoning Parliament. And nothing, in fact, could have been a more eloquent demonstration of Wolsey's growing desperation. Neither recognising its evolving status nor appreciating its growing self-confidence, Wolsey was particularly contemptuous of the institution whose support he now so badly needed. Long accustomed to swift and sweeping action, the noisy quibbling of squires and burgesses was an unwelcome distraction and potential obstacle to the smooth running of high state affairs. This, indeed, would be the first time that Parliament had assembled in eight years – the first time, significantly, that it had been summoned since the cardinal assumed full control. So when Wolsey made his way to the House of Commons in April 1523 an almighty clash of wills was imminent.

Two weeks after the formal opening of the session, at which Wolsey had sat at the king's feet, directly to his right, he came once more before the Commons to set out the Crown's specific needs. Initially, he explained why the king 'in his honour' could no longer endure the treachery of the French king who 'had broken his promises to England by making war with the emperor', 'had refused to pay the French queen's dowry', 'had withholden the payment of money agreed on as to the delivering up of Tournay' and had lately sent the Duke of Albany into Scotland to stir up war. But the mortal sting in Wolsey's address came next, for he then exhorted his audience to 'cheerfully assist' the king by granting him the sum of £800,000. Amounting to four shillings in the pound on the value of lands and goods, this was a truly grievous levy, and as the cardinal beat a swift but suitably imperious retreat from the chamber, leaving listeners to reflect at leisure upon the time bomb that had just been casually deposited in their midst, there was a predictable hum of stunned disapproval.

The following day when the Speaker, Sir Thomas More, urged that payment should indeed be made for duty's sake, complaints and counter-arguments flew thick and fast. Loyal subjects, it was said, would be reduced 'to barter clothes for victuals and bread and cheese', and if the sum were conceded 'the realm itself for want of money would grow in a sort barbarous and ignoble'. When, moreover, the Commons appointed a committee in the hope that Wolsey might persuade the king to accept less, he is said to have 'currishly answered' that he would rather have his tongue plucked from his head with pincers than do so. Yet stalemate prevailed, leaving the cardinal with no other choice than to attempt to impose the irresistible force of his personal presence upon the seemingly immovable resistance of a refractory Parliament. This, after all, was a man who had not only hobnobbed on equal terms with kings and emperors, but had arrested foreign ambassadors, spurned papal legates, and on one occasion seen fit to manhandle a papal nuncio. If reason could not prevail, therefore, Wolsey would descend upon his detractors 'in all his pomp, with his maces, his pillars, his poleaxes, his crosses and his great seal, too' and thereby cow them into awed submission.

In truth, there was little choice, and behind the show of strength lay all the inner misgivings of a tightrope walker who was focused more and more acutely upon what lay below rather than the way ahead. Wolsey had rarely, if ever, had the moral stamina or weight of genuine influence to swing the king from any cause upon which he had firmly set his sights, and for all his vaunted power was impotent without his master. Now, however, with that master exulting ever more fully and demandingly in his own pulsating sense of kingship, Wolsey's sense of usefulness was increasingly under challenge. Even before the negotiations at Calais in 1521, Henry had instructed his secretary to inform the cardinal that younger men should be duly trained and prepared in the skills of diplomacy. 'Whereas old men do now decay greatly within this realm,' wrote the secretary on behalf of the king, 'his mind is to acquaint other young men with his great affairs, and therefore he desireth your Grace to make Sir William Sandys and Sir Thomas More privy to all such matters as your Grace shall treat at Calais' – an innocent and reasonable enough request, perhaps, but nevertheless all too redolent of ebbing tides and shifting sands.

So when Wolsey subsequently surrounded himself with his trusty acolytes and puffed himself to full extension before Parliament in a show of intimidating majesty, the response was, perhaps, the most important test of his self-assurance to date. Much else, too, would depend upon the outcome, for without his unwavering confidence and panache, his instinctive knack for weighing situations and calculating odds, not to mention his conjuror's gift for plucking ingenious solutions to thorny problems from the confines of a cardinal's hat, the king's chief minister might well appear distinctly mortal. If his touch was as sure as ever, he would prevail as he always had in previous displays of brinkmanship. And if the actor's flourish and stage manager's imagination, so important for any statesman, were still at his disposal, they might yet be brought to bear with overpowering effect. He was playing, after all, a favourite card, one of many that he had previously brandished with exquisite timing. But if the time, and more importantly the place were on this occasion wrong, the consequent loss of face could well prove lasting.

In the event, the parliamentary response was crushing. For Wolsey was neither contradicted nor debated, nor greeted with derision, but met with what he himself termed a 'marvellous obstinate silence'. Previously he had berated Parliament for its idle babble and complained how its wearisome arguments were 'blown abroad in every alehouse'. Now, however, Sir Thomas More was left to explain a devastating dumb show. It was clearly no easy task and left even him, to all appearances, a blathering, cringing heap. When Wolsey turned at last in the Speaker's direction, Sir Thomas suggested, in fact, that members were simply 'abashed at the presence of so noble a personage'. It was not, moreover, in accordance with their privileges to debate with strangers. Thus vanquished, the hitherto invincible cardinal bore himself from the scene of carnage with whatever small composure he could muster.

Over the next sixteen days there followed weighty speeches on the costs and risks of invading France, though better advocates than Wolsey, it seems, remained to argue the case for at least some form of payment to the king. For 'after long persuading and the privy labouring of friends', the Commons agreed to vote supplies, albeit on a far less generous scale than first requested. Those with incomes of £20 and over were to provide 2 shillings in the pound, while those with between £1 and £20 would pay 1 shilling. The king's poorest subjects, in their turn, would contribute fourpence per head. Under the circumstances, Wolsey had little alternative beyond accepting the inevitable and feigning satisfaction with the outcome. Even the king was prepared to do likewise, though no doubt through firmly gritted teeth. Yet in the country at large there remained seething discontent, as murky rumours of resistance circulated freely. From Norfolk came talk of insurrection, and in Coventry there were plans, apparently, to 'seize and rob the collectors of the subsidy, and then to hold Kenilworth against the king'. True, the rumours proved idle, but their significance could not have been lost upon Wolsey himself. For they reflected the hostility of the common people all too clearly and demonstrated beyond any shadow of doubt that he now had far more than the enmity of lords and nobles to disturb his meagre slumbers.

In his desperation, the cardinal had been no less high-handed over clerical taxation to finance the current war emergency that he and his master had largely generated themselves. Technically, such funding could only be voted separately by the convocations of Canterbury and York. But by invoking his legatine authority, Wolsey ordered the Canterbury convocation, which Archbishop Warham had summoned to St Paul's, to join members from York at a legatine synod called to Westminster. In the event, he was actually forced to issue a second demand for attendance before the clergy duly complied. The opposition, moreover, was wholly understandable, for never before had England's convocations been superseded in this way, and the resulting levy of 50 per cent of one year's revenue of all benefices in England, to be levied over five years, was equally unprecedented. 'Gentle Paul, lay down thy sword,' wrote John Skelton, 'for Peter of Westminster hath shaven thy beard.'

15

'Violence and Puissance'

The grand military strategy to which Thomas Wolsey now found himself irrevocably committed was both far-flung and far-fetched. As the cardinal well knew, the decisive arena of the Franco-imperial struggle was Italy, where the pope, Venice, Florence and Genoa – all facing the imminent threat of Turkish attack – were in alliance with Charles V against the French. Spanish forces, however, were now intended to pile further pressure upon France along the Pyrenees border, as an English army, working in close co-operation with the newly enlisted Duke of Bourbon, plunged deep into the enemy's heartland. Bourbon, who had recently defected from his sovereign's service, was to advance against Lyons at the head of a force of Burgundians and German *Landsknechte*, while the Duke of Suffolk was to take his army of some 20,000 men from Calais to the maximum limit of penetration that he could manage. The plain intention was a show of crushing force delivered to a bewildered and floundering foe in a series of deadly assaults, each designed to bleed France dry before the clinical dismemberment of her broken corpse.

Central to Wolsey's strategy was the role of the traitor in the French camp. Charles, Duke of Bourbon, was, after all, a major recruit to the Anglo-imperial cause, and Wolsey, much to his master's delight, had in the past been able to weave the most romantic dreams of prospective glory from altogether humbler threads than he. In his youth, Bourbon had distinguished himself at the Battle of Marignano and gone on to become Constable of France. But he was proud, frustrated and prone to disloyalty, as his behaviour towards his ruler had already amply demonstrated. Inevitably, his ancient family and great possessions had aroused Francis's suspicions and when accused by the king of jealousy, Bourbon's response could not have betrayed his pretensions more eloquently. 'How,' he retorted, 'can your Majesty believe that I feel jealousy of a gentleman whose ancestors were only too happy to be squires of mine?' Nor was this the only example of the duke's stubborn refusal to kowtow, for in 1520, at the Field of Cloth of Gold, the King of England had been so struck by his strutting arrogance that he freely admitted to Francis that any Englishman behaving thus would not long keep his head.

Yet it was this individual upon whom both Henry and Wolsey now staked so much. When Bourbon, at the age of 31, scorned the amorous advances of the king's 45-year-old mother, saying that he would not marry her for all the riches of Christendom, he was deprived not only of his lands and rank but even of the sable and cloth-of-gold cloak he had worn as Constable. And thus ripened for defection, he was duly plucked by Wolsey. Sir John Russell, a rising Dorsetshire gentleman who was making a successful career as a soldier, diplomat and courtier, was soon dispatched for a secret meeting, and a deal was sealed, notwithstanding the personal interference of Henry himself, who foolishly proposed that Bourbon should kidnap the French king while the intended victim was on one of his well-known libidinous excursions at dead of night.

The tenuous arrangement with Bourbon was, however, only the starting point of a long and heavy chain of problems facing Wolsey. Not only were there fears that the duke might be hatching counter-plans with Emperor Charles, there were also other more pressing concerns to contend with. In July, Wolsey had reported that the 'poore souldgiers' of Calais were 'far behinde unpayde of their wages' and that the town's defences and supplies were largely inadequate for the forthcoming conflict. More worryingly still, he found himself at odds with the king's military thinking, which, for once, proved eminently sound. In Henry's view, the primary objective should be both traditional and limited. Like Wolsey, he suspected that his Burgundian allies might well be tempted to 'stay' upon their frontiers 'to the end that our money be spent upon them'. But, unlike his chief minister, he concluded that the wisest option was to 'have the siege of Boulogne experimented'. By his own admission, he knew all too well what it meant to march an army through the 'wet weather and rotten ways of Picardy' and he claimed to have heard 'on the faith of a gentleman' that Francis had sworn he would defeat his English enemy at any cost. Worse still, it was reported that the French king had equipped Richard de la Pole, the rival claimant to the English throne, with a force 12,000 strong.

Yet the emperor had objected that Boulogne was impregnable and Wolsey soon found himself concurring with both this and the further suggestion that the Duke of Suffolk's army should attempt nothing less than the capture of Paris itself. For once, moreover, the English king deferred to his minister's judgement. Faced with a potentially fateful decision, he seems to have shed his usual intransigence, and even went so far as to praise the cardinal for having the strength to differ. As Thomas More wrote on Henry's behalf:

> His Highness esteemeth nothing in counsel more perilous than for one to persevere in the maintenance of his advice because he hath once given it. He therefore commendeth and most affectuously thanketh your faithful diligence and high wisdom in advertising him of the reasons which have moved you to change your opinion.

The irony, however, could not have more been delicious. For on the one occasion that Wolsey's master had agreed to change his mind, his original thinking was in all respects sound, possibly more so than ever before. As events would prove, the king's fears about sending his army into a 'distant land', dependent on people well known for their 'slackness and hard handling', were entirely justified. So, too, were his concerns about Suffolk's abominably late departure from Calais on 21 September. Henry had stated his reservations about the prospect of 'harsh weather' to Wolsey only the day before, in fact, along with the concern that the English army might have to 'forbear the profit of the spoil'. And then there was the further worry that Bourbon's force would be dispersed before it could combine with Suffolk's. On all points the king was proved right, especially with regard to Bourbon, whose treason was discovered by Francis before any effective aid had been offered. But it was Wolsey who prevailed, and prevailed in the one area of affairs where his own expertise was most limited. Well beyond his comfort zone in all senses of the term, he would therefore be more and more inclined henceforth to rely upon that most deadly of political expedients: the gambler's throw.

Initially, however, Suffolk and his men made good progress as they headed for their goal. Advancing without serious hindrance, they met and defeated two French armies, and before the end of the month appeared to have gained 'free entry into the bowels of France'. By the end of October, indeed, Suffolk had crossed the Somme and taken Montdidier. 'When they were all armed,' wrote the chronicler Edward Hall, 'the trumpets blew; then towards the bray marched these valiant gentlemen with pikes and swords and cried Har! Har!' There was, he added, 'foining, lashing and striking', as the invading force swept all before it.

Brandon, too, was for the time being in full cry, informing Henry from his camp at Compiègne that there was 'good likelihood' of his attaining 'his ancient right and title to the crown of France to his singular comfort and eternal honour'. Four weeks later the English were only 40 miles from the French capital.

But now the weather intervened with a vengeance. A 'fervent' frost hampered all movement and over two days killed more than a hundred troops. Thereafter, when the temperature rose, the army foundered in the mud and, as provisions grew scarce, whispers of mutiny circulated ominously. The imperialists in Suffolk's army went home, the Burgundians disbanded, as predicted, and the duke, in desperation, sent an emissary to the king to explain 'that his people which were in the French ground abode much misery'. The weather, he said, was wet, 'the ways deep' and there were also 'long nights, short days, great journeys and little victual' to endure, 'which caused the soldiers daily to die'. Nevertheless, the king was adamant. And as the very scenario that he had predicted unfolded before his eyes, Henry became increasingly indignant at Suffolk's apparent unwillingness to persevere. 'We will in no wise,' the king informed him, 'that the army should break.' A force of 6,000 men under Lord Moulsey was, he claimed, being organised to relieve the beleaguered duke.

Yet by December Suffolk was back in England, and it was he rather than Wolsey who seems to have borne the brunt of the king's anger. Henry had, after all, been willingly converted to the revised plan and could not now – openly, at least – accept its error. There was also the possibility, gratefully seized upon by Wolsey as he grasped at any shortening straw available, that the setback was merely temporary; no more than might be expected by any great commander involved with the chance of war. For the time being, therefore, the blame would have to rest upon the executant rather than the deviser of the whole fiasco. The royal wrath, moreover, had been magnified by the contrasting fortunes of the emperor, who had achieved all his objectives in the south-west, while failing to invade Guienne as promised. In consequence, as Wolsey breathed a heavy, if fleeting, sigh of relief, Suffolk and his captains were left to languish in semi-disgrace. They 'came not to the king's presence a long season,' we are told, 'to their great heaviness and displeasure'.

In the meantime, the cardinal had found himself with yet another plate to juggle. On 14 September Pope Adrian VI had raised himself wearily in his sickbed and announced, 'like a man fatigated', to the cardinals attending him that he was going to die. Weary of their unequal struggle with chronic disease, his wretched kidneys had finally done for him and plunged Thomas Wolsey once more into a race for the papacy that remained little more than an irksome distraction from his main business. Learning of the news at his favourite residence, the More, he immediately wrote to the king expressing both his misgivings and submission to his master's wishes. He felt himself 'unmeet and unable to so high and great a dignity', he told Henry, and would much rather continue in the king's service 'than to be ten popes'. Nevertheless, his letter continued, he knew the king's mind on this matter and dutifully accepted his decision. He acknowledged, he said, that the king's interests would be well served by his presence in Rome and was therefore composing written instructions to the English agent in the Holy City, which would be in Henry's hands by the next post.

Nor, once again, was there any false modesty or any other kind of insincerity at the heart of this letter. Nothing had occurred to lessen Wolsey's reluctance since the last abortive attempt in 1521 and there had certainly been no time for him to develop any kind of 'English faction' in the Roman curia. Writing privately to Richard Pace, he once more protested his wish to end his days in Henry's service, remaining on familiar ground, instead of 'mine old days approaching, to enter into new things', and confirmed, too, that the king was the driving force behind his involvement. 'The mind and entire desire of His Highness, above all earthly things,' he admitted to Pace, 'is that I shall attain to the said dignity.' Hoist as before by his own petard, he clearly had no alternative but to pander to his master's ego as earnestly and energetically as his waning resources allowed.

In the autumn of 1523, therefore, while Suffolk's wagons were floundering vainly in French mud, Wolsey began his own equally pointless quest. Among the papers he had dispatched to Henry so swiftly was also 'a familiar letter in the king's name to the emperor', which he intended his master to rewrite in his own hand, 'putting thereunto your secret sign and mark'. The primary intention here was a straightforward reminder to Charles of his earlier promise to advance Wolsey's cause in the College of Cardinals. But other correspondence, which was duly forwarded to Rome, detailed the English candidate's credentials. His diplomatic ability was emphasised and he was praised especially as a statesman who had striven hard for international harmony: someone whose main desire now was to bring 'final rest, peace and quiet' to Christendom. Nor, it was suggested, were his fellow cardinals to expect the blandness and austerity of his predecessor, if he were to be elected. On the contrary, he would bring energy and imagination to his office, and would arrive in Rome within three months, raring to lead a crusade against the Turk with the aid of the King of England.

For a self-composed testimonial, it did not hold back for modesty's sake. Nor, of course, could it, since the inexorable logic of events, which had by now entirely overtaken Wolsey, clearly dictated otherwise. Even so, however, the die was already cast in another's favour, for Charles had once more played his allies false and Wolsey, too, had sent alternative instructions in support of another candidate. When the emperor wrote later of the 'zeal and diligence' he had exercised on the English candidate's behalf, he was therefore dealing in little more than cynical word games. He had, it is true, written a letter of recommendation to the Duke of Sessa, his ambassador in Rome, but he had also taken the cunning precaution of delaying its dispatch so that it would fail to reach its destination until long after the election was over. Wolsey, meanwhile, had made it clear to his own agents in Rome that they were to support the candidacy of Giulio de Medici as soon as there could be no further doubt that his own bid was irrelevant.

As the cardinals in the Sistine Chapel settled in to their cramped wooden cells, confined and watched over by their Swiss guards, the familiar intrigues duly ran their chaotic course. A dash of mirth lifted the gloom momentarily when the French cardinals arrived late in riding boots, spurs, and feathered hats. But the roof cracked during the early voting and the unprecedented intrusion of an architect had to be permitted to ensure the building's safety. By the eighth day, moreover, rations were being cut down and twelve days later the Roman mob was said to be threatening the conclave with bread and water. There were darker rumours, too. For when word spread that arms had been hidden by malcontents, a search was made and the doors were walled up and windows locked. Thus secure under the guidance and protection of the indefatigable Holy Ghost, the Sacred College continued its deliberations.

The chief shapers and movers were cardinals Campeggio, Colonna, Pucci and, above all, Medici. Yet on this occasion some energetic canvassing was conducted for Wolsey himself, though mainly, it must be said, for tactical reasons. Certainly, John Clerk proffered some words of encouragement to the English candidate. 'One thing we be right sure of,' Clerk reported, 'if your Grace were here present ye should be as sure of it as ye be of York.' Some cardinals, he added, would rather 'go to Jerusalem upon their thumbs' than pass the Englishman over. And in one of the scrutinies on 16 November, Wolsey did indeed fare better than on any previous occasion, since the French-backed candidate, Cardinal Colonna, who had hitherto opposed him, became determined to prevent the election of a Medici at any cost.

Yet Colonna's ploy failed and the bastard scion of one of Italy's most notorious noble houses was duly elevated to the papal chair. The son of Cardinal de Grassis, who was himself a bishop, claimed in a dream to have seen Medici playing the pipes on the high altar as the other cardinals danced to his tune. And this, coupled to desperate weariness on the part of all concerned after twenty-one days of numbing deadlock and Medici's utter refusal to compromise, seems to have swung the balance. For when Colonna asked him whether he intended 'to stay in that prison forever', the Italian confirmed that he would never yield. And after learning that he had been deserted by his French patrons, Colonna duly opted for freedom and fresh air by switching his decisive vote to Medici.

After a conclave of record duration, Giulio de Medici therefore became Clement VII. He 'loves money' and 'coquettes with the French', wrote the Spanish ambassador. But Wolsey was soon congratulating the new pope as 'his singular and especial lover and friend' and telling him how his election was merited 'above all spiritual persons living'. Nor, once again, was he lying when he told his Holy Father how he was 'far more joyful' at the appointment 'than if it had happened upon mine own person'. Indeed, if his position in England had been more comfortable at that time, he would doubtless have been a truly happy man. Yet, even though the failure of English arms remained an open sore, he was still continuing to ride the storm, and the poison chalice of long and painful exile in Rome had at least been taken from his lips. More importantly, it had been withdrawn once and for all, for his master would never again have reason for him to step into the papal breach.

Clearly the emperor had not lived up to his promise of support. But this did not deflect the King of England's allegiance or alter his determination to prosecute the war that had begun so disappointingly. Nor does it explain the curious twist of policy that Wolsey now began to ponder in spite of his master's inclinations. Notwithstanding the previous impasse with Parliament, Henry was soon contriving a double offensive in France, involving a vast force of 20,000 men led by him in person and another army under the control of none other than the Duke of Bourbon, who was now free again, it seems, to emulate the military escapades of his youth. In all, 100,000 ducats were to be furnished for the duke's intended campaign in Provence, and in the early weeks of 1524 a merchant was bribed to smuggle sacks of coins to the continent to pay for mercenaries. The money, we are told, was sewn into 'coats of brigandines fashion' – a type of light body armour – and carried undetected across several borders, the merchant having been paid well 'not to meddle with it'. Some time later, the ever-willing and ever-suffering Richard Pace was also dispatched to the Franco-Italian border to seal arrangements. Having traversed the Alpine pass over the Col di Tenda, 'so upright to ascend and stand that it made us creep on all four', he complained from Lucca in July of the 'molestious passage' of his baggage. At one point, indeed, he had not 'dared to turn his horse for all worldly riches, nor even look down for proclivity and deepness of the valley'.

But while Pace was loyally shredding his nerves in pursuit of the royal fancy, both the council and the cardinal were bent on undermining his efforts. On the one hand, the king's councillors were eager to obstruct any attempt to prolong the conflict. Beyond the obvious hazard of death in battle for a king who had no heir, they could see no profitable outcome from another costly adventure across the Channel – a view widely shared by other observers in Europe itself. When the Bishop of Capua's secretary wrote to him in March 1524, for instance, he was puzzled by the King of England's apparent obsession with combat for combat's sake. The aims of the emperor and his French counterpart were, he argued, coolly logical, but King Henry's motives made little sense. Was a personal vendetta involved or had he simply been deluded by the emperor's blandishments? Perhaps he was seeking revenge for French assistance to the Scots. Surely he was not seriously expecting to make good his claims to territory in France itself. The only plausible conclusion, it seemed, was that the king 'had no clear object in view'.

While Henry flailed, however, and his council attempted to limit the damage, Wolsey was already contemplating a much more radical deviation from the king's chosen path – nothing less, indeed, than a reaccommodation with Francis I himself. In theory, of course, there were sturdy grounds for personal animus against the Holy Roman Emperor. Not only had he failed to procure the papacy as promised, he was also failing to deliver the pension of 9,000 ducats previously offered to Wolsey. According to the cardinal's agent at the imperial court, it was as easy 'to get money from a stone as cash from these people'. The new pope, meanwhile, was also known to be keen for reconciliation with France and this, too – just like the claim that Wolsey was still pursuing a balance of power in the quest for peace – has been suggested as a possible motive for what now transpired. All, indeed, may have played some role, to a greater or lesser degree, in determining his actions.

But pragmatism, opportunism and the flexibility that went with both were always Wolsey's watchwords in pursuit of his overriding priorities: the king's and England's self-interest, and the increasingly pressing matter of his own political survival. The emperor had, after all, already failed to fulfil the obligations agreed at Windsor for the campaign of 1523. Yet now, with Milan in imperial lands, he was beginning to appear as much of a threat to the papacy as Francis himself, and while Wolsey was no blind slave to Rome, he had every reason from England's perspective to maintain the independence of the pope. Above all, however, it was crucial for the representative of a comparatively lightweight power like England to keep the major combatants guessing. If Charles became too confident of his ally's friendship and Francis too resigned to her enmity, the only result could be a diminution of influence. For England to thrive, the balance of power must be utilised – not in the interests of peace, but in the natural pursuit of advantage.

And with this in mind, while Richard Pace was clambering precariously among the windswept Alpine peaks, Wolsey was exploring the altogether greener and more fertile foothills of a new understanding with the ancient enemy.

By June 1524, in fact, the cardinal had already approached Clement VII with an informal appeal for peace and opened furtive communications with Louise of Savoy, the Queen Mother of France. The failures of the Duke of Bourbon, moreover, seemed to make this policy a sensible one. He had duly invaded Provence at the end of June and laid siege to Marseille, attempting to open a passage between Spain and Italy for the emperor. Imperial funds arrived only in driblets, however, and not a penny of English money made its way through. Nor did the King of England's promised onslaught from Calais materialise, with the consequence that after forty days Bourbon's army was forced to retire in confusion along the steep and twisting Aurelian Way. The headlong flight of his troops became, in fact, a source of wry amusement to John Clerk. 'If they had made as good speed outwards as they have made homewards,' he informed Wolsey, 'they might have been at Calais long afore this time.'

But far from sweetening the French to English overtures, as Wolsey had hoped, the shifting situation now convinced Francis I that the time was ripe for an onslaught of his own. The Duke of Bourbon's treachery naturally demanded revenge and, to increase the temptation, the emperor was currently in poor health. Sources in Spain, where Charles now lay, suggested that he was 'very feeble and nothing apt for war' and the Spaniards themselves were said to be 'very desirous of peace' since Bourbon's defeat. The 'rashness of his enemies' had therefore presented the King of France with a window of opportunity that he was determined to exploit to the full. 'I am concluded,' he declared in October, 'and am resolved to pass in person into Italy; and whoever shall advise me to the contrary shall not only be blamed, but incur my displeasure.' The objective was the Duchy of Milan and, in particular, the main imperial stronghold at Pavia. If this were to fall, the conquest of all Italy could be completed at leisure.

As events unfolded, Wolsey found himself for the first time a passive spectator on the European stage, since reality had at long last descended and the two main protagonists, freed from distraction and unimpeded by impudent schemes and interventions from across the English Channel, now openly squared for a decisive showdown. Even before October was out, the city of Milan had fallen to the French and the audacity of their king once more placed him on the threshold of sweeping success. Yet plague swiftly took hold inside the walls of his new conquest and in November the first assault upon Pavia failed. With the river Po swollen by autumn rain, Francis had been defied by Dom Antonio de Leyva, losing 3,000 infantry infantry in the process. At which point this doughty Spanish veteran, so crippled by gout that it was his custom to be borne into battle upon a chair, resolved to defend his high-towered fortress at any cost.

The onset of winter proved cruel for the besiegers and Wolsey's recent overtures to his former enemies seemed increasingly mistimed. 'The King of France,' reported one observer, 'has made a very hasty invasion of Italy, and it will not be easy for him to return without risking his life and all that he has.' A chicken, it seems, now cost a French gentleman all of 15s, while 'the infantry lie in the trenches and dare not leave them lest they die of hunger and cold'. 'All the great lords,' it was said, 'are obliged to warm themselves in the king's kitchen.' And when in January 1525, against all odds, an enemy army led by none other than the Duke of Bourbon was reported nearby, the French king was faced with a fateful decision. Egged on by stubborn pride and foolish counsel, he decided to maintain his position before an oncoming force and the resolute will of de Leyva's hardy garrison.

Accordingly, at dawn on 24 February, Francis I found his army caught between 3,000 German and Spanish infantry and a horde of onrushing imperialists who had decided at long last to sally forth from the gates of Pavia. As the French, with the king at their head, charged the Spanish pikemen and arqebusiers, they quickly found themselves entrapped in a gory killing zone. Francis distinguished himself by his bravery and succeeded in bringing down one of the imperial standard bearers by his own hand. But by the time he approached a bridge which might have carried him to safety, his escort had dwindled and he was rudely grappled from his horse. Though the Abbot of Narjara later told the emperor that he had 'no wounds at all save a contusion of the leg, and a mere scratch between the fingers of his hand', he was now at his enemy's mercy. So when an imperial knight clapped his sword on an exposed joint of the royal armour, Francis accepted the inevitable. 'Give me my life, for I am the king', he is said to have declared. 'I yield myself up to the emperor.' And with that, the European balance of power upon which Thomas Wolsey's machinations had so utterly depended came to a shattering and irrevocable end.

Yet the King of England, utterly failing to appreciate the broader implications, met the news with an uncontrollable outburst of boyish glee. In early March, the Archduchess Margaret greeted an English envoy with word of what had passed. 'We have this morning heard from Italy the best news in the world', she declared. 'The King of France is prisoner, 13,000 of his people slain.' And when Henry finally learned of the victory in his bedchamber some time later, he exclaimed to the archduchess's messenger that he was 'as welcome as the angel Gabriel was to the Virgin Mary'. Springing up to tell his queen the glad tidings, he was already laying heady plans for the future. 'Now is the time,' he told imperial officials, 'for the emperor and myself to devise full satisfaction from France. Not an hour is to be lost!'

From Henry's perspective, moreover, 'full satisfaction' could mean only one thing – the unconditional recovery of 'his' French crown by the sword. As he now told Sir Robert Wingfield, his permanent ambassador to the emperor:

> So long as the realm of France shall remain in the hands of those who cannot, nor never will, cease to apply their wits, powers, thoughts and studies, to ampliate and extend their limits and dominions, never satiate nor contented with enough, there can never be rest, quiet and tranquillity in Christendom.

It was 'notorious and manifest', Henry went on, that the crown of France was morally his, though he would settle for possession of Normandy, Gascony, Guienne, Anjou, Maine and Poitou, which were his by right of lineal succession. And since these could only be taken by 'violence and puissance', the time was apparently ripe for a hare-brained joint invasion. Henry and Charles would enter Paris together, whereupon the English ruler would be crowned anew at Notre Dame. Thereafter, he would accompany his nephew, friend and ally to Rome itself to 'see the Crown imperial set upon his head'. The Princess Mary, meanwhile, was to be 'transported' to the French capital, where her long-anticipated marriage to Charles could be solemnised.

The impact of such delirium upon Wolsey may well be imagined. For the cardinal was all too painfully aware that a project of this kind could no longer appeal to the spindly, lantern-jawed ruler whose machinations and double-dealings had already resoundingly trumped his own. As Holy Roman Emperor, Charles now dominated Europe and had neither need nor inclination for English help. Though his own slender finances made it politic to keep his ally dangling for the time being, there could be, in fact, but one long-term outcome. He would use the English while it pleased him and leave Wolsey, at imperial convenience, to execute his master's folly. Nor was there any hope of escaping such an outcome, for Henry was by now hell-bent upon invasion, with or without the emperor's feigned assistance. Richard Sampson, English ambassador at Madrid, had, it seems, already detected evidence of Charles's half-heartedness. 'They think here,' he observed, 'that the king should make the rest of any conquest at his own charge.' And now, of course, the dreadful task of procuring the king's 'charge' would fall once more on Thomas Wolsey.

After the outright hostility and intense embarrassment of 1523, there was certainly no possibility of a return to Parliament for a further round of taxation, especially when time was such a crucial consideration. Instead, Wolsey found himself forced to opt for an alternative expedient; though one, it must be said, which also carried with it every likelihood of failure. On this occasion, he would attempt to fleece both laity and clergy alike by means of ancient feudal custom, which laid down a public obligation to support the king with an appropriate 'aid' when he led an army abroad in person. To sweeten the pill, this new levy was to be presented as a 'loan' based upon assessments of income made two years earlier, and like the arrangements stipulated at that time it would be graduated according to the ability to pay. Three shillings and fourpence in the pound would be raised on incomes of £50 and above, 2s 8d on those with £20 and upwards, and 1s in the pound on the poorer groups boasting only £1 or more.

But this more enlightened aspect of the so-called 'Amicable Grant' did nothing to make it more acceptable to those who had to suffer it. Wolsey himself was responsible for collecting the levy in London and soon found himself entirely reliant upon the kind of bullying with which his name was already synonymous. When the Mayor and corporation demurred, they were reminded in no uncertain terms how 'it were better that some should suffer indigence than that the king should lack'. More ominously still, they were told to 'ruffle not in this case', since 'it might fortune to cost some their heads'. The implication was clear enough. Far from being the imperious decree of a minister confident of carrying all before him, this was the anguished outburst of a desperate skater flailing wildly on the thinnest possible ice. The shriller his bluster, moreover, the greater grew the number of cracks around him, for as Edward Hall observed, 'the poor cursed, the rich repugned, the light wits railed'. All, indeed, now saw the cardinal and his 'co-adherents' as 'subversors of the law and liberty of England'.

Nor was the resistance confined to London. On the contrary, there was 'muttering throughout the realm' and Wolsey's other commissioners faced even greater resistance. Sir Thomas Boleyn was roughly handled in Maidstone, while East Anglia teetered on the edge of outright civil war. When the new Duke of Norfolk, who had succeeded his father the previous year, came to Suffolk he was met with stiff opposition at Lavenham and Sudbury in particular. Church bells were rung in alarm and, after attempting to identify the leader of the Thetford protesters, the duke was told by one John Green, a 'well-aged man', that their captain's name was 'Poverty', 'for he and his cousin Necessity have brought us to this doing'. In Cambridge, students rioted and in Kent, where men suggested they 'would have no rest' as long as Wolsey lived, every secular priest in the diocese of Salisbury refused to make the grant. Elsewhere, Huntingdonshire rumbled and Essex reeled as the men of Chelmsford and Stansted refused to pay and commissioners reported that 'some fear to be hewn in pieces if they make any grant'. 'If any insurrection follow,' Wolsey was now informed, 'the blame shall be only against you.'

Such fears of rebellion were reinforced, moreover, by parallel events in Germany, where the pent-up frustration of thousands of marauding peasants had been wreaking havoc on a scale never witnessed before. Armed with pikes and firearms, the German rebels were protesting the loss of their ancient manorial rights and in doing so had laid waste to much of Swabia, Franconia and Thuringia. In Frankfurt alone they had destroyed thirty fortresses and sacked eighty monasteries as rulers throughout Europe watched on anxiously lest the contagion sweeping the Holy Roman Empire should spread to their own kingdoms. And now the spectre of anarchy seemed to many to be rearing its monstrous head in Henry VIII's island realm. Writing to the imperial ambassador in Florence, a Swiss cleric related how his English friends had said that Henry's subjects were everywhere turning against him and that no-one could say where the ferment might end. In France, too, Louise of Savoy was confidently asserting that England was facing meltdown. Her spies, it seems, had told her that the whole country was in such a state of mutiny that there was now no possibility whatsoever of a successful attack against her own homeland.

Under such circumstances, even Henry was impelled to tread carefully, urging his agents to 'proceed doucely rather than by violence' in their money-gathering efforts. By May, however, he was prepared to capitulate entirely, withdrawing the levy altogether and heaping further execration upon the man who was already blamed by one and all. 'Well,' he complained, 'some have informed me that my realm was never so rich and that men would pay at the first request, but now I find all the contrary.' 'I will no more of this trouble', he continued. 'Let letters be sent to all shires that the matter be no more spoken of. I will pardon all.' Though the king still claimed to require funds for an impending campaign that would never actually materialise, the element of compulsion was nevertheless decisively shelved. Instead, he would ask only for 'such as his loving subjects would grant to him of their good minds'. Thus, it seemed, was the tyranny of the cardinal duly righted by the fair-minded and bounteous intervention of his master.

Nor, by this stage, did Wolsey expect or seek any other outcome. When he faced the council, indeed, his defence was little more than token. 'Because every man layeth the burden from him,' he told his audience, 'I am content to take it on me, and to endure the fume and noise of the people, for my good will towards the king, and comfort of you my lords, and other king's councillors.' 'But,' he could not resist adding, 'the eternal God knoweth all.' Predictably, the concluding profession of good faith found no more sympathy among his peers than it did in the country at large, where the cardinal was 'known well enough'. Abroad, too, Wolsey now stood naked – execrated by those whom he had formerly sought to manipulate as friends and exposed to the painful realities of an international situation forever beyond his control. When he encouraged Sir Thomas More to intercept the dispatches of the new imperial ambassador, Louis de Praet, his worst fears were immediately confirmed, since de Praet was determined that the emperor should 'escape the danger of such friends and confederates as he hath hitherto had'. As for Wolsey, the ambassador hoped to see his master 'properly avenged on his man'.

The position, in fact, could not have been more clear-cut or the emperor's reaction – with or without his ambassador's prompting – more inevitable. In the very same week that Wolsey had dispatched his commissioners to collect the Amicable Grant, Charles had begun to compose his response to the King of England's hopes of permanent alliance and swingeing military retribution upon France. His dislike for the cardinal was plainly personal and he had already told de Praet that he would be 'revenged' on him 'in proper time'. The cardinal was, after all, the arrogant alter ego of his equally arrogant master – a base-born upstart and compulsive intriguer whom he knew to be in daily consultation with Giovanni Ciovacchino, a Genoese agent of the French, posing unconvincingly as a merchant. But there were more practical reasons for the emperor's wish to cut his ties: finance and marauding German peasants, to name but two. Italy, more importantly, was already at his mercy and the restoration of the French king to his throne – albeit on the stiffest possible terms – was infinitely preferable to the succession of Henry VIII. Indeed, Charles was already in contact with Dowager Queen Louise of France, determined to rescue her son at any cost from his imprisonment at the castle of Pizzigitone under 1,300 Spanish infantry.

So it was that the screw began to tighten. Initially, it was requested that the Princess Mary, now aged 9, be sent to Spain at once 'to learn the language' and with a huge dowry, in the full knowledge that such appeals would never be met. Then followed a message delivered in person by de Praet that if the English wished to fight, they would have to do so alone. The emperor would not, Henry learned, disarm altogether, but his energies were for now entirely directed towards peace with France. And, as if the bitterness of the pill could be made even greater, Charles also told Henry that his prospective union with Mary was actually no longer of interest to him. Instead, he had set his heart upon a new, 19-year-old bride and her lavish dowry. 'I see no way,' he wrote in June, 'except for me to marry Isabella of Portugal, with whom the king offers a million ducats, but I shall not take any step without the consent of the King of England, as I have sent him my word.' 'I wish for no war this year,' he reminded his victim, 'but to attend to my marriage.'

The impact upon Henry of this appalling affront may well be imagined. The man whom he considered his brother-in-arms, the one chosen to be his son-in-law and potential successor, the friend and nephew to whom he had offered loans nearing half a million ducats had not only deserted him, but was seeking reconciliation with the ancient enemy. After Pavia, Henry had informed Charles that he rejoiced 'as if he himself had been the victor'. His ambassadors had carried a ring from the Princess Mary, which the emperor had 'put upon his little finger', saying that he would wear it 'for her sake'. The King of England had even admitted his readiness to send Wolsey on this errand of love, though he had neglected to do so for fear that the cardinal was now 'so growing towards age' that 'so long a journey by sea and land would prove dangerous to him'. What more could therefore have been done to prove his honour and good faith? Yet an insult and betrayal had been delivered which was every bit as dishonourable as the repeated treachery of Charles's grandfathers, Ferdinand and Maximilian. Spaniards, Flemings, Habsburgs: all were clearly spun from the same twisted yarn. And now they would pay, or so at least Henry hoped.

Recompense for his debts to the English crown was at once demanded from the emperor and the Treaty of Windsor was cancelled. On 14 August, moreover, Henry's realm sold its allegiance to Francis, and cashed in on growing fears in Italy of imperial domination. Though Venice, Florence, Siena, Mantua and the pope had been pleased at the routing of the French, all were now in league once more. This time, however, they were uniting against their new foe, and it was with great satisfaction that in September the King of England received the first instalment of a lifetime pension of 100,000 crowns a year from the French. It had been guaranteed by the Treaty of the More, signed at Wolsey's own residence on 30 August, as a result of which several of Henry's councillors, including the cardinal, received generous pensions of their own and the King of England agreed to mediate for the release of his French counterpart.

Once again Wolsey had escaped and, in doing so, he had taken shelter in the very imperial treachery which, under other circumstances, might have been thought likely to consume him. Indeed, the desertion of the emperor had actually deflected attention from the catastrophe of the Amicable Grant – Wolsey's first unequivocal failure in ten eventful years as the king's chief servant. With a new enemy, moreover, the cardinal's expertise still seemed indispensable. He had fumed in unison with his master when the emperor was officially repudiated, and his earlier leanings towards France now assumed a credibility that they had formerly lacked. All hope of future 'amity and good feeling' between England

and the Holy Roman Empire was now dead, he declared emphatically to two Flemish envoys representing the Archduchess Margaret. 'I know full well,' he went on, 'that we shall never get assistance from you; but we shall do our best, either by contracting alliance with the Turk, or making peace with the French, or by giving the Princess Mary's hand to the Dauphin.' Every harm, he swore, would be delivered upon the emperor and his confederates, 'so that war between us may last a whole century'.

It was another well-worn display of political posturing, which coincided with a rather more constructive and altogether more personal triumph of sorts. For, on 15 July, as tumult reigned behind the closed doors of government, the foundation stone of Wolsey's very own Cardinal College had finally been laid at Oxford: a fitting testament, or so he hoped, to his higher sentiments and legacy to posterity. In all, 200 scholars in theology, civil law, physics, philosophy, mathematics, Greek and rhetoric were now to receive the finest possible tuition in the grandest possible setting. He planned, not least of all, to equip the new library with copies of manuscripts from the Vatican, 'transcribed for that purpose' and had already asked the Venetian Doge for 'transcripts, for the college library, of the Greek manuscripts which had belonged to Cardinals Grimaldi and Bessarion'. But besides the construction of a great courtyard surrounded by a cloister with an imposing dining hall extending down one side of the yard, Wolsey had also guaranteed that the college's larders, pastry houses and other amenities would be 'so goodly done that no two of the best colleges in Oxford had rooms to compare with them'. With such largesse and nobility of purpose, it was little wonder, of course, that the university was inclined to sing its benefactor's praises. 'We cannot, most Worshipful Father in Christ, after so many and noble gifts received from you, but give you our everlasting thanks', began the formal vote of gratitude.

In spite of everything, therefore, the mask of domination remained in place, though not all commentators would prove so generous regarding Wolsey's precious venture. 'A fine piece of business,' observed one sneering wag before long. 'This Cardinal projected a college and has built a tavern.' Eventually, nearly every stone of the handsome walls of Wolsey's college would be emblazoned with his arms. Towards the street, moreover, the king's arms and the cardinal's were soon proudly displayed above the gate, the latter in gold and colour. And the undercurrent of opposition to his vanity swelled accordingly, as ballads lampooning him circulated more and more freely. For, as the walls of Cardinal College rose, the extravagance of the edifice once again matched the extravagance of its patron. Twenty-one minor monasteries had been dissolved the year before to help meet the cost, and in one fortnight alone the numbers employed in construction included no fewer than 122 masons, twenty-five handhewers, forty-seven roughlayers, thirty-two carpenters, twelve sawyers and 228 labourers. This too drew the usual comparisons between Wolsey's appetite for magnificence and the king's own; comparisons which may now, perhaps, have been assuming increasing significance even for Henry himself.

If the Amicable Grant, along with the cardinal's other recent failings, were to be thoroughly swept from view, a grand and generous gesture might therefore be deemed politic. And with this in mind, Wolsey duly agreed to gift his splendid Hampton Court, with all its furnishings, its treasures and its trappings, to his royal master in exchange for the king's markedly inferior dwelling at Richmond. It was a grand enough symbolic gesture, though Wolsey would retain the right to use his former pride and joy whenever occasion demanded or time allowed. But whether such generosity would protect him from the brunt of further failure was far from certain, and the risk of further failure was, if anything, more tangible than ever. In the first place, he was now bound to an alliance with France that was as problematic as it was unlikely. 'The cardinal,' wrote de Praet in October, 'has two ends in view, first to obtain great sums of money for the King of England under pretence of war; second to keep the French king and the emperor in perpetual war and distrust.' Neither undertaking was enviable. Yet Wolsey was also facing his most formidable and desperate task of all – the unravelling of a royal marriage that had long grown barren and cold.

16

The Cardinal's 'Great Matter'

In the early morning of 18 June 1525, the 6-year-old Lord Henry Fitzroy, bastard son of England's king, was brought by barge from Wolsey's mansion of Durham Place, near Charing Cross, to what may well have seemed an appointment with destiny. Accompanied by a bustling host of knights, squires and other gentlemen he had arrived as planned at Bridewell Palace's water gate by nine o'clock, and passed at once through richly decorated galleries to the king's lodgings, flanked at every turn by bishops, earls, dukes and ambassadors. Nor was the splendour of the setting in any way unfitting. For the illegitimate son of Bessie Blount was about to be showered with honours and openly presented as prospective heir to the English throne. Closely attended by the earls of Oxford and Arundel as well as the Earl of Northumberland, who carried the Sword of State, he was first created Earl of Nottingham in a lengthy ceremony, and then made ready to receive the self-same titles that his father had held in boyhood. As Sir Thomas More read out the patents of nobility within the palace's great chamber, young Fitzroy knelt before the king, who formally invested him with the robe and sword, cap and circlet of his new rank. And in rising to his feet, he did so as Duke of Richmond and Somerset.

King Henry himself had designed his son's new arms, and upon his departure, dressed in crimson and blue velvet, the boy now travelled in a gorgeous litter upholstered in cloth of silver, a gift from his godfather, Thomas Wolsey. Henceforth, his riding horse would be draped in black velvet with gilt reins and his household increased to a complement of almost 200 officers and servants.

Two cloths of estate, four state chairs of cloth of gold and velvet, four great carpets and vast quantities of linen were only some of the other trappings which went with this new household. For its upkeep and maintenance was henceforth allocated the genuinely princely sum of £4,000 a year – a figure far exceeding that made over for the Princess Mary's. Eighty manors also came with Fitzroy's new titles, and appointments to nominal high office followed thick and fast: Warden of the Cinque Ports, Lord of Ireland, High Admiral of England, Warden General of the Scottish Marches. Before long a well-known tutor, Richard Croke, was found to equip him with the full rigour of a Renaissance education apt and fitting for any royal heir.

Not since 1188, when Henry II first acknowledged William Longsword, had an illegitimate son been raised to the peerage thus. And the implications could not have been clearer: bastard or not, Fitzroy would succeed his father unless a suitable alternative could be found. Nor at the moment was any such alternative in sight. As the Venetian ambassador Lorenzo Orio freely acknowledged, Henry loved his son 'like his soul' and proudly treated him 'next in rank to his majesty'. While the boy bathed in his father's hope and affection, moreover, the Princess Mary was packed off to Ludlow to begin her duties as Princess of Wales, away from her mother and increasingly compromised on all fronts. For if a suitably dazzling imperial marriage was not without its attractions, her newly conceived union with the dauphin was certain to be intensely unpopular. No French prince, after all, would come to share the throne of England easily, even as consort, while marriage to a native nobleman raised nagging fears of civil war upon her accession.

But the timing of the king's action, as his wife well understood, was no mere matter of policy alone. On the contrary, it was partly the result of cold anger – anger at the queen's consistent failure to produce an heir to safeguard the succession, anger at the consequent challenge to her spouse's virility and, above all, anger at the recent treachery of her nephew, Charles. In the meantime, however, Catherine's own deep bitterness and suspicion at this most difficult of times seems to have been mainly reserved for her husband's chief minister. The decline in the queen's political influence had, of course, coincided with the cardinal's rise and she had long resented his intrusions. As a fervent advocate of the imperial cause she had come, on the one hand, to despise his pro-French inclinations, first exemplified by the marriage of her sister-in-law to Louis XII and then made infinitely worse by the recent betrothal of her own daughter to the dauphin. She blamed him, too, for the elevation of his godson, Henry Fitzroy, to the dukedom of Richmond and reviled him as a corrupt and worldly representative of the Church to which she was so deeply committed. Even more, perhaps, she detested him for the Princess Mary's removal to Ludlow, a place which had such bitter memories for her personally.

There were, however, further grievances on Queen Catherine's part. She felt humiliated, for instance, when Wolsey contrived, on the pretext of economy, to dismiss her favourite ladies-in-waiting and replaced them with women of his own choosing who, it seemed, had been instructed to spy upon her. Nor, in fairness, was this particular suspicion any more unreasonable than her other misgivings, since the cardinal now consistently prevented her from seeing the Spanish ambassador alone and frequently intercepted her correspondence. Most worryingly of all, the queen had little doubt by this time that Wolsey was steadily exploiting her infertility. By 1525 it was clear for all to see that the queen's childbearing days were over and, to compound matters, her political leverage had lessened still further as the Anglo-imperial alliance foundered hopelessly. In short, she had become a tiresome irrelevance in all but her ability to impede her husband's plans and those of the cardinal. This the queen knew. This the queen feared. And this she continued to resent – laying all blame, like the rest of the court, upon the king's willing scapegoat.

But while Catherine smarted and smouldered during the Christmas revelries of what had been a particularly bad year, the target of her ill will chose to dwell upon altogether more humdrum affairs – a convenient shelter, perhaps, from the animus surrounding him and even more welcome relief from the fearsome complexity of the international scene, which he would soon have to address with redoubled energy. In 1519 he had made some attempt to reform the operation of the king's household. Abuses still abounded, however, and as the need for order and tighter control of expenditure became ever more urgent and the midwinter weather brought a temporary lull in his other distractions, Wolsey drew up proposals for reform and retrenchment, which eventually bore fruit in 1526 as the so-called 'Eltham Ordinances'.

The royal household had expanded significantly over the years, and in the process had developed numerous chaotic hierarchies of officials and servants which seriously impeded efficiency. Worse still, they were responsible for waste as well as indiscipline, and it was with this in mind that Wolsey now sought to combat 'the great confusion, annoyance, infection, trouble and dishonour that ensueth by the numbers as well of sickly, impotent, inable, and unmeet persons, as of rascals and vagabonds […] in all the court'. There were altogether too many carvers, servers, cup bearers, ushers and yeomen of the guard, and even when some officials were no more than absentee sinecurists, their servants retained the right to free board and lodging. Locks had been stolen from doors. Plate had disappeared. Food was left to rot upon floors, while half-filled cups and dishes were left to gather mould in darkened corners. Brawling was commonplace. Scullions sometimes worked naked or were clad in garments of 'vileness'. Those with duties to perform often collected their fees but had their functions discharged by deputies, all of whom brought their own tribes of supernumeraries and hangers-on.

In short, the court had become a den of costly disorder, which deprived the king of due formality and ran counter to all the orderly instincts of Wolsey's fastidious mind. Henceforth, however, there would be change. Gentlemen ushers, for instance, were to exercise keen vigilance to discourage wholesale theft and every effort made 'to banish lewd women from the household'. Likewise, fines were now imposed for 'the leaving of dishes, saucers, or vessels about the house, or throwing away of any reliques of meat', and all courts, galleries and chambers were to be cleaned twice daily 'for the better avoiding of corruption and all uncleanness […] which doth engender danger of infection, and is very noisome and displeasant'. Sensibly enough mastiffs, greyhounds and ferrets were to be turned out of doors, and the king's privy chamber kept clear of 'rascals, boys and others' who had been accustomed to stand, stare, beg and, on occasion, steal. Pages, in their turn, were told to moderate their language, not to make a noise when playing cards or chess, and to stop their games upon the king's entry, while unnecessary officials – much to their 'lamentation' – were to be removed without ceremony. Promotion by merit was to be encouraged. Consumption of food, fuel and candles was to be reduced. And even Penny, the king's barber, became compelled to tighten his act. Now he was to be ready every morning with cloths, combs, scissors and water scented with cloves, and required not only to be more scrupulous about his own cleanliness but to avoid bad company.

The ordinances offer a fascinating glimpse into the unseen world of contemporary court life. But they offer, too, an intimate insight into both the operation of Wolsey's mind and the full breadth of his undertakings. Neither the crushing rejection of the Amicable Grant nor the wholesale failure of the Anglo-imperial alliance had prevented him from tending his wider chores. And these wider involvements continued to extend far beyond his current preoccupation with daily rations of firewood, bread and beer at royal palaces. It was Wolsey, for instance, who had to give judgement when the fences of the Marquess of Dorest were broken and his deer slain. It was he, too, who supervised the casting of the king's funeral monument, which was to be at least a quarter larger than his father's. Then there were problems of trade, both domestic and foreign, to manage, including the allocation of import and export patents. In any one day, in fact, Wolsey might well find himself settling compensation for those whose ships had been seized by pirates or juggling with the contested rights of towns like Ross and Waterford to an obscure wine franchise. The load remained as relentless as the man who bore it almost single-handedly. And now, inch by inch and turn by grinding turn, the full force of his reputation would carry him towards the abyss.

Before the ink was dry on his household reforms Wolsey heard news from the continent that snatched him, like a weary sleepwalker, back to cold reality. In February 1526 the French king, who had been moved from Italy to Spain, was visited amid high ceremony by Charles V and accepted the terms of the Treaty of Madrid for his release. He had failed to make good his escape in the wake of Pavia and now, after a period of illness, succumbed to a truly harrowing settlement. In swearing to keep the peace, he was forced to surrender the whole of Burgundy – the emperor's most prized objective – and to renounce his claims over Flanders, Artois and the rest of the Low Countries, as well as his rights in Naples, Sicily and Milan. He was also to marry Charles's sister, Eleanor, and discharge the emperor's debt to the King of England, while providing 5,000 men-at-arms and 10,000 infantry to accompany his enemy to Rome, when he went there to receive the imperial crown formally. Finally, Francis was compelled to hand over his two eldest sons, the dauphin and the Duke of Orléans, as hostages for the proper execution of the treaty.

It was, ostensibly, the greatest possible victory for the emperor and one which appeared to seal the conclusion of a conflict that had dragged on for more than thirty years. It had certain unexpected side-effects for Wolsey, too, since Francis immediately wrote to declare that he owed his freedom solely to the cardinal's intervention; in a curious burst of euphoria he added to the English ambassador that he would honour his rescuer as a father all his life. But when Henry VIII ordered a *Te Deum* at St Paul's, he did so with ill-concealed resentment, and the bonfires grudgingly lit across his realm could not convince his subjects that peace would be long-lived. For the emperor's victory would prove as hollow as it was spectacular, and by the time that Francis boarded the boat at Bildassoa, which carried him home, he was already bent on renewing the struggle. Upon reaching the French shore, indeed, he rode flat out for St Jean de Luz and Bayonne, convinced that promises made in captivity carried no authority in either conscience or law. He was soon buoyed, too, by the most powerful legal minds of his realm, who declared unequivocally that he had not the power to give away French territory without due consultation with his subjects, and by the further encouragement of the King of England, who congratulated him upon his release and expressed his 'stupefaction' at the emperor's demands. For good measure, Wolsey even dispatched John Taylor, Deputy Master of the Rolls, to confirm the English view that Francis was under no compulsion to observe the terms of a treaty signed while he was a prisoner and under condition that his sons should be made hostages.

So, while Charles V was travelling at leisure and in high spirits towards Seville to marry Isabella of Portugal and thereby secure her family's accumulated riches in Brazil and the East, his vanquished foe was already laying breakneck plans for retribution. By May 1526 Francis had enlisted the pope, Florence, Venice and the exiled Ludovico Sforza, Duke of Milan, into the so-called League of Cognac, which the King of England cautiously endorsed by becoming before long its 'Protector'. For, though Wolsey had no real desire to wage war against the emperor, and did not wish to interfere with trade between England and the Netherlands, which was so essential to both countries, he was determined nevertheless to injure Charles and weaken his power. And since Italy was the only place he could do this, he had given the inception of the new league every encouragement – not least because France was to meet two-thirds of the cost of any military operation and Venice the rest. The fact that Henry's involvement as Protector would not be announced until the cardinal saw fit was, of course, another considerable bonus.

From the ashes of his former policy, therefore, Wolsey appeared to have conceived a typically sublime volte-face, holding out the serious prospect that England might once again exert diplomatic mastery while others did her dirty work for her. He had, it is true, promised the pope that Henry would join the league fully as soon as the emperor provided him with ample excuse and he had also offered £20,000 to pay for mercenaries in the league's service. But the initiative, or so it appeared, lay squarely with him, since France and her Italian allies were, on the one hand, as supple to his plans as they were desperate, and the emperor, in spite of his recent triumphs, remained vulnerable. Important German cities, after all, were turning Lutheran and in February the Protestant League of Torgau had been formed to further complicate Charles's predicament within his own territories. Only that spring, moreover, the crescent-tipped battle standards of the Turks, draped with human hair, had surged into Hungary, and by the end of August the flower of the Hungarian aristocracy would lie dead on the battlefield of Mohács, either slain by Sipahi cavalry or massacred before the Turkish pasha's tent, where the head of the Bishop of Colocz stood impaled upon a spear.

With such imminent threats to his security, might not the dominance of the emperor thus be thwarted even yet? In Italy too, Wolsey reasoned, Charles's position remained assailable. His forces were large, but he could neither pay nor discipline them effectively. Had he not, after all, once joked to English ambassadors that men are not always as rich as they seem and that he himself was 'poor indeed'? And did he not live, for that matter, in little more than ostentatious poverty – his household servants unpaid, his Spanish and imperial troops left to plunder and ravage the Italian countryside while they waited for their wages? The Spaniards were well known and hated for their unremitting cruelty, while the Lutheran contingents in Charles's army had the further ingredient of religious fanaticism to fuel their own brutality. Would not such a combination of insolvency and wanton barbarism surely loosen the imperial grip in Italy before long? If so, then England might once again reap the benefits of Wolsey's grand designs. The portents were favourable, the circumstances right, the tree of opportunity waiting to be cheaply plucked – or so a desperate man might somehow convince himself. For, in his subtlest planning, Wolsey had merely fashioned one more house of cards. And while Europe was waiting to confound his efforts, the sharpest dagger of all was now heading unerringly towards his throat.

Not without some irony, the gathering winds of Wolsey's schemes for war had already blown Mistress Anne Boleyn back to England some years earlier. For, as the military campaign of 1522 began to loom, she had abandoned the French court in haste and soon found herself a maid of honour to Henry VIII's own Queen Catherine. Upon her return, she was already a self-aware young woman of about 20 – dark-haired, olive-skinned, graceful, elegant, vivacious and 'likely enough to have children' – who had learnt much about the wider world since her departure across the Channel some six years earlier. She had, on the one hand, become fluent in the language of her hosts and acquired a taste for literature, music and art. But she had also savoured the relaxed decadence of Francis I's gilded Renaissance court, where rakish young nobles in silken doublets and glittering earrings, guided and mentored by the king himself, rejoiced in amorous liaisons and erotic adventures. 'Alexander the Great saw women when there was no business to be looked after', wrote one contemporary. 'Francis I,' he added, 'looks after business when there are no women.' 'Rarely or never,' observed Brantôme, 'did any maid or wife leave that court chaste.'

Thus equipped, a nubile and provocative young woman like Anne with 'black and beautiful' almond-shaped eyes and a fund of vitality to match her natural magnetism was always likely to stand out upon her homecoming, particularly among the grey and upright ladies of the lonely queen, who hastened to cross themselves at every pious opportunity and remained closeted with their needlework while the king made merry. She had the example to follow, moreover, of her elder sister, Mary, who was also now snugly ensconced at the English court after a similar stay in France, where she had not only lost her innocence, but become renowned for her sexual generosity. Long after she left his court the French king remembered her as the 'hackney' or 'English mare' that he and his companions had often ridden. And soon after her return to England and marriage to the king's esquire of the body, William Carey, she was once again installed as royal mistress, this time to Henry VIII himself. When Anne surveyed her new home, therefore, she was already familiar with its landscape and fully attuned to its possibilities. Indeed, with her sister, four other girls and Mary Brandon, she distinguished herself almost at once in a courtly spectacle entitled 'Le Château Vert'. Wearing a white satin gown and jewelled bonnet and pretending to defend a mock castle with missiles made of sugarplums, she gaily repelled a horde of eager assailants, among whom none was more boisterous than the king himself.

But Anne had more than charms and worldly wisdom to recommend her, since she was also propelled forward by the most powerful of family ties. Her uncle, Thomas Howard, who had not long ago succeeded to the dukedom of Norfolk, was limited, hidebound and deadly. A short, dark soldier with a wary eye, hatchet face and cruel mouth, he had married Elizabeth, daughter of the executed Duke of Buckingham, and was now the most powerful noble in the realm, with all the prejudices and narrow-mindedness of his class. Wholly convinced that England was 'merrier before the New Learning came up', he prided himself that he had never read the Scriptures, nor ever would. And though he was an untiring henchman of his sovereign and would prove the ever-willing executioner of the king's enemies, he served the crown, in reality, mainly out of prudence. Stridently proud of his pedigree, he conveniently ignored the fact that his Howard forebears were grasping East Anglian gentry who had married into the great medieval family of Mowbray, and now posed boldly as the personification of feudal family rights and landed power. As such, he was the undisputed figurehead of the noble interest on the king's council – and mortal enemy to Thomas Wolsey.

Yet Anne Boleyn's father was also a figure of considerable substance in his own right. The grandson of a wealthy silk and wool mercer who had gone on to become Lord Mayor of London, Sir Thomas Boleyn had married Lady Elizabeth Howard, eldest daughter of the Duke of Norfolk, in 1499 and made rapid progress thereafter. He had been keeper of the Foreign Exchange and ambassador to Francis I, and by 1522 he was treasurer to the royal household, with substantial estates in Kent and East Anglia and lucrative timber mills at Rochford in Essex. In 1525, moreover – at the same time that Henry Fitzroy had been elevated to the dukedom of Richmond – he had been made Viscount Rochford, the only commoner to hold such a title. In the same year, he was receiving a pension of 1,000 crowns a year from the imperial court, a sum as high as that paid to Norfolk and Brandon. Rich, pliable, cunning and methodical, he, too, was a self-seeker of the first order: someone who, in the words of a French diplomat, 'would sooner act from interest than from any other motive'. And he, too, was no lover of Thomas Wolsey, for in addition to his Howard allegiances he bore a personal grudge from the time in 1519 that Wolsey had succeeded in postponing his appointment as treasurer of the royal household and barred him from the lesser role of comptroller.

Nor would the Boleyns' personal grudges subside once Anne had returned from her French sojourn, since the cardinal's first sally into the lady's affairs was an abrupt and insensitive one, which left both a painful scar and residing bitterness. To her considerable misfortune, the object of Anne's early passion was Henry Percy, heir to the Earl of Northumberland and, more significantly still, a member of Wolsey's household. Already promised to Mary Talbot, a daughter of the Earl of Shrewsbury, Percy nevertheless pursued his new quarry with gusto until Wolsey angrily put paid to the liaison, telling him in no uncertain terms that he must forget 'that foolish girl yonder in the court'. Acting, it seems, upon his master's instructions, the cardinal commanded Percy 'in the king's name […] not once to resort to her company, as thou intendest to avoid the king's high indignation'.

But if Henry was already experiencing his own first inklings of infatuation, this did not deter Wolsey from taking further harsh action against the lovelorn lady herself, for she was 'commanded to avoid the court and sent home again to her father for a season'. 'Whereat,' we hear, 'she smoked.' Banished to the Boleyn country home at Hever, her sophistication and allure were clearly wasted on the local Kentish gentry. Worse still, she was accustomed to excitement and gaiety, so that her exile at Wolsey's hands must have seemed, in effect, a prison sentence during which countless opportunities were passing her by. Heartsick, angry and resentful, crushed by a dull and uneventful existence made even worse by the stigma and humiliation of disgrace, she would neither forgive nor forget. 'If ever it lay in her power,' Anne is said to have sworn, 'she would work the cardinal as much displeasure' as he had wrought for her.

By the time of her return to court in 1525 or 1526, the good lady was soon enjoying every opportunity to live up to her word. For it seems that sometime in 1526 Henry was, to use his own phrase, 'struck with the dart of love'. His dalliance with the older sister had ended perhaps a year earlier, and the realignment of his affections was plainly signalled in the royal military accounts, which refer to the commissioning of a new ship, the *Anne Boleyn*, duly superseding the one that had been launched in her sister's name only a little earlier. There were payments, too, to his goldsmiths for four gold brooches, one of Venus surrounded by cupids, one of a lady holding a heart in her hand, a third of a gentleman lying in a lady's lap, and another – significantly enough – of a lady holding a crown. And like a lovestruck teenager the king began to preen and posture on a scale that exceeded even his usual vanity. Posing in black velvet suits lined with sables and adorned with studs and buttons made of diamonds and pearls, he doused himself more copiously than ever with his favourite perfume – a pungent concoction of musk, ambergris, sugar and rosewater – and made no secret of the object of his newfound desire.

That Henry should have been thus smitten is hardly difficult to explain. He was held fast, in the first place, by chivalric delusions that he had never managed to outgrow, and since Anne refused to succumb to his advances he dangled hopelessly like a worm on a line, ensnaring himself more and more securely with every effort expended and parry received. He was galvanised too, of course, by the ongoing frustration of his fruitless and colourless marriage. Almost pitifully, Queen Catherine's life was steadily shrinking into a dreary round of religious devotions and meditations, and now, to cap all, she had taken to wearing a penitential habit under her court robes after becoming a professed sister of the Third Order of St Francis. But, if the queen's devotions made her a 'mirror of goodness' among her ladies, she was certainly no longer the fairest of them all or even, for that matter, remotely appealing to her husband. With every passing day, indeed, she appeared more preoccupied with the afterlife than the tiresome demands of this one. Writing to Wolsey about the proposed marriage of one of her maids, Catherine wistfully confided around this time that she was concerned to provide for her attendants while she still could, 'before God called her to account'.

Yet there was another more curious but equally compelling reason for the king's obsession with Mistress Anne Boleyn. His concerns about the lawfulness of his current marriage had first arisen well before this time, of course, but they had gradually reached crisis point as the queen's dismal record of stillbirths and miscarriages dragged on without remedy. With an ever-supple conscience that could be readily moulded to convenience, Henry had therefore begun to appreciate the new significance of the 'protest' about marrying his brother's widow that he had been made to submit by his father as long ago as 1505. What had been at the time nothing more than a tactical ploy to gain more favourable marriage terms from Catherine's father now became a serious pretext for questioning anew the validity of Pope Julius II's 20-year-old dispensation. And as Henry's penchant for theological dabbling assumed a new intensity and fuelled his latent insecurity and naturally superstitious tendencies, the arrival at court of a vivacious, healthy and apparently fecund substitute for his current wife sealed the process that had been germinating since as early as 1518. If the king required a moral platform for demolishing his marriage and degrading his wife, then his elastic principles and self-serving intellect could be relied upon to furnish the necessary tools.

Always attracted to theological problems, Henry had, after all, become extremely knowledgeable about the canon law of divorce, so much so, indeed, that Cardinal Campeggio was not entirely flattering him in claiming that the king knew more about the subject than any divine. And by the spring of 1527 his study of Scripture left him in no doubt whatsoever that in God's eyes he was still a bachelor and for this reason denied a legitimate son. In his view, the Book of Leviticus (ch. 20, v. 21) could not have contained a clearer prohibition against what he had done or a plainer explanation of his present predicament. 'And if a man shall take his brother's wife,' ran the crucial passage, 'it is an unclean thing: he hath uncovered his brother's nakedness; they shall be childless.' Irrespective, therefore, of whether the Jewish law of the Old Testament was binding upon Christians or whether, as some suggested, the injunction of Leviticus was superseded by Deuteronomy (ch. 25, v. 5) – which actually contained a direct command for a man to marry his deceased brother's wife when that brother had died without children – Henry would not budge from his course. That learned men had agonised for years about the self-same issues without reaching any kind of consensus was neatly overlooked; as, indeed, was the fact that the king's prior relationship with Mary Boleyn now placed similar theological shadows over his intended union with her sister.

When the time was ripe, therefore, Henry needed no persuading, least of all from Wolsey, whose name has long been unfairly darkened on this account. According to Edward Hall the cardinal gained his opportunity to strike against the queen in February 1527, as his pro-French strategy gathered momentum. When the Bishop of Tarbes arrived to negotiate the betrothal of the Princess Mary to one of the French princes, he raised – apparently in collaboration with Wolsey – certain doubts about the status of the princess and 'whether the marriage between the king and her mother, being his brother's wife, was good or no: of which the first motion grew much business or it were ended'. In consequence, the king's confessor, John Longland, Bishop of Lincoln, and 'other great clerks' were in a position to inform the king later that spring 'that the marriage between him and the Lady Katherine, late wife of his brother, was not good but damnable'. From Edward Hall's perspective, therefore, Wolsey had contrived and engineered the whole plan to ditch the queen, thus neutralising her pro-imperial sympathies and dealing with Henry's succession problems in one fell swoop – a view firmly endorsed by Polydore Vergil, who, in Book XXVII of his history has Wolsey scheming 'to arrange a divorce at the earliest moment', so that the king might marry a French princess.

Not altogether surprisingly, the imperialists themselves harboured similar suspicions and did not hesitate, moreover, to tell the queen as much. Catherine had, of course, long endeavoured to foster England's relations with her nephew, Charles, and though she had now been out of contact with him for years, she nevertheless continued to look upon herself as his agent at the English court. Her letters, it is true, occasionally reproached him for his neglect, but she never failed to assure him of her 'readiness for his service' and was horrified to learn from the imperial ambassador in April that for six weeks she had been facing a growing threat to her marriage. Indeed, according to the ambassador, Wolsey had been hatching plans to undermine both her and her daughter for more than a year. 'The Cardinal,' Catherine learned, 'to crown his iniquities' was 'working to separate the King and Queen [...] and the plot was so far advanced that a number of bishops and lawyers had already gathered secretly to declare her marriage null and void'.

Yet the myth of Wolsey's responsibility for the divorce, however plausible superficially, remains unconvincing. Certainly, his pro-French sympathies at this time were plain enough. Indeed, to judge from the days of jousting and pageantry in London in the early months of 1527, the newfound amity with the French surpassed all previous diplomatic accords in importance. At Hampton Court, French envoys feasted in luxury upon fantastic creations of battling soldiers, leaping knights, guns and crossbows, all brought to life by Wolsey's chefs, and on one occasion – in recognition of the cardinal's gifts as a chess player – a special chessboard, complete with chessmen made entirely of sweetmeats, was set before the guests and then placed in a case specially constructed for transport to France. Clearly, then, Wolsey made no secret whatsoever of his newly acquired allegiances. On the contrary, every effort was expended to overwhelm the representatives of the French king, in order 'to make them such triumphant cheer as they may not only wonder at it here, but also make a glorious report in their country to the king's honour and of this realm'.

Nor, it must be said, was Wolsey comfortable with Queen Catherine's influence. Surrounded by her Spanish ladies and household servants, she preserved a clear cultural distance between herself and the English. Speaking her adopted language only haltingly, she referred to Greenwich as 'Granuche' and Hampton Court as 'Antoncourt'. But, much more worryingly from Wolsey's point of view, she demonstrated a shrewd objectivity and clear-headed insight that belied her apparent passivity and matched her unswerving loyalty to the Habsburg cause. 'A small advantage renders them overbearing, and a little adversity makes them despondent', she once remarked of her husband's diplomatic advisers, and it was opinions such as these, coupled to her willingness to express them, that made her the target of Wolsey's spies. By March 1527, therefore, she was left with no other choice than to abandon her letters to her nephew and communicate with him purely verbally by means of her physician, Ferdinand de Vittoria.

But Wolsey neither wished nor needed to destroy the queen's marriage. Though suspect, she remained sufficiently hamstrung to be left largely unmolested in her current state of limbo, especially when the complexity and potential pitfalls of divorce proceedings, not to mention the implicit threat to the pope's authority, were taken into account. In any event the king's own mind was certainly made up long before the much-vaunted visit of the Bishop of Tarbes, since the first approach to Rome had actually been made in secret at some point before 13 September 1526, when John Clerk wrote from the Holy City to confirm that 'the cursed divorce' will not be easily granted. Nor, it seems, were all negotiations carried out with Wolsey's full knowledge. Even by the middle of 1527 Henry was telling the French ambassador that he had 'some things to communicate to your master of which Wolsey knows nothing'.

So when Henry later absolved Wolsey of any responsibility, there is little need to distrust him. 'Marry,' he openly declared, 'ye have been rather against me in attempting or setting forth thereof.' There seems scant reason to discount this last claim either, since the risk that dissolving the union with Catherine might well lead to much more menacing links with Anne Boleyn rather than marriage to an altogether more pliable and accommodating French princess cannot have been lost upon the cardinal. Significantly, Bishop Longland, who features so prominently in the accounts of Hall and Vergil, left no doubt that it was the king rather than the cardinal who first discussed the matter of the divorce with him 'and never left urging him until he had won him to give his consent'. And George Cavendish's account of his master's reaction to the news of the king's 'long hid and secret love' for Anne Boleyn has a definite ring of authenticity to it. The king, wrote Cavendish, was so 'amorously affectionate' that the cardinal, in spite of his 'persuasion contrary', could not dissuade him, though he made his pleas 'upon his knees'. If, therefore, Wolsey was left with no other choice, he was enough of a realist to do his master's bidding, but from his perspective the divorce remained neither necessary nor desirable.

It was not, of course, the first time that that the cardinal had been presented with such a perplexing conundrum, and on previous occasions – whether by imagination, timing, outright luck or a combination of all three – an accommodation of sorts, if not an outright victory, had usually secured his position. As an all-time master of political escapology, he may even have felt that this particular chore might be easier to execute than some of those he had attempted previously. So when in May 1527 Wolsey summoned Henry to appear before him at York House, 'charged' with living in sin with his brother's widow, he had firm grounds for confidence that he was about to achieve another decisive coup. Acting in his capacity as legate *a latere* and duly presiding over a legatine court in the company of Archbishop Warham, who had long ago harboured doubts about Pope Julius's 1503 bull of dispensation, Wolsey believed he could conduct a swift, unfussy and comparatively painless excision of the king from his troublesome bond.

In the build-up to the hearing, however, the pressure on the cardinal continued to mount on all fronts. One evening in April, as a party of French envoys returned from dining with the Tailors' Guild at Blackfriars, a lackey of the Count of Touraine was unintentionally splashed with filth from a gutter being cleaned by two apprentices. Though the man was unhurt, the Frenchmen complained to Wolsey and the cardinal's response betrayed, perhaps, his growing stress. Being 'too hasty of credence', he gave vent to his notorious temper and ordered the Lord Mayor to arrest not only the two offending boys, but everyone else in the house concerned. The apprentices were consigned to the Tower, where one died and the other 'fell lame' from the fetters which had bound his legs and ankles before he was freed. 'Of the cruelty of the cardinal, and of the pride of the Frenchmen,' observed Edward Hall, 'much people spake, and would have been revenged on the Frenchmen, if wise men in the city had not appeased it with fair words.'

There were murmurs, too, of vengeance upon Wolsey himself, and with the approach of May Day – traditionally the occasion for general disorder – he put the capital on guard. Nightly watches were set at some half-dozen points throughout the city and, at Westminster, soldiers with cannon stood ready to break up any budding disorder. Yet handbills critical of the king's council and especially Wolsey continued to circulate nightly, condemning the proposed French marriage and threatening the cardinal with punishment as 'an enemy to the king and the realm'. By mid-May, moreover, the campaign of slander had escalated to the point where it was widely rumoured that the king intended to be done with his favourite adviser once and for all – a rumour made plausible by the cardinal's temporary disappearance from court.

In reality, however, Wolsey was unwell, and had been for weeks. Beneath the ice-cool logic and stonewall confidence he presented to the world, there lay the usual carping doubts and insecurities, and the further fear that his French allies might still betray him. The strain of frequent 'high words' with the Duke of Norfolk and Bishop Tunstall, his chief opponents on the council, had also taken their toll. And, when not laid low by indigestion or fever, the cardinal continued to storm through his crushing schedule. Now, therefore, he became increasingly inclined to lash out, even at his trusted secretaries, and unusually prone to inconsistency. Appearing to thrive on detail just as he had done in the past, orders might well be drawn up for the detention of all ships carrying goods to Flanders and Spain, or any number of other matters relating to the impending war. Soon afterwards, however, the same orders were sometimes reversed even more emphatically. It was at this time, too, that he reacted 'in a great fury' to news of his ridicule in a 'disguising' staged by the students of Gray's Inn. And though Wolsey insisted that the ringleader's imprisonment in the Fleet Prison was conducted at the behest of the king, who was 'sorely displeased' by such disrespect, the more obvious conclusion seems hard to dismiss.

Yet the strategy for achieving the annulment of the king's marriage still showed no clear sign of being devised at breaking point. On the contrary, it bore all the usual hallmarks of craft, detachment and boldness. The queen's attendance at the impending hearing was, for example, carefully circumvented. Nor was it even deemed necessary for her to be represented, which meant she need have no suspicion that proceedings against her marriage were actually underway at all. Henry, moreover, was to appear before the court not as petitioner but defendant – not so much the instigator of a treacherous act as the unwitting victim of a misconceived dispensation framed more than twenty years ago. Explaining to Henry that, as legate, he was duty bound to investigate the validity of his marriage, Wolsey, too, could neatly sanitise his own role, posing as no more than the righteous executant of canon law and noble guardian of his sovereign's spiritual welfare. Warham, meanwhile, was deftly presented as the final arbiter of whether the king was living openly in sin with his brother's widow. By the time, therefore, that Henry was respectfully requested to attend the inquest, hardly a single loose end remained untied.

Accordingly in mid-May the whole elaborate ruse unfolded as Wolsey once again assumed the guise of earnest impartiality and Archbishop Warham settled into his familiar niche of exalted irrelevance. The king too, however, was a masterful actor when occasion required – so much so, in fact, that even at this stage Wolsey had no inkling of his longer-term inclination to marry Anne – and he showed no hesitation in presenting a feigned protest to the effect that he was legally married to his wife. With cold-blooded gall he duly produced Pope Julius's dispensation and then employed Dr John Bell, his proctor, to defend its validity. Thereafter, Wolsey's court pored over Henry's union with Catherine for all of two weeks, during which time Bell's arguments were conveniently dismantled by the prosecutor, Dr Richard Wolman, and witnesses produced to challenge their soundness. There were concerns, it is true, over the queen's eventual reaction, and the likelihood that she would insist upon appealing her case to the pope and the emperor, thus transforming into an international crisis what Wolsey was hoping to present as a merely domestic matter. But the court itself seemed neatly insulated from all such external interference, and therefore appeared to be performing its function precisely as intended. Over its four sessions, indeed, it seemed to be proceeding inexorably to its preordained conclusion that the king had been living in 'open sin' for the last seventeen years.

By the time that the court adjourned abruptly for its last session on 31 May, however, a thunderbolt from Italy had robbed Wolsey once and for all of any illusion that this most delicate of tasks could be settled so neatly. Rome, he now learned, had been captured by Spanish and imperial troops more than a fortnight earlier, even before his legatine court had convened, and to increase the irony the capture had been effected by none other than England's former confederate, the Duke of Bourbon. Though Bourbon himself had been shot in the thigh during the onslaught and eventually died in the Sistine Chapel, his famished and unpaid troops had nevertheless taken a fearful toll upon the Holy City. 'Never,' wrote one commentator, 'was Rome so pilled neither by Goths nor Vandals.' Holy relics and sacred shrines were destroyed, virgins despoiled and wives ravished, with perhaps a quarter of the entire population killed, while rampaging soldiers 'punished citizens by the privy members to cause them to confess their treasure'. Pope Clement, in the meantime, had fled in fear of his life to the castle of San Angelo and was now under siege.

Under such circumstances Wolsey's legatine court was utterly impotent, since a pope at the emperor's mercy was a pope incapable of sanctioning any action intolerable to the emperor's aunt. While Clement cowered before her nephew, therefore, Catherine was no longer to be lightly dismissed, let alone casually discarded. And Wolsey's task had gone from difficult to desperate in the brief time it takes a breathless messenger to deliver his tale of disaster. Ruling that it could not provide an authoritative decision on so intricate a point of canon law as the king's marriage, the legatine court – of which so much had been expected – therefore confined itself ultimately to a finding that the dispensation of 1503 was no more than 'open to doubt'. Only two days later, moreover, the beleaguered cardinal was expressing to his royal master the full gravity of the new situation as he wrote:

And surely sire, if the Pope's Holiness fortune either to be slain or taken, as God forbid, it shall not a little hinder your Grace's affairs, which I now have in hand; wherein such good and substantial order and process hath hitherto been made and used.

Nevertheless, within those same two days, Wolsey had conceived another grand enterprise – perhaps his grandest to date – shot full with complex crossing threads and diverse linking outcomes, all of which, he believed, might rescue an all-but-hopeless situation and redound once more to both his sovereign's and his own greater glory. Exhorted on all sides to rescue the pope, Henry was at a loss as to how this might be achieved. 'What should I do?' he complained. 'My person nor my people cannot him rescue, but if my treasure may help him, take that which to you seemeth most convenient.' Certainly, the treasure would indeed be convenient, since the first plank of Wolsey's proposed solution involved consolidating the alliance with the French. But something much more sweeping still was now required, for with the pope subservient to a secular power, the Church itself was in urgent need of a rescuer. The cardinal would therefore go to France in person, where Louise of Savoy was already suggesting that the princes of Christendom should withdraw their allegiance to the Bishop of Rome until his release. And he, in all his glory, would duly proceed to take over the government of Christendom on Pope Clement's behalf.

Though Wolsey's behaviour was probably indicative of a curious state of euphoria born of utter desperation, the charge of megalomania is easy enough to level. This, it should be remembered, was a man who wished to be buried, like the king, at Windsor and whose tomb was to match in splendour that of Henry VII. A black marble sarcophagus would hold the carved bronze figure of the cardinal lying in repose. Kneeling angels bearing the symbols of Wolsey's dignities, his cross and cardinal's hat, were to guard his head and feet, while four more angels bearing candlesticks were to be perched atop thick bronze pillars 9ft high. This too, of course, was an individual used to the most extravagant deference. It had long been customary, in fact, for visitors at the English court to kiss the cardinal's hand before kissing the king's – an acknowledgement of the higher respect due to the divine office, but in practice as much a bow to Wolsey the person as to his rank within the Church.

Yet, as the leading churchman of the West not under imperial sway and as a figure whom the pope claimed to regard not merely as a brother but as a colleague, Wolsey was not entirely without hope. To resolve the crisis he would travel to France in person and convoke an assembly of cardinals at Avignon, which was to oversee the administration of papal affairs during the pope's captivity.

Then by deft diplomacy he would secure Pope Clement's freedom and thereby guarantee the Church's compliance in the annulment of King Henry's marriage. And this was not the limit of Wolsey's finest ploy, for by bringing liberty to the Holy See and peace to Europe, he would make his master the most respected prince within the Church's mighty ambit. From some perspectives, therefore, it was a plan of grand, magisterial vision and elegance: sweeping in concept and bold in content, a masterpiece of intricacy and simplicity combined. Nor could its nature and timing have been more apt, as the icy flood of events began to reach the cardinal's nostrils. That it would eventually founder on the king's own folly was something, however, that not even Wolsey could have envisaged in his most baleful of calculations.

There could be no question, of course, that the king's sledgehammer tendencies would have to be carefully curtailed in such a delicate situation. Henry's preferred approach to his predicament was, for instance, to contend that Catherine's previous marriage to his brother had indeed been consummated, in spite of her resolute denials, and to insist that the pope had not the authority to grant a dispensation that challenged divine law as laid down in Scripture. To argue thus, as Wolsey well knew, cast doubt not only on the queen's integrity, but upon papal authority in general, and was therefore bound both to inflame and complicate matters considerably. The cardinal's own solution, by contrast, was to accept the non-consummation of the marriage, and therefore to invalidate the dispensation on much less provocative, but wholly effective, technical grounds. If, Wolsey reasoned, the marriage had not been consummated in the first place, then the dispensation had dealt with a non-existent impediment and was therefore without authority. As a further flourish, it might also be pointed out that Julius II's measure had not dealt with the issue of 'public honesty' or, in other words, the fact that Arthur and Catherine had indeed been formally married in a Church ceremony. In addressing a non-existent impediment, the original dispensation had therefore also neglected a real one. If the king could be persuaded to leave well alone and allow his minister a free hand to execute his plans across the Channel, all, it seemed, might still be executed with surgical precision and minimal collateral damage.

Before leaving for France on 22 July, amid tremendous pomp, Wolsey had drawn up a communication for the pope to sign, bestowing upon him absolute power as if he were indeed pope – power 'even to relax, limit or moderate divine law' – which meant that Clement would be undertaking to ratify all Wolsey's actions upon regaining his freedom. The cardinal had troubled, too, to consult with his astrologer about the most favourable date for his departure, and on the appointed day his splendid retinue duly formed its ranks and set off for Dover, spreading out along the narrow road for over three-quarters of a mile. Hundreds of gentlemen and yeomen in black and tawny liveries rode in the vanguard, along with closely guarded carts and carriages loaded down with 'barrels of gold' and Wolsey's travel furnishings. While the cardinal rode as always on muleback, his rich cardinal's robes blending with the red velvet trappings of his mount, seven attendants rode before him bearing the usual paraphernalia of his office and a gold-embroidered bag that held his scarlet cloak.

There were also errands to perform and prayers to recite as the would-be man of the hour passed on his way. At Canterbury, for instance, he paused to join a special litany for the captive pope. 'Saint Mary, pray for our Pope Clement', intoned the monks, while Wolsey knelt and 'wept very tenderly'. There was time, too, to visit Archbishop Warham, whom the cardinal feared might be inclined to Catherine's side in any impending struggle, though the aged bishop's words were reassuring. 'However displeasant it may be to the queen,' he declared, 'truth and law must prevail.' And though a further meeting with Bishop John Fisher of Rochester promised more tension, it likewise passed off without incident. In a cogent tract on the divorce, Fisher had already made it clear that he considered Pope Julius's dispensation valid and further inquiry needless. So without debating the issue Wolsey merely explained the king's view more fully, adding that Catherine had spoken harshly to her husband – which Fisher condemned – and urging him not to take any further action of any kind without the king's consent.

By the time that Wolsey reached Calais, moreover, he was given further grounds for optimism. In April he had induced Henry to write to his French counterpart as his 'brother and perfect friend', thanking him 'for some birds you have sent me for the pursuit of the heron'. According to a Hungarian envoy, however, the King of France was now at a clear disadvantage in the coming negotiations. He was, Wolsey heard, 'destitute of good captains and money', and this was not all, since 'the said French king considering the captivity of the pope, the detention of his children with the emperor', and the likelihood of imperial generals 'attaining Italy' was 'marvellous perplexed, not knowing what to do'. As such, the sealing of the Anglo-French treaties agreed to in England three months earlier and the arrangement of a marriage between Henry and a French princess, such as Renée, Francis I's sister-in-law, seemed a matter of course. Nor was Wolsey disappointed, for when he finally arrived at Amiens in August to conclude business, the French king – surrounded by Greek and Albanian mercenaries, 'drawn up in a great piece of oats, all in harness, upon light horses' – was swift to agree a full alliance. And though Renée, somewhat to Wolsey's regret, was eventually spared a marriage contract with Henry, there was at least the considerable consolation of the Princess Mary's engagement to Francis's younger son.

For all its early success, however, Wolsey's time in France was punctuated with petty frustrations and apparent ill omens. At Boulogne he had been greeted by pageants at the city gate, one depicting 'a nun called Holy Church whom the Spaniards and Almayns had violated, but whom the cardinal had rescued and set up again' and another of the pope 'lying under the emperor sitting in majesty, whom the cardinal pulled down'. Yet the mule that Wolsey was riding shied at the sound of cannon fire and nearly threw him to the ground. Furthermore, insulting graffiti were found in his lodgings. In one place, a cardinal's hat was carved into a stone windowsill, with a gallows over it, and to compound his problems he was subject to repeated thefts from his chamber, which included a valuable silver dish and other items kept for his personal use. Perhaps the worst loss of all came at Compiègne, however, when the truly indispensable silver and gilt inkpot, with which he composed his dispatches to Henry, went missing. The culprit, it emerged, was the protégé of a professional thief in Paris – a 12-year-old 'ruffian's page' – who was found hiding under a stairwell when the alarm was raised. Prior to being placed in the pillory, moreover, the boy confessed how he had not only taken the precious inkpot, but everything else pilfered from the cardinal in recent days.

An even more curious incident marred the banqueting that followed the meeting with Francis. Accompanying Wolsey as part of his travelling household was a group of highly skilled musicians, including a particularly gifted but ill-fated shalm-player. So impressed was Francis by their virtuosity that he subsequently borrowed the entire ensemble for a visit to the house of a nobleman, where they played on throughout the night and so captivated their audience that they were said to have thoroughly surpassed even the king's own players – none more so, indeed, than the celebrated shalm-player himself. Two days later, however, Wolsey's most revered musician was left breathless in the most literal sense of the term – a stone-cold corpse, who had died, it was said, 'either with extreme labour of blowing or with poisoning'. For the hapless cardinal, it seems, there was simply no escape on earth from envy.

Much more importantly there was no respite either from the King of England's misjudgment and indiscretion. In London, the angry talk was that Wolsey was 'all French', and the commercial interests of the City were scarcely concealing their concerns about the threat to trade with the Low Countries posed by any new alliance with France. When Wolsey defended it, wrote Edward Hall, 'some knocked the other on the elbow and said softly "he lieth"'. But now Sir Thomas More was reporting to the cardinal how the king, too, was restive about the same thing. Pointing out 'how loath the Low Countries were to have any war with him', Henry had also commanded Lord Sandys to 'hold back his troops at Guisnes', lest his reluctant enemies 'reaped the goods of the English merchants' and began 'some business upon the English Pale'. As Wolsey proceeded to build bridges with the French, then, their foundations were being steadily undermined at home.

But these particular developments did not remotely match the much more troublesome and ominous events that had also begun to unfold in the cardinal's absence. In spite of Wolsey's appeals that Henry should proceed 'both gently and doucely' with the queen – at least 'till it were known what should succeed of the pope' – the king had continued to bluster and bully. Indeed, a month before the cardinal's departure, he had impulsively confronted Catherine with his doubts about their marriage, which, he declared, must make their separation inevitable. In the aftermath of this shockwave, moreover, she had managed to obtain a passport for her trusted servant of thirty years, Francisco Felipez, whom she now dispatched to her nephew in Spain. Though Henry had informed the French of Felipez's mission in the hope that he would be captured en route, the Spaniard nevertheless evaded his pursuers and duly reached Valladolid to inform the emperor of his aunt's predicament. Now, therefore, Charles V was not only apprised of what he termed 'this ugly affair', but became irrevocably committed to Catherine's cause. 'Nothing shall be omitted on my part to help you in your present tribulation', he told her, and to confirm his promise he followed her suggestion and urged the pope to revoke Wolsey's legatine power, which would leave him powerless in the matter of the marriage.

Meanwhile, the cardinal's enemies at the English court had also been making hay. Much to his dismay, Wolsey learned that the king had enjoyed supper in his privy chamber with the dukes of Norfolk and Suffolk, the Marquess of Exeter and Sir Thomas Boleyn. Given Henry's susceptibility to influence and proneness to whim, the possibilities were obvious and, with this in mind, John Clerk was therefore returned at once to England to emphasise Wolsey's progress and explain his plans for the future. He returned, too, with a personal letter from the cardinal, couched in the most obsequious terms, assuring the king that it was his unstinting desire to bring to pass 'your secret matter' with the pope. The letter was written, Wolsey assured Henry, 'with the rude and shaking hand of your must humble, subject and chaplain'.

But the cardinal's hands would not be steadied by the bad news which next came his way, for he soon learned that the king was intending to bypass him with a direct appeal of his own to the pope. William Knight, the special envoy appointed for the task, was ostensibly to convey the king's condolences for

Clement's captivity and to assist Wolsey's current efforts to oversee papal affairs. He was instructed, further, to meet Wolsey at Compiègne, pretending all the while that his journey to Italy had nothing to do with the divorce and making every effort to conceal his true objectives from 'any craft that the Cardinal [...] can find'. In reality, however, Knight was to carry two draft bulls for the pope to consider: one permitting the king to marry any woman he chose once freed from Catherine, the other looking ahead to the possibility that the pope might not be able to declare Henry's marriage invalid. In the latter eventuality, the pope was to permit the King of England to enjoy a second, simultaneous, marriage with Anne Boleyn.

When Wolsey learned of these plans from a member of the king's household, the impact was nothing short of seismic. He had left England on his greatest and most critical mission to date, and now he had been decisively undermined by the master he was striving to serve against all odds. And not only was that master now courting disaster, he was also, it seemed, mistrustful of the only man who could help him. Without informing Wolsey, Henry had for good measure foolishly resolved to propose a marriage – and a bigamous one at that – to the very woman who could be guaranteed to seek the cardinal's destruction. It was one of the cardinal's residing superstitions that his fall would be brought about by a woman, and now his worst fears were being realised. That the king should have sunk to such duplicity was the worst blow he had suffered and for the first time in Wolsey's long career the threat to his pre-eminence stood out starkly. His master had struck out independently and in the process left him both stranded and exposed. For not only was he now expected to feign ignorance of the king's subterfuge but to connive in a scheme that was as ominous for him personally as it was ill-conceived.

To compound an already dire situation, the projected meeting of cardinals at Avignon was already foundering hopelessly. With the King of France's half-hearted persuasion, six cardinals eventually answered the appeal to protest the imprisonment of Clement VII and pledge their refusal to any act he might make under compulsion. But no more ripples of support were forthcoming. On the contrary, the College of Cardinals, in spite of lukewarm French pressure and Wolsey's bribes, stood icily aloof from the man whom they had already twice rejected for the papacy. Bad luck – in this case at least – was little in evidence. It was true that both English agents and Italian agents in English pay had experienced great difficulty in obtaining access to the pope now that news of the annulment had reached the emperor. But the simple truth was that Wolsey's motives had quite simply proven too transparent and fear of imperial reprisals too strong. The pope, in any case, had rejected any delegation of power and by December was enjoying a liberty of sorts at Orvieto after being allowed to escape his more blatant captivity at Rome. If ever Wolsey's conclave had been a viable option, now it was wholly superfluous.

After a desultory attempt to prevent Knight's passage to Rome on the quite legitimate grounds that he 'had no colour or acquaintance there', and a predictably futile appeal that the king 'take a little patience' and trust instead to the efforts of Girolamo Ghinucci, Bishop of Worcester, Wolsey was squarely thwarted. Henry's reply had, it is true, been polite, expressing gratitude at his servant's efforts, 'which service cannot be by any kind master forgotten, of which fault I trust I shall never be accused, especially to youward, which so laboriously do serve me'. But it was clear that Wolsey would need to return, if he were to have any realistic chance of salvaging the imminent shipwreck. Knight's errand in Rome was bound for wholesale failure, and when king and minister were once again together, there was still perhaps an outside possibility that Henry's thoughts might be guided as in earlier days. Above all, Wolsey must revive the old and easy familiarity, the crucial bond of trust that had for so long held fast against all adversity.

On 13 September, therefore, the careworn traveller informed his master that he was making for home as speedily 'as mine old and cracked body may endure'. Predictably, the months of travel had worn him down as he rushed from city to city enduring French heat and French impudence, and, as summer gave way to autumn in more senses than one, so Wolsey gave way to self-pity, bemoaning 'the travails and pains which I daily and hourly sustain, without any regard to the continuance of my life or death'. If, however, Wolsey's energies were indeed ebbing, his ability to frame a well-turned phrase of flattery remained robust, for he added, with a characteristic dash of timely smarm, that 'there was never love more desirous of the sight of his lady than I am of your royal person'.

Yet the time when tinsel talk could carry the day was indeed rapidly disappearing and when Wolsey set sail for Dover four days later an altogether altered scene awaited him. In his absence, the slip of a girl whom he had once rudely separated from Henry Percy had become exalted. Now she indulged her passion for carp and shrimps at the king's high table, while he in turn expressed unbounded passion for her. 'For what joy in this world,' wrote Henry, 'can be greater than to have the company of her who is the most dearly loved, knowing likewise that she by her choice holds the same, the thought of which greatly delights me.' Though the king continued to maintain civilities with his wife and queen, Mistress Anne Boleyn was nevertheless firmly ensconced at Windsor, joining him when hawking or upon his afternoon walks in the surrounding parkland. 'Darling,' ran another of the king's letters, 'you and I shall [soon] have our desired end, which should be more to my heart's ease, and more quietness to my mind than any other thing in the world.'

Wolsey, of course, was still a formidable figure, who had discharged a string of high offices and managed the affairs of princes far too long to be lightly discounted. Furthermore, he was still ostensibly the king's friend. Certainly, he knew his master's ways and whims, as well as his secret needs and wishes. He knew his weak points, too – his fears and insecurities, his volatility, his proneness to flattery and passing fancy. And though Wolsey's enemies continued to whisper against him, they did so mainly in corners. Nor did they offer any viable alternative to his primacy. Yet now, in spite of all, he was in uncharted territory – the world of private passion and impulse – and the doubt remained whether the affairs of the royal bedroom could be managed as objectively and rationally as the subtleties of international diplomacy or the logistics of any military campaign. 'It was supposed among us,' wrote George Cavendish, 'that the Cardinal would be joyfully received at his homecoming, as well of the King as of all other noblemen; but we were deceived in our expectation.'

17

Bereft, Beleaguered and Bedevilled

As the dark waters of the late-September Channel swell heaved beneath him, Thomas Wolsey was still staking all upon a swift, joyous and decisive reconciliation with the king, and with this in mind he rode immediately from Dover to Richmond upon his arrival. Bearing rich gifts from Francis – a golden chalice and paten, gold and silk altar cloths and tapestries worth 30,000 ducats – he planned to tame his master with a potent mixture of material enticements and heady promises for the alliance he had so recently secured with France. But it was with wicked delight that the Spanish ambassador, Inigo de Mendoza, recorded the cardinal's sudden discomfiture. Sending as always advance notice of his arrival and expecting to be received by the king in a 'private closet', where he might discuss 'affairs of state', Wolsey now received a rebuff no less sharp than the shocking revelation which went with it. For 'the lady called Anna de Bolaine', who, suggested Mendoza, 'seems to have no great affection for the Cardinal', was waiting imperiously with her royal lover. And it was she rather than Henry who now had the temerity to block Wolsey's request. Pre-empting any prospect of a cosy reconciliation behind closed doors, she left the cardinal's messenger in no doubt about the new balance of influence at court. 'Where else should the Cardinal come?' she interjected. 'Tell him he may come here where the king is.'

The signs were unmistakable. But in spite of Anne's precocious self-confidence, Wolsey was not yet entirely undone. In due course, he did indeed talk at length with his master and eventually remained at court some two or three days. His lines of communication with the king, though threatened, were still partially intact and for the time being he retained what amounted, in effect, to the boldness of no option. Paradoxically, Wolsey had never been proud where his treatment by the king was concerned, and if he now had to endure slights and indifference, he was well equipped to do so. Faced, moreover, with a rival like Anne – who was daily derided in the capital as the king's 'night crow' and 'mare' – he could afford to wait and endure. It was no small consolation, of course, that the king's bad temper was still mainly directed against Pope Clement in Rome and the emperor who held his reins. And there was one further card in Wolsey's hands. For, if the pope feared Charles, he could in turn be made to fear the King of England. The potential loss of the English Church was, after all, no light thought for any pope to bear and with a man like Clement VII, who cowered and teetered by nature, the pressure of Wolsey's lieutenants might yet reap rich rewards.

Pope Clement had, in fact, remained a layman until the age of 35, when his Medici cousin, Leo X, appointed him Archbishop of Florence. A decade later he had gone from being a quick-witted and respected cardinal to a hard-pressed pope of small esteem. Though his private life was comparatively innocuous, he was nevertheless 'the most secretive man in the world' and notoriously indecisive to boot: 'the greatest of all delayers', as one of Wolsey's agents put it. He was also inclined to give way easily under pressure, promising publicly to fulfil whatever was asked of him before betraying any agreement to which he had pledged himself. As such, Clement was ill-suited to settle even the pettiest of disputes. But now, shaken to numbness by his captivity and standing astride two fast-parting ice flows, he was stricken. He had escaped from captivity in a long false beard, wearing the tattered tunic and threadbare hat of a household menial, but his release had been engineered rather than won. And his days in the tumbledown palace at Orvieto, a day's journey from Rome, where he now resided, were as troubled as ever. A helpless morsel between slathering hounds, his only options were subterfuge, prayer and delay.

While William Knight was still in Rome, ploughing his hapless furrow, Wolsey was therefore laying further plans of his own. He had known from the outset that the ways of the pope and the Roman curia were far beyond Knight's competence and that if any genuine progress were to be made, it required the services of someone well versed in the vice and venality of the Eternal City. To Richard Pace, Rome was a perversion of everything sacred, a monstrosity 'full of shame and scandal'. 'There,' he wrote, 'all faith, honesty and religion seem to have vanished from the earth.' Englishmen, it seems, were particularly ineffectual in this dragons' den of self-aggrandisement – which may explain why one cardinal wrote in 1517 that they did nothing but gorge, drink, run riot and abuse each other. All this Wolsey knew. And it was for this reason that he now enlisted the services of Gregorio Casali for one last effort at 'friendly' persuasion of the papal see.

Later falsely rumoured to be the poisoner of Catherine of Aragon, Casale was in fact the archetypal exponent of sixteenth-century espionage and political 'fixing' in a mysterious, undercover world of secret cyphers, kidnapping, blackmail and murky midnight missions to the high and mighty. Wolsey's instructions were explicit. Casali was to go in disguise to Orvieto and persuade Clement to comply with a crucial request, 'without disclosing the affair to anyone'. 'You should change your dress,' wrote Wolsey on 5 December 1527, 'and as if you were in some other person's employ, or had some commission from the Duke of Ferrara, obtain a secret interview with the pope.' The objective was a document empowering Wolsey and one other cardinal to determine in England whether the 1503 bull of dispensation was valid in canon law. And though Wolsey continued to maintain his own integrity unflinchingly, the presence of an additional judge still provided little more than the thinnest veneer of objectivity. 'Since I am a cardinal and legate *a latere*,' he declared, 'the honour of the pope and the integrity of his conscience can come to no harm in my hands.' Whereupon he duly furnished Casali with letters of credit to Venetian bankers for 10,000 ducats, which were to be used for bribery of 'any person whatever that can secure you the interview' or to buy off any third party who might catch wind of the affair.

There were threats and dire prognostications, too – not least concerning Wolsey himself. In a further letter to Casali, dispatched the following day, the cardinal left no doubt about the stakes involved. 'Among all the arguments I can think of,' he wrote, 'none is stronger than the friendship with which I have inspired the king towards His Holiness.' 'A friendship,' he added with time-honoured gangster finesse, 'which will be permanent, unless some occasion should be offered for alienating the king's mind, in which event it will never be in my power to serve his holiness.' But this was not by any means the sum of Wolsey's concerns, for the hidden agenda, which was weighing so heavily on his private thoughts, also surfaced starkly. 'If the pope is not compliant,' he admitted, 'my own life will be shortened, and I dread to anticipate the consequences.' In a hushed-up letter to a shadowy figure on a pitch-dark, subterranean mission, Wolsey had therefore finally unburdened himself. By steady degrees, he had been sucked inexorably into a mortal struggle, which would have to be conducted, come what may, to the bitter end or until, in other words, the corner in which he was increasingly tightly confined was finally painted over.

Yet in spite of Casali's best efforts the pope proceeded to parry him with his usual – and in this case quite intentional – indecision. What the English cardinal proposed was, of course, entirely unacceptable, for though Wolsey might quite successfully pose as devil to the beleaguered pontiff, there was still the much deeper, bluer sea of imperial wrath for Clement to consider. The draft document prepared in England had limited the judges of the nullity suit to consideration solely of the points in Henry's case that were favourable to him. Furthermore, it empowered Wolsey alone, if need be, to deliver judgement and committed the pope to ratify whatever he decided. In the opinion of Cardinal Lorenzo Pucci, such a strategy would have served to disgrace all parties, pope, king and cardinal. Even by the curia's own slender standards, therefore, this was chicanery of the crudest kind and not to be countenanced. The pope, moreover, agreed with his advisers entirely. But rather than reject the proposal outright and risk immediate consequences, he proposed amendments, subtly framed by his own Cardinal St Quatuor, which proved, naturally enough, wholly insufficient.

Faced, then, with obfuscation and delay, Wolsey now opted – as was often his wont in circumstances of utter deadlock – for naked intimidation. And on 12 February 1528 Edward Fox and Stephen Gardiner, two lawyers from the cardinal's own secretariat, duly set out to browbeat Clement into granting all the powers for which he had earlier been asked. Delayed at Dover by wind and storms and narrowly escaping shipwreck during the crossing, they took eight days to reach Calais. Whereupon they visited the French king at St Germain-en-Laye, and travelled on by Lyons, Genoa and Lucca with all possible speed, always beginning their day's journey before sunrise and never spending two nights in the same place. Even so, they did not reach Orvieto until 21 March and the figure they cut by that time was altogether less than impressive, since they arrived 'with no garments but the coats they rode in, which were much worn and defaced by the foul weather'. And since the squalor in Orvieto was such that few men had 'more garments than one' and new ones could not be purchased, the two envoys were left with no other choice than to postpone their audience with the pope until their clothes were mended.

But if, in the meantime, Fox and Gardiner were clad like nomads, their diplomatic teeth were already keenly honed and sharpened for the impending onslaught, and by the time of their arrival they found a pope apparently ripe for consumption. 'I cannot tell,' observed Gardiner, 'how the pope should be described as being at liberty here, where hunger, scarcity, bad lodgings, and ill air keep him as much confined as he was in the Castle Angelo.' On the way to their audience, the Englishmen passed through three rooms 'all naked and unhanged, the roofs fallen down, and, as we can guess 30 persons, riffraff and other, standing in the chamber for a garnishment'. When they met the Holy Father himself, moreover, they found him, according to Gardiner, upon a couch covered with a rug not worth 20s. As the meeting progressed, Pope Clement paced up and down in undisguised agitation, sighing and wiping his eyes and bemoaning his fate. With the Spaniards at his doorstep, he found himself, he said, 'in the power of dogs'.

Yet the envoys, true to their instructions, displayed little sympathy and 'on the morrow' returned to the pope and 'spoke roundly to him', making it clear that their king would, if necessary, 'do without him'. First, however, they denied any suggestion that Henry's nullity suit was prompted by 'vain affection and undue love' for Anne Boleyn, or what the pope termed 'private reasons'. The envoys also countered rumours at the papal court that the king's mistress was already pregnant. No doubt feeling the ink curdle upon his pen, Wolsey had indeed already instructed his men to speak up ardently in Anne's defence, emphasising:

> The excellent virtuous [qualities] of the said gentlewoman, the purity of her life, her constant virginity, her maidenly and womanly pudicity, her soberness, chasteness, meekness, humility, wisdom, descent of right noble and high thorough regal blood, education in all good and laudable [qualities] and manners [and] apparent aptness to procreation of children.

Clearly, if the cardinal's survival depended upon it, even he would have to worship at Anne's altar for the time being. And it was no coincidence that this particular encomium to the royal mistress was prominently displayed in the recorded instructions to Fox and Gardiner, where it would be seen by the king himself.

Predictably, however, the discussions dragged on wearily day after day and often night after night as Gardiner answered all qualms and quibbles extempore in Latin. 'Discussed the matter warmly for five hours until one in the morning,' Gardiner informed Wolsey, 'when we departed with no other answer but that we should have a definite reply the next day before dinner.' But no reply came. On another occasion, the pope sent a canonist and his protonotary, Gambara, out to the houses of his cardinals for a speedy judgement, only to receive the answer that they would study the matter on the morrow. The pope, complained Gardiner, 'sees all that is spoken sooner and better than any other, but no man is so slow to give an answer'. 'Fearing a scorpion in every word', the pope's advisers were equally obstructive. Only the ongoing threat that the King of England might be forced to look elsewhere for a solution to his predicament – to 'live out of the laws of Holy Church', as it was said – seemed to afford any appreciable leverage.

Relentless pressure, combined with the advance of a French army in Northern Italy and the threat to imperial Naples from Andrea Doria's galleys, did indeed give Clement the will to act at last. With the emperor's troops increasingly demoralised and the prospect of a new and healthier balance of force in his homelands, the pope finally submitted on 7 April with a typical display of amateur dramatics. Walking frantically up and down the great audience chamber, with tears dripping down his copious beard and 'casting now and then his arms abroad', Clement duly agreed that the king's case could be heard at a legatine court in London headed by Wolsey and Lorenzo Campeggio, the Englishman's personal choice for co-adjudicator. There remained, it is true, the need for further clarification of certain details, which Wolsey was immediately alive to. Clement's initial agreement omitted, for instance, any reference to the binding authority of the court's decisions and did not preclude the possibility of revoking the case to Rome at a later date. But in a secret letter dated 23 July 1528 the necessary assurances were delivered on all such scores. Campeggio was, moreover, to travel to England, fully equipped with a decretal bull sanctioning an annulment of the king's marriage, something which Wolsey considered absolutely essential.

Not surprisingly, when news of the long-awaited breakthrough reached Henry at Greenwich, he received it, we are told, 'marvellously thankfully, and made marvellous demonstrations of joy and gladness'. Nor did Fox, the bringer of glad tidings, minimise Wolsey's part in the apparent victory. It was through the cardinal's letters, he said, that the pope had finally 'leaned to justice, and showed himself marvellous prone and glad to satisfy the king's requests'. And Wolsey, too, was eventually satisfied with the outcome of his ambassadors' efforts. Receiving the news in his bed at Durham House, the cardinal was at first circumspect and considered the papal commission little better than the one procured earlier by Casali. But after further discussion with Dr Bell, his proctor, he became better contented. If the arrangement was not by any means the cast-iron solution the king believed it to be, for the cardinal it was at least a lifeline.

The fact that his co-legate to hear and determine the 'Great Matter' was none other than Cardinal Campeggio was certainly heartening news. 'One of the best and most learned men living', according to Erasmus, Campeggio was an expert in both canon and civil law, and a man of considerable worldly experience to boot. He had, after all, been married to one Francesca Guastevallani until her death in 1509 and had the unusual distinction of producing five sons *before* entering ecclesiastical service during the pontificate of Julius II. Thereafter, he had performed both diligently and effectively as cardinal-protector of the Holy Roman Empire, during which time he also became well acquainted with the English king and court as an expert cadger of English benefices and absentee Bishop of Salisbury. It was Campeggio, too, who visited England in 1518 to propose the launch of a new crusade against the Turks. Above all, however, the Italian appeared to be Wolsey's creature; a man whom Wolsey had decisively upstaged, almost bullied, a decade earlier. And though he was bound to represent the pope and therefore avoid offence to the emperor, he was nevertheless known to be one of the more ambivalent supporters of imperial interests, not least, perhaps, because his own house and possessions had been destroyed during the sack of Rome only a year earlier.

But the double game was still afoot and Wolsey now found himself the victim of what would amount to slow diplomatic strangulation: more drawn out, more frustrating, more ingenious, more inexorable and more excruciating than even he might have devised for an unwitting quarry of his own. It was Wolsey, of course, who had kept Campeggio waiting interminably in Calais in 1518, as he applied pressure for his appointment as a papal legate. Now, however, the roles were reversed, as the Italian exploited every opportunity to loiter and obstruct. Acting under strict instructions from Clement, even his martyrdom to gout became from this time forth an invaluable asset. Unable either to walk or ride, it was all he could do, it seems, to sit confined in his litter, enduring the purgatory of unpaved roads and stifling summer heat as he trundled across Europe. Such, indeed, was his discomfort that curious villagers who caught sight of him along the way saw only a shrunken figure hunched in pain with a long untrimmed beard – a sign, they thought, of mourning for the English Church. But every shock and jar of his journey meant further delay and further opportunity for some unforeseen development which might somehow release the pope from the Gordian knot currently binding him.

In England, however, Wolsey's own path was proving bumpier still. The respite afforded by the pope's submission had initially prompted even Anne Boleyn's goodwill. Not long before Campeggio began his creaky descent upon her homeland, she wrote to Wolsey, thanking him 'for the great pains and troubles that you have taken for me both day and night' and assuring him of the love she bore him 'next unto the King's Grace, above all creatures living'. Such, it seems, is the fickleness engendered by welcome news and relief from long waiting. But the reverse is also true, and as days turned to weeks and weeks to months the sky darkened. The temporary renewal of war in

January 1528 had, for instance, already stirred further hatred of Wolsey in the country at large. Four clothmakers, joined by a fuller and a fiddler – along with 150 men from Frykenden and Cranbrook – had conspired to kidnap the cardinal and drown him. 'We will bring him to the sea side,' explained one of the conspirators, 'and there will put him in a boat, in the which shall be bored four great holes.' The harsh winter had also taken its toll on common folk's patience. 'Either the people must die for famine,' wrote the Lord Mayor of London to Wolsey, 'or else they with strong hand will fetch corn from them that have it.'

But it was the king who dominated Wolsey's thoughts and, in particular, the fear that Campeggio's journey would not only be interminably drawn out but ultimately fruitless. By August, Henry was so utterly committed to his cause, declared the French ambassador du Bellay, 'that none but God can get him out of it' and Wolsey's pleas that Henry be both patient and prepared for further compromise now provoked only 'terrible language'. It was small wonder, perhaps, that the cardinal wrote plaintively to du Bellay of his wish to be done with public office. 'Sometimes in walking with me,' wrote the ambassador, 'while speaking of his affairs and life up to that time, he has said to me […] that, without any doubt, on the first honourable occasion he could find, he would give up politics.' Should the king's suit fail to produce the desired outcome, as the cardinal increasingly anticipated, there was of course no doubt where the blame would fall, and if the king's protection was ever lost there would be no shortage of waiting enemies to rip at the fallen minister's flesh. It would take 'a terrible alchemy and dexterity', Wolsey told the Frenchman, to overcome the onslaught of those ranged against him.

Perhaps it was for this reason that the cardinal continued, even *in extremis*, to derive such consolation from his patronage of education, the one area where he could reasonably hope for a legacy free from political taint and accusations of self-interest and personal gain. Less than a month before Campeggio's arrival the College of St Mary had been opened in Ipswich at his inspiration, with the express intention of outshining Eton and serving as a feeder institution to Cardinal College at Oxford. In the event, Wolsey had considered no detail of the school's development too small for his attention, including the question of discipline. 'We admonish particularly,' he had written, 'that tender youth be not effected by severe stripes or threatening countenance or by any species of tyranny.' Nor, for that matter, did he neglect to urge parents to provide warm winter clothing for their boys. The faculty, meanwhile, would include a dean, twelve canons, a choir of eight men and eight boys, and for the basic curriculum Wolsey ordered the use of William Lily's *Latin Grammar*, for which he produced a special preface. Unable, of course, to forego the opportunity, he began the preface with a characteristic flourish of self-affirmation:

> We imagine no body can be ignorant of the care, study, and industry of mind, with which we have hitherto directed our labours, not for our own private interest, but that of our country, and all our citizens, which we shall deem ourselves to have been most amply gratified, if, by any divine blessing, we should improve the minds of the people.

But he was equally keen to emphasise that 'it avails little to have built a school, however magnificent it might be, unless it be furnished with skilful masters', and the appointment of William Capon, former Master of Jesus College Cambridge, as the college's first dean confirmed that Wolsey was as good as his word.

The possibility that Wolsey might have so little time to fulfil the school's potential could not have escaped him, however. Outwardly as pre-eminent as ever, he was nevertheless living on appearances and his inner confidence was seriously challenged. Such was Henry's growing frustration, moreover, that only an outbreak of sweating sickness – to which Anne herself briefly fell victim on 16 June – served to distract him in some small measure from his predicament. As he snatched at straws, Wolsey appeased his master as best he could with news of proven remedies gleaned from the dowager Duchess of Norfolk. Those with pains around the heart or groin, he informed the king, had been doused with treacle and 'imperial water', while others with stomach cramps had been saved by a herb to purge the swelling and a fast of sixteen hours' duration. To keep him well while visiting infected areas, the duchess had also advised the cardinal to keep a linen cloth before his nose, containing a mixture of vinegar, wormwood, rosewater and crumbs of brown bread. It was desperate stuff, indeed, on Wolsey's part, though Henry, still infinitely malleable when either his own or a loved one's wellbeing was at stake, responded keenly with cures of his own, sending his minister 'manus Christi', an efficacious herb, and instructing him to eat lightly, drink little wine and fortify himself with 'pills of Rasis'.

By August the king was buoyed at last by more-promising news. As a nod to discretion in anticipation of Campeggio's arrival, Anne had been encouraged to take up new apartments at Greenwich, especially prepared for her by Wolsey, to separate her from her lover. The apartments still allowed easy access, however, and while briefly absent on a hunting trip, Henry now informed her of the Italian's approach. Writing at eleven o'clock after a hard day's chase and 'the killing of a hart', the message to 'mine own darling' was encouraging. 'The legate which we most desire arrived at Paris on Sunday or Monday last past,' wrote the king, 'so that I trust by the next Monday to hear of his arrival in Calais; and then I trust with a while to enjoy that which I have so longed for, to God's pleasure, and our both comforts.' The 'while', however, would still be a long one. For it was not until the first week of October that the Italian finally reached London to be housed, first, in the Duke of Suffolk's residence and then the Bishop of Bath's palace.

Campeggio would arrive at Canterbury on 1 October and as he continued to make his agonising way through the autumn English countryside, he was confounded by news of further developments on the continent. Now, for instance, he would have to bear in mind that Andrea Dorea's naval initiative against the emperor in Naples had been bought off by imperial gold and that the advancing French army had ultimately surrendered, rotten with plague and fever. To cast further gloom upon an already furrowed papal brow, Genoa – so vital to French supply lines and so vital, too, to the emperor – had just changed sides. In consequence, Campeggio's mission in London could not possibly bring any prospect of quick or neat solutions. On the contrary, it was once more hopelessly mired in the vagaries of war and stuck fast between an unprecedented conjunction of immovable objects, irresistible forces and mutually incompatible objectives. To all intents and purposes, it was doomed to inexorable failure, over before it had begun.

In the meantime, however, both Henry and Anne remained utterly oblivious to any such prospect. The significance of Campeggio's late arrival was, indeed, completely lost upon them, as they pondered their joint futures with fond elation. The optimism of Fox and Gardiner had raised their hopes and, with typical duplicity, Clement himself had sent word that he would do his best to satisfy their wishes. Petitioners at court had also begun to seek out Anne, just as they had once been drawn to Catherine, to gain the king's favour. Any thought, therefore, that Campeggio's gouty odyssey from Rome was only one part of a broader papal policy to delay and frustrate their plans entirely escaped them. Like all accomplished statesmen, moreover, Campeggio was a consummate actor, and from the moment of his arrival the earnest posturing and strict maintenance of formalities, which became his trademark, was unwavering. To all outward appearances, he arrived as nothing more than an amenable executant of Wolsey's wishes, while in secret he was loaded with crafty ploys and counter-instructions straight from the pope's own lips.

By overwhelming weight of circumstance, then, Campeggio arrived in England as a trader in false hope – for Henry and Anne, for Wolsey, for Catherine, and for all indeed but the pope himself and the emperor who held him fast, since the hard facts of Clement's predicament placed him beyond illusions and

Charles was so firmly ascendant that he needed none. Certainly, if the queen took any consolation from the arrival of a learned, ethical arbiter from Rome to hear her case and find in her favour, she was sorely mistaken, for Campeggio was neither her saviour nor even her advocate. On the contrary, his favoured ploy upon arrival was to persuade Catherine to abandon her marriage willingly by entering a convent – just as Jeanne de Valois, Queen of France, had done before her. More insensitively still, he was also prepared to talk, if nothing more, of marriage between Henry Fitzroy and the Princess Mary and of satisfying the king's need for a legitimate heir by recognising any children born to Anne out of wedlock. He would even listen, albeit equally imperviously, to Henry's own suggestion made in January that he be allowed to have two wives. If, therefore, by some miracle – and nothing less would suffice – events in Europe somehow contrived to loosen the emperor's stranglehold, the conjugal knot tying Catherine to her faithless husband would have been snipped without hesitation. That it was not, of course, had little to do with virtue, justice or loyalty.

Nevertheless, Campeggio was struck at once by the King of England's absolute determination to have his way. When Wolsey met him on 9 October for preliminary discussions, he emphasised the acute danger to all concerned if Henry did not secure a favourable judgement. 'There would speedily follow,' as Campeggio made clear in his report of Wolsey's claims, 'the complete ruin of the Kingdom, of his Right Reverend Lordship and of the prestige of the Church throughout the Kingdom.' Linking his own survival to the continued wellbeing of the Church in England, Wolsey was therefore not only advertising his own importance but establishing the highest possible stakes from the outset. And the Italian's first meetings with Henry did nothing to suggest that his fellow legate was exaggerating on either count.

The king's desire for an annulment was 'most ardent', Campeggio wrote a week after his arrival. Ego, logic and self-righteousness – all reinforced by a typically selective show of hard learning – left Henry in no doubt about the virtue of his case. 'His Majesty has so diligently studied this matter,' observed Campeggio, 'that I believe in this case he knows more than a great theologian or jurist.' But if the king was well acquainted with what he considered the letter of the law, he was less familiar with the true scholar's preference for patience, balance and, above all, listening, and his learning remained, to all intents and purposes, as self-serving as his conscience. For four hours he had held forth as Campeggio played the role of sponge and nodding student. But the real lesson emerging from the interview was neither legal nor theological. Reflecting on the king's intransigence, Campeggio drew the only possible conclusion. 'I believe that an angel descending from heaven would be unable to persuade him otherwise,' he noted wistfully. And on the following Sunday he was persuaded to reveal the decretal bull, which appeared to sanction all that the king desired.

What Campeggio did not reveal, however, was the elaborate ruse which centred upon this document. For, in spite of previous assurances to the contrary, the pope had left him in no doubt that the bull should be shown only to Henry and Wolsey and could not be produced in court. More importantly still, it was on no account to be executed. As such, its unveiling was nothing more than a sop to starving men – an appetiser for a non-existent meal and a prelude to further delay as Campeggio now took to his sickbed whenever convenient. Neither hero nor genius, the Italian knew at least how to lose slowly and to save what could be saved from a no-win situation, since Wolsey, too, had proved unbending. 'I have no more success in persuading the cardinal,' wrote Campeggio, 'than if I had spoken to a rock.' Thus, with king and cardinal alike insisting that they would 'endure no procrastination' since 'the affairs of the kingdom are at a standstill', the Italian duly procrastinated, fighting hot air with a steady cooling stream of paltry excuses and chill indifference.

Only when Campeggio suggested that Catherine might opt for convenient seclusion within a nunnery had Henry's impatience temporarily abated. But she, too, remained another immovable object in the stone wall maze confronting Wolsey. Ever desperate to probe any and every avenue, he had met in August with Robert Shorton, the queen's almoner, to debate her case, but was told once more that Catherine had never known Prince Arthur as her husband. Worse still, Wolsey also learned of her conviction that no court in England could offer her justice and of her determination to make use of certain papal bulls existing in Spain that allegedly removed all impediments to her present marriage. When, therefore, Wolsey claimed to have proof of consummation, centring on fears that Catherine had been pregnant at the time of Arthur's death, he was already clutching at straws. Nor was the queen any more convinced by the cardinal's even lamer assertion that the current impasse cast a stigma upon all the learned men of England who had found the marriage invalid. For, although she had been left to hammer out her defence alone, she was nevertheless secure in conscience, convinced of her cause and raring to fight.

Yet this, of course, did not prevent Wolsey and Campeggio from persevering with Catherine. On one of their three visits, she listened patiently over the space of two hours to the inducements offered her: the beauties of a life of religious contemplation; the guarantee that she would retain her dowry; the promise that she would retain the guardianship of her daughter. But her only response was to request legal counsel. And at the end of the discussion, it was to Campeggio rather than Wolsey that she chose to make her confession. What Catherine subsequently revealed, moreover, she urged him to communicate to the pope, even though it was rendered under the sacred seal of the confessional. Covering the whole of her life from the time of her arrival in England, she made it clear that she had not slept in the same bed with Arthur 'more than seven nights' and 'that he had left her as he had found her – a virgin'. She affirmed, too, that 'she intended to live and die in the estate of matrimony, to which God had called her' and that 'she would always remain of that opinion and never change it'.

Meanwhile, on their next visit to the queen, Wolsey and Campeggio found her flanked by advisers, and as adamant as ever that she would do nothing either to condemn her soul or violate God's laws. And as Wolsey raised himself from his knees after one final flourish in which he pleaded that she listen to the voice of the Church, the course before him was clear. With the queen's assent out of the question once and for all, the scene was now irrevocably set for all the high and public drama of his legatine court – though not, predictably, before further random obstacles and painful twists and turns had run their weary course. In mid-November, Catherine did indeed produce a copy of a further dispensation, hitherto unknown in England and dating from 1505, which appeared to undermine the whole case upon which Campeggio's decretal bull was based. Then, as Sir Francis Bryan headed for Rome at Wolsey's behest to prove the document spurious, news came that the pope was mortally ill and that 'another lapse will finish him', though Wolsey's desperate fantasies of yet another personal bid for the papacy and subsequent plans for hefty bribes proved fleeting, since Clement survived, and neither Stephen Gardiner's ongoing pressure at Rome throughout the spring of 1529 nor Bryan's best efforts yielded any progress. By Easter, indeed, Bryan had concluded that Henry's cause was hopeless and, unlike Gardiner who had been manfully gnawing at granite for all of fifteenth months, he was prepared to say as much. 'Neither fair means nor foul' could now prevail upon the pope, he reported to Henry. And 'if the cardinal feels aggrieved at the truth,' the message concluded, then 'let him'.

On 29 May, therefore, Henry duly instructed Campeggio and Wolsey to proceed under the terms of Clement's original commission, and two days later formal arrangements were drawn up for Henry and Catherine to appear at Blackfriars on 18 June. Yet Wolsey, 'betwixt hope and fear', still wondered whether Clement might well renege upon his earlier guarantee and revoke the case to Rome. He had received further confirmation, too, of his own increasingly brittle relationship with the king. During the previous summer he had blocked the appointment of Eleanor Carey as Abbess of Wilton and in doing so forestalled the wishes of Anne Boleyn. The result was a wholly unfamiliar barb from his royal master. 'Ah! my lord,' wrote Henry, 'it is a double offence, both to do ill and colour it, too; but with men that have wit it cannot be accepted so. Wherefore, good my lord, use no more that way with me, for there is no man living that more hateth it.' Nor was this all, for Henry then proceeded to twist the knife by questioning both Wolsey's closure of certain monasteries and subsequent decision to redistribute the resulting funds to his beloved colleges at Oxford and Ipswich.

It was with no little trepidation, therefore, that Wolsey must have made his way to the long-awaited legatine court at Blackfriars on Friday, 18 June 1529. He was faced with the critical moment of his career and, though he only feared as much as yet, neither he nor Campeggio could actually deliver the favourable outcome on which all hinged. For, as the two scarlet-robed princes of the Universal Church, hatted, gloved and ringed, moved majestically to their chairs of state behind a railed and carpeted table, both were hopelessly at odds. As such, the great hall of the Dominican priory at Blackfriars, decked out 'like a solemn court' with carpets and wall tapestries, may already have seemed more like a place of judgement for Wolsey personally; the queen's eleven advocates – seven English, four foreign – more like his prosecutors than her defenders. And then, of course, there was Catherine herself to consider, by her own confession 'a poor ignorant woman' unversed in the law, but idolised nevertheless by the Londoners who thronged outside the building. She had wooed them, as Wolsey bitterly acknowledged, 'by beckoning with her head and smiling' – 'which she had not been accustomed to do in times past' – and now she was to have her moment.

To the astonishment of all concerned, it was not the queen's lawyers but Catherine herself who entered the court on the day appointed for her defence. Though Henry was represented only by proxy she was determined to lodge her complaints about the court's competence in person. And though her protest was carefully worded, she pulled no punches. Leaning on the arm of one of her oldest retainers, Griffith ap Rhys, she had smiled and nodded her head to the noisy crowd outside in what the French ambassador termed 'a display of Castilianisms', before delivering a withering surgical strike against her judges. Since Campeggio was Bishop of Winchester, he like Wolsey was, she claimed, a subject of her husband and therefore partial. Furthermore, the second papal dispensation of 1505 – which she had refused to produce in the original for fear that it would be destroyed by her enemies – was indisputably valid, and twenty years of married life with her husband lent it a *de facto* legitimacy that no legal artifice could undermine. Most important of all, she remained a virgin at the time of Prince Arthur's death, and this too, in her opinion, was beyond all challenge.

When Henry appeared in person on 21 June to argue the justice of his own case, Catherine's objections were swiftly overruled. Yet this was only the prelude to the queen's most spectacular gesture of all. If she had delivered measured defiance three days earlier, her husband now opted for a stream of cloying hypocrisy. 'I most heartily beseech you to ponder my mind and intent,' he told the judges, 'which is to have a final end to the discharge of my conscience, for every good Christian man knoweth what pain and what unquietness he suffereth that hath a conscience grieved.' No prince had a worthier queen, he admitted, but he was now so troubled that he could no longer exercise his duty of rule effectively. At which point, Catherine made her own, altogether more dramatic, appeal.

Rising from her chair and sweeping across the court, she knelt at Henry's feet and contradicted him flatly in what George Cavendish described as 'broken English'. 'I take God to witness that I have been a true, humble and obedient wife,' she declared, 'and when you had me first, I take God to be my judge, I was a true maid, without touch of man.' Striking at the king's most sensitive spot, she then delivered her most telling blow. Having affirmed her maidenhood at the time of their marriage, she offered the king a chance to say otherwise: 'and whether this be true or not I put to your conscience'. The response was silence and a fixed gaze straight before him – a gaze that was maintained while Catherine then begged him to consider her honour, her daughter's and his own.

Making her reverence to the court with a final curtsey, the queen then ignored three requests from the court crier to remain and withdrew imperiously. When Griffith ap Rhys suggested she turn back, his appeal was squarely rebuffed. 'On, on,' she rejoined, 'it makes no matter, for it is no indifferent court for me. Therefore I will not tarry, go on your ways.' Wolsey's response, meanwhile, betrayed his consternation. Addressing the king, his first priority now was to cover his own back as best he could, while maintaining the deceit that Henry was driven purely by conscience. There had long been whispers that he had prompted the divorce and as cheers from outside greeted the abandoned queen, all was geared to self-defence. 'Sire,' he pleaded, 'I most humbly beseech your highness to declare me before all this audience whether I have been the chief inventor or first mover of this matter unto your Majesty, for I am greatly suspected of all men herein.' And much to his relief, he received not only the answer he wanted but also the one that best reflected the truth. For the king had needed no persuasion from first to last.

The crumbs from Henry's lips did nothing to solve the cardinal's greater dilemma, however. Certainly, the significance of the cheering women who had gathered outside the court in support of Catherine was not lost upon the French ambassador, du Bellay. Had the matter been decided by them, he wrote, the king would have lost his battle there and then, for they 'did not fail to encourage the queen on her entrance and departure by their cries'. And though nothing that followed could match the drama of that day, there was no substantial progress for Wolsey to offer the king during the arduous weeks ahead. The Marquess of Dorset, Sir Anthony Willoughby and Sir William Thomas of Caernarvon all trundled forth as material witnesses to the likely loss of Catherine's maidenhood in Arthur's bed. Had the prince not told Willoughby, for instance, to bring him a cup of ale 'for I have tonight been in the midst of Spain'? But Lord Mountjoy and the Bishop of Ely refused to commit themselves, and John Fisher offered steely defiance. When Warham cited his name among the signatures of those supporting the king's case, Fisher was quick to object, in fact. 'No sir, not so, under your correction', he countered, before claiming that he was ready to stake his own life, like John the Baptist, on the sanctity of the queen's marriage.

Yet one week before Fisher's tirade, the fate of Wolsey's legatine court and indeed the fate of Wolsey himself had in any case been sealed. Though none present knew it, the crushing Spanish victory over the French at Landriano on 21 June had confirmed Habsburg rule in Italy and finally halted Pope Clement's agonising. Addressing the Archbishop of Capua shortly after news of the battle reached him, the old waverer at last accepted the inevitable. 'I have quite made up my mind,' he declared, 'to become an Imperialist and live and die as such.' Nor, on this occasion at least, was he anything other than true to his word. For on 29 June pope and emperor were reconciled by the Treaty of Barcelona. Extending the kind of generosity that was altogether beyond the slender means of Wolsey, Charles V duly restored Florence to Clement's House of Medici and sweetened the pope even further by the return of Ravenna and Cervia to his grateful grasp.

Now, as a willing puppet of the emperor, Clement could never permit the abandonment of his new friend's embattled aunt in England. The pope had even pledged his nephew to the hand of Charles's illegitimate daughter, Margaret of Parma. So when Catherine's personal appeal against proceedings at Blackfriars arrived in Rome on 5 July, there could be but one outcome. Accordingly, on 13 July, from the warmth of his sickbed, Clement formally decided to abandon his guarantees to the King of England and duly revoked the case to the Eternal City. But even this was not the final dart for Wolsey to endure. For the French horse that he had backed so desperately was soon to prove not only a loser but a turncoat into the bargain. Only one month later Francis I bade his mother, Louise, to sign the Peace of Cambrai with Margaret of Austria, Regent of Burgundy, and with that parting insult, Wolsey's house of straw, so artfully crafted with so many interlocking layers of 'mights' and 'would-bes', received its final crushing blow.

The irony, however, was that Wolsey still had no appreciation of events in Europe as he continued to press the king's case throughout this same period. On 23 July the king's proctor made his formal request for judgement from the two legates at Blackfriars, and just over one week later, on 31 July, the court was packed in anticipation. Sitting in a gallery near the door, from which he had a commanding view of the judges, Henry awaited the long-overdue end to his agonies. Courtiers and churchmen, too, thronged the chamber and balconies for what was bound to be a defining event in Henry's reign. He had wriggled, wheedled, endured and blustered over many long months and, with uncharacteristic consistency, he had remained committed – at least nominally – to his chief minister, even sometimes trusting that minister's judgement over his own.

So the king's outright incredulity and seismic fury at what followed may well be imagined. Rising to his feet and delivering his brief address in elegant Latin, Campeggio suavely announced that since no cases were, by long custom, heard at Rome during the summer vacation, the legatine court assembled in London under Roman rules must therefore be adjourned until October. Though no mention was made of revoking the case to the Holy City, the implication was entirely clear and the response of the audience left no doubt of this. Giving 'a great clap on the table' and bearing 'a hard countenance', the Duke of Suffolk ranted how 'it was never merry in England while we had cardinals among us'. And Wolsey's angry response was as much a token of final defeat as any gesture of genuine defiance. Referring back to the time when he had helped the duke survive the king's wrath after his hasty marriage to Mary Tudor, the vanquished minister struck out vainly one last time. 'Sir,' he is said to have countered, 'of all men in this realm, ye have least cause to dispraise or be offended with cardinals; for if I, poor cardinal, had not been, you should have had at this present no head upon your shoulders.'

But the once-invincible legate had nevertheless been utterly dished and deserted, and this time he knew it. Outplayed at his own game by the man he considered his protégé, Wolsey had allowed his Italian counterpart to steal the initiative piece by piece until this final glorious twist. Nor, as he well knew, was there any virtue in trying to overrule Campeggio, since the hope that he could deliver a satisfactory verdict of his liking was always premised in reality upon their joint agreement. In effect, the pope had placed him on a paper tiger, and left him to ride it to his own destruction. Only the month before, Ipswich's grand panjandrum had acknowledged that if the case was removed to Rome it would 'utterly destroy him for ever'. And now, as Campeggio affected a doddering return to his seat, that dreadful possibility had become accomplished fact. Not long hence, Wolsey would be hounded from his office by his enemies at court. Shortly, too, he would be deserted by the king to whom he had promised the moon. And, as that same king retired to Greenwich to nourish his wrath, there was even the distant prospect that Campeggio's final ploy had rendered an epitaph for the entire medieval church in England.

18

'Tyrants' Sepulchre'

While Wolsey's torn and bleeding nails maintained a slender grasp on power during May and June of 1529, his clients still saw fit to ply him with gifts and dainties. The prior of Christ Church sent four Avon salmon and nineteen lobsters, while Sir Giles Strangeways was pleased to offer a great horse, a peacock, forty rabbits, six heron and two dozen quails. Thomas Trenchard, too, had dispatched heron, along with cygnets and shoveller ducks, and Sir John Rogers a further four pheasants and six gulls. The Mayor of Salisbury, in his turn, had presented beef and mutton; the Mayor of Poole, a tun of white wine; the town of Wareham, a hogshead of claret; and the vicar of Canford, two lambs, four capon and two geese. There were also two kids, a peacock, a peahen and a moorhen from a certain Master Philips. Other tokens, too, might well have suggested that Wolsey's ship remained afloat, even after its drastic holing at Blackfriars. Still his pillars and his poleaxes and all the other lofty luggage of high office went before him as he sleepwalked his way through the more menial tasks left to his charge. Still he received new bulls from the pope, allowing him to dissolve monasteries, and still he dreamed ambitious dreams for his college at Ipswich. To all outward appearances, it was business as usual, as the waning momentum of the cardinal's reputation nevertheless carried him slowly forward, like a great, creaking juggernaut, on its final crushing descent.

But by August it was widely broadcast that the divorce case had been revoked to Rome and before the month was out the so-called 'Ladies' Peace' of Cambrai was also common knowledge. Now, when Wolsey sent Rowland Phillips, the

Vicar of Croydon, to press the Abbot of Wigmore in Herefordshire to surrender his monastery, the offer was casually refused. Even a yearly pension of 40 marks was impudently spurned by the normally pliant monk. For, as Phillips told Wolsey on 31 August – with not a little insensitivity of his own – the abbot would not long since have gladly accepted, but now anticipated the cardinal's extinction. Furthermore, on 10 September it was reported to Wolsey by one of his agents that the Vicar of Southampton had appointed a chantry priest without proper consultation, in flagrant disregard for his authority as Bishop of Winchester. And even those closer to the cardinal were no longer dependable. 'I have less hope of his maintaining his influence, since my talk with him, than I had before,' wrote du Bellay at this time, 'for I see he trusts in some of his own creatures, who, I am sure, have turned their coats.' Clearly, the worms were stirring at every level as the impending landslide approached.

Much more obvious was the king's intense displeasure with his former favourite. Having gone on progress to Woodstock and Grafton, he appointed Stephen Gardiner as chief secretary and now refused to write to Wolsey in person. He also abruptly declined the cardinal's invitation to stay at the manor of the More, and would not allow him to come to court, in spite of a string of abject entreaties. As early as May, the French ambassador was reporting how 'Wolsey is in the greatest pain he ever was in', simply because Henry had been persuaded by the Dukes of Norfolk and Suffolk and Viscount Rochford that the cardinal had not been doing all he might to advance his marriage to Anne Boleyn. But by the time that Eustace Chapuys, the new imperial ambassador, arrived in late August, the situation had deteriorated immeasurably. 'It is generally and almost publicly stated,' he noted, 'that the affairs of the cardinal are getting worse and worse every day.' The two dukes, it seemed, 'transact all business', and though not long ago 'no one dared to say a word against the cardinal', now 'the tables were turned and his name is in everybody's mouth.' True, like a wounded lion, Wolsey was still feared. His relationship with the king had, after all, been long and in its day deeply personal, and there remained good reason, too, to distrust the abilities of those who sought to replace him. But his wounds were not only grievous. They were mortal. And as autumn's cusp approached, Henry shaped to strike.

Not until Sunday, 19 September, almost two months after the adjournment at Blackfriars, did Wolsey finally gain an audience with the king – and only then on the occasion of Campeggio's final farewell to the ruler whom he had so woefully frustrated. At the Italian's specific request, his fellow legate travelled with him to Grafton, though both were warned to travel without their wonted display of status. And upon their arrival Wolsey found no lodging prepared for him. Whether this last indignity was a conscious slight remains uncertain. Yet Cavendish, the cardinal's gentleman usher, leaves no doubt that prominent courtiers were already making wagers on whether the king would see his Lord Chancellor in person at all, and only the kindly sacrifice of his own chamber by the Groom of the Stool, Sir Henry Norris, produced a temporary space for Wolsey to remove his riding apparel and receive a handful of visitors, all of whom regaled him with depressing details of the king's displeasure.

Even so, the meeting with Henry that followed was ostensibly cordial, if tense. In the great chamber, Wolsey saluted the attendant councillors with unusual deference and was greeted by the king 'with as amiable cheer as ever he did' before being raised from his knees and led away to a great window for a private discussion. Whereupon, Cavendish tells us, Henry produced a letter and, with increasing emphasis, asked the cardinal, 'How can this be? Is not this your own hand?' It was presumably linked to the annulment proceedings, and Wolsey was left to explain the contents as best he could, although there was still no clear-cut sign of dissatisfaction with his response. Instead, the cardinal was instructed to go to dinner with the lords, after which, said Henry, 'we will commune further with you on this matter'.

In the afternoon session, too, the king appeared pensive rather than accusatory, taking Wolsey to the same great window and then retiring with him to the privy chamber until nightfall – something, says Cavendish, 'that blanked his enemies very sore, and made them stir the coals'. Yet Wolsey was certainly no nearer glorious resurrection than he had been upon his arrival. On the contrary, he appears to have been the willing dupe in a tantalising game of cat and mouse that would become cruelly familiar to others who fell foul of the king down the years. Picturing himself as the fount of all justice and fair-doing and enjoying the theatrical element of keeping his minions on edge, Henry was not infrequently inclined to coat his retribution in shows of temporary fellowship and goodwill. And now, with the favourite who had promised so much and ultimately delivered so little, he was prepared to turn the spit a little longer. Certainly, his performance on this occasion appears to have been particularly skilful, for Cavendish tells us how 'to behold the countenances' of those who were hoping for swift and cudgel-like satisfaction 'would have made you smile'. But if the king remained sufficiently personable to disconcert the cardinal's enemies, they would not have long to wait to savour altogether better news.

If Cavendish's reports of servants' whispers are to be believed, Anne Boleyn had been one of those particularly aggrieved by the apparent leniency of Wolsey's treatment. At a private dinner with the king that day, she urged him, it seems, to consider 'what debt and danger the Cardinal hath brought you in, with all your subjects'. 'There is never a nobleman within this realm,' she declared, 'if he had done but half so much as he hath done, but he were well worthy to lose his head.' Yet, if the vehemence of Anne's protests was suggestive of any lingering doubts about her enemy's fate, the events of the following morning could not have relieved her misgivings more conclusively. For, in spite of his teasing and apparently genial excuses for some of his minister's shortcomings – 'for I know that matter better than you or any other' – Henry's preferred course of action was as clear now as it had been from the final day of July onwards. And he needed neither prompting from his dukes nor pleading from his mistress to do what in any case came so naturally.

Next morning, therefore, when Wolsey rose at dawn to ride the 3 miles back to Grafton from the house at Easton where he had lodged that night, he could have saved himself the trouble. Gardiner, it seems, had visited him the night before 'to dissemble a certain obedience and love towards him, or else to espy his behaviour and to hear his communication at supper', so Cavendish tells us, and they had talked at first of greyhounds before conferring 'secretly together'. But while Gardiner primed the victim, Henry was planning, quite literally, his final farewell. For when Wolsey arrived to see him, he was already leaving with Anne Boleyn for a day's hunting in his new park at Hartwell. The trip, Wolsey learned, would be a long one and he was therefore curtly instructed to return to London in Campeggio's company. In retrospect, the king's gesture could not have sent a clearer signal of his new direction. Nor could it have been cooler, more abrupt, more impersonal, or more utterly final, for though Henry now appeared to leave Wolsey 'amiably in the sight of men', he would never set eyes upon him again.

On their uneasy journey back to the capital the two cardinals stopped first at St Albans and then at the More, where they assumed once again the trappings of their legatine office to travel in the full dignity denied them by Henry. Arriving at York Place and still stranded for the moment in an eerie state of nagging expectancy and forlorn hope, Wolsey prepared himself for the opening of the Michaelmas legal term, while Campeggio made for Dover on the first leg of his return journey to Rome. In a day or so the king would move on to Westminster to complete preparations for the new Parliament on 3 November, and in the meantime Wolsey's only option was to feign indifference to events beyond his control and play out the vestiges of his former status as best he could. On 6 October, for instance, he received the imperial ambassador with other councillors. But the writs of summons for the forthcoming Parliament had been dispatched to the shires 'by the hand and advice of the Duke of

Norfolk' and according to Edward Hall, the cardinal now 'showed himself much more humblier than he was wont to be, and the Lords showed themselves more higher and stronger'.

When Henry made a flying visit to London two days later, moreover, Wolsey was ignorant of it, and du Bellay sounded another ominous note at precisely the same time. 'At present,' the ambassador observed, 'the king takes the management of everything himself.' For the first time since his succession, then, Henry considered himself his own master and his heavy hand was already being felt – not least by Campeggio. There had been a lengthy delay in the legate's passage to Calais and though it had been said that a shortage of ships was responsible, two individuals close to Wolsey's household had heard that the Italian had been detained under the king's warrant, so that his baggage could be searched. Henry, it appeared, had been informed that the legate was carrying large sums of silver and gold, as well as secret documents belonging to Wolsey, which were to be transported to Rome – 'whither,' says Cavendish, 'they surmised my lord would secretly convey himself out of this realm.' In fact, the king's men found only chests filled with 'old hosen, old coats, and such vile stuff as no honest man would care to have it'. Yet, if a report of Wolsey's imminent flight could be credited and acted upon by the king, it was another clear indication of how low the cardinal's stock had sunk. Nor did Henry's response to Campeggio's complaints leave any doubt about the depth to which events at Blackfriars had cut him. How could he help it, wrote the king, 'if certain porters of ours had been rough'? 'You may infer from this,' he added archly, 'that my subjects are not well pleased that my case has come to no better conclusion.'

Now, however, Wolsey was to feel the full force of Henry's suspicion in person. On 9 October, the first day of the new legal term, he came to Westminster Hall with rather less pomp than usual, we are told, since 'none of the King's servants would go before him'. And even as he assumed his familiar place in the Court of Chancery, the Attorney-General, Christopher Hales, was preparing a charge of *praemunire* against him in the Court of King's Bench next door. That the charge was wholly spurious made little difference, and Henry's most diligent servant was duly accused of abusing the powers of the legatine court to the detriment of his sovereign. He had allegedly received bulls from Rome in direct contravention of the Statutes of Provisors and Praemunire, and on this basis was to defend himself before either the Court of King's Bench or Parliament itself. The choice was his.

In the event, Wolsey opted without hesitation to surrender to the common law, since an Act of Attainder rendered by Parliament might well cost him his life, and he chose with equal wisdom to rely upon abject appeals to the king's pity rather than an energetic assertion of innocence. For he knew his accuser well enough to realise that the die was already cast and that any sturdy attempt at defence could only impugn his master's judgement and justice. The key was total, unconditional and unremitting self-abasement, which Wolsey now proceeded to deliver in lavish helpings. 'Most gracious and merciful sovereign lord,' he wrote from York Place that same evening, 'next unto God, I desire nor covet anything in this world but the attaining of your gracious favour and forgiveness of my trespass.' Citing the Sermon on the Mount, he begged for 'grace, mercy, remission and pardon' and professed how 'the sharp sword of the king's displeasure hath penetrated my heart'. In appending his signature, moreover, he duly described himself as 'Your Grace's most prostrated, poor chaplain, creature and bedesman. *T. Cardinalis, Ebor, Miserimus.*'

Until almost the very end, there would be occasional dying flickers of bravado, but no-one – least of all Wolsey himself – could seriously credit his current hope that he would eventually 'discharge himself of all these light flea bitings and flies' stingings' and 'so handle the matter that he should reign in more authority than ever he did and all quake and repent that had meddled against him'. On the contrary, the charges against him mounted as the clamour against his great '*orgueil*', or odious pride, intensified. More than ever, he was reviled for impoverishing the nobility and the king's servants, 'yea and the whole community, like for many years to be irrecoverable'. Increasingly, too, he was blamed for the expense of his wars, for the inflation that had begun to rack the kingdom and all other aspects of 'the great decay and enorme ruin, scarceness and poverty' that had followed upon the 'advancing of his own high and prodigal palm'. Meanwhile, for one Protestant exile writing from Strasbourg, he was 'the Proude Cardinall [...] Borne up between two angels off Sathan [...] Gnawinge with his teth a kynges crowne'.

Yet with a temerity fully worthy of his modern-day counterparts, he refused to bow before the general contempt that rained down from all directions. Despite his indictment, he remained Chancellor for another week and it was not until the dukes of Suffolk and Norfolk arrived at York Place to demand the Great Seal from him that he finally faltered. Even then, he insisted on seeing the king's own signature for their authority and, 'after many great and heinous words', they were made to return the next day. Thereafter, upon finally receiving an official royal instruction to deliver the seal into the custody of Dr John Taylor, Master of the Rolls, he broke down and wept – the greatest example 'of fortune that one could see', wrote du Bellay. Utterly distraught, he later pleaded his case to the French ambassador 'in the worst rhetoric I ever witnessed', since 'his heart and tongue failed him completely'. He desired neither 'legateship, seal of authority, nor influence', observed du Bellay, and was ready 'to abandon everything, even to his shirt, and to live in a hermitage, provided his King will not hold him in disfavour'. It was a measure of Wolsey's desperation, indeed, that he even expressed a hope that the French king might 'withdraw his faithful servant from the gate of hell'. In England, he expected perpetual imprisonment at the very least and would therefore, it seems, seek salvation from any available quarter.

Even Wolsey, however, was unable to plot the subsequent course of events with entire accuracy. Certainly, Henry took good care not to see him, and it was no coincidence either that the king would deliver the final blows to his former servant through intermediaries, since eye-to-eye condemnation of an adversary – especially one whom he had previously favoured – never came easily to him. Instead, like many puffed-up despots, he preferred the critical thrust to be delivered by any other hand than his, irrespective of honour, fair play or due process. And Wolsey, who had served him for the best part of two decades, would have to suffer the full impact of this unfortunate trait. That the opening sally had come not from the king directly but from the Court of King's Bench was galling. That Wolsey had learned his fate from Suffolk and Norfolk made it doubly so. But that Henry now chose to hide behind his mistress's silken skirts was the final indignity. For 'Mademoiselle de Boulen,' wrote the French ambassador, 'has made her Friend promise that he will never give Wolsey a hearing, for she thinks he could not help having pity on him'.

Nevertheless, while Henry hid his face, he and his workmen were keenly dismantling the edifice of Wolsey's power and refashioning it along more congenial lines. 'My legacy is gone' Wolsey is said to have cried when news of his indictment first reached him, and he was not mistaken. Since another churchman was ruled out as Lord Chancellor and the Duke of Norfolk was adamant that his counterpart, Suffolk, should not succeed, the obvious candidate was the one English lawyer with an international reputation, Sir Thomas More, who accepted the post on 26 October. The two dukes, meanwhile, duly announced in Star Chamber that they were henceforth responsible for delivering judgement to any subject seeking justice, and the very same day Wolsey signed a document in which he acknowledged that through his legatine authority he had 'vexed the prelates and others of the realm unlawfully', thus incurring the full vigour the Act of Praemunire of 1353. Now, therefore, he faced dismissal from all state offices, the loss of his personal property and the prospect of lengthy confinement at the king's discretion.

Wolsey's ecclesiastical posts remained, it is true, beyond Henry's grasp, but he could make no fight for his secular ones or, for that matter, his material possessions. Making a somewhat half-hearted virtue of the inevitable, therefore, he duly begged the king to accept his worldly goods in atonement for his misdemeanours, and drew up a detailed inventory. Accordingly, the 'goodly rich stuffs', which he had accumulated in such profusion over many long years, were duly heaped on long tables in the gallery of York Place. The cloth of gold and silver, the gorgeous vestments and expensive tapestries were hung along the walls and carefully itemised. Chairs in black velvet, embroidered with cardinal's hats and double crosses in crimson satin and Venetian gold were stacked and recorded. And there were further long lists of gold and silver plate, curtains of 'changeable sarcenet', blankets furred with white lamb's wool and black silk pillowcases embroidered with fleurs-de-lys. Fifteen great beds, sixty Venetian carpets, fifty-nine counterpanes of satin and damask and a variety of altar frontals, all intended for service in the chapels of his colleges at Oxford and Ipswich, were wistfully abandoned.

Shortly after Wolsey received the order to move to a small house belonging to the see of Winchester at Esher, York Place itself became the king's. For many years Henry had envied its central position and grandeur, and now it was his to transform by turns into what would become Whitehall. As Wolsey left it for the last time to board his barge at the privy stairs, he found that great numbers of Londoners had turned out on the river in small boats to enjoy the spectacle. 'I cannot but see,' observed the faithful Cavendish, 'that it is the inclination and natural disposition of Englishmen to desire change of men in authority – most of all where such men have administered justice impartially.' Some had expected him to be travelling downstream to the Tower rather than upstream to Putney, and that, it seems, was also the misapprehension of his treasurer, who condoled with his likely fate. 'Is that the good counsel and comfort that you can give your master in adversity?' came the reply – half frosty, half submissive – along with a wry reference to the cardinal's long-held belief that 'a woman should be his confusion'. Drawing upon the dun cow emblem of the Tudors and the bull of the Boleyns, a prophetic rhyme, which Wolsey now mentioned, had been circulating widely. 'When the Cowe doth ride the Bull,' it ran, 'Then Priest beware thy skull.'

Yet, at the very time when Wolsey was facing the prospect of ignominious exile, the king was preparing an oddly ironic gesture. Whether to salve a scratchy conscience or satisfy one of those sentimental impulses to which he was not infrequently prone, Henry dispatched Sir Henry Norris with a golden ring as a parting keepsake and guarantee that Wolsey could not be arrested without the king's personal authority. Taken aback by his sovereign's apparent kindness, the cardinal was so overwhelmed that he knelt down on the filthy road to give thanks, before giving Norris a little gold crucifix, containing a piece of the true cross, which the cardinal always wore around his neck. More importantly, he then offered the king his 'poor Foole', nicknamed Patch, since he now had nothing more valuable to give. 'I trust', Wolsey is said to have told the messenger, that the king 'will accept him – for he is for a nobleman's pleasure [...] worth a thousand pounds'. And though the fool 'took on like a tyrant' and required six tall yeomen to drag him, shrieking, from the cardinal's service, the king, it seems, was delighted with his new acquisition.

It had, of course, been a sadly vulnerable response to a largely empty gesture from the king. Rather more sickeningly, the ring had also been accompanied, it seems, by a cringing message from Henry that Wolsey had been undone 'only to satisfy more the minds of some (which he knoweth be not your friends)' rather than through 'any indignation' of his own. There was even, Cavendish tells us, a further suggestion from Norris that the king might yet recompense his former favourite 'with twice as much as your goods amounteth unto' and see him 'in better estate than ever ye were'. It was certainly enough to give the cardinal a further pulse of false hope – and all the more cruel, perhaps, for that reason, since Henry's message was not only over-egged, but whimsical. On the evening of All Saints' Day, just before Parliament opened, Wolsey was brought another of the king's rings by Sir John Russell, which this time encouraged him to write to Henry in the vain hope that before long 'it may openly be known to my poor friends and servants that Your Highness hath forgiven me mine offence and trespass and delivered me from the danger of your laws'. But, as events of the following day would demonstrate, this particular ring was no less misleading than its predecessor.

Just an hour or so before Parliament opened on 3 November Henry read another letter that Wolsey had written with his 'rude and trembling hand' and then stood by impassively as his subjects tore into the cardinal's flesh with all the pent-up fury of starving hounds. Even the elegance of Sir Thomas More's opening oration did little to lessen its cutting impact. Presenting a travesty of the parable of the Good Shepherd, the normally accommodating Lord Chancellor now displayed his own set of finely filed teeth. The king, he said, like a good shepherd had seen the need for reform and just as any great flock contained creatures that were 'rotten or faulty', so he had rightly seen fit to cast out the 'great wether which is of late fallen, as you all know'. Wolsey, the new Chancellor continued, had 'so craftily, so scabbedly, yea, and so untruly juggled with the King' that men must surely think he was either unable to see his wrongdoing or had counted on his master's ignorance. But, More concluded, 'he was deceived, for his Grace's sight was so quick and penetrable that he saw him, yea and saw through him'. Accordingly, Wolsey had been treated to a 'gentle correction'.

This 'gentle correction' was not, however, nearly adequate for More's hearers, as they proceeded to frame a bill listing multiple charges, which were originally drafted by Lord Darcy, an intimate of the Howards who now bore his own personal grudge against the fallen cardinal for earlier removing him from the captaincy of Berwick. The committee enlisted to draw up the detailed articles was, of course, no more impartial. Including Darcy himself, along with Norfolk, Suffolk, Rochford, Northumberland and More, it comprised fourteen peers, as well as two judges and two officials of the royal household who were also members of the Commons. It was no small irony either that the Marquess of Dorset, who had been a pupil of Wolsey's at Oxford some years earlier, was a further eventual signatory. Nor was much dirt left unthrown. For, whereas the proceedings in King's Bench had been confined to breaches of law perpetrated by Wolsey as papal legate, the peers now ranged freely over the whole panorama of his alleged misdeeds.

Forty-four articles were listed in all, though they were declared to be 'but a few in comparison of all his enormities, excuses and trespasses against Your Grace's laws'. Some were real, some were false, some serious, some trivial. But together they represented a flood tide, which the king, for all his rings and former messages of apparent reassurance, did nothing to stem. On the contrary, Henry looked on blankly into the blue horizon – much as he had done at Blackfriars when his wife confronted him – as the cardinal was accused of making wrongful appointments to benefices, pillaging monastic foundations, depriving them of free elections and impeding bishops in their attempts to stamp out heresy. There was no flicker of defence either when the king's sometime confidant was accused of embezzling the goods of his predecessors in the archbishopric of York as well as the sees of Lincoln, Durham and Winchester. He had, it seems, pillaged the Church as papal legate, and now he would be left to face the music alone.

Even more serious, however, were the more wide-ranging offences of which Wolsey was also accused. He had, it was said, concluded treaties with both the pope and the King of France, as well as the Duke of Ferrara, without Henry's authority. In his correspondence with foreigners he had used the expression the 'King and I', demonstrating that 'he used himself more like a fellow to Your Highness than like a subject', something that was also confirmed by the appearance of a cardinal's hat on the coinage of the realm. He had even, it seems, endangered the king's health. For, knowing that he had 'the foul and contagious disease of the great pox broken out upon him in divers places of his body', he nevertheless 'came daily to Your Grace, rowning in your ear and blowing upon your most noble Grace with his perilous and infective breath'. And while the charges mounted, the king lifted not a finger. Accused of withholding ambassadorial letters to his sovereign, of granting himself licences to export grain for personal profit, of stifling debate on the king's council and of interfering with the decisions of common law judges, he received no glimmer of sympathy. Equally, when spiteful reference was made to his former mistress, Joan Lark – 'which woman the said lord cardinal kept, and had with her two children' – there was no attempt to mitigate the onslaught. On the contrary, the articles were presented to the King on 1 December and thereafter sent, without amendment, directly to the Commons.

There was, it is true, no promise on Henry's part to bar Wolsey from office forever, in spite of the bill's request that 'he be so provided for that he never have any power, jurisdiction or authority hereafter'. Indeed, by the time that Parliament was prorogued just before Christmas, the king was committed to no other course of action than that which he might deem fit. But the bill had served its purpose merely by being drafted, since it provided a public platform for Wolsey's enemies, which rounded off his disgrace and in doing so confirmed not only the king's wisdom but also his glorious and inevitable triumph over the enemy within. Unconditional acceptance of Parliament's wishes was, of course, a potential sign of weakness and Henry had other reasons, too, for keeping Wolsey in what amounted to a state of cryogenic suspension. Not least of all, he rightly saw the Duke of Norfolk as a self-centred opportunist, whose ongoing fear of the cardinal would serve as a handy bridle upon his ambition. Handy too, at least potentially, was the continued existence of an English papal legate who in any case enjoyed the protection of the Church. Why, then, destroy a broken tool, which even in its obsolete condition might yet perform some menial function? If the tool had lost forever its higher purpose, it might at least be used to prop a chair or jam a door. If not, there was always the scrapheap – or the fire – at some later date.

This, then, was not as is sometimes suggested a remorseful, hesitant monarch drawing back from the consequences of an earlier rash decision, which he later hoped to rectify. On the contrary, it was actually the selfsame ruthless egotist who continued as always to calculate his own best advantage before all else, irrespective of the worm so hopelessly impaled upon his hook. Indeed, only Wolsey's rising servant Thomas Cromwell seemed to offer any sustained defence on the cardinal's behalf, both in and out of Parliament. To every charge levelled, said Cavendish, Cromwell 'was ever ready furnished with a sufficient answer, so that at length, for his honest behaviour in his master's cause, he grew into such estimation in every man's opinion' and 'was of all men greatly commended'. Even this, however, was little more than cupboard love, it seems. For when Cavendish found Cromwell weeping copious tears at Esher with a prayer book in his hands – 'which,' said Cavendish, 'had been a strange sight in him afore' – the truth was soon forthcoming. 'Why Mr Cromwell,' said the gentleman usher, 'what meaneth this dole. Is my lord in any danger?' Cromwell's main concern, however, was Cromwell. 'I am like to lose all that I have ever laboured for', he confessed, since he was already 'disdained for his master's sake', and an 'evil name, once gotten', was not to be 'lightly put away'.

Yet still that master – that 'maggot born of a flesh fly' – continued to wriggle. When Parliament was prorogued Wolsey implored Cromwell to use all his influence to obtain the best possible financial provision from the king, both for himself and for his household, and was equally grateful for his champion's readiness to draft appropriate letters to the king. Signing himself 'your assured lover', he called Cromwell in one letter his 'most assured refuge in this my calamity' and at the same time endeavoured to curry favour in less likely quarters. Appreciating the need to salvage what little he could by offering bribes in the right places, Wolsey initially gave pensions of £200 a year from the bishopric of Winchester and 200 marks a year from the Abbey of St Albans to Anne Boleyn's ill-fated brother, George. When, moreover, Thomas More requested the fallen cardinal to grant him a house which he owned in Battersea for the use of his son-in-law, Wolsey saw good reason to comply. Indeed, even Thomas Winter, his bastard son, now found himself surrendering lands and benefices to various clerics and courtiers who might respond to similar sweetening.

Nevertheless, Wolsey's current exile at Esher remained a bitter one. At one point, even Norfolk was invited to dinner and cagily refused to assume precedence at table for fear of the accusation that, in excelling a papal legate, he was assuming a higher rank than that accorded him by the king. But entertaining his enemies in the hope of securing some meagre advantage was the least of Wolsey's indignities. For, in spite of two more rings from Henry – one of them an item that Wolsey had given him some years earlier – Cavendish and other members of the cardinal's household believed that his enemies at court were deliberately attempting to injure his health by causing him daily annoyance. The king himself, however, was probably the main culprit in this regard, since Wolsey's pressing concern – and one common to all great figures at this time – was that the number of his servants would be steadily reduced, thereby lowering his status. Even so, Sir John Russell and other representatives of the king regularly arrived at Esher to conscript the services of members of the cardinal's household, usually in connection with the string of confiscated properties, which appeared to grow daily.

Wolsey was, moreover, desperately short of money to pay those servants who remained, and even, it seems, lacked linen, crockery and a host of everyday items. Winchester and St Albans Abbey were soon taken from him and his colleges at Oxford and Ipswich now fell into imminent danger of dissolution. Likewise, when he reminded Stephen Gardiner, the king's secretary, that he had only the revenues of York to meet his expenditure – so that 'approaching death, I must begin this world again' – he was met with blank indifference. Indeed, to add insult to injury, the new gallery he had built at Esher was dismantled before his eyes and taken in sections to Westminster to be incorporated into Henry's new palace of Whitehall. Nor was the cardinal left free from the further blight of gossip and daily rumour, for each day stinging messages were brought from court, together with talk of fresh charges against him 'to persecute his mind'. 'This order of life,' wrote Cavendish, who was with him throughout, 'he had continually.' There was, indeed, 'no one day or even he went to bed, that he had not an occasion greatly to chafe or fret the heart out of his body'.

Only once, however, did Wolsey's exasperation show through. By his conviction for *praemunire* he had forfeited all property to the king, but when Chief Justice Shelley of the Court of Common Pleas came to receive formal submission of York Place, the sometime Lord Chancellor could not resist the temptation to flex his muscles. Since he alone and not his successors were guilty, he could not, he claimed, render up the property voluntarily, as this would give the king ownership in perpetuity. Not to be browbeaten, he continued to insist that the archbishop's residence was not his to give on such terms and warned the king's lawyers 'to put no more into his head than the law may stand with good conscience'. It was a final theatrical flourish towards an official he still viewed as a natural underling. But as a result of this legal technicality Shelley was forced to offer, at the king's behest, a valuable – and almost unheard of – *quid pro quo*. If Wolsey would offer York Place as required, then the king, said Shelley, would return to him all property from the archbishopric of York, already forfeited. Even so, in spite of his vulnerability, the cardinal could not resist a fleeting last word of defiance. The king, he told Shelley, should 'call to his most gracious remembrance that there is both heaven and hell'.

Yet, in spite of this notable outburst, which the Chief Justice was probably wise to keep to himself, the wind was continuing to blow in one direction only. And, if any further proof were needed, the elevation of Anne Boleyn's father to the earldom of Wiltshire on 8 December confirmed it. When Wolsey fell ill, just before Christmas, it therefore came as no surprise. He had suffered a night-time loss of breath so serious that his physician, the Venetian Agostino degli Agostini, had sought help from the king's physicians, and Henry lost no time, we are told, in dispatching Dr William Butts and three of his colleagues to minister to the stricken cardinal. 'God forbid that he should die, for I would not lose him for £20,000', the king is said to have declared with no apparent sense of irony or compunction, though Wolsey, fearing that the doctors might poison him, was considerably relieved to discover that one was a Scot whom he had once befriended.

In Butts' view, the illness was at least partly psychological. 'Sir,' he told the king – no doubt with a little prompting from the patient himself – 'if you would have him dead, I warrant he will be dead within these four days if he receive not comfort from you, and Mistress Anne.' However, the plain suspicion that Wolsey had exaggerated his symptoms merely to exploit the king's alleged unease at his disgrace can never be proven. Certainly, the king seems once more to have gushed concern, as he often did when the full consequences of any momentous decision finally came home to roost. Another ring was therefore duly dispatched, while Anne Boleyn of all people was now prevailed upon to send her *bête noire* the 'tassel of gold hanging from her girdle'. There followed, too, cartloads of furnishings, plate and other items valued at £6,300 before a comprehensive cure of the cardinal's condition was finally achieved after four days of rest and the generous application of leeches and 'vomitive electuaries' by Agostini.

Early in February Wolsey was well enough to be given the use of the Lodge in Richmond Park, since the air at Esher was too damp. And he was soon well enough, too, to renew his scrambling search for salvation. There was, for example, a futile attempt at rapprochement with the Boleyns, whom he regarded as much more influential with the king than Norfolk. 'If the pleasure of my Lady Anne be somewhat assuaged, as I pray God the case may be,' he informed Cromwell, 'then should it be well that by some correct mean she be further laboured with, for this is the only help and remedy.' 'All possible means,' he added, 'must be employed for attaining of her favour.' There were also overtures to the French and imperial courts, as well as the pope. But such approaches were perhaps only to be expected, and their main result at this stage was to infuriate rather than disquiet his enemies. Were Wolsey somehow to succeed in engineering a return to court, Norfolk told Sir John Russell amid numerous country curses, 'he would eat him up alive'. Nevertheless, as the duke realised, the safest and most convenient option for the moment was simply to remove the fallen troublemaker to the north, far away not only from the king but from the foreign envoys he was hoping to enlist.

Accordingly Stephen Gardiner, on behalf of the king and council, was appointed to broker an arrangement which would neutralise Wolsey in the most amenable fashion to all concerned by saving his face in return for effective political oblivion. Since his current 'crimes' had already been punished to the maximum extent of the law, as expressed by the king's will, there seemed little other option. Moreover, Wolsey had already asked Cromwell to make clear that £4,000 a year was the least – 'mine degree considered' – upon which he could possibly live. Perhaps, therefore, the most effective way of silencing the cardinal was to fill his mouth with silver. Suitably sweetened, he could then be hurtled far from court and all contact with the centre of political gravity. The king would be both relieved and gratified by such an option, and the cardinal's enemies could clear their decks and bide their time. If Wolsey did not accept his good fortune, he could then be treated to less generous fare whenever the need arose.

For any other individual in Wolsey's dire condition, the offer might surely have seemed heaven sent. On 10 February the king granted him a general pardon, and four days later he was officially provided with all property belonging to the archbishopric of York, excepting York Place. He was also given £3,000 in coin, a pension of 1,000 marks (£666) a year and personal furnishings fitting to an archbishop's status: enough tapestry and plate to equip five rooms. A further £300 was earmarked for his clothing and he was provided with enough livestock – fifty-two oxen and seventy sheep – to keep his household fed, at least for many months. It was, in truth, hardly largesse on the grand scale, but in view of the altogether more dreadful alternative, the offer was certainly a viable one. Yet far-off, penurious York was limbo and purgatory combined, and fifty-two oxen and seventy sheep were hardly signs of wealth unbounded, even by his father's standards.

So it was small wonder, perhaps, that Wolsey loitered over his departure to the dreary wastelands of the north and the city he had never yet visited, although he had held its archbishopric for all of fifteen years. Pressing Stephen Gardiner to intercede with the king for extra funds for the journey, he was given short shrift. As king's secretary, Gardiner pointed out, he had 'no such trade', adding that if Wolsey now had not enough money to live upon, it was his fault alone. The Archbishop of York also dallied, it seems, over the condition of his archiepiscopal residences at Southwell and Cawood, which were genuinely in sorest need of repair. While equipment and belongings were loaded into coastal craft bound for Hull, Wolsey delayed further, so that by Lent he was not only still present but had actually moved from the Lodge in Richmond Park to the Carthusian monastery at the same location. Here, we are told, he indulged a more spiritual interest in religion, even sampling a hair shirt from time to time at the monks' invitation. Mainly, however, he seems to have spent his time seeking solace in prayer and whiling away many long hours in earnest theological discussion. 'Methinks,' complained Norfolk to Cromwell, 'that the cardinal, thy master, maketh no haste to go northward.' 'Tell him,' the message continued, 'if he go not away, but shall tarry longer, I shall tear him with my teeth.'

At last, however, on 5 April Wolsey set out on his long trek north to what might have been a comparatively honourable, if humble, retirement. Certainly his retinue reflected his fallen fortunes. Only 160 attendants this time made the journey with him – a far cry from the pomp of his heyday – and twelve carts carried his baggage. But his itinerary was not without highlights and Sir Thomas More and other members of the council had informed his hosts that he should be treated with all the honours due to an Archbishop of York. The first night was spent at the Abbot of Westminster's house at Hendon, the second at Lady Parr's Rye House, the third at the monastery in Royston, the fourth at Huntingdon Abbey. Then, on Palm Sunday, Wolsey arrived at Peterborough Abbey, where he stayed several days and on Maundy Thursday washed the feet of fifty-nine beggars. Moving further north, he subsequently stayed at the house of Sir William Fitzwilliam, an old colleague on the council, before reaching Southwell on 28 April.

The king had confirmed to Lord Dacre that the archbishop should be treated according to his dignity, but Wolsey, it seems, was already feeling the pangs of deprivation. When he wrote to Henry to report his arrival, he made no attempt to hide his anguish. 'According to your pleasure,' he moaned, 'I have come into my diocese unfurnished, to my extreme heaviness, of everything that I and my poor folks should be entertained with.' The episcopal residence at Southwell was so decayed and leaky that he took up residence in the canon's house nearby and experienced a variety of other inconveniences. Complaining to Cromwell and his agents in London that the bargemen at Hull were remiss in delivering the additional baggage that he had sent by sea, he highlighted, too, the quails he wanted for his table. Before long, indeed, he found himself 'wrapped in misery and need on every side, not knowing where to be succoured or relieved'. And there were other, more wounding barbs for him to endure.

On 20 July he learned that the king had dissolved his college at Ipswich and appropriated the property to his own use, and although Cardinal College at Oxford was eventually spared at the eleventh hour, even this news was not without a taint of sadness. For Henry had decided to remove Wolsey's coat-of-arms, which adorned each and every gate and window, and renamed the place 'King Henry VIII's College'. 'I am in such disposition of body and mind,'

Wolsey informed Cromwell, 'by the reason of such great heaviness as I am in, being put from my sleep and eat, for such advertisements as I have had from you of the dissolution of my colleges.' Indeed, broken in health and consequently tormented once more with leeches, which he described as 'very hungry ones', Wolsey was soon signing his correspondence with Stephen Gardiner as 'Thomas the miserable, Cardinal of York'.

Yet initially, at least, he had shown no intention of actually making for York itself. His orders, after all, had been only to 'repair to his diocese', with no more specific reference, and he took the opportunity to stay at Southwell for several months, refurbishing it and, so some believed, awaiting a call from London. 'The Cardinal has not yet gone to York', wrote Eustace Chapuys to Charles V. 'Probably he does not wish to remove so far from court, as he would then have less facility for watching his opportunity and returning to it.' In spite of his straitened circumstances, Wolsey also, it seems, took the opportunity to entertain lavishly, so much so that on 18 August Cromwell issued a word of warning. 'Sir,' he wrote, 'some there be that doth allege that Your Grace doth keep too great a house and family and that ye are continually building.' Therefore, suggested Cromwell, it was time to curtail any familiar excess and 'put to silence some persons that much speaketh of the same'.

In May, Cromwell had also advised him to be much more circumspect in what he said and wrote, since the king was aware of his wish to undermine Norfolk. This, Cromwell warned, was a risky enterprise. And it was not, to his great misfortune, the only gamble that Wolsey now undertook. Too long accustomed to greatness, he could not resist the temptation to meddle and now attempted to enlist the favour of Catherine of Aragon, who, like him, had suffered so grievously at the hands of the Norfolk–Boleyn faction. In early June the imperial ambassador received a letter from Wolsey's physician, Agostini, which seemed to imply that his patient was willing to supply information beneficial to the former queen. And before the end of the month Wolsey had dispatched another letter, this time asking how the queen's divorce case was progressing and urging the ambassador that strong action – presumably by the emperor and the pope – should be taken on her behalf. By August, indeed, the cardinal was sending messages to Chapuys on an almost daily basis. 'He disliked delay above all,' wrote the ambassador to his emperor, 'for he thinks that, this business settled, he has a good chance of returning to power.'

In the meantime, rumours of the cardinal's subterfuge were causing increasing unease and upon his sudden departure from Southwell to York on 1 September, orders were issued for the ports to be closed, though the chances of his flight were remote. Curiously, however, he was more and more warmly received the further north he travelled. As Henry had observed earlier, York had been 'long destitute of an archbishop there resident' and the arrival of even a fallen celebrity seems to have galvanised high and low alike. Between 6 and 30 September he stayed at his house at Scrooby, from which he visited various churches and 'ministered many deeds of charity', which Norfolk typically dismissed as a scam to cover the cardinal's intrigues with the French ambassador. On his way from Scrooby to Cawood, moreover, Wolsey confirmed large numbers of children, first at St Oswald's Abbey and then by the stone cross on a village green near Ferrybridge. Thereafter, on 2 October, he finally reached his palace at Cawood, by the river Ouse, some 7 miles from the city of York.

Nor could the welcome awaiting Wolsey have been more cordial. The dean and canons of York were all on hand and he gladly informed his audience that he had come not for a fleeting stay but 'to spend my life with you as a very father and mutual brother'. He was quick, too, both to order plans for his enthronement on 7 November and to summon a full convocation of his northern province on the same day – even though this last gesture could only properly be executed by royal mandate. The enthronement, he insisted, was to be a comparatively humble affair, with no processional carpet and the archbishop himself going, in all humility, on foot, 'in the raumpes of his hosen'. In the meantime, however, all peers, abbots, priors, knights and esquires of the diocese were to escort him to York 'with all manner of pomp and solemnity'. And when Bishop Tunstall of Durham, who had been purposely installed as President of the Council of the North to watch upon the cardinal's activities, attempted to prevent the calling of convocation without royal assent, he was calmly brushed aside.

Wolsey's fate, however, was already sealed. Though York was distant, it remained the second city in the kingdom and was still the spiritual home of what remained of the 'White Rose' party. There were dizzy rumours, moreover, that Wolsey intended descending upon the place with 800 horsemen and 'returning to his ancient pomp and corrupting the people'. The arrival of a papal nuncio in England did nothing to ease tension, particularly when the Venetian ambassador claimed to have heard that Wolsey had sent secret letters to Rome, which urged the king's excommunication if he did not banish Anne Boleyn from court, reconcile himself with Queen Catherine, and respect the rights of the Church. The truth of such claims was by now increasingly irrelevant. What did matter, though, was the obvious fact that Wolsey was incapable of keeping his side of a bargain that was, with hindsight, wholly beyond his slender resources of self-control. Addicted to status and stricken by a dreamlike self-confidence that was, in his case, a feature of this addiction, he had finally exposed his soft underbelly to his enemies and, most important of all, exhausted the patience of the one man who had so far spared him his life: the king.

Not long since Henry had, it seems, lost his temper in the council room and in a spiteful outburst berated his advisers, telling them that 'the Cardinal was a better man than any of them for managing matters'. 'Repeating this twice,' observed Chapuys, 'he flung himself out of the room', since when 'the Duke [of Norfolk], the Lady Anne and her father have not ceased to plot against the Cardinal, especially the Lady.' But the king by now needed little persuasion, for a report had reached him on 23 October that a papal brief had already been issued forbidding him to marry while his divorce was still under litigation. More provocatively still, he had heard further rumours that Pope Clement intended to excommunicate him and banish Anne Boleyn from court. All this, coupled to Wolsey's summons of the northern convocation without royal permission, convinced him that the archbishop's intended enthronement on 7 November might well become the occasion for the formal publication of a bull of excommunication. Always more than capable of mistaking the smoke from smouldering ashes for forest fire, Henry therefore panicked and came to the conclusion that Wolsey must be guilty of 'presumptuous sinister practices made to the court of Rome'.

There was, it is true, further evidence, gleaned by the Duke of Norfolk from Wolsey's Italian physician, which helped to seal the cardinal's fate. Arrested and subjected to the kind of official grilling that was likely to produce only one outcome, Agostini freely admitted that he had been employed in negotiations with the French ambassadors and others. In fact, he could hardly do otherwise since a number of his letters, written in cypher, had already been intercepted. Yet this confession was not obtained until after the commission for Wolsey's arrest had already been issued by the king on 1 November, as a result of which the Earl of Northumberland and Walter Walsh, a groom of the privy chamber, were swiftly dispatched north. For the former, above all, it was a sweet moment. Ever since his days as Wolsey's ward, when the cardinal had made him abandon his courtship of Anne Boleyn, he had harboured a deep resentment, which had finally turned to hatred 'after a sharp remonstrance discharged to him by Wolsey for real or imagined misconduct in the north'. Now, however, the wrong could be righted with interest.

One day earlier, on All Souls' Eve, Wolsey is said to have received a premonition of his impending misfortune. Sitting at dinner with various members of his household, the great silver cross of York positioned at one end of the table, Wolsey received his warning just as the meal reached its end. Rising to take his leave, none other than Dr Agostini, wearing a 'boisterous black gown of velvet', seems to have swept against the cross, causing it to fall upon the head of Edmund Bonner, the cardinal's personal chaplain. 'Hath it drawn any blood?' asked Wolsey of George Cavendish after a moment's stunned silence. 'Yea, forsooth, my lord,' responded the gentleman usher, whereupon the cardinal looked long and sombrely at his servant. *'Malum omen'* – ill luck – came his final comment at last, as he made for his bedchamber, heavy, Cavendish tells us, with foreboding.

The following Friday, 4 November, again at the end of dinner, when Wolsey was 'at his fruites' in his private room, the young Earl of Northumberland, accompanied by a gaggle of eager gentry, entered the great hall at Cawood after taking the keys from the porter and sealing the gates with sentries. Told of their arrival Wolsey appeared unperturbed, whether through genuine sang-froid or, more likely, utter ignorance of the intruders' real purpose. Apologising that he had dined already and regretting that there was not enough fish left, he even bade the earl a hearty welcome, led him to the roaring fire and remarked how well his former charge had followed his advice and kept his father's servants about him, for he recognised a number of those present. 'My Lord,' came Northumberland's hushed reply, 'I arrest you of high treason.' And laying his hand upon the victim's arm he rendered him dumbstruck.

Before long, however, Wolsey seems to have recovered himself and when Northumberland refused the cardinal's request that he produce the king's commission, he was met with defiance. Indeed, only when Walsh entered after the arrest of Agostini did Wolsey accept the inevitable. Recognising him as a gentleman of the privy chamber, he thereby acknowledged Walsh as a due representative of the king and complied. Even now, however, he could not resist the final word, pointing out that the lowliest of the king's servants nevertheless had full right to arrest even 'the greatest peer of the realm'. Then, no doubt relishing the snub delivered to the earl, he placed himself in Walsh's custody and surrendered the keys of his coffers. 'I am left here bare and wretched,' he told Cavendish the next day, 'without help or succour.' The accusations, he claimed, were false. Yet he knew that he could not expect 'indifferent justice'. On the contrary, he observed with resignation, 'they will rather seek some other sinister ways to destroy me'.

The following day, on the very eve of the date designated for his enthronement at York Minster, the broken cardinal was taken under guard to Pontefract amid the lamentations of the townspeople of Cawood, who, like many other northerners, had warmed to him since his arrival. Accompanied now by only five retainers, he left the archbishop's palace to cries from common folk that 'the foul fiend might catch' his captors – perhaps the only occasion, ironically, that he had enjoyed such public sympathy. But he feared his destination, for Richard II had met his fate at Pontefract Castle, dying there 'like a beast'. And it was for this reason, perhaps, that Wolsey asked for someone to be sent back to Cawood to fetch the 'red buckram bag lying in my almonry in my chamber sealed with my seal'. When opened that night it was found to contain three hair shirts to sanctify his penance, though it was to the abbey at Pontefract rather than the castle that he eventually found himself taken, and thence to Doncaster and the Earl of Shrewsbury's lodge at Sheffield Park, where he was civilly entertained for nearly three weeks, even being invited to 'kill a hart' by his hospitable host.

The lengthy respite was, however, mainly for his enemies' benefit, since the evidence against him was being sifted all the while in London. Besides which, Wolsey was in neither the mood nor the condition for further recreation. Elderly and weak, he was now, it seems, 'taken with a thing about his stomach as cold as a whetstone', which turned before long into full-blown dysentery. In spite of medicinal powders administered to him by Shrewsbury's physician – which he would only accept, for fear of poison, after Cavendish and the physician himself had tasted them – he showed no sign of improvement. Ominously, too, he was delivered at Sheffield Park into the custody of Sir William Kingston, Constable of the Tower, who arrived with twenty-four royal guards.

Nor did the constable's generous attempts to console his pathetic captive have any effect. When he suggested that Wolsey was at last to achieve his wish to see the king and might even be acquitted at his impending trial, the cardinal remained unmoved. Instead, he lingered on another long-held superstitious belief that he was due to meet his end at Kingston-on-Thames, something which gave the constable's surname a particular significance for him. 'Mr Kingston, Mr Kingston', he reiterated, before heaving a great sigh and admitting that he was 'a wretch replete with misery' whose case was hopeless. Perhaps recalling Buckingham's fate, he politely but firmly rejected Kingston's reassurances as a 'fool's paradise'. 'I know what is provided for me', he concluded darkly.

That night the dysentery – or so-called 'bloody flux' – grew appallingly worse. 'In so much from the time that his disease took him unto the next day,' Cavendish tells us, 'he had fifty stools, so that he was next day very weak.' 'The matter that he voided,' it seems, 'was wondrous black, the which physicians call *choler adustum*.' Such was his weakness and fever, in fact, that he could not resume his journey for twenty-four hours, and on the way from Hardwick Hall 'he waxed so sick that he was divers times likely to have fallen from his mule'. Even so, he continued his journey from Hardwick to Nottingham and from there to Leicester Abbey, which he reached on the evening of Saturday the

26 November. Propped up on both sides by yeomen and greeted with torches at the abbey gate by Abbot Pexall, it was plain to all, and especially him, that his condition was fatal. 'Father Abbot,' he told Pexall, 'I am come hither to leave my bones among you.'

Nevertheless, by Monday Kingston was questioning the dying cardinal about the sum of £1,500 which Northumberland had reported to the king could not be found at Cawood. For, in spite of Wolsey's abject condition, Henry had nevertheless seen fit to dispatch a message that he should not be spared a final cross-examination – at the very time, in fact, that Dr Agostini, was presently emptying his heart to Norfolk in London, in return for a royal pardon. Even so, it was not the manner of Kingston's questioning that finally killed the cardinal. On the contrary, the Tower's constable seems to have gone as lightly with him as he could, bidding him very early on Tuesday morning to 'be of good heart, and then he would surely recover'. Wolsey had, indeed, actually taken a little chicken broth around four o'clock before recognising the taste and refusing any more on the grounds that it was St Andrew's Eve and therefore a fast day. But the cardinal claimed to have 'some experience in my disease' and had already made clear that, without improvement after eight days, such a flux and fever could only result in death. And surely enough, those few paltry sips of broth would prove his final nourishment.

After receiving absolution from his confessor, Wolsey is said to have delivered his final words to Kingston. By now, if the pious canons of Norwich can be relied upon, a great storm was sweeping over the country – a sign, they claimed, that the Prince of Darkness himself had arrived in person to carry off one of his own. Yet Wolsey's final words were calm and apparently unlaboured. 'If I had served God as diligently as I have done the king,' the dying cardinal is said to have muttered, 'He would not have given me over in my grey hairs.' The king, however, was in his opinion 'a prince of royal courage, and hath a royal heart', albeit one who would 'hazard the loss of one half of his realm', in order to achieve his ends. 'I assure you,' he told Kingston, 'I have often kneeled before him in his privy chamber the space of an hour or two, to persuade him from his will and appetite, but I could never dissuade him.' Therefore, the constable was informed, he should be most careful about any idea he might put into the king's head, 'for ye shall never pull it out again'.

If Cavendish's account of this lengthy deathbed speech is taken on its merits, there was a further call upon the king to stamp out Lutheranism before Wolsey finally called upon Kingston to take careful note of his comments, 'for when I am dead ye shall peradventure remember my words much better'. Then, Cavendish tells us, as the clock struck eight he died, and by Kingston's orders was buried with full honours, though as quietly as possible. Just before dawn, the Mayor of Leicester and his aldermen were invited to view the mitred body, dressed in all its archiepiscopal robes within a coffin of boards. And thus identified, the Cardinal of York was then carried to the Lady Chapel to lie open and barefaced, 'that all men might see him there dead without feigning'. Throughout the night, too, the body lay on display amid wax tapers and mournful dirges before it was brought to its final resting place in the abbey's main aisle – not far, we are told, from the body of Richard III in what, according to the imperial ambassador, was commonly called 'the tyrants' sepulchre'.

Epilogue

Long before his death, Wolsey had planned to be regally interred at St George's Chapel, Windsor. But the magnificent tomb, designed by Benedetto da Rovezzano of Florence to rival that of Henry VII, was never completed. And though Henry VIII had subsequently planned to use it for his own uneasy appointment with eternity, he too had eventually spurned the opportunity, preferring instead the somewhat humbler accommodation provided by Jane Seymour's grave. Only the sarcophagus of black marble, originally intended to be the base for a magnificent recumbent statue of the cardinal in gilt bronze, ultimately survived – minus, of course, the 9ft pillars, the angels bearing candlesticks, the legatine emblems, the archiepiscopal cross and cardinal's hat intended for its decoration. And only centuries later would a suitable use be found for the grand but empty shell, when it was adapted for service in Nelson's tomb at St Paul's.

Nevertheless, a timely if agonising death at Leicester Abbey had at least spared the fallen minister from the final ignominy of a state trial and a verdict which was a foregone conclusion. It had also saved the king from another inconvenient assault upon his conscience, not unlike that inflicted by Buckingham's execution eight years earlier. When George Cavendish was eventually summoned to Hampton Court to relate the events of his master's final hours, he had already been warned that he should not mention all of the cardinal's deathbed comments. And he was treated subsequently to the full measure of the king's grief. Told by Henry that he would give £20,000 to have Wolsey still alive, the gentleman usher was then interrogated about the possible whereabouts of the missing £1,500 that the much-missed minister was alleged to have salted away.

Not all responses to the hated minister's death were quite so conspicuously ambivalent, however. Instead, most contemporaries flagrantly ignored his earlier diplomatic wizardry and worthy quests for European peace, and scoffed dismissively at his administration of justice, which ensured that England would never again endure a clerical Lord Chancellor. Meanwhile, as the king's new palaces at Whitehall and Hampton Court were widely praised for their lavish splendour, their creator was derided for his worldly excesses. Even those whom Wolsey had genuinely tried to court were deeply scornful – none more so, perhaps, than the King of France. Finally rid of his '*bon ami*', Francis I was quick to tell the English ambassador, Sir Francis Bryan, of his long-held conviction that 'so pompous and vicious a heart, sprung out of so vile a stock, would once show forth the baseness of his nature' and eventually rise against the very sovereign who 'hath raised him from low degree to high dignity'. Thus, continued Francis, 'by his outrageous misbehaviours he had well merited either a life worse than death, or else of all deaths the most cruel'.

For sheer exuberance at the cardinal's passing, however, the Boleyns exceeded all. Anne herself was 'now as brave as a lion', and at the behest of her father, a company of actors was commissioned to play out a farce celebrating the demise of his family's bitterest enemy. Performed with great gusto before the king himself and subsequently printed and distributed upon the Duke of Norfolk's order, its title, *Of the Descent of the Cardinal into Hell*, spoke as eloquently of its patrons as it did of its target. Stripped of power, vainly intriguing to regain his lost authority, Wolsey had at last given the victors the opportunity they craved for gleeful triumph. Yet even in defeat within his bare wood coffin, there remained, for better or worse, something altogether more substantial about the fallen prelate than the smaller men who sought to fill his place. And only his influence, for all its imperfections, had proffered passing hope of shelter from the far more treacherous course to come.

Sources and Bibliographical Information

Contemporary and near-contemporary accounts

George Cavendish (1500–61?), whose work *The Life and Death of Cardinal Wolsey* has earned rightful recognition as one of the earliest biographies in the English language, became gentleman-usher to Wolsey around 1522, 'abandoning,' said the cardinal, 'his own country, wife and children, his own house and family, his rest and quietness, only to serve me'. From that time forth Cavendish was his master's faithful and intimate companion and he began to write his account of Wolsey's life during the reign of Queen Mary. One of the few contemporaries to acknowledge the cardinal's merits in print, Cavendish would begin his own biography by castigating all those who 'with their blasphemous trump' had spread 'innumerable lies' about his former master. And the ensuing work clearly presents a more favourable view of its subject than had resulted from earlier, much more vitriolic treatments produced by the likes of Polydore Vergil and John Skelton. Circulated at first in manuscript, Cavendish's biography was eventually published in a garbled state in 1641, since when it has been frequently reprinted. The standard modern version remains R.S. Sylvester and D.P. Harding (eds), *Two Early Tudor Lives* (New Haven, 1962).

Polydore Vergil's *Anglica Historia*, translated and edited by David Hay, Camden Society, LXXIV (1950), is the first chronicle of English history by a Renaissance humanist. It appeared initially in 1534 and is important for the reigns of both

Henry VII and Henry VIII up to 1537. It glorifies the Tudors and is unashamedly hostile to Wolsey. Vergil's life and work is fully discussed in D. Hay, *Polydore Vergil: Renaissance Historian and Man of Letters* (Oxford, 1952).

Further material is be found in H. Ellis (ed.), *The Union of the Two Noble and Illustre Famelies of Lancastre and York* (London, 1809). First published in 1542, Hall's chronicle is heavily influenced by Vergil's *Anglica Historia*, though militantly Protestant and nationalistic in outlook. It is possible that the theme of Wolsey's tyranny and corruption, which unites Hall's account of the decade before 1529, was the product of later refashioning. Yet it was hostility to the cardinal, and in particular his financial demands upon the City, which appears to have turned Hall into a critic of the Church in the first place. Hall was an MP and lawyer of Gray's Inn.

Sebastiano Giustiniani's *Four Years at the Court of Henry VIII*, R. Brown (trans.) (2 vols, London, 1854) is also valuable. The Venetian diplomat's 226 letters from England convey the complexities of contemporary diplomacy and are equally interesting in terms of the social observations they contain. He assesses Wolsey with both hostility and admiration, noting in particular the cardinal's efforts to intimidate and upset him.

Collections of documents

The starting-point for any serious student of Thomas Wolsey's activities remains J.S. Brewer (ed.), *Letters and Papers, Foreign and Domestic, of the Reign of Henry VIII, 1509–47*, 1–4 (London, 1862–76), henceforth referred to as *L&P*. In addition to *State Papers Published under the Authority of His Majesty's Commission, King Henry VIII* (11 vols, London, 1830–52), two collections of foreign documents are also of particular worth: R. Brown *et al.* (eds) *Calendar of State Papers, Venetian* (9 vols, London, 1864–98) and G.A. Bergenroth *et al.* (eds), *Calendar of State Papers, Spanish* (13 vols and 2 supplements, London, 1862–9). A.B. Hinds (ed.), *Calendar of State Papers, Milan* (London, 1913) is also of considerable interest.

Other collections of contemporary source material include:

G. Burnet, *History of the Reformation of the Church of England*, N. Pocock (ed.) (6 vols, Oxford, 1865)

J.R. Dasent (ed.), *Acts of the Privy Council of England* (46 vols, London, 1890–1907)

H. Ellis (ed.), *Original Letters, Illustrative of English History* (London, 1824–6)

J. Gairdner (ed.), *Letters and Papers, Foreign and Domestic, of the Reigns of Richard III and Henry VII* (2 vols, Rolls Series, 1861–63)

H. Nicholas (ed.), *Proceedings and Ordinances of the Privy Council, 1386–1542* (7 vols, London, 1837)

N. Pocock (ed.), *Records of the Reformation, the divorce 1527–33* (2 vols, Oxford, 1870)

J.M. Rigg (ed.), *Calendar of State Papers Relating to English Affairs Preserved Principally at Rome in the Vatican Archives Library* (London, 1916–26)

T. Rymer (ed.), *Foedera, Conventiones, Litterae,* etc. (London, 1704–35)

J. Strype, *Ecclesiastical Memorials, Relating Chiefly to Religion, and the Reformation ... under King Henry VIII, King Edward VI, and Queen Mary I* (3 vols, Oxford, 1822)

D. Wilkins, *Concilia magna Britanniae et Hiberniae a synodo Verulamiens A.D. 446 ad Londiniensem, A.D. 1717,* vol. 3 (4 vols, London, 1737).

Other relevant sources

P.S. and H.M. Allen (eds), *The Letters of Richard Fox, 1486–1527* (Oxford, 1928)

P.S. Allen *et al.* (eds), *Opus Epistolarum Des. Erasmi Roterodami* (Oxford, 1906–58)

B. André, *Annales Henrici Septimi,* printed in *Memorials of King Henry the Seventh,* J. Gairdner (ed.) (London, 1858)

J. Bain (ed.), *Hamilton Papers: Letters and Papers Illustrating the Political Relations of England and Scotland in the Sixteenth Century* (2 vols, Edinburgh, 1890–2)

J. du Bellay, *Ambassades en Angleterre,* V.L. Bourilly and P. de Vaissire (eds) (Archives de l'histoire religieuse de la France, Paris, 1905)

J. du Bellay, *Correspondence du Cardinal Jean du Bellay,* R. Scheiner (ed.) (Société de l'histoire de France, Paris, 1969)

W. Bradford, *Correspondence of the Emperor Charles V* (8 vols, London, 1850)

H. Chitty, *Registrum Thome Wolsey,* Canterbury and York Society, 32 (London, 1926)

W. Cobbett, D. Jardine and T.J. Howell (eds), *A Complete Collection of State Trials* (London, 1972)

A.G. Dickens (ed.), *The Register and Chronicle of Butley Priory, Suffolk, 1510–1535* (Warren, London, 1951)

A.G. Dickens (ed.), *Clifford Letters of the Sixteenth Century,* Surtees Society, clxxii (Durham, 1962)

Ellis Gruffyd's Chronicle, MS. Mostyn (Nat. Lib. Wales) 158, fol. 410

F. Godwin, *Annals of England* (London, 1630)

N. Harpsfield, *A treatise on the Pretended Divorce between Henry VIII and Catherine of Aragon,* Camden Society, 2nd series, 21 (London, 1878).

J. Harrington, *A Brief View of the State of the Church of England* (1653)

Herbert, Edward Lord of Cherbury, *The History of England under Henry VIII* (1719, reprinted London, 1870)

R. Holinshed, *The Chronicles of England, Scotland and Ireland*, ed. Sir H. Ellis (6 vols, London, 1807–8)

P.L. Hughes and J.F. Larkin (eds), *Tudor Royal Proclamations* (3 vols, 1964–9)

W. Jordan (ed.), *The Rutland Papers* (1842)

I.S. Leadam (ed.), *Select Cases before the King's Council in Star Chamber, 1509–44*, *SS*, 75 (1958)

H.C. Maxwell-Lyte, *Registers of Thomas Wolsey, John Clerke*, etc., Somerset Record Society, 55 (1940)

J.A. Muller (ed.), *The Letters of Stephen Gardiner* (Cambridge, 1933)

J.G. Nichols (ed.), *Chronicle of the Grey Friars of London*, Camden Society, 53 (London, 1852)

E.F. Rogers (ed.), *Correspondence of Sir Thomas More* (Princeton, 1947)

M. St Clare Byrne (ed.), *The Letters of King Henry VIII* (London, 1936)

M. St Clare Byrne (ed.), *Lisle Letters* (6 vols, 1982)

W. Tyndale, *The Practice of Prelates*, H. Walker (ed.), Parker Society, 43 (1849)

W. Warham, *'Letters of,' AC*, 1, 2 (1858–9).

Early and modern biographical works

One of the most significant early biographies of the cardinal was produced by Richard Fiddes, a Yorkshire rector and associate of Jonathan Swift. His *Life of Wolsey*, published in 1724, was founded upon an intimate knowledge of the times and a close acquaintance with the documentary evidence then available. But its aim of rescuing the cardinal's memory from the obloquy which had persistently pursued it resulted in widespread condemnation. Dr Knight, Prebendary of Ely, accused Fiddes of 'throwing dirt upon the happy reformation of religion among us'.

Over the next two centuries a number of other biographical works followed, which include:

M. Creighton, *Cardinal Wolsey* (London, 1888)

J. Galt, *The Life and Administration of Cardinal Wolsey* (London, 1812)

J. Grove, *The History of the Life and Times of Cardinal Wolsey Prime Minister to Henry VIII* (4 vols, London, 1742–4)

G. Howard, *Wolsey: The Cardinal and his Times, Courtly, Political and Ecclesiastical* (London, 1814)

E. Law, *England's First Great War Minister* (London, 1916).

E.L. Taunton, *Thomas Wolsey, Legate and Reformer* (London and New York, 1902)

Popular studies which followed include:

C.W. Ferguson, *Naked to Mine Enemies: The Life of Cardinal Wolsey* (Boston, 1958)

N.L. Harvey, *Thomas Cardinal Wolsey* (New York, 1980).

N. Williams, *The Cardinal and the Secretary: Thomas Wolsey and Thomas Cromwell* (New York, 1976)

One of the first modern works to present a more sympathetic view was J.G. Ridley, *The Statesman and the Fanatic: Thomas Wolsey and Thomas More* (London, 1982). But the main credit for challenging long-established misconceptions belongs to P.J. Gwyn, *The King's Cardinal: The Rise and Fall of Thomas Wolsey* (London, 1990), which has become the standard work. A more recent treatment is S. Fletcher, *Cardinal Wolsey: A Life in Renaissance Europe* (London, 2009).

A variety of important essays on aspects of Wolsey's life and career can be found in S.J. Gunn and P.G. Lindley, *Cardinal Wolsey: Church, State and Art* (Cambridge and New York, 1991).

★ ★ ★

There follows a summary of material specifically relevant to each chapter. Most of the books mentioned are secondary works, but there are also references to particular contemporary sources not cited in the preceding section.

1. 'This Ipswich Fellow'

As Wolsey's family home was eventually demolished in the eighteenth century, we know comparatively little about it. Its location, however, was mentioned in W. Camden, *Britannia*, R. Gough (ed.) (London, 1789), and further information about the house, the contemporary town and its school can be gleaned from the following sources:

Nathaniell Bacon, *Annalls of Ipswich* (1654), W.H. Richardson (ed.) (Ipswich, 1884)

J. Blatchly, *A Famous Ancient Seed-plot of Learning: A History of Ipswich School* (Ipswich, 2003)

T.W. Cameron, 'The early life of Thomas Wolsey', *English Historical Review*, 3 (1888)

R. Cobbold, *Freston Tower; or the Early Days of Cardinal Wolsey* (London, 1850)

V.B. Redstone, 'The Parents of Cardinal Wolsey', *The Athenaeum*, 1 (London, 1900)

V.B. Redstone, 'Wulcy of Suffolk', *Suffolk Institute of Archaeology and Natural History*, 16 (1918)

S. Smith, *The Madonna of Ipswich* (East Anglian Magazine Limited, 1980).

The date of Wolsey's birth has been the subject of much imaginative, but ultimately unavailing, speculation. Early in the twentieth century A.F. Pollard suggested some time in 1472 or 1473 and more recently P. Gwyn has settled on a similar time frame. Although George Cavendish makes no specific reference to Wolsey's birth year, he does mention the number of feet washed by Wolsey during the Maundy Thursday ceremony of 1530. Given that the figure – in this case, 59 – was supposed to equate with the age of the individual presiding, some historians have suggested that Wolsey's birth year should be put at 1471, although even this has been disputed on the grounds that the figure may denote the number of years *lived through* rather than the more obvious sense. The current *Oxford Dictionary of National Biography* suggests that Wolsey was born in either 1470 or 1471, while the ominous events of early 1471 are described in 'Warkworth's Chronicle' in J. Bohn, (ed.), *Chronicles of the White Rose of York* (London, 1945), and J. Gairdner, (ed.), *The Paston Letters 1422–1509* (London, 1873).

For details of Wolsey's stay at Oxford, see the following:

T.H. Aston, 'Oxford's medieval alumni', *Past and Present*, 74 (1977)

J.I. Catto and T.A.R. Evans (eds.), *The History of the University of Oxford, 2: Late Medieval Oxford* (Oxford, 1992)

A.B. Emden, *A Biographical Register of the University of Oxford to 1500* (Oxford, 1957 to 1959)

A.B. Emden, *A Biographical Register of the University of Oxford, 1501–40* (Oxford, 1974)

J. McConica (ed.), *The History of the University of Oxford, 3: The Collegiate University* (Oxford, 1986)

C.E. Mallet, *A History of the University of Oxford* (London, 1924)

D. Roberts and R. Shepherd (eds), *Hidden Magdalen* (Oxford, 2008)

H. Trevor-Roper, *Christ Church Oxford*, 3rd edn (Oxford, 1989).

It is also worth noting that Wolsey will have been resident at Magdalen when Prince Arthur was entertained there during his two visits of 1495 and 1496. Records of the prince's visits are scanty, but it may have been for his amusement that two marmosets were brought to the college on the latter occasion.

2. The Wide Ocean of Opportunity

It was the scholar Richard Pace who noted in his chief literary work, *De Fructu Qui ex Doctrina Precipitur* (Basel, 1517), the contempt for learning exhibited by certain gentlemen, while Wolsey's central role in the education of the Marquess of Dorset's sons features in both Vergil and Cavendish. For more on the marquess himself, consult T.B. Pugh, 'Grey, Thomas, first marquess of Dorset (c. 1455–1501)', *Dictionary of National Biography*.

Records relating to Wolsey's stay at Limington can be found in F.W. Weaver, *Somerset Incumbents* (Somerset Record Society, 1889) and the topic is comprehensively covered in T.W. Cameron, *op. cit.*, C.W. Ferguson, *op. cit.* and J.G. Ridley *op. cit.* His confinement in the stocks is also mentioned in Thomas Storer's sixteenth-century metrical 'Life and Death of Thomas Wolsey', while the later confinement of Sir Amyas Paulet is recorded in C.H. Hopwood (ed.), *A Calendar of Middle Temple Records* (London, 1903). Curiously, the individual charged with occult divination and baptising a cat at Magdalen was none other than John Stokesley, Vice-President of the college and later Bishop of London. Stokesley was also accused simultaneously of adultery with the wife of the college organist.

For more on Archbishop Deane, consult:

J.B. Deane, 'The will of Henry Deane, archbishop of Canterbury, deceased 15 February 1502–3', *Archaeological Journal*, 18 (1861), pp. 256–67
W.F. Hook, *Lives of the Archbishops of Canterbury*, 2nd edn, 12 vols (1861–84)
T.F. Tout, 'Deane, Henry', *Dictionary of National Biography*, vol. 14 (1885–1900)

References to Sir Richard Nanfan's service as Deputy of Calais are to be found in J. Gairdner (ed.), *Letters and Papers, op. cit.* and an explanation of the post itself can be found in R.B. Calton, *Annals and Legends of Calais* (London, 1852). For further material relating to contemporary Calais, see J.G. Nichols (ed.), *The Chronicle of Calais in the Reigns of Henry VII and Henry VIII to the Year 1540*, Camden Society, Old Series, 35 (London, 1846) and D. Grummitt, *The Calais Garrison: War and Military Service in England, 1436–1558* (Woodbridge, 2008).

30. 'At Anchor in the Port of Promotion'

Collections of sources dealing with this period of the reign of Henry VII include:

W. Campbell (ed.), *Materials for a History of the Reign of Henry VII* (London, 1873)
J. Gairdner (ed.), *Letters and Papers, op. cit.*
J. Gairdner (ed.), *Memorials of Henry VII* (London, 1858)
A.F. Pollard, *The Reign of Henry VII from Contemporary Sources* (London, 1913) vols 1 and 3

For further information on Henry VII, see:

S.B. Chrimes, *Henry VII* (London, 1981)
S. Cunningham, *Henry VII* (London, 2007)
R.L. Storey, *The Reign of Henry VII* (London, 1968).

Wolsey's arrival at court and relationships with Thomas Lovell and Richard Fox are alluded to by Cavendish, though P.J. Gwyn, *op. cit.*, denies that there was any serious personal tension between Fox and the Earl of Surrey, and concludes that this undermines Cavendish's suggestion that the former sought to push Wolsey forward on behalf of the clerical interest at court. However, if Gwyn is correct on the first count, his conclusion does not necessarily follow. For, if Howard himself was not a potential threat in his own right, the noble interest that he himself represented most certainly remained so.

Wolsey's mission to Scotland is described in J. Pinkerton, *The History of Scotland from the Accession of the House of Stuart to that of Mary* (London, 1797) and T.W. Cameron, *op. cit.*

The letter from Lord Darcy of Templehurst was written on 15 January 1514 and can be found in *L&P*, 3, pp. 4652. The mission to the Emperor Maximilian is also discussed by Cameron*, op. cit.*, C.W. Ferguson, *op. cit.*, and J. G. Ridley, *op. cit.*

4. The Threshold of All Things Great

For Henry VIII's background and personality, and the balance of political forces at the opening of the new reign, see:

J. Matusiak, *Henry VIII: The Life and Rule of England's Nero* (Stroud, 2013)
J.J. Scarisbrick, *Henry VIII* (New Haven, 1968; 2nd edn, 1997)
D. Starkey, *Virtuous Prince* (London, 2008).

Another useful starting point is S.J. Gunn, 'The accession of Henry VIII', *Historical Research* 64 (1991). Lady Margaret Beaufort's influence is considered in E.M.G. Routh, *Lady Margaret, Mother of Henry VII* (Oxford, 1924), and more recently by M.K. Jones and M.G. Underwood, *The King's Mother* (Cambridge, 1993). Fox's early importance is suggested by Nicholas Harpsfield, *The Pretended Divorce between Henry VIII and Catherine of Aragon*, Camden Society, 2nd series, 21 (1878), and Polydore Vergil also emphasises Fox's role in advancing Wolsey.

Initial concerns about the king's marriage are discussed in J. Matusiak, *op. cit.*, J.J. Scarisbrick, *op. cit.* and D. Starkey, *op. cit.*, as well as D. Starkey, *Six Wives: The Queens of Henry VIII* (London, 2004) and Alison Weir, *The Six Wives of Henry VIII* (London, 1991). See also G. Mattingly, *Catherine of Aragon* (London, 1942). Details of the coronation are given in A.H. Thomas and I.D. Thornley (eds), *The Great Chronicle of London* (London, 1938), while Wolsey's absence from the coronation lists emerges from *L&P,* 1. 82.

The character of Henry VIII's court at the outset of the reign is well known, but the less advertised craze for cutting purses is revealed in *Ellis Gruffyd, op. cit.* The practice may have been connected with the frivolous stripping of the king's person, which was encouraged by Henry himself in 1511 and is described in *The Great Chronicle of London*.

Sir William Paulet's account of the debate concerning the role of the young king in the conduct of policy and administration is given in H. Ellis (ed.), *Original Letters, op. cit.*, pp. 3369–72.

5. Service and High Favour

The accusation that Wolsey's eye had been disfigured by the pox can be found in J. Skelton, *The Complete English Poems*, J. Scattergood (ed.) (1978), p. 308, 2, 1169–70. There is also a related reference elsewhere (*Spanish Calendar, F.S.*, p. 164) to Wolsey being, at some point, in danger of losing an eye. It was the historian Garret Mattingly who created the myth of Wolsey's 'coarse red face' more than sixty years ago.

The Marquess of Dorset's recommendation of Wolsey to the king is mentioned in J.C. Campbell, *Lives of the Lord Chancellors* (New York, 1848), 1. p. 445. However, little more has come to light about 'Mistress Lark' since the time of A. Pollard, *op. cit.* Thomas Wynter, by contrast, now merits his own entry, written by Julian Lock, in the *Dictionary of National Biography*. He would be heard of finally in 1543, in connection with the revenues of the archdeaconry of Cornwall, which he was still enjoying, and apparently survived for a further decade. For guidance in interpreting all Skelton's criticisms of Wolsey`s alleged moral failings, see G. Walker, *John Skelton and the Politics of the 1520s* (Cambridge, 2002). The articles of the House of Lords made against Wolsey on 1 December 1529 can be found in W. Kennet, *A Complete History of England with the lives of the Kings and Queens thereof* (London, 1706), 2, p. 128.

All aspects of the international situation are discussed fully in:

S. Doran, *England and Europe in the Sixteenth Century* (New York, 1999)

S. Doran and G. Richardson (eds), *Tudor England and its Neighbours* (Basingstoke, 2005)

M. Mallett and C. Shaw, *The Italian Wars, 1494–1559: War, State and Society in Early Modern Europe* (Harlow, 2012).

6. Mars Ascendant

For a flavour of the growing war fever in England at this time, see J. Matusiak *op. cit.* There is, in fact, no conclusive evidence that Wolsey consciously set out to remove Fox from influence. Certainly, by this time the bishop was feeling the weight of his own years pile upon him and was already becoming increasingly keen to return to the humbler task of pastoral care at Winchester. But though his anti-war stance was undermining his influence, he was still a substantial political figure and remained so at least until 1516 when he finally resigned as Lord Privy Seal. The correspondence between the two men can be studied in P.S. and H.M. Allen (eds), *op. cit.*

The classic case for Wolsey's subservience to the papacy was put forward by A.F. Pollard and countered by J.J. Scarisbrick, who argued that any apparent link was purely coincidental. The relationship between Henry and Wolsey is also fully explored, from contrasting perspectives, by Pollard, Scarisbrick and P.J. Gwyn, *op. cit.*

Wolsey's painstaking preparations for the 1513 campaign are described in E. Law, *England's Great War Minister* (London, 1916) and C.G. Cruickshank, *Army Royal: Henry VIII's Invasion of France, 1513* (Oxford, 1969). 'The king's book of payments', relating to the campaign, can be found in *L&P*, 2, pp. 1441–1518.

For the history of Anglo-Scottish relations, see N. Macdougall, *James IV* (Edinburgh, 2004) and J. Sadler, *Border Fury: England and Scotland at War, 1296–1568* (London, 2004). Sir Edward Howard's military career is surveyed by D. Loades in the *Dictionary of National Biography.*

7. To Tournay's Towered Walls

The most comprehensive study of Henry VIII's campaign of 1513 remains C. Cruickshank, *Army Royal, op.cit.*, although Sir Charles Oman's *A History of the Art of War in the Sixteenth Century* (London, 1937) also remains valuable. From the French perspective, there are the *Memoires du Chevalier Bayard dit le Chevalier sans peur et sans reproche: Memoires particuliers relatifs a l'histoire de France*, xv (London and Paris, 1786), as well as the *Memoires du maréchal de Florange dit le jeune adventureux*, R. Goubaux and P.-A. Lemoisne (eds) (Paris, 1913). For further information on the origins and consequences of Henry VIII's preoccupation with the conquest of France, see J. Matusiak, *op. cit.*, while those seeking a more general discussion of the contemporary military ethos should consult J.R. Hale: *The Art of War and Renaissance England* (Washington, 1961) and 'Sixteenth-century explanations of war and violence', *Past and Present*, 1971. The scale of the English invasion fleet of 1513 was described by Dr John Taylor, rector of Coldingham in Lincolnshire, the king's chaplain and clerk to the English Parliament.

A. Hocquet, *Tournai et l'occupation anglaise* (Bilbliothèque de l'École des chartes, 1900) contains a good deal of interesting information, as does C.G. Cruickshank, *The English Occupation of Tournai* (Oxford, 1971). Similarly, much light is thrown on the Battle of Flodden by:

N. Bevor, *The Scottish Invasion of Henry VIII's England* (Stroud, 2001)

G. Goodwin, *Fatal Rivalry: James IV and the Battle for Renaissance Britain, Flodden 1513* (London, 2013)

W. Mackenzie, *The Secret of Flodden* (Edinburgh, 1931).

8. Author of Peace

The financial and strategic consequences of the 1513 campaign are discussed by C.G. Cruickshank, *op. cit.*, and J. Matusiak, *op. cit.* Further discussion of the subsequent diplomatic manoeuvring can be found in S. Doran and G. Richardson (eds), *op. cit.,* and M. Mallett and C. Shaw, *op. cit.* For further information on the 'perpetual peace' and Louis XII's marriage to Princess Mary, see F.J. Baumgartner, *Louis XII* (Basingstoke, 1996). The impact of the 1514 treaty upon Wolsey's reputation and career is discussed in the all the major biographical works cited above.

Matters relating to Cardinal Bainbridge are covered in D.S. Chambers, *Cardinal Bainbridge in the Court of Rome, 1509–14* (Oxford, 1965), while William Tyndale's belief in Wolsey's use of the occult is made clear in *Exposition and Notes on Sundry*

Portions of the Scriptures. John Skelton also ascribed Wolsey's ascendancy to 'sorcery or such other loselry', as is demonstrated in Chapter 13.

9. Thomas Cardinalis

The context of Wolsey's quest for the cardinalate is covered in W.E. Wilkie, *The Cardinal Protectors of England: Rome and the Tudors before the Reformation* (Cambridge, 1974). Other relevant books include M.M. Harvey, *England, Rome and the Papacy, 1417–1464: the Study of a Relationship* (Manchester, 1993) and H. Hynes, *The Privileges of Cardinals* (Washington, 1945).

The only available full biography of the Duke of Suffolk is S.J. Gunn, *Charles Brandon, Duke of Suffolk, c.1484–1545* (Oxford, 1988), although there are further details on his relationship with Henry's sister Mary in:

W. Hester Chapman, *The Sisters of Henry VIII* (London, 1969)
M. Perry, *The Sisters of Henry VIII: The Tumultuous Lives of Margaret of Scotland and Mary of France* (London, 1998)
W.C. Richardson, *Mary Tudor, The White Queen* (London, 1970).

For Mary's French marriage, see C. Giry-Deloison, 'Mary Tudor's marriage to Louis XII' in D. Grummitt (ed.), *The English Experience in France, c. 1450–1558* (Basingstoke, 2000), pp. 132–59.

The standard biography of Francis I remains R.J. Knecht, *Renaissance Warrior and Patron: The Reign of Francis I* (Cambridge, 1996). See also G. Richardson, *Renaissance Monarchy: The Reigns of Henry VIII, Francis I and Charles V* (London, 2002).

10. Pillar of Church and State

The best starting point for a study of the 'Hunne case' is possibly G.W. Bernard, *The Late Medieval English Church: Vitality and Vulnerability before the Break with Rome* (New Haven and London, 2012), chapter 1: 'The Hunne Affair'. Other useful material includes:

E.J. Davis, 'The authorities for the case of Richard Hunne', *English Historical Review*, 30 (1915)
E.J. Davis, 'The enquiry of the death of Richard Hunne', *The Library*, 3rd series, 17 (1914)

S.F.C. Milsom, 'Richard Hunne's "praemunire"', *English Historical Review*, 86 (1961);

S.J. Smart, 'John Foxe and "The Story of Richard Hun, Martyr"', *Journal of Ecclesiastical History*, 37 (1986)

R. Wunderli, 'Pre-Reformation London Summoners and the Murder of Richard Hunne', *Journal of Ecclesiastical History*, 33 (1982).

For Wolsey's performance as Lord Chancellor, see J. Guy, *The Cardinal's Court: The Impact of Thomas Wolsey in Star Chamber* (Hassocks, 1977) and 'Wolsey, the Council and the Council Courts', *English Historical Review*, 91 (1976). Meanwhile, an interesting account of 'Evil May Day' is provided by G. Noble '"Evil May Day": Re-examining the Race Riot of 1517', *History Review* (2008).

Further perspectives on the condition of the Church in England at this time can be gleaned from P. Marshall, *Reformation England 1480–1642* (London, 2012) and R. Houlbrooke, *Church Courts and the People during the English Reformation, 1520–70* (Oxford, 1979).

11. 'Glorious Peacock'

Valuable insights into Wolsey's possession of precious objects are to be gained from P. Glanville, 'Wolsey and the Goldsmiths', in S.J. Gunn and P.G. Lindley (eds), *op. cit.*, and T. Campbell, 'Cardinal Wolsey's tapestry collection', *Antiquaries Journal*, 76 (1996). His grand building projects, meanwhile, are discussed in:

J.H. Harvey, 'The building works and architects of Cardinal Wolsey', *Journal of the British Archaeological Association*, 3rd ser., 8 (1943)

E. Law, *A Short History of Hampton Court* (London, 1929)

S. Thurley, 'The domestic building works of Cardinal Wolsey', in S.J. Gunn and P.G. Lindley (eds), *op. cit.*

S. Thurley, *Hampton Court: A Social and Architectural History* (New Haven and London, 2003)

S. Thurley, *The Lost Palace of Whitehall* (London, 1998)

L. Worsley and D. Souden, *Hampton Court Palace: The Official Illustrated History* (London and New York, 2005).

For Wolsey's plans for his tomb, consult A. Higgins, 'On the work of Florentine sculptors in the early part of the sixteenth century: with special reference to the tombs of Cardinal Wolsey and King Henry VIII', *Archaeological Journal*, 51 (1894). Note that the ducat had an average value in Wolsey's time of around 4s 6d.

The fragility of Wolsey's health was widely recorded by contemporaries and his limited involvement in physical activity is not in doubt either. There is, in fact, only one reference to his involvement in hunting (*L&P*, 4, p. 1473), and this occurs only late on in his life.

12. 'Arbiter of Christendom'

M. Mallett and C. Shaw, *op.cit.* is the best introduction to the context of Wolsey's diplomacy and deals with both the background to the Battle of Marignano and its consequences. One of the more recent and more interesting studies of the Emperor Maximilian is L. Silver, *Marketing Maximilian: The Visual Ideology of a Holy Roman Emperor* (Princeton, 2008). The intriguing life of the Duke of Albany is covered in M.W. Stuart, *The Scot Who Was a Frenchman, the Life of John Stewart, Duke of Albany*, William Hodge (Edinburgh, 1940).

The Treaty of London is discussed in T.A. Morris, *Europe and England in the Sixteenth Century* (London, 1998) and the nature of the Holy Roman Empire and the electoral process is dealt with in H.G. Koenigsburger, *The Habsburgs and Europe, 1516–1660* (London, 1971). Charles V's eventual success is explained in K. Brandi, *The Emperor Charles V*, C.V. Wedgewood (trans.) (London, 1965).

The *Spanish Calendar, Venetian Calendar* and *The Chronicle of Calais* contain a wealth of material on the Field of Cloth of Gold, as well as the preliminary meeting between Henry and Charles. There is an interesting account by S. Anglo, *Le Camp du Drap d'Or et les Entrevues d'Henri VIII et de Charles Quint* (Paris, 1959), although the best general account in English remains J.G. Russell, *The Field of Cloth of Gold: Men and Manners in 1520* (London, 1969).

13. 'Butcher's Cur'

Wolsey's expulsion of the 'minions' in 1519 is discussed in G. Walker, 'The "expulsion of the minions" of 1519 reconsidered', *Historical Journal*, 32 (1989), and further analysis of his approach towards enclosures is provided by J.J. Scarisbrick, 'Cardinal Wolsey and the common weal', in E.W. Ives, R.J. Knecht and J.J. Scarisbrick (eds), *Wealth and Power in Tudor England: Essays Presented to S.T. Bindoff* (London, 1978).

G. Walker, 'Cardinal Wolsey and the satirists: the case of Godly Queen Hester reopened', in S.J. Gunn and P.G. Lindley (eds), *op. cit.*, deals with the literary onslaught, while Skelton's specific role is the subject of G. Walker, *John Skelton, op. cit.*

A useful edition of Skelton's works is *John Skelton*, selected works, G. Walker (ed.) (London, 1997), while other hostile works are reproduced in:

The Eclogues of Alexander Barclay, B. White (ed.), Early English Text Society, original ser., 175 (London, 1928)

J. Barlow, *The Burial of the Mass*, in E. Arber (ed.), *English Reprints* (London, 1871).

J. Barlow and W. Roy, *Rede me and be not Wrothe*, D.H. Parker (ed.) (Toronto, 1992)

See W.A. Clebsch, *England's Earliest Protestants, 1520–1535* with regard to Robert Barnes; and for more on the activities of Polydore Vergil, consult D. Hay, 'The Life of Polydore Vergil of Urbino', *Journal of the Warburg and Courtauld Institutes*, 12 (1949).

The most authoritative modern evaluation of Anne Boleyn's rise to influence and later life is provided by E.W. Ives, *The Life and Death of Anne Boleyn: The Most Happy* (Oxford, 2005). The story of Bessie Blount's bastard son, the Duke of Richmond, is told in B.A. Murphy, *Bastard Prince: Henry VIII's Lost Son* (Stroud, 2001).

Further information on the Duke of Buckingham can be obtained from:

B.J. Harris, *Edward Stafford, Third Duke of Buckingham, 1478–1521* (Stanford, 1986)

B.J. Harris, 'The trial of the third duke of Buckingham: a revisionist view', *American Journal of Legal History*, 20 (1976)

M. Levine, 'The fall of Edward Duke of Buckingham' in *Tudor Men and Institutions*, A.J. Flavin (ed.) (Louisiana, 1972)

C. Rawcliffe, *The Staffords, Earls of Stafford and Dukes of Buckingham, 1394–1521* (Cambridge, 1978)

14. Neither Glory nor Gain

The diplomacy of 1521 is discussed in P.J. Gwyn, 'Wolsey's foreign policy: the conferences at Calais and Bruges reconsidered', *Historical Journal*, 23 (1980) and J.G. Russell, 'The search for universal peace: the conferences at Calais and Bruges in 1521', *Bulletin of the Institute of Historical Research*, 44 (1971). Wolsey's involvement in the papal elections of 1521 and 1523, on the other hand, is covered in two works by D.S. Chambers: 'Cardinal Wolsey and the papal tiara', *Bulletin of the Institute of Historical Research*, 38 (1965) and 'Papal conclaves and prophetic mystery in the Sistine Chapel', *Journal of the Warburg and Courtauld Institutes*, 41 (1978). See also F.J. Baumgartner, *Behind Closed Doors: A History of the Papal Elections* (Basingstoke, 2003).

M.H. Keen, *The Laws of War in the Late Middle Ages* (London, 1965) helps to set Surrey's campaign of 1522 in perspective, while the broader context is outlined by S.J. Gunn's essay 'The French wars of Henry VIII', in *The Origins of War in Early Modern Europe*, J. Black (ed.) (Edinburgh, 1987).

The most authoritative source for Wolsey's clash with the Parliament of 1523 remains J.A. Guy, 'Wolsey and the Parliament of 1523' in C. Cross, D. Loades and J.J. Scarisbrick (eds), *Law and Government in Tudor England: Essays Presented to Sir Geoffrey Elton* (Cambridge, 1988). See also R.S. Schofield, *Taxation under the Early Tudors, 1485–1547* (Cambridge, 2004).

15. 'Violence and Puissance'

For the military campaign of 1523 see S.J. Gunn, 'The duke of Suffolk's march on Paris in 1523', *English Historical Review*, 101 (1986). Further information on Clement VII's election to the papacy is available in K. Gouwens and S.E. Reiss (eds), *The Pontificate of Clement VII: History, Politics, Culture* (Aldershot and Burlington, 2005); and the resounding imperial victory of 1525 is dealt with in A. Konstan, *Pavia, 1525: The Climax of the Italian Wars* (Oxford, 1996). The Amicable Grant is discussed in G.W. Bernard, *War, Taxation and Rebellion in Early Tudor England: Henry VIII, Cardinal Wolsey and the Amicable Grant of 1525* (Brighton, 1983), while comparisons with the situation in Germany can be made by reading P. Blickle, *The Revolution of 1525: The German Peasants' War from a new perspective* (Baltimore and London, 1981). Further information on Charles V's desertion of his English ally will be found in W. Blockmans, *Emperor Charles V, 1500–1558* (London, 2002) and J.D. Tracy, *Emperor Charles V, Impresario of War: Campaign Strategy, International Finance and Domestic Politics* (Cambridge, 2002). See also W. Bradford (ed.) *op cit.*

The foundation of Cardinal College, Oxford, is discussed in:

J.H. Harvey and J.G. Milne, 'The building of Cardinal College, Oxford', *Oxoniensia*, 8–9 (1943–4)

J. Newman, 'Cardinal Wolsey's collegiate foundations', in S.J. Gunn and P.G. Lindley (eds), *op. cit.*

H. Trevor-Roper, *op. cit.*

16. The Cardinal's 'Great Matter'

The entire story of Bessie Blount's bastard son, Henry Fitzroy, is told in B.A. Murphy, *op. cit.* Further detail on the nature of the Henrician household and the Eltham Ordinances is available in A. Weir, *Henry VIII: King and Court* (London, 2002). Wolsey's foreign policy machinations around this time are discussed in C. Giry-Deloison, 'A diplomatic revolution? Anglo–French relations and the treaties of 1527', and D. Starkey (ed.), *Henry VIII: A European Court in England* (London, 1991). E. W. Ives, *op. cit.*, should be consulted for all material relevant to Anne Boleyn.

The main technicalities of Henry's divorce case are covered in G. de C. Parmiter, *The King's Great Matter: A Study of Anglo-Papal Relations* (London, 1967) and H. Thurston, 'The canon law of divorce', *English Historical Review*, 19 (1904). There is also a great deal of technical detail in N. Harpsfield, *op. cit.* See also E. Surtz and V. Murphy (eds), *The Divorce Tracts of Henry VIII* (Angers, 1988) and H.A. Kelly, *The Matrimonial Trials of Henry VIII* (Stanford, 1976). Chapter 7 of J.J. Scarisbrick, *op. cit.*, remains the best starting point for any exploration of the canon law of the divorce.

For the key event in the collapse of English diplomacy, see:

A. Chastel, *The Sack of Rome* (Princeton, 1983)
L. Guicciardini, *The Sack of Rome*, J.H. McGregor (ed.) (New York, 1993)
J. Hook, *The Sack of Rome, 1527* (Basingstoke, 2004).

An interesting account of the hidden mechanics of English diplomacy is to be found in C. Fletcher, *Our Man in Rome: Henry VIII and his Italian Ambassador* (London, 2012).

17. Bereft, Beleaguered and Bedevilled

A fuller picture of Clement VII can be obtained from K. Gouwens and S.E. Reiss (eds), *op. cit.* For other material relating to Anglo-papal relations at this time, consult:

V. Murphy, 'The Literature and Propaganda of Henry VIII's First Divorce', in D. MacCulloch (ed.), *The Reign of Henry VIII* (Basingstoke, 1995)
G. de C. Parmiter, *op. cit.*
G. Redworth, *In Defence of the Church Catholic: The Life of Stephen Gardiner* (Oxford, 1990)
J. Sharkey, 'Between king and pope: Thomas Wolsey and the Knight mission', *Historical Research*, 84 (2011).

The most comprehensive life of Cardinal Campeggio remains E.V. Cardinal, *Cardinal Lorenzo Campeggio, Legate to the Courts of Henry VIII and Charles V* (Boston, 1935). The legatine court of 1529 is also extensively discussed in all the main biographies of Henry VIII and Thomas Wolsey already cited. For the Peace of Cambrai see F. Guicciardini, *The History of Italy*, trans. S. Alexander (Princeton, 1984).

18. 'Tyrants' Sepulchre'

Wolsey's fall is discussed in E.W. Ives, 'The Fall of Wolsey', in S.J. Gunn and P.G. Lindley (eds), *op. cit.*, and G.W. Bernard, 'The Fall of Wolsey Reconsidered', *Journal of British Studies*, 35 (1996). See also L.R. Gardiner, 'Further news of Cardinal Wolsey's end, November–December 1530', *Bulletin of the Institute of Historical Research*, 57 (1984).

Author's Note

At a point when old stereotypes stubbornly persist and outright misrepresentations have been widely construed as fact, a new biography of Catholic England's last and most memorable cardinal is surely more than timely, particularly when it is remembered that there has been no truly popular account of his life for more than three decades. During that period, a range of fresh perspectives have emerged among the academic community, which have enriched our understanding, and served to place both the man and his career in a more sympathetic light. But these, more often than not, have failed to achieve general currency and have, in any case, sometimes served to over-compensate for the centuries of opprobrium that have been heaped upon the cardinal's head. The search for objectivity frequently involves more than one swing of the pendulum, it seems, and only now perhaps – some five hundred years after Thomas Wolsey secured his position of primacy at Henry VIII's court – are we truly able to survey such an extraordinary life impartially. Politicians, as we are reminded almost daily, are all too human. Yet their load is nevertheless a heavy one and no life demonstrates this more aptly than Thomas Wolsey's. Its fascination is undiminished and its lessons abide.

Acknowledgements

Authors, like nations, can only admit their debts rather than hope to pay them. But in their case, regrettably, there is the added complication of even quantifying what they owe. In effect, this book has taken all of thirty years to gestate and a host of influences played their role along the way: some direct, some not; some tangible, some less so. Friends, family, colleagues, teachers, students, other books and writers all contributed, so that in trying to isolate, identify and prioritise at a time when my memory is not, in any case, all that it once was, I am faced with a task that is more than daunting. To Barbara, my wife, I give my deepest thanks, especially for her help at a time when she was already caring for her elderly mother. To the excellent team at The History Press and, in particular, Mark Beynon and Lauren Newby, I am also much obliged. Nor must I neglect to mention a string of earlier popular biographers, such as Charles Ferguson, Jasper Ridley, Neville Williams and Nancy Lenz Harvey, though their academic counterparts, who shaped my overall understanding, are too numerous to mention individually. Suffice it to say that the practice of history remains as restless as ever and that the efforts of the various experts, who make it so, have in the case of Thomas Wolsey carried us to clearer, richer and more plausible perspectives than ever. Without such expertise, the humbler efforts of biographers like this one would be largely fruitless.

Index

Visit our website and discover thousands of other History Press books.

www.thehistorypress.co.uk